Marie Jones

582-5870
SLC

581-6017

Marriott
Lib.
U. of U

Background Readings
in
Building Library Collections

Second Edition

edited by
Phyllis Van Orden
and
Edith B. Phillips

The Scarecrow Press, Inc.
Metuchen, N.J. & London
1979

Library of Congress Cataloging in Publication Data

Main entry under title:

Background readings in building library collections.

    First ed. compiled by M. V. Gaver.
    Includes bibliographies and index.
    1. Collection development (Libraries) I. Gaver,
Mary Virginia, 1906-   comp. Background readings in
building library collections. II. Van Orden, Phyllis.
III. Phillips, Edith.
Z687.B33 1979   025.2'1   78-31263
ISBN 0-8108-1200-2

TABLE OF CONTENTS

v

ACKNOWLEDGMENTS

The editors appreciate the confidence and trust extended to them by Mary Gaver, the editor of the first edition of this work. We hope that we have maintained her high standards.

We are also grateful to the many editors and publishers who assisted us in the process of obtaining permission to reprint these selections. A special word of appreciation must be given to the people whose individual or collective thinking is represented here. To each of them we are grateful that they took time to put their ideas into print and then were willing to share their thoughts with our readers.

PREFACE

The task of revising the well-known Background Readings in Building Library Collections, Volumes I & II by Mary Virginia Gaver presented a challenge. Unlike the original volumes, which reflected Miss Gaver's teaching, the present work is not a reflection of any specific course. Rather, the editors identified themes basic to an understanding of one of the library's key functions, that of creating, maintaining, and evaluating collections. The literature was then examined for works on these themes which would be of value to individuals enrolled in formal coursework, as well as those concerned with or engaged in these activities.

As Gaver noted in her work, the literature on collection development is diverse and frequently not readily accessible except through reserve reading collections. By bringing this collection together, the editors hope to make a portion of that literature accessible.

There are many parallels in the purposes and coverage of the two editions. Specific changes in scope, organization, and arrangement are enumerated in Chapter 1.

CHAPTER 1

INTRODUCTION

The building of library collections is a task common to all librarians, regardless of their institutional affiliation or specific job assignment. Asheim notes that "... it is here [selection of materials] that we exert however indirectly, our greatest influence on the public we serve and the total society of which the public is a part."[1] The editors of this collection of readings agree that the provision of materials and information remains the basic purpose of libraries. The existence and quality of a library's services and programs are dependent upon the collection and its appropriateness to the goals and objectives of that particular library.

The implications of these opening remarks provide the essence of the professional activities of the librarian. Librarians' activities are reflections of their philosophical attitudes, their goals for library service and their cognizance of the needs of their community. Librarians are decision-makers who have developed skills in deciding what should be in the collection and what should be maintained. That is, they have learned to weigh the many factors that must be considered if the collection is to be a viable one. Mere application of the knowledge of what makes a "good" book or a "good" film does not create a viable collection. Without a commitment to beliefs, such as that of the individual's right to information, decisions about the collection may become acts without meaning.

These general overriding beliefs are the focus of Chapter 2, entitled "Theory of Collection Development." The essays discuss the theoretical foundations for collection development, the concept of intellectual freedom, and the role of the library as one provider of information in our society.

These beliefs provide some of the reasons for the "why" of selection policies. In Chapter 3, "Development of Selection Policy," the writers address questions such as who should be responsible for writing and implementing policies as well as what should be included. In addition, they suggest procedures for formulating policies.

A library's selection policy is a reflection of the goals and objectives of that particular library. This relationship of the library and its setting is the theme of Chapter 4, "The Selection En-

1

vironment: the Community and the Collection." Writers speak of methods of community analysis, as well as methods of analyzing, evaluating and maintaining the collection. Other essays identify the needs of libraries within different settings and the consequential implications for the selection of materials.

The process of building collections involves several activities that may be carried out simultaneously. The editors have differentiated these activities into two major aspects: (1) selection and (2) evaluation. Each is treated in a separate chapter. The articles in Chapter 5, "The Selection Process," deal with the operational aspects of selection. Some of the writers deal with this theme from the viewpoint of the broad/overall concerns of selectors. Some deal with the question of who should be involved in the process, and others write of the sources of guidance; that is, the reviewing/previewing process, be it through use of reviewing media, approval plans, or examination centers.

While legitimate arguments can be made that evaluation does not take place until a user interacts with a specific item, the editors use the term "The Evaluation Process" (Chapter 6) as the title for articles that deal with criteria which need to be applied during the activity of judging specific materials. Although librarians must consider the special criteria that different formats demand, their decisions as to the potential worth of an item cannot be made without consideration of the total collection and the factors outlined in earlier chapters. The writers in Chapter 6 focus on the range of criteria one must apply when judging a variety of formats, such as books, nonprint materials, realia, microforms and pamphlets.

Throughout these processes librarians are not operating in a vacuum. In Chapter 7, "Role of Publishers, Producers, and Distributors," many factors which influence the provision of materials are discussed. For librarians to be knowledgeable selectors they must be aware of their relationship to the producers and distributors of materials, as well as the conditions under which these companies carry on their work.

Events within and outside the field of librarianship also influence the whole process. Some of these concerns and their implications for the future are addressed by the writers in Chapter 8, "Issues Affecting the Practice of Collection Development." Some of these issues, such as libraries receiving payment for information services, could be considered philosophical in nature. Others, like "zero growth," can be considered managerial in nature, and yet other issues deal with legal matters including copyright regulations.

In order to provide coverage of these themes, six factors influenced the choice of articles for inclusion in this work. First, the processes, policies and philosophies identified as aspects of the themes and scope statements given above served as the "content" criteria.

Second, the editors looked for articles that applied to all types of libraries. Preference was given to articles written at a theoretical level, rather than those that reported on the practice of a specific library. This is not to say that various types of libraries are not represented in the writings. There are articles written from the viewpoint of librarians in academic settings, in public libraries, in schools, in hospitals, etc. The authors of these articles are people holding a variety of positions: administrators, special librarians, library educators, publishers, reviewers, trustees, etc. What these writers have in common is a concern about problems of selection and collection development which transcends a particular type of library or a specific function within a library.

A third consideration for inclusion of articles was whether or not the article would "speak" to students of the problems of collection building. The term "students" certainly includes those engaged in the formal education process, but to limit the term to that category of people prohibits the inclusion of many others who are interested in or involved with this process. The editors perceive "students" as being a broad group: preservice/inservice librarians, members of boards of trustees, publishers, and others who share this interest and who may have missed these works at the time of their original appearance.

Fourth, the selections were limited to the library literature of the United States and Canada. This is not to say that there are not common concerns about collection development at the international level. Indeed, there are, but in limiting this collection to one volume the editors were unable to provide as comprehensive and as widely based selections as were found in the earlier edition. The literature base was also restricted to periodical literature, books, and related documents issued during the period of 1969 through the spring of 1978. An exception is the inclusion of Lester Asheim's article, "Professional Division," originally published in Asheim's 2 Library Lectures by the Kansas State Teachers College in 1959. Although Asheim wrote the editors that if he were to write the speech today he "would broaden [it] to cover materials in many formats"[2] and would use recent titles for his references, the editors think that the issues raised in this article are basic to any discussion of the topic and are worthy of today's reader's considerations.

Fifth, materials which appear in other collections of readings are generally not repeated here. References to such collections are made in the "Recommended Readings" at the end of appropriate chapters.

Sixth, the item needed to be available for reprinting. The selections include articles and excerpts from books and journals published for the national audience, as well as ones produced for association members or by state libraries. In a number of cases the selections were originally given as speeches. A few of the selections represent unpublished works by individuals or groups.

The selections represent, in part, the patterns found in the literature. However, the coverage of a topic in the literature is not reflected by the number of articles on that topic chosen for this collection. Topics such as intellectual freedom, the reviewing process and approval plans have had wide coverage in the literature. In contrast, some topics, such as composite criteria to use in judging materials regardless of format or combination of formats, have received minimum attention. With still other topics, the literature search revealed greater attention to a given topic from the viewpoint of one kind of library than from another, even when the problems and issues are faced by all libraries. Within this category falls the literature about studying a community and that about evaluating collections. Both topics have received more attention from academic and public librarians than from school librarians.

There are a number of activities involved in collection development which are not represented in the selected readings. Citations are given in the "Recommended Readings" for some of these. Such omissions include "weeding" or de-evaluation, actual selection policies, and standards for various types of libraries.

A large body of literature not represented in this collection deals with the "Evaluation Process" discussed in Chapter 6. Criteria for materials for different audiences or by genre and the literature which represents criteria advanced by special interest groups are not included. In the latter case, the nature of the issues raised calls for a more comprehensive treatment than the current work is able to provide. The decision to consider these issues as outside the scope of the current work is not to be interpreted as an editorial oversight. Indeed, the editors do consider these writings to be of vital significance to librarians, but space limitations impose omissions.

In attempting to condense the size of the work, several topics that were treated as separate sections in the earlier edition have been integrated with other topics or dropped from this edition. For instance, "Developing special collections and collections of special materials" (Chapter 9 in the first edition) is integrated in the current work under a variety of broader headings. The topic "Aids in selection of materials--retrospective and current" is handled from the viewpoints of those who create such works and from that of those who use them. This broader approach negates attention to specific titles. The editors think that comprehensive and "up-to-the-minute" coverage is needed to cover such tools adequately. Since there are numerous sources that provide current information on these tools, no attempt was made to include them in this work.

The historical survey of collection development, as found in the earlier edition's Chapter 1, "Theory of building library collections, " and in that edition's chronological arrangement of some sections is absent from the current work. The editors want to emphasize a thematic approach to the subject as reflected in the literature of 1969 through 1977.

Each chapter includes three parts. The first is an introductory essay which provides an overview and highlights the contribution of the individual selections. The second part consists of the
actual readings with a note of the source of their initial appearance
in the literature. The third section, "Recommended Readings," provides citations to related articles or documents that expand on or
refute comments in the readings. Thus, to gain a full impact of
the thinking of this period of time, the reader is advised to consider
not only the included readings, but also the additional sources cited.

Information about the authors is found in the section entitled
"Biographical Sketches of Contributors," located at the end of the
book. The integrated author, title and subject index provides further
access to the readings through the listing of the titles and authors
of the selected works, as well as works mentioned in the "Recommended Readings." Subject entries are provided for concepts, issues, practices, policies, types of libraries, and material formats
referred to in the chapters.

In summary, if the act of building library collections is an
intellectual activity which leads to viable collections, then librarians
must develop attitudes, skills and the knowledge needed to perform
this complex process.

Notes

1. Lester Asheim, "Professional Decision," 2 Library Lectures
   (Kansas State Teachers College, 1959), p. 14.
2. Correspondence, April 4, 1978.

CHAPTER 2

THEORY OF COLLECTION DEVELOPMENT

The practice of materials selection and collection development for any library is based upon a foundation of beliefs and attitudes as well as skills. These together come into focus when a selection decision is made.

Important among these attitudes for the librarian is the recognition of his or her professional competence to evaluate the essential features of an item, to place the evaluation in context with the other factors of the library situation and to come to a valid decision, in terms of the current information needs and possible future demands upon the collection. This ability is one of the most significant skills of the librarian.

Another attitude of importance for the librarian is an understanding of the part he or she plays in the provision of access to information, unrestricted by considerations of the controversiality of the subject matter or of the author. The "Library Bill of Rights" and similar policy statements of the American Library Association need interpretation and thoughtful consideration for their underlying beliefs to become part of the professional attitude. Though restrictions and limitations perforce exist, the motivation behind the final decision for selection or rejection should be thoroughly understood.

In this chapter, material contributing to the formation of a theoretical and attitudinal base for library selection is presented. Much more exists than could be included here, and the librarian and student should benefit from wide reading in this field.

In the first article, "The Professional Decision, " Lester Asheim delineates the special abilities of the librarian/selector, drawing an analogy between the selector's work and that of the publisher. Further, he differentiates between literary criticism and library selection, a question that does arise in a consideration of library selection. Though first published in 1959, Asheim's description of the librarian's role still holds validity and inspiration for the contemporary librarian.

Besides the professional attitudes and beliefs, a sense of the purpose and goals of library service enters into a philosophy of selection and collection development. An examination of how we view the library's contribution to society will help to develop that sense, and may assist in making specific selection decisions. Are the immediate, strongly-expressed demands of patrons the only or the foremost ones that librarians can attempt to meet? Or should the librarian consider also the potential needs, either for "special" materials that might be attractive to the unserved, or for the items of recognized, lasting value to build the collection's worth?

The positions presented in the "demand" and "value" theories are discussed by LeRoy Merritt in "Book Selection and Intellectual Freedom, " which also deals with other aspects and problems of intellectual freedom and censorship. Much solid advice upon particular problems and in the different subject fields is offered.

In the following articles, the concept of intellectual freedom receives further examination and development. The introduction to the A. L. A. Intellectual Freedom Manual, a standard tool in this subject field, is given a strong challenge in Leo N. Flanagan's "Defending the Indefensible, the Limits of Intellectual Freedom, " wherein he questions the manual's definition of intellectual freedom and aligns freedom of expression with freedom of action and its limitations. In addition, he criticizes the introduction for over-simplification, anti-intellectualism, and contrasts its statements with that of the National Commission on Libraries and Information Science in regard to freedom of access to information. He does, however, allot some kind words to the "Historic Overview" of the Manual.

Flanagan's article naturally did not go unanswered, and in the "Recommended Readings" at the end of this chapter are citations for some of the responses.

In another selection, that of Elaine Fain, "Selection and Soapboxes: an Ideological Primer, " the concept of intellectual freedom is examined from the classic expression of it in John Stuart Mill's On Liberty to its application in library selection. The writer believes this to have been a misapplication, but also questions the viewpoints of Flanagan (above) and of those who take "the high road of moral guardianship. " She carefully separates the selection process from liberal doctrine on intellectual freedom in a way that provokes thought.

The freer provision of materials to children and young people in the last several years has been the cause of much controversy, attempted censorship, and extensive, impassioned discourse, as most librarians are aware. In the article by Judith Krug, "Intellectual Freedom and the Rights of Children, " she looks at the "in loco parentis" concept and traces the development of children's rights in other arenas than the library. Judicial decisions are cited, some of them relating to freedom of expression for minors, and the relationship of this development to the "Library Bill of Rights" is traced.

A glimpse into the censorship of non-print media is provided

by the next selection, "Censoring the Censors," an editorial from
Previews by Tina Novaseda.   Content of films, such as sex and violence, that has aroused demonstrations and debate in United States
communities is discussed and a position in favor of freedom of choice
is stated.

In the concluding selection, "The Changing Capacities of Print
and the Varying Utilities of Libraries," the impact of different technologies on library service and the range of materials collected is
discussed by Kathleen Molz.   The role of print and attitudes toward
reading are traced historically, and arguments made for the recognition of contemporary means of communication in library education
and professional retraining.

THE PROFESSIONAL DECISION

By Lester Asheim

Yesterday, assured of a really captive audience, I took advantage of the occasion to let off some long-accumulated steam about the librarian's own view of his professional importance. To many of you who were there, it may have seemed that I was guilty, at least of ill-becoming immodesty, if not of downright unscientific exaggeration. My claims about the importance of the librarian to his community and about the professional character of librarianship may have been flattering to voice and to hear, but some of you may have wondered how great the actual distance is between the ideal professional stature I was claiming, and the reality of practice for most librarians. After all, I made things easy for myself by speaking in broad general terms of the aims and objectives of librarianship as I see them. If I were to look a little more intensively at what librarians accomplish instead of what they profess, would we still look so good?

For those of you who were not in yesterday's audience, let me say merely that I called for stronger conviction on the part of librarians themselves that we are engaged in a truly professional activity dedicated to the performance of an essential and unselfish service to others; that this service is of sufficient social value for us to acknowledge it with pride rather than with apologies; that the word "only" should be dropped from the all-too-frequent disclaimer, "I'm only a librarian, " and that not until we ourselves recognize the importance of our calling will we be able to expect such recognition from others. I deplored the tendency of many librarians to defend their choice of a career on the grounds that it is so much fun, because it seems to me that librarianship is so much more than that, that the pleasure we get from it goes without saying. Our social value gives us satisfaction and fulfillment (not just fun), and I think we do the profession of librarianship a disservice when we minimize what librarianship does for other people to concentrate on what it does for us.

I think I can make my point most clearly by taking a really searching look at the one task of librarianship for which every librarian, whether in a special library, a university library, the public library or a children's collection is held responsible: the practice of book selection. For it is here that we exert, however indirectly, our greatest influence on the public we serve and the total society of which that public is a part. For one of the most impor-

Reprinted from 2 Library Lectures, Kansas State Teachers College, 1959, pp. 14-24 by permission of the author and publisher.

tant factors in determining what people will read, listen to, and watch, is Accessibility--having the material ready to hand. It is a factor which has been shown to be even more important than the reader's own professed interest in most cases of free-choice selection of communication experiences. There are few instances where the individual is so interested in a particular book that he will walk a mile, wait a week, or brave a storm for it. If he can't get the specific item he will take what is there. And when his interest is more general, which is frequently the case, when he just wants a good book to read or some general information on a broad subject-- he certainly will select from what is available. The librarian, by determining what shall be available through the library, defines the field from which the average reader will make his choice.

It is my claim that this is an important responsibility--and that the librarian has discharged it (and will continue to discharge it) with a great deal more insight, tolerance, and efficiency than could a person with another kind of training. One has only to compare the quality and the variety of materials available through the average (not even the best, but just the average) public library, with that made available through any of the other communication agencies serving the public at large; the news stand, the radio and TV station, the moving picture theatre, and even most book stores.

One frequently hears the question--and the reason I'm holding forth in this vein today is that one frequently hears it from librarians themselves: "But who are we to decide what the patrons of the library should read?" The answer to that question is, obviously: "You are the librarians." Nobody--but nobody--is better qualified to make that decision. The library and the attainment of its objectives are the responsibility of the head librarian. In larger systems he delegates aspects of that responsibility to the other librarians on his staff. They are accountable to him; he is accountable to the public. If there is an abrogation of this accountability anywhere along the line then our claims to professional status are without foundation. Not to decide what the patrons of the library should read is not to be the librarian at all.

Now the librarian is quite right in pointing out that he cannot be an expert in all subject fields; that the authenticity, truth, and sincerity of certain works in subject fields in which he is not an expert can be established only by the experts in those fields. But the librarian is--or should be--the expert on the state of his library book collection and its adequacy for serving the needs of its patrons. Whether a certain book is needed in the library--quite apart from the enthusiastic endorsement of someone with a vested interest in it --is the decision the librarian must make.

To buy or not to buy--that is the question. Only the librarian really knows anything about the kinds of books that are needed for different kinds of readers; only the librarian knows what the present collection in the field is like and what gaps need to be filled; only the librarian knows what in the collection has been useful in the past,

and what is being called for now.   And most important of all--and
this is a point about which I feel very strongly--only the librarian,
of all the subject experts you can name, has that breadth of view
which sees books in relation to the needs of others, all others, and
not just to the particular subject specialty he himself professes.   Advice from non-librarians can be very useful; much of it can and
should be followed, but to decide whether to follow it or not--all
things considered--is the librarian's assignment.

"All things considered" is the key phrase and it is in relation
to it that the librarian stands head and shoulders above other experts whose subject specialization defines the limit of their attention.
Any librarian who has ever relied upon the assistance of outside experts, or who has accepted suggestions from patrons, has run into
the complete indifference and the complete ignorance they exhibit of
fields outside their own special interests.   If you wish to test my
assumption here, take any authoritative subject expert you choose,
and show him the list of titles in the "Weekly Record" of the Publishers' Weekly.   It is my firm belief that, as he goes down the
list, he will say much more frequently than any librarian ever
would, "Who'd ever want to read something like that?"   For the librarian is, in the familiar phrase, "a specialist in the general," and
it is this specialization which is his particular strength, the key to
his contribution, and the safeguard he provides for the preservation
of the library's unique role in promoting freedom of inquiry.

This broad awareness of the many potential users for whom
the librarian chooses books is absolutely essential in the selection
process for the general library.   And because it is, I believe that
many of the library schools may be making a serious tactical mistake in basing their book selection courses on the premise that book
selection for the library should be approached as though it were like
the work of the literary critic.   Many practicing librarians continue
after library school to cling to this theory also, even though all of
their experience tells them differently.   It would help a great deal,
I think, if librarians made their analogy, not with the work of the
literary critic, but with the work of the responsible publisher.   For
the critic is fundamentally concerned with the book's adherence to a
set of standards primarily literary; ideally his evaluation should be
of the book for its own sake and in its own terms rather than for
the sake of its users and in terms of its social utility.

On the other hand, what does a publisher do?   He tries to
meet the needs of readers--a variety of readers with a variety of
interests and backgrounds--with books of quality.   He tries to keep
his list broad, and he is content to satisfy immediate needs as well
as long-term ones.   He is glad when he can publish a permanent
classic, but he does not insist that all the books he publishes be
classics.   There are books of value as information, as recreation,
as tools of education which may well be superseded in fifty years,
or ten, or five, or one, which nevertheless deserve the chance to
have their say now.   He exists to serve, not only the particular demands of Art, but the individual and group demands of Tom, Dick

and Harry.   And thus the definition of "quality" in the publisher's
vocabulary has connotations quite different from those carried by the
term in the critic's lexicon.

A perfect example of this conflict in meaning was apparent in
a University of Chicago Round Table broadcast a few years ago
which featured the ALA's list of notable books.   The chairman of the
notable books committee was on the panel, as was a professor of
literature in the College of the University.   And it soon became
abundantly clear that whereas both were using the phrase "notable
books," they were not at all talking about the same things.   By the
definition of the term as used by the professor of literature there
were not likely to be fifty notable books in the past twenty-five
years.   By the librarian's definition, the limitation to only fifty
books was a stringent restriction when one considers the output of
any one year.   The professor never did seem to understand why the
panelists, although they were talking to each other, were not communicating.   But the librarians here, I am sure, can see what the
trouble was immediately.   For we know what the librarian's
"notable books" concept is, and we know that the books that
are selected as notable for the annual list are not necessarily
monumental in the history of human thought.   They are useful,
they are well written, they are of value to our readers. Is this
not indeed notable?

Do not be pushed by this anecdote into imagining that somehow
the "quality" definition of the librarian is not really as good as that
of the professor.   The standards are different, not because the librarian is less serious in his approach to books, but because his aims
are different.   The librarian cannot be content with reaching a small,
selective group of highly motivated readers with an intensive analysis
of a few prescribed texts.   The library is expected to have these, of
course, but it is also expected--even by the college professor--to
have the supplementary materials, the non-required readings, the
books which will meet the needs of a lifetime of reading, not just
those of the quarter, the semester, or the term.   The professor has
the freedom to work intensively with a limited selection of books precisely because the library exists--to broaden the reading interests of
his students outside the classroom.

More importantly, of course, the public library serves
many other readers besides the small group in the classroom;
for many people it is a substitute for the kind of introduction
that the classroom provides; for many others it is not related
to classroom kinds of interests at all.   Each of these groups
is of equal importance in the eyes of the librarian, and this is
what I meant when I said that only the librarian has the particular
breadth of view necessary to make the final decisions about book purchase.   For the college professor thinks in terms of his course objectives; the scholar in terms of his research aims; the subject expert in terms of the specialist's highly intensive needs.   But the librarian thinks in terms of his publics--and notice that the word is
plural.

It is important to emphasize the plural form of the word, because a trap into which librarians sometimes fall is to accept the mass medium notion that the "public" is a kind of single entity. It is not, of course, and because it is not, the library must diligently work to perform the individualized service which the mass media ignore. Most of the other media of communication today deliberately design their services to fit an audience--a vast, undifferentiated, faceless audience. The library still serves the individuals who make up the audience and they are all different. This is a most important distinction to preserve; if ever we lose that, the brave new world of 1984 will really have arrived.

To many--and again, strangely enough, this seems to be true of some librarians as well as laymen--the provision of materials on all sides of an issue, the inclusion of all kinds of subject matter, and the receptability to the unpopular things as well as to the popular ones is seen as the absence of selection. Selection is interpreted to mean the careful elimination of some points of view and the complete provision of others. But a much more complicated job of selection is involved in the building of a collection on the basis of some kind of qualitative standards which will represent a great variety of interests, opinions and attitudes. This is real selection, for it involves professional judgment rather than mere recognition of subject content. It requires search to uncover the several kinds of materials which will guarantee the broad coverage we seek. It requires critical analysis to compare different treatments of similar topics and to select from them those which will represent fairly, and on a certain quality level, the different points of view which deserve a hearing. It requires control and broadmindedness to recognize the value of a viewpoint with which one disagrees, and to anticipate interest in areas which are new or of limited appeal or downright unpopular. For the provision of all points of view is not the same thing as the provision of "everything"; it means the selection of a representative sampling of "everything"--which is quite a delicate and much more difficult process. More than that, the obligation of the librarian implies the imposition of a qualitative standard--not just representation of all points of view, but the best representative that can be found for each. How can this be designated the absence of selection?

Now the exercise of selection is forced upon the librarian whether or not he wishes to accept the responsibility it entails. Ideally he might wish that the principle of providing all points of view could be carried to its logical extreme to mean providing every book. Unfortunately the laws of physics make this ideal--supposing it were desirable--impossible practically. No library in the world is large enough to house even one copy of every printed publication, and since in order to serve its publics, the library must have more than one copy of many of the books, we must defer to the limitations of space and eliminate some books from our collections.

But physical limitations, real as they are, are of secondary importance, as any practicing librarian knows. Few public librarians have as much as $2 per year to spend for each person in the community, and this will not buy many books even in inexpensive formats. But the librarian is charged with the responsibility of having available the more expensive rather than the less expensive books: the reference works, the illustrated volumes, the many volumed sets, the serious works of limited appeal. So again the librarian must select; 1000 new titles, let us say, from the more than 11,000 published (in the U.S. alone) in a single year.

I should think that the librarian would embrace the challenge which selection implies. If building a library collection meant merely to place a standing order for one copy of each title published, the librarian would need to be only a bookkeeper, not a keeper of books. But a library is more than an indiscriminate conglomeration of print; it is an agency with a specific purpose: the enlightenment and improvement of its community. The library virtually by definition is destined to be selective.

The nature of the selection is also in a way predestined. For one thing, libraries are not--as are the other agencies and channels for the dissemination of ideas--money making enterprises. If twice as many books were to circulate this month as circulated last, not a single additional cent would be added to the library's coffers. Thus the library need not worry about pleasing the greatest possible number of readers, or increasing its Hooper rating, or swelling the box office take. Ideas can be evaluated as ideas rather than as gimmicks; values can be judged on other bases than dollar and cents return. To stay in business, the other agencies of communication usually feel that they must reflect the most widely popular notions and avoid controversy or challenge. The library is the only agency which is so organized and so privileged that it can do just the opposite. And I suggest that, in order for the library to justify its continuation in business, it has an obligation to do that which none of the other agencies can do: be better than the common denominator.

For it is important to remember that a reader learns, not only from the facts presented, but from the manner of presentation. If we make available to our citizens the second rate, the diluted, the inadequate, we are weakening their ability to distinguish between the meretricious and the valuable, the banal and the creative, the false and the true. Thus it is not enough that all sides be represented, but that they be represented by a presentation, the form and manner of which is in itself enlightening.

Remember that those of us who provide communication to the public are helping to create public demand for the kind of content we make available. Meeting public demand is not the simple one-way process we sometimes claim. People learn to like what they get-- and if what they get is second rate, those who provide it are more at fault than the public whose second rate taste they condemn. How often have we, as enlightened citizens, attacked those who control the content of the mass media for their failure to exercise a "proper" control? How often have we condemned the sensational press, and asked why editors do not take a greater responsibility for selecting

the matter which shall be emphasized and the manner in which news
is presented? How often have we condemned the low level sameness
of films, radio, and TV--and demanded that those in control take
greater responsibility for elevating quality and introducing variety,
even though vast audiences do not demand it? In so doing we are
not attempting to curtail the freedom of the press. We are not advocating that news be suppressed, that entertainment be abandoned,
or that popular interests be ignored. We are asking merely that
those with authority accept responsibility.

I submit, that as librarians, our authority, and therefore our
responsibility, are as great. For the reader who chooses his reading from what we make available to him can get the second rate from
us only if we have it. A process of selection by the librarian should
take place before the process of selection by the patron.

It is at this point that the analogy with publishing becomes
even more clear. You will remember that I suggested that the librarian's selection obligations are like those of a "responsible" publisher, with responsible underlined. While the general publisher is anxious to serve the many interests of his potential readers, and while
he is quite willing to select materials at a great many levels of pro-
fundity, difficulty, erudition, and permanent worth, he also has the
obligation to impose standards upon his selection. We do not consider it wrong for the editor of Harper's Magazine to reject a manuscript on the ground that its proper market is Confidential. As a
matter of fact we would consider him to be a very poor publisher indeed if he indiscriminately accepted for publication anything that anyone might under any set of conceivable circumstances wish to read.
The editor--the publisher--has a public service to perform, and the
public he wishes to serve is certainly as broad as possible. But this
does not mean that he is obliged, on the basis of his public service
obligations, to have something for everybody no matter how substan-
dard some of the tastes to which he caters. An even more important public service to perform than the provision of something for
everybody, is the imposition of standards.

So it is with the librarian. The stamp of the library's name
on page 99 is like the publisher's imprint on the title page: it is, in
effect, a kind of seal of approval by those experts who have been appointed to their positions because they are deemed to be capable of
judging a book's worth. We abrogate our responsibility and are untrue to the public service ideal if we give that stamp to books that
do not deserve it.

This, of course, is what makes book selection a professional
process and not a clerical routine. And it is this--the emphasis on
the positive rather than on the negative--which makes it selection and
not censorship. It is not easy--and it may even lead to as many
problems as it solves. For every selection we make--and more especially every rejection we make--is sure to render someone unhappy. Standards of quality, no matter how carefully arrived at, are
still dependent upon subjective factors which may or may not be

shared by all members of the community we serve. But the responsibility of leadership always entails this kind of problem. So long
as we accept the necessity for making decisions at all (and that is
what a professional person does), we must be prepared for the disagreement to which our decision is bound to give rise in some quarters. If we do not buy a book for good and sufficient reasons, we
make unhappy the potential borrower who wanted to read it. And if,
giving in to pressures from him, we add the book to the collection,
we make unhappy those borrowers who agree with our original good
and sufficient reasons. It is my belief that our position is strongest
if we stand on our good and sufficient reasons--and that means, of
course, that we ought to have a good reason for every decision we
make, either to accept or reject.

The reasons may be of many kinds: selection is not based on
the simple either/or which usually characterizes the discussions
about selection. It is not a matter of having either important books
or popular ones--we should have both, and sometimes they are the
same books. It is not a matter of having a serious book or a recreational book--we should have both and sometimes they are the
same books. It is not a matter of serving this public or that pub-
lic--we should serve them all. But much as it may seem that we
are by such reasoning sanctioning the inclusion of anything, remember that the standards we establish still must be imposed upon this
variety of selections. Whatever the purposes we wish to serve by
our book collection--and there are many of them--we must try to
make sure that we are serving them with the best books for the purpose and not mediocre or poor ones.

The identification of the mediocre or poor book is not limited
to literary criteria alone, although literary criteria are important.
There are reasons why a public library should have some books
which would not be on the reading list of a college course in literature. The library wishes to help meet some of the everyday practical needs of a great variety of readers: thus reliable and informative how-to-do-it books of all kinds have a logical place in our collections. The library wishes to provide insights into current problems and mores: thus a great many books which are reportage
rather than history, journalism rather than sociology, have a logical
place in our collections. The library wishes to help people understand themselves and those around them: thus a great many books of
popular as well as academic psychology have a logical place in our
collections. If a book has the power to provoke thought in the reader
(as for example do books as widely divergent as The Voices of Silence and The Insolent Chariots); if it is of some significance in social or literary history (as are the works of the Beat Generation and
the Angry Young Men); if it provides factual information in a context
which sharpens its meaning and relevance to the life of today (something let us say, like Stuart Chase's Some Things Worth Knowing);
if it is distinguished by the quality of its insights into human character (and here we might well raise the question of Lolita, no matter
how distasteful we may find the insights to be); if it has the ability
to recreate vividly a time, place, attitude, or way of life (as does a

good history or even a good travel book); or if indeed it carries the reflection of a sharp and witty mind (not only that of a Spinoza but also that of a Jean Kerr or a Stephen Potter), then certainly it demands that we give it serious consideration for inclusion in our collections. If we can give a positive yes to any one or any combination of the above characteristics, we are on pretty strong ground for defending our choices. Note that we do not reject a book which cannot meet all of these criteria, but surely it should meet at least one. If it does not, I should think we need not be too embarrassed if the book does not appear in our collections, even if a public demand arises for it. Since we can't have everything, everything we have should be defensible.

It is clear, I suppose, that I am implicitly arguing for a statement of book selection policy: a clearly stated listing of the standards which govern the choices the library makes. One of the main reasons why book selection is difficult is that we are often called upon to justify it; it would not be difficult at all if we never had to answer for our decisions. When we are thus called upon, a forthright statement of the principles that guided us is an indispensable backstop. Do not for a moment imagine that it will necessarily satisfy those who raise the question, but it will certainly help to keep the level of the discourse on the points at issue, and not on irrelevancies.

The points at issue should be the objectives which your library aims to foster, and the contribution that your book selection makes to the achievement of those objectives. Or--to state that fancy phraseology in more commonplace terms--the librarian ought to know what he is doing and why.

What he is doing--it seems to me--is bringing all of his special expert knowledge to bear on the provision of reading and other materials of communication which will serve the needs and the interests of the community he or she serves. These needs are not always openly expressed; part of the librarian's problem is to discover the needs of the community which the members of the community themselves have not recognized. The reverse of the problem is even harder: to know when an expressed demand does not serve the community's true interest.

In other words, while demand is an important factor in library book selection, certain criteria of quality and value may outweigh demand in the final decision. Remember that a demand made in public is not necessarily evidence of a public demand; the influence of a single person, or a small number of vocal patrons, may give the effect of a great spontaneous movement. But even if the spontaneous movement does appear, the librarian should heed it only if he is convinced that it expresses needs that his library exists to serve. There are many needs in the community--even some reading needs--that may not be the library's obligation to meet.

On the other hand, be careful to avoid the snobbish notion that "popular" must of necessity be somewhat different from "good. " We have fallen into a bad habit of equating "best seller" with pot-boiler; of assuming that anything which is liked by a great number of people must inevitably be less good than something with a narrower appeal. We sometimes forget that the best seller lists have carried first rate writers as well as third rate ones; we should remember that Dickens, Twain, Zola, Tolstoy, Wells, Cather, Toynbee, Hemingway, Faulkner are not of less value because they reached a wide readership.

In other words, popular demand in itself is really not a good enough reason either to purchase or to reject; it is merely one consideration among many that must be taken into account when the merits of any individual title are being weighed.

You will notice that in one way or another, we constantly come back to the same conclusion: the librarian must be a person capable of making decisions on the basis of informed judgments, and with the courage to stand back of his decisions once he has made them. It is this that makes librarianship a true profession and not just a skilled trade: the fact that it calls for judgment, decision, responsibility; that it is dedicated to high standards of performance; and that it is based upon a code of ethical practice devoted to service to others. Of course it is difficult, and demanding, and challenging--would you really have it otherwise?

I hope not. The day may not yet be gone, but let us all do everything we can to hasten its going, when the appeal of librarianship is that it is such nice, clean, ladylike, undemanding work. I like to think that the appeal of librarianship to the young people of today is not that but this: its ideal of service, its importance in the fight for freedom of expression, its position of leadership and educational force in its community. To be a part of that kind of social contribution will inevitably require trouble and effort, but it is well worth it.

BOOK SELECTION AND INTELLECTUAL FREEDOM

By LeRoy Charles Merritt

In very general terms, it may be said that there are two theories of public library book selection which are almost as diametrically opposed to each other as the two poles. Too simply, perhaps, they may be designated as the value theory and the demand theory. The value theory posits the public library as an educational institution containing books that provide inspiration, information, and recreation, with insistence that even the last-mentioned should embody some measure of creative imagination. The collection should include only those books which one way or another tend toward the development and enrichment of life. In short, "give them what they should have. "

The demand theory, on the other hand, sees the public library as a democratic institution, supported by taxes paid by the whole community, each member of which has an equal right to find what he wishes to read in the library collection. In short, "give them what they want. " Just as no man can live well or for long at either pole, so no librarian can espouse either the value theory or the demand theory to the exclusion of the other. Nor is life on the equator especially salutary or easily possible. So it is that each librarian works out some sort of "temperate" compromise, and if all goes well, his library acquires and holds a clientele which is comfortable with the collection it finds.

The relative weight of the two theories varies from field to field within a given library, varies somewhat between libraries of the same type, and may vary greatly between different types of libraries. In the context of intellectual freedom, the librarian needs to be in the position of being able to argue for the value of his collection to his community and, by corollary, for the place of every book in that collection as being of value to some group of readers in the community.

Acting in good conscience and without fear of intimidation, the librarian must select each book as being in fact a positive contribution to the collection and of potential benefit or usefulness to some portion of the library's clientele. He must select each book not because it will do no harm but because it may do some good. There is an important corollary to this. A book is selected because of its usefulness to a group of readers, even though it may not be useful

---

to others, or may even be distasteful, repugnant, or objectionable
to them. It is selected for its positive value to a certain group of
patrons, despite the possibility of another patron's objecting or the
likelihood of controversy.

It is important also that the librarian harbor no fear that he
is engaging in censorship himself when a title is rejected as not be-
longing in the library according to established policy. The distinction made by Asheim between selection and censorship on the librarian's part[1] is a valid one and must be completely understood, felt,
and believed if the librarian is to be in a proper frame of mind to
withstand an onslaught from people with tendencies toward censorship.
The librarian who feels, believes, or suspects that he himself engages in a measure of censorship in the process of selection is in a
poor psychological position when the real thing comes, either as a
request to remove a book or to add one the librarian considers un-
acceptable.

That some librarians consciously or unconsciously do engage
in censorship in the selection process is an unfortunate irrelevancy.
The Fiske report,[2] with its evidence of conscious and subconscious
censorship by librarians engaged in book selection, stands on its own
merits. The Newsletter on Intellectual Freedom gives almost issue-
by-issue testimony that Fiske's findings are as valid now as they
were a decade ago, and not only in California but in all parts of the
country. The purpose of this chapter is to assist the librarian in
moving toward a firm and sound position on intellectual freedom in
the selection process. The remainder of the volume is devoted to
precepts, techniques, and practices which it is hoped will assist the
librarian to withstand tendencies toward censorship from outside the
library. This chapter is primarily concerned with those sensitive
areas of book selection where librarians are divided in theory and
in practice, where they find a conflict between selection theory and
legal requirements, and where their selection policies and practices
have been challenged.

Obscenity and Pornography. Let us begin by attempting to define the indefinable. Etymologically, pornography, which is derived
from the Greek, means writing about prostitutes or prostitution. In
common usage it is defined as meaning "a depiction (as in writing or
painting) of licentiousness or lewdness: a portrayal of erotic behavior designed to cause sexual excitement."[3] The definition is clear,
but it reveals that the application of the term to any work is bound
to be subjective. Only the author himself can say what effect a particular work or passage in a work is "designed" to produce. What
the reader concludes about the author's intentions can only be an in-
ference.

Obscene, from the Latin, applies to whatever is indecent, dis-
gusting, or grossly offensive, including, although not limited to,
things sexual or scatological. What is considered obscene varies
greatly from culture to culture, from time to time, from place to
place, from art form to art form. Hardly any instrumental music

could be considered obscene. Much that would be regarded as obscene if performed on stage is portrayed in books, the reading of which is essentially a private activity. This is still broadly true, even though there is now much more freedom in regard to nudity and erotic behavior on stage and screen than would have seemed possible a generation ago.

In law, the word obscene may be described as indefinable. The best legal minds, including those on the Supreme Court, have labored mightily, and failed. They will continue to fail, for like beauty, obscenity is in the eye of the beholder (as noted above, pornography is an equally subjective term). In literature the effort at definition is just as impossible, and as pointless. Books fall above or below the level of critical acceptability according to contemporary theories and standards of literary criticism, of which obscenity is not one. A book achieves critical acceptance on criteria other than the amount or the frankness of its sexual content. A book with little or no other content fails to achieve acceptance on those same literary criteria.

So it is also with library book selection. An actual or theoretical obscenity quotient is not a criterion of selection. Neither Haines, nor Carter and Bonk, nor Ranganathan mention it. The librarian who rejects Valley of the Dolls or The Arrangement as trash is on firm literary ground; the librarian who rejects either because of its sexual content must in consistency withdraw a host of much better books from his collections. The librarian willing to work at selecting fiction and other creative writing by good literary standards will be in a sound position to defend any of his selections against charges of their alleged obscenity.

Sex Education. Broderick reported that three quarters of the public libraries buying books on sex consider it necessary to keep them in protective custody. [4] Libraries not buying such books gave as a reason that "This type material disappears from shelves." Conversely, libraries keeping the books on open shelves reported little or no theft or mutilation. Some librarians expressed annoyance that such books wear out and need to be replaced. These differences in practice can possibly be explained by differences in clientele in various parts of the country and in communities of various sizes. The more probable explanation, however, is the difference in attitude on the part of the librarians concerned. The importance of having such books in the library was disputed by none of Broderick's respondents. Considering the known reluctance on the part of many library patrons to ask for books on sex education, there is a correspondingly strong argument for keeping them on the open shelves. Providing for a certain amount of loss by theft must be considered part of the cost of purveying authoritative information in this sensitive area in our society.

Religion. The paragraph on religion in the composite selection policy in Chapter 3 sets forth a standard library position on the selection of religious books in the public library. The field is usually not touched on in school library selection policies, but no school library can be considered complete without the Bible and some histories of religion, both ancient and modern. Religion is a major part of our culture and can be dealt with as such without being presented as doctrine.

Not covered in public library selection policies, probably because their occurrence is rare, are the occasional books critical of a particular religion. Paul Blanshard's critical works on Roman Catholicism will serve as cases in point of books which should be in public libraries in communities where there is public interest in them. Members of a faith are not all of a piece in their attitude toward such works. Even a devout Catholic may want to know what a sincere critic has to say about his faith. The librarian need only follow the normal selection criteria for nonfiction in this sensitive area; and having thus selected such titles, he will be in a strong position to defend their presence in the collection.

The obverse problem may be more difficult--that of the citizen who protests the absence of books which have not been selected. Such protests almost invariably come not from people who wish to read the books but from those who want them in the library for other people to read. They want the library to serve their propagandistic purposes. Suggested here is possibly a new principle of book selection. All public librarians consider very carefully every request from a patron for the addition of a particular title when it is clear that the patron wants to read the book. When it seems unlikely that anyone else in the community will want to read the title in question, the book is borrowed from another library. There is no reason, however, either to buy the book or borrow it because an interested citizen wants it to be available for others to read. The principle applies not only to books in the field of religion but to all other areas in which the patron may have an ulterior motive, be it politics, his views on the fluoridation of water, or parental interest in his own deathless prose or poetry. It applies equally to books offered as gifts. The librarian who would not buy a volume presented with the author's compliments should feel under no compulsion to add it to his library's collection.

Politics. "The Myth of Library Impartiality," first so described by Berelson, [5] is here generally recognized as such. Libraries cannot supply an equal number of titles on both or all sides of every political issue. They must follow the pattern of book publication and cannot wait for a title to appear on the "other" side before making a purchase. It is necessary, however, that the authentic and important books on every political issue which meets the normal selection criteria be acquired as they are published. And certain landmark books need to be added regardless of those criteria. The Communist Manifesto, Mein Kampf, and the Blue Book of the John Birch Society are classic examples.

The ulterior motive principle is relevant here also, particularly during presidential campaign years. A Texan Looks at Lyndon, by J. Evetts Haley, is only one example of books which many public libraries were urged to add to their collections for the propagandistic purposes of the donors. Some libraries added them; some did not; some placed them in pamphlet files as being "ephemeral" material--not a bad hiding place. One librarian added them with a flourish of local newspaper publicity as to why he did so.[6] This may have been good public relations but seems clearly inconsistent with the ALA Statement on Labelling.

Books as News. It happens occasionally that a book which does not meet the normal selection criteria of a public library is added later when, for one reason or another, it becomes news. Peyton Place will serve as an example. Literary trash by almost anyone's standards, this book was rejected by many public libraries following the normal selection process. "But," as one librarian has said, "when a book sells seven million copies, it becomes news as a literary phenomenon, and should be added so that readers in general can discover what the fuss is all about."

In another area, Race and Reason, by Carleton Putnam, was not bought by the Arlington (Virginia) County Public Library because it gave biased, inaccurate information on the alleged basic inferiority of Negroes. The book's supporters protested vehemently to the library, then placed a bill before the Virginia General Assembly requiring mandatory inclusion of the book on the Board of Education's approved list for public schools. Thus the title acquired news value, and it became important for libraries to have it so that interested citizens could form their own opinions about the controversy. The director of the Arlington County Public Library then added Race and Reason to the book collection. Neither Peyton Place nor Race and Reason acquired intrinsic value because of their topical interest. One remains trash and the other remains inaccurate, and now that they are no longer in the limelight, no librarian should feel any compulsion to add them in violation of normal selection criteria.

Closed Shelves and Locked Cases. A substantial number of librarians whose book selection policies are relatively unrestrictive limit the practice of intellectual freedom by restricting the circulation of certain titles and certain classes of books. To say the books are shown in the card catalog and are available at the desk on request still places a barrier between book and patron. Nearly 80 per cent of public library patrons do not come to the library to obtain a specific book;[7] hence the book which cannot be found by browsing through the open shelves is lost to the overwhelming majority of library patrons.

Many of the titles which are not freely available on the open shelves are precisely the ones which ought to be there to be found and read by the patron who has no one to ask or consult for the needed information and who is too timid to allow a librarian to become aware of his need. Once the selection decision has been made to add a title to a library collection, that title should find its rightful place on the open shelves of the library.

Such closed shelf collections are justified in the minds of many librarians by a real or alleged need for the library to protect the books from theft or mutilation. The need may well be real for some books, including those which must be segregated for reasons other than their possible controversiality.

Segregation to protect the book, however, is probably over-emphasized. To have several copies of a ten-dollar book stolen in a single year is a painful experience for library personnel and involves both budgetary and processing costs; a librarian's natural response is to find a way of putting a stop to it--such as placing all such books on closed shelves. The fact of the matter is that we have no evidence that titles with an alleged high theft potential are stolen at a greater rate than the average volume in the collection. It just seems that way. Some loss by theft is part of the cost of doing business on an open shelf basis and should be budgeted for in the same manner as losses by depreciation and obsolescence. Good unrestrictive selection policies developed in the cause of intellectual freedom should not be vitiated by restrictive administrative practices.

Age of Reader. Closed shelves are sometimes considered necessary as a means of keeping children and young people from finding books considered suitable only for adults. Other administrative practices are used to the same end under the presumption that some books are harmful to the young or in an effort to avoid controversy with parents who might think so. Indeed, the protest of only one patron about a book on the open shelves has served as a jail sentence for many books in many libraries. Librarians generally resist the withdrawal or destruction of a book, but too many do not hesitate to place it under lock and key.

Beginning on June 27, 1967, when the American Library Association Council unanimously approved a revised Library Bill of Rights as "basic policies which should govern the services of all libraries," any restriction on the use of the library by reason of the reader's age clearly became contrary to ALA policy. Paragraph 5 of the Library Bill of Rights now reads: "The rights of an individual to the use of a library should not be denied or abridged because of his age, race, religion, national origins or social or political views."

The insertion of the word "age" was a direct result of the 1967 Preconference Institute on Intellectual Freedom and the Teenager, sponsored by the Intellectual Freedom Committee, the American Association of School Librarians, and the Young Adult Services Division. Beginning with a brilliant address by Edgar Z. Friedenberg, then Professor of Sociology on the Davis campus of the University of California, speaker after speaker brought authority to bear on the fact that no evidence exists of a correlation between the reading of allegedly obscene materials and juvenile delinquency, and that, in

fact, the typical juvenile delinquent reads hardly anything at all. A
summary by Intellectual Freedom Committee chairman Ervin J.
Gaines of the conference papers ... may be found in the September
1967 issue of the Newsletter on Intellectual Freedom. In brief, the
young person who is ready for the content of a book is also ready to
handle that content; if he is not ready he will either not be interested
in the book or will not understand and will pass over the portions his
elders are concerned about on his behalf.

The librarian who would restrict the availability of books to
young people because of actual or suspected parental objection to certain books being freely available to young people on the open shelves
needs to bear in mind that he is not in loco parentis in his position
as librarian. The job of the public and school librarian is to select
books for a particular clientele in accordance with established policy.
Not all books can be suitable for all members of a clientele, but all
must be there for the use of those who can and want to read them.
The parent who would rather his child did not read certain
books or certain categories of books should advise the child,
not the librarian.

Health and Medicine. Librarians are from time to time
charged with censorship for not adding to their collections in the
field of health, nutrition, and medicine books not regarded by the
medical profession as authentic and reliable. Dianetics, by L. Ronald Hubbard, for example, was not added to the collections of the
Brooklyn Public Library on the basis of a negative review in the
Journal of the American Medical Association. More recently the
Madison, Wisconsin, Public Library came under criticism for not
stocking the books on nutrition written by Adele Davis. In a letter
dated October 4, 1966, Assistant Director Orrilla Blackshear responded as follows:

> When a person comes to the public library to obtain books
> on nutrition or on health, he has a right to expect that the
> books he receives will fall within the broad area of accepted
> nutritional and medical practice. Anyone using the library
> to obtain technical information has the right to assume that
> the library will furnish such information from authoritative
> sources. In technical matters, we must depend upon autho-
> rities in the field for evaluation.

This problem was also touched on by Broderick, who noted
that some librarians responding to her questionnaire about problem
nonfiction were caught in a dilemma in connection with books in the
field of nutrition. [8] One librarian who considered Taller's Calories
Don't Count to be dangerous said the reserve list was too heavy for
the library to withdraw the book. On the other hand, six libraries
holding the book withdrew it from circulation when the United States
Government instituted action against it. [9] Both situations point up a
failure to think through the principles involved and reveal a lack of

confidence in the librarian's own book selection judgment. Certainly a book which is dangerous should not be circulated by a library no matter how long the reserve list. Nor, when a library has decided a book is a desirable addition to the collection, should it be withdrawn just because a legal action has been instituted against it. Let librarians not be guilty of equating accusation with a formal determination of guilt by a court of competent jurisdiction.

In General. Other subject areas which librarians consider sensitive could be adduced, but enough examples have been presented to work toward some generalizations in behalf of complete intellectual freedom in the book selection process by the wholly intellectually honest librarian. A few words more need to be said in criticism of efforts by school administrators and public librarians to rationalize a restrictive attitude or position.

The pressure toward censorship in school libraries has sometimes been alleviated or eliminated by a compromise: the reading of the book in question is permitted rather than required. This serves to remove the impasse between the parent who objects to a particular book and his child who feels he must read it because it is in his school assignment. Thus a strong parental protest against one of four books on a required reading list in a Philadelphia high school was resolved amicably by the addition of three to the list and the requirement that any four of the seven be read. In Oceanside, California, when parents representing nine families requested that their children be kept out of the school library because of the presence of the Dictionary of American Slang, the request was denied; but school authorities agreed that the Dictionary would not be made available to these children, in accordance with general district policy to deny children access to books their own parents deemed objectionable. This practice seems to remove or to alleviate pressure, but it does not solve the problem concerning those materials which librarians or teachers believe every student should have access to or should be required to read. Were the principle to be generally extended to permit adjustment of curriculum and library resources for each individual child according to the predilections of his parents, public education soon would be a mockery and the school library an administrative shambles. School authorities and librarians must realize that there is no easy way to escape around the pressures toward censorship. Inevitably, sooner or later, they must be met head-on with a forthright defense of the principle of the freedom to read along with a very sincere and dedicated effort to educate the public concerned in the importance of the principle and the value of the books to which a vocal minority objects.

The public librarian frequently states that his reason for not buying a particular book is "lack of funds." The reason is used almost indiscriminately for books the librarian considers of dubious worth, those potentially a subject of controversy, and those so obviously superior as to be very expensive. Art books are a usual example. While most readers allow themselves to be put off by this specious answer, the reader who chooses to argue can almost invariably

place the librarian in an untenable position. If the book in question
is of dubious value the reader can find a host of volumes already on
the shelves equally if not more dubious.

It is the same with the potentially controversial book. Any
good collection already contains many books which have been involved
in controversy and a good many more which may be.

Even in the case of the expensive art book, the librarian who
says he cannot afford it because there are other needs that take precedence at a particular time is saying only that he considers those
other needs to be more important to his community than the art book.
There can hardly be a library so poor that it could not purchase a
one-hundred-dollar art book if the selector considered that book to be
more important to the community than the twenty or thirty other
books the same one hundred dollars could buy. The plea of poverty
is one which librarians must learn to avoid as being too easy an answer to an important question and one which only the casual inquirer
will accept and which the intelligent reader considers either evasive
or dishonest.

Another frequently stated reason for not purchasing a book is
that there is no demand for it. The joker in the sentence is the absent modifier known. Some books are so obviously important or potentially of such great value that they must be purchased even if there
is no known demand. Furthermore, since most books borrowed from
the public library are found on the shelf by borrowers who did not
know of their existence upon entering the library, the librarian has
the obligation to provide the good and important books of our time so
that his clientele may have the opportunity of finding them while browsing. Thus the argument of demand, or lack of demand, is equally
specious. It causes the librarian to say or imply that no one in his
community has the wit or the will to read the book in question--a stand
no librarian can afford to take.

The librarian who understands Asheim's distinction between
selection and censorship, who is wholly serious and conscientious in
the process of selection need have no fear of a censor's success in
a legal determination of an issue by a competent court. This position
was admirably set forth by Edward de Grazia at the Washington Conference on Intellectual Freedom:

> It is my opinion that under present law no book selected by
> a librarian for his shelves can constitutionally be found ob-
> scene. Why? Because any such book must have at least
> some slight redeeming social importance. The very act of
> library selection testifies to and engrafts such importance
> upon it.

> This is why, for example, the Kinsey Institute was able to
> vindicate in court its constitutional right to import even so-
> called hard-core pornography. The process of selection,
> the institutional interest, can lend even otherwise "worth-

less" material the kind of importance necessary to activate the constitutional guarantees of free expression. Therefore, I believe that libraries must have something like total immunity from prosecution or external coercion in the exercise of their vital functions.

The basic principle for librarians might best be described thus: Any material selected by a librarian, in the exercise of his function as a librarian, is protected. The protection extends both to his acquisition and retention of the material, and also precludes any valid prosecution of the librarian for acquiring or retaining it.[10]

Notes

1. Lester Asheim. "Not Censorship but Selection," Wilson Library Bulletin, 28 (September 1953), 63-67.
2. Marjorie Fiske. Book Selection and Censorship (Berkeley: University of California Press, 1959).
3. Webster's Third New International Dictionary, under "pornography," sense 2.
4. Dorothy Broderick. "Problem Nonfiction," Library Journal, 87 (October 1, 1962), 3373-8.
5. Bernard Berelson. "The Myth of Library Impartiality," Wilson Library Bulletin, 13 (October 1938), 87-90.
6. "Dayton Tests Selection Policy Against Election Campaign Books," Library Journal, 89 (December 1, 1964), 4765.
7. Mary Lee Bundy. "Metropolitan Public Library Use," Wilson Library Bulletin, 41 (May 1967), 956.
8. Broderick. "Problem Nonfiction," 3373-8.
9. Dr. Herman Taller was found guilty by a federal jury in New York City on twelve counts of mail fraud, one count of conspiracy, and violation of the Food, Drug and Cosmetics Law. See "Calories Author Guilty," Publishers' Weekly (May 22, 1967), 40.
10. Edward de Grazia. "Defending the Freedom to Read in the Courts," ALA Bulletin, 59 (June 1965), 507-15.

DEFENDING THE INDEFENSIBLE:
THE LIMITS OF INTELLECTUAL FREEDOM

By Leo N. Flanagan

It is now more than a year since the American Library Association's national office for Intellectual Freedom issued its Intellectual Freedom Manual.[1] With the exception of Rhode Island's local intellectual freedom committee, which issued a position paper at the spring conference of the state library association, no one has seen fit, to my knowledge to comment on the impracticality, oversimplification, legal difficulties, anti-intellectualism, and want of professionalism manifest in the Manual's Introduction.

Perhaps less attention has been paid to the Manual's Introduction simply because it is both brief and confusing. Its confusion is only an exaggeration of the typical confusion attendant on library discussions of intellectual freedom, and the great remainder of the Manual has already proven to be a valuable addition to the literature of librarianship. Overall, the Manual gathers together in one place the many ALA pronouncements of nearly the last four decades on intellectual freedom and summarizes them well in a "Historical Overview." Included are the Association's Library Bill of Rights and the Freedom To Read Statement. While these and most other documents in the Manual lack some precision, some social and technological currency, and some everyday usefulness, in regard to the controversial role of the librarian as change agent and advocate, and in regard to the even more controversial effects of newer media technologies, it is helpful to have all ALA position papers on intellectual freedom and censorship brought together.

Using this Manual, the deficiencies of the overall ALA position can be determined. With Gerald Shields' new draft of the Library Bill of Rights about to appear at ALA's Midwinter Conference, it is time that the ALA membership address the inadequacies of the old Library Bill and related ALA papers.

The reason for concern over the Introduction is that from its position in the Manual, its content, and the anonymity of its authorship, it has every appearance of being intended to serve as the latest, most definitive philosophic interpretation of the numerous documents on intellectual freedom that follow. Given its limitations, it thus becomes a dangerous document. The specific problems in the Introduction are five, each of which I will explore in some detail.

Impracticality

The Introduction defines intellectual freedom to mean "the right of any person to believe whatever he wants on any subject and to express his beliefs or ideas in whatever way he thinks appropriate." This is patently impractical. John Stuart Mill made an elaborate defense of allowing ideas to compete in the marketplace, and the Freedom To Read Statement reaffirms that stand in its concept of the "free enterprise" of ideas. But Mill would not have countenanced expressing ideas in any way an individual wished, because Mill again and again restricted the freedom he defended by noting that no one had the freedom to injure another. A century later anthropologist J. C. Carothers tells us, "No existing society really allows free speech" because of the harm it would do itself. [2] No society can remain intact and allow an individual the right to express his ideas in any way he thinks appropriate. Two years ago in LJ Patrick Williams and J. T. Pearce said:

> Freedom of expression and freedom of inquiry are species of freedom of action. Just as freedom of action is subject to all manner of limitation by the rights of others and the best interests of society, so also are freedom of expression and inquiry. [3]

Necessary limitation on the freedom of expression and inquiry come to mind at once. No one in the United States during World War II was permitted to inform the Germans of the position of American naval bases or even to advocate such disclosure, however sincerely he believed in the cause of Germany. Most people would consider that a reasonable restriction of individual freedom of expression. San Francisco Major Joseph Alioto was lately enjoined by a California court from commenting on the recent Zebra murders, lest he endanger the right of certain defendants to a fair trial. B'nai B'rith's recent recourse to law to force the Mutual Broadcasting Company to cancel anti-Semitic Liberty Lobby broadcasts on 80 radio stations did not seem unfair to most people of liberal sympathies. So, too, have many liberal Americans striven for laws against fraudulent advertising. And most of us abide by the laws of copyright limiting our rights to repeat what has cost others time and money to express initially. Similarly, we do not fault the law that says no one of us is allowed to accuse a neighbor of crimes or misdemeanors, without evidence, however deep our beliefs in another's guilt may be. If we do, and are sued for libel, most people would not say our freedom of expression had been unfairly restricted.

There are necessary limitations on individual freedom of expression, and sensible people allow for some regulation of such expression for the overall social order. Overzealous application of the First Amendment, to the detriment of others, will do as much damage to the rights of free exercise of religion, freedom of speech, freedom of the press, and freedom of assembly and petition as outright attack on these principles.

Lord Kenneth Clark finds that civilizations are distinguished by the kind and subtlety of their regulations. Our own civilization is presently regarding a number of subtleties in its regulations. For example, social psychologists are carefully investigating the damage certain free expression in the media may be doing to the society. In the matter of television, the Surgeon General's Scientific Advisory Committee on Television and Social Behavior has found that the causal relation between televised violence and antisocial behavior is sufficient to warrant immediate remedial guidelines. [4] The people of Boston felt the same way in 1973. Only a few days after a television program had portrayed teenage boys burning a young woman to death with gasoline, several Boston youths duplicated the crime. Like television producers, journalists are now considering self-regulation in reporting sensational news in light of a rash of plane hijackings and terrorist kidnappings. Within the past year, two conferences of journalists considered the possibility that certain types of reporting suggest, encourage, and multiply crimes and that self-imposed guidelines may be necessary. [5] Some librarians in support of an absolute, simplistic position on intellectual freedom remain in ignorance of regulatory developments in other fields and occupations. As Dorothy Broderick said it, in the conclusion of a fine article: "Having decided once and for all to be in favor of intellectual freedom, a segment of our profession has then closed its mind to all consideration of the opposing view. "[6]

A purist position on intellectual freedom today is similar to a purist position on free enterprise. The laissez faire approach to economics--and ideas and media--is absurd at this time, when Western civilization is more than ever committed to social responsibility. Responsibility implies choice of judgment and control of members of a society by the members themselves for their common good. Such control would limit individual expression and the opportunity to hear and see some things. Most reasonable people recognize that, albeit sadly, as a condition of living in a less than perfect world.

Oversimplification

A second difficulty with the Introduction to the Intellectual Freedom Manual--and for that matter with many ALA documents on the subject--is gross oversimplification. The Introduction affirms the individual's right to express one's beliefs or ideas through "any mode of communication. " Any mode of communication is a phrase of such sweeping magnitude that it is immediately suspect. Would librarians defend physical blows, torture, enforced starvation, economic or racial exploitation, all of which are especially dramatic modes of human communication of some kinds of ideas? Do librarians wish to be apologists for the literature of mutilation, flagellation, and bondage? Do librarians want to protect acts of civilian bombing and strafing, which certainly became a mode of communication in Indo-China? Do librarians want to, as Betty Friedan puts it, hide behind the First Amendment in promotion of sexist stereotypes in text books?[7] Do librarians, concerned about the position of

women today, wish to condone the bottom drawer pornography which
feminist Robin Morgan calls "visual rape"? I think most of the library community would answer nay to each of these questions. Yet
the simplicity of the Introduction's definition, its failure, and the
failure of many ALA documents to make realistic distinctions in addressing the complicated subject of intellectual freedom diminishes
community respect for the intelligence of librarians.

Speaking of oversimplification, are no distinctions to be called
for in discussing the degree of intellectual freedom, in the sense of
freedom of inquiry, that one might have in an academic as distinct
from a public library of the same size? In the public library might
one not expect far less opportunity for real freedom of inquiry,
since so much of the collection would be devoted to the literature of
entertainment rather than information? In the academic library,
with its collections deliberately designed for the widest pursuit of
all types of information and all types of views in depth, might one not
well expect more freedom of inquiry?

Looking at the subject of types of libraries from the librarian's view, can the public librarian with some obligation to the vagaries of the tax-paying reader exercise as much personal intellectual
freedom in book selection as the academic librarian concerned only
with the fullest range of serious and scholarly arguments? Are not
distinctions needed here?

Another ALA problem in distinction proceeds from failure to
note the differences among a reader's right to free access to ideas,
to information, and to entertainment. In fact, many state library
networks, such as Connecticut's, make the distinction in guaranteeing
circulation of nonfiction but not of fiction.

Should there not be some distinctions made in regard to the
differing effects or influences on audiences of different media? A
television program of questionable content may reach 60 million
people in an evening, while a bestselling book with the same message may never reach a tenth of that audience and will not reach that
audience at the same time. Is it not plausible that novels may affect,
for better or worse, general audiences more profoundly than poetry?
The government has thought so for years, and so, as Ernest Hemingway noted in Men at War, the government has not arrested critical
poets as quickly as critical novelists in war time. [8] Is it not possible that realistic motion pictures may affect audiences more profoundly than books? After all, reading is a highly abstract experience
while a motion picture is a far better "imitation of an action" (to borrow from Aristotle's definition of drama). Concern with many subtle
but real differences in media effect has not been an ALA preoccupation in the discussion of intellectual freedom. It is extremely difficult to see how librarians avoid this responsibility.

Legal Difficulties

The Introduction also states that the definition of Intellectual

Freedom includes a second integral part, "the right of unrestricted access to all information and ideas regardless of the medium of communication used." This assertion poses two problems. One, it pledges librarians to more than they can actually deliver. Secondly, and more importantly, it flies in the face of the Constitution of the United States and the law of the land. The Constitution mandates free access to information by implication in the first Amendment of the Bill of Rights, but that free access is in fact restricted by Amendments Four, Five, and Six, guaranteeing the right to privacy, fair trial, and freedom from self-incrimination. No one's right to information allows him to make an unwarranted search of another's home, to force another to testify against himself, or to extricate information by torture.

As a sidelight the Office of Intellectual Freedom's "unrestricted access to all information" ignores not only the law, but the latest development within the field of librarianship itself. The National Commission on Libraries and Information Science, aware of the law and the restrictions it mandates, has made a recommendation in direct opposition to the Office of Intellectual Freedom. NCLIS recommends that libraries be linked in computer, audiovisual, and telecommunications systems to create a national information pool, and it recommends establishment of "security protocols" to exclude some of the pooled information from some individuals. [9] The National Commission assumes only that "all of the people of the United States have the right, according to their individual needs, to realistic and convenient access" to the national information resource, and that they have the right only for their "personal enrichment and achievement." [10] Ironically, intellectual freedom slogans notwithstanding, librarians themselves already use "security protocols" in admitting only scholars to university race or pornography collections, and in not even building such collections in public libraries. It may be true that many governments abuse security systems of classifying information, but abuse does not deny the original need for methods of protecting national or individual security.

Anti-intellectualism

In paragraph two of the Introduction, the Office for Intellectual Freedom contradicts its definition of intellectual freedom in paragraph 1, sentence 1, now defining intellectual freedom as only freedom of the mind, necessary to action but separate from it. What does freedom of the mind mean? If intellectual freedom is not action, how can it be freedom of expression as well as thought? What is expression if it is not action? The difficulty appears to lie in the Manual's partial attempt to divide thought from action, a recent attempt in human history, and one with unfortunate implications. To believe that ideas can be separated from action, and that such ideas when promulgated will have no effect on action, is to undervalue the power of ideas considerably. It is an anti-intellectual stance to assert that ideas are ineffective! To believe that only "good" ideas are effective and not evil ones is to be illogical and unrealistic. Or as Irving Kristol said, if no one has ever been corrupted by a book (movie, television program), then no one has been improved by one either.[11] To believe that it does not matter what effect ideas have is to believe in no values or standards, to be nihilistic. This perpetuates racist, sexist, and exploitative views which hinder human growth, which dehumanize, and which consequently reduce what freedom is possible. The refusal to regulate (not repress) freedom in the United States today has led to an abuse of freedom by the military in Vietnam, government leaders in the White House, and big business in the competitive economy, and has resulted in attempts by such agencies to obliterate the freedom of all of us. To believe that good ideas--that is, ideas fostering human growth--will automatically triumph over evil ones is simply to be ignorant of the lessons of history.

Want of Professionalism

To refuse to impose some values in the world of ideas and information, and on the means of expression--to undertake, as the Introduction advises, to provide all points of view on all questions--is to avoid doing what professionals in other fields actually do, that is, to avoid judging what is conducive to human growth and what is not. To "give 'em what they want, " as Judy Krug of the Office for Intellectual Freedom advised graduate library students at Simmons College, is to avoid constructive judgment.[12]

To abrogate the responsibility for decision in the selection and exclusion of materials, and for counsel of readers, is to miss the whole point of professionalism. For what is a professional librarian but one who believes in the goodness and worthiness of improving human communication through symbol-carrying objects or media?[13] It is no accident that for 2000 years librarians were priests very much aware that ideas, language, literature, information, and entertainment had definite moral influences on society. What is a professional librarian but one who holds such belief, who because of this belief acquires substantive knowledge, who with such knowledge maintains independence of judgment even within institutional settings, who joins fellow professionals in a strong organization to insure development of the field's knowledge and its humane application in the community interest?[14] What is a professional librarian but one who on the basis of a substantive knowledge of the means of communication, knowledge greater than that of the general community, judges what media is necessary to improve provision of ideas and information in the community, and who judges what counsel and advice would be helpful to individual members of the community? The Library Bill of Rights itself exhorts librarians to choose library materials "for values of interest, information, and enlightenment, " and choice of those values certainly requires judgment. If it does not, chimpanzees might as well be doing it.

Unfortunately, many librarians doubt their ability to make decided judgments regarding materials and patrons. Again and again I hear the question, from librarians, at library conferences, "Who are we to judge?" A better question might be, "Who else is to judge?" Doctors judge illness and the means of curing it, and they strongly recommend but do not force the cure. Lawyers judge the nature of individual human conflict and recommend courses of action to conclude it to the satisfaction of their clients. Generals judge the conflicts of nations and recommend campaigns to end them. And we trust them because they have greater expertise in their areas of specialty than we do as laymen. Do we trust librarians? Do librarians trust themselves?

In that the answer to the latter question appears to be "no" lies the single greatest tragedy of librarianship. Most librarians hide behind a definition of intellectual freedom which demands no responsibility, which simply commands them to do nothing. And I would suggest that is because they are fearful of making decisions about materials and people with the low level of substantive knowledge that they possess.[15] Few librarians have more than a year's graduate work in the field. Most have no undergraduate preparation for the work. Few pursue continuing education in librarianship or related fields. Few read in the serious literature of the field.[16] For that matter, there is little serious literature because, as Paul Wasserman says again and again, there are rather poor scholarly foundations for the field. I believe that librarians do not think they can judge because not only don't they develop the knowledge to do so but knowledge in the way of reliable research, surveys, and statistics is not available in librarianship. I have even heard librarians go so far as to say that the issues of intellectual freedom cannot be defined any more than the issues of tragedy and comedy. Yet in fact tragedy and comedy are rather well defined in literary criticism, and there is general agreement on the major components. Librarians who tend to operate only in a world of opinion and assumption unfortunately believe that the same weakness bedevils laborers in other vineyards.

The doctrine of intellectual freedom is, therefore, a facesaving device to avoid responsible judgments on complex issues by librarians who lack the knowledge to make them. What can be done about it is surprisingly simple. If librarians wish to be clerks, caretakers, and technicians, transferring objects between people, they can continue to make no decisions. If they wish to be professional, then they, and ALA, must place an emphasis on acquisition of considerably more substantive knowledge by each librarian. To properly choose materials and relate them to people, librarians will need intensive continuous education in the technology of communication, in learning psychology, in human engineering, and in much more. This may well require a basic education of three years, an internship, ALA certification, and recertification every several years.

If there existed enough librarians with real substantive knowledge, who could make reliable, responsible judgments most of the time, no major difficulties would exist with the current issues of the intellectual freedom debate. There would, for example, be no problem for such librarians in regard to censorship. Where censors attempt to <u>suppress</u> ideas or information that they find dangerous or objectionable, knowledgeable librarians, with the help of experts in virtually every learned field, would <u>select</u> <u>and</u> <u>promote</u> published materials that either clearly or probably encourage human growth or development, that do not turn people to objects as do racism and pornography. Every effort would be made to include the controversial and disputatious in general collections so long as it was not destructive or probably destructive of the public safety. Such materials could be housed in research centers where expert guidance by knowledgeable librarians would be used to aid responsible patrons with ascertained need to know. In fact, librarianship is already well on this course, with librarians relying on experts through reviews in choosing materials, and in the placement of highly controversial materials in research libraries. Ultimately, with sufficient knowledge, librarians could select for their own collections and patrons the materials their training showed were sound. And they could avoid just as much as doctors any sweeping defenses of pornographic movies in Los Angeles or political rebellions in Afghanistan, both of which are beyond their profession.

With substantive knowledge amongst librarians, many of the problems of the library users' intellectual freedom would disappear. If the community indeed found that librarians had the ability to choose, and did choose fairly and intelligently a range of materials providing ideas and information necessary to the community, the community would not fear repression of its intellectual freedom. If more research centers were open to the responsible public that could demonstrate its research interest, there would actually be an expansion of freedom of inquiry. If the community respected librarians' knowledge as much as that of doctors, there would be no serious challenge of librarians' selections for children. Nor would knowledgeable librarians open any materials to children without guidance.

There would be no question of librarians' right to intellectual freedom in personal and professional matters if their knowledge of communication and media were well in advance of that of other segments of the community.

Lastly, amongst current issues on intellectual freedom there would be no difficulty with advocacy. Librarians well trained would be expected to judge the need for and undertake advocacy of any procedure or idea within their professional purview. Hence, the demonstrated observation that some portion of the community received inadequate information would lead to establishment of orthodox or unorthodox methods of bringing information to the disadvantaged population. Librarians would still be expected to avoid pronouncements on brain surgery just as neurosurgeons would avoid pronouncements on television as a public learning tool.

Overall, knowledgeable librarians would treat intellectual freedom as any freedom, regulating it responsibly in the best joint interests of the individual and the public order, never mistaking it for license, never destroying it by undue restriction. While such a bal-

Leo N. Flanagan / 37

anced position is agonizingly difficult to maintain, and must continually be reevaluated and regained, the only other choices are to sacrifice the social good to anarchy or the individual to autocracy.

Presently the only problem is that librarians find themselves between technical roles, processing and transferring learning materials with no concern for the effect of that work, and professional roles, judging library materials and users and the effect of materials on users. ALA only has to recommend respectable education for librarians to make professional judgment sound, responsible, and credible, to allow librarians to exploit a special knowledge for the good of others without that knowledge. This is a great but necessary burden. And those who assume it rightfully know that freedom is not an end, but only a means to such ends as individual development and a benevolent society. Librarians who undertake responsibility for creating such a society are like other creators and artists, unafraid of controls. Art is after all the controlled expression in a medium of a significant human experience. A benevolent society does not happen. It is only the result of controlled, deliberate, thoughtful expression. It is a work of art.

The original occasion of this article, the Introduction to the Intellectual Freedom Manual, demonstrates little appreciation of deliberated action, of thoughtful control. That Introduction and many other intellectual freedom documents reveal no confidence in the beauty, truth, or goodness of the imposition of human decision on reality. Heaven knows human decision and action is far from infallible. However, human decision, the willingness to collect good evidence and to decide on the basis of it for ourselves and others has gotten us out of the caves.

Perhaps the Manual's Introduction was to be expected, given many of the inadequacies in education for librarianship. Yet while it might be expected, it is hardly to be accepted in its blind optimism, timidity, naivete, absolutism, imprecision, confusion, simplification, and anti-intellectualism. As an unqualified series of slogans it is hardly to be accepted as the final interpretation of a complicated reality. Its inadequacies are so great that the "Historic Overview" which follows it stands out by virtue of its common sense and its contradiction of the Introduction. By contrast, this "Historic Overview" by Krug and Harvey simply recognizes the complexities involved with intellectual freedom. The "Overview" recognizes that there are limits upon the First Amendment, that the concept of advocacy cannot be dismissed easily, that opposition to censorship is tempered by law and by librarians' sense of personal responsibility, and that full access to information for minors is still a controversial issue. In sum the strengths of the "Historic Overview" so overshadow the deficiencies of the Introduction that it may be hoped that the Office of Intellectual Freedom will delete the Introduction from future printings of the Intellectual Freedom Manual, and allow the "Overview" to remain alone as an adequate introduction for the present. It may also be hoped that the limitations of many of the documents contained in the Manual will provoke a more enlightened examination of intellectual freedom and censorship amongst librarians.

38 / Collection Development

Notes

1. Office for Intellectual Freedom of the American Library Association. Intellectual Freedom Manual (American Library Assn., 1974).
2. Carothers, J. C. "Culture, Psychiatry, and the Written Word," Psychiatry, November 1949, p. 307-20.
3. Williams, Patrick & J. J. Pearce. "Common Sense and Censorship; a Call for Revision," Library Journal, September 1, 1973, p. 2399-2400.
4. Pastore, John. "Blood in American Living Rooms," Pawtucket (Rhode Island) Times, June 18, 1974, p. 34.
5. Dickinson, Brian. "A Free Press and the Law," Providence Sunday Journal, June 23, 1974, p. 15. And Donald Goldfarb. "The Effects of News Publication Pose a Serious Dilemma," Providence Journal, May 2, 1974: p. A-25.
6. Broderick, Dorothy. "Censorship-Reevaluated," School Library Journal, November 15, 1971, p. 3816-18.
7. Nyren, Karl. "Those Female Stereotypes," LJ/SLJ Hotline, November 4, 1974, p. 4.
8. Hemingway, Ernest, ed. Men at War (Crown, 1942), p. 7.
9. The National Commission on Libraries and Information Science. A National Program for Library and Information Services: a Synopsis of the Second Draft Proposal. GPO, June 1974, p. 7.
10. _____. Toward a National Program for Libraries, and Information Services: Goals for Action. GPO, 1975, p. x.
11. Kristol, Irving. "Pornography, Obscenity and the Case for Censorship," N.Y. Times Magazine, March 28, 1971, p. 24-25 & p. 112-16.
12. Krug, Judy. "Intellectual Freedom and the ALA," a lecture at Simmons College, Boston, Massachusetts, December 6, 1972.
13. Flanagan, L. N. "Comment on Librarians and Libraries," Catholic Library World, November 1974, p. 177-78.
14. Bundy, Mary Lee & Paul Wasserman. "Professionalism Reconsidered," College and Research Libraries, January 1968, p. 4-26. Also L. N. Flanagan. "Professionalism Dismissed," CRL, May 1973, p. 209-14.
15. Broderick, p. 3818.
16. Goldstein, Samuel. "Using the Literature of Librarianship," Conference on Writing and Publishing for Librarians, Brandeis University, Waltham, Massachusetts, April 4, 1975.

SELECTION AND SOAPBOXES:
AN IDEOLOGICAL PRIMER

By Elaine Fain

Libraries cannot buy everything; librarians are the officially designated "selectors" or "collectors" who must determine what their institutions can afford to acquire. That much is clear. Very little else is clear, however, when it comes to what I shall call "the selection-censorship muddle." Incredible confusion has been generated in the selection policy area because of a pair of concepts endorsed by the ALA: the freedom to read and intellectual freedom.

At first glance the muddle seems to be the outcome of a collision course between two opposite traditions: 1) the liberal tradition, with its emphasis on complete freedom of thought and expression (no matter how wrong or repulsive or evil those thoughts and expressions might be), and 2) the educational-moral uplift tradition of libraries, with its emphasis on "quality" selection of library materials. The collision need not have occurred, however; it only appears to have been inevitable in retrospect because the arguments for liberalism have been misapplied to selection policy.

Let us begin the untangling of the muddle by reexamining the most eloquent expression of the liberal position on freedom of thought--that presented by John Stuart Mill in his classic On Liberty. Mill endeavored to carve out an inviolate area of individual liberty, a province of thought and action immune from social censure and suppression. Mill's basic theme, a corollary of his Utilitarianism, was that attempts to suppress an individual's freedom of thought or action would in the long run cause greater harm to society than the harm that might result from allowing that freedom. The only justification, Mill argued, for social interference with an individual's freedom of expression or action was either self-protection or the prevention of harm to others.

Mill's critics were many, both in his day and ours. Some disapproved entirely of his concept of individual liberty; others approved but found his supporting arguments inadequate or misguided. (See, for example, the essay section entitled "The Case Against Mill" in the 1975 Norton critical edition of On Liberty or the well known chapter, "Liberty," in Robert Paul Wolff's The Poverty of Liberalism, published in 1968.)

Mill believed it possible to distinguish between those individual

actions that involved others and those that did not; with regard to
the latter, there could be no defensible ground whatever for interference. "In the part which merely concerns himself," wrote Mill,
"the independence is, of right, absolute. Over himself, over his
own body and mind, the individual is sovereign." Mill, who abhorred
the temperance movement that had gained ground in England during
his lifetime, held that

> no person ought to be punished for simply being drunk....
> His [the drunk's] own good, either physical or moral, is
> not a sufficient warrant. He cannot rightfully be compelled
> to do or forbear because it will make him happier, because,
> in the opinions of others, to do so would be wise, or even
> right....

If a person's conduct involved others, however, then a limited case
for control might be made on the basis of the protection of society.
Thus, Mill found it consistent with his idea of liberty that "a soldier
or policeman should be punished for being drunk on duty." Children
and barbarians, he added, did not come under the umbrella of liberty at all.

Mill's doctrine was held by him to apply to the following
spheres: 1) the inward domain of consciousness, including thought
and feeling, and 2) the liberty of tastes and pursuits. A third liberty, that of adults uniting voluntarily for any purpose, followed as a
consequence of the first two liberties. Under category one, which
is the area of special interest for librarians, Mill included the freedom to express and publish opinions. He admitted that the expression of opinions did indeed involve other people, but insisted that it
was quite impossible to separate the expression and publication of
opinions from the freedom of thought.

Mill's assumption that a sharp distinction can be drawn between actions that affect others and those that do not is, to say the
least, troublesome. One might well balk at the simplistic notion that
when someone reads a book on the construction of Molotov cocktails
and then proceeds to make one and throw it, the action of reading
had concerned only the bomb-thrower. Nonetheless, one might still
hold Mill's general libertarian position, arguing that the suppression
of books on Molotov cocktails would in the long run be more destructive to a free society than the bomb explosion itself. To take another case, one might be thoroughly convinced that the viewing of certain films incites spectators to violence (a conviction held in Norway,
where Bonnie and Clyde, The Wild Ones, and other films have been
totally banned on the grounds that violent films incite violent behavior), but be equally firm in the conviction that film censorship
would, in the long run, be more socially damaging than possible acts
of violence induced by motion pictures.

It is essential to stress that what Mill and the liberals wanted
was really a "permanent floating" soapbox, a movable Hyde Park
Corner, a traveling free marketplace of ideas. These could naturally

emerge, Mill thought, once the social suppression of unpopular ideas was abandoned. Mill designated no guardian institution to function as an official platform for the free expression of ideas. He envisioned neither university nor library as a guarantor of liberty. The liberals, let us remember, were opposed to governmental interference with individual affairs, even when the motives for interfering were admirable. Mill stated in On Liberty that "a general State education is a mere contrivance for moulding people to be exactly like one another...." He was in favor of the state requiring some kind of education for all children, but adamant in the opinion that the state itself should never actually operate schools except as "one among many competing experiments, carried on for the purpose of example and stimulus...."

Now when the ALA Council declared that "in a free society each individual is free to determine for himself what he wishes to read" (The Freedom to Read), it was endorsing a concept of individual freedom straight out of Mill's On Liberty. Here was the classic liberal stance: People ought to be able to read what they want without interference. "If one takes On Liberty as a guide," Robert Paul Wolff has commented,

> ... then the right of adults to indulge their lascivious desires by reading deliberately provocative pornography or by viewing lewd movies ought to be completely unregulated by government or society ... the doctrine of the liberty of the inner life dictates that each person be left to make his own decision regarding so manifestly private a choice. (The Poverty of Liberalism, p. 39)

Justice William O. Douglas steadfastly endorsed this position during his long tenure on the Supreme Court. In his June 21, 1973 dissent in Paris Adult Theatre I v. Slaton, Douglas wrote:

> I never read or see the materials coming to the Court under charges of 'obscenity,' because I have thought the First Amendment made it unconstitutional for me to act as a censor.... Our society--unlike most of the world-- presupposes that freedom and liberty are in a frame of reference that make the individual, not government, the keeper of his tastes, beliefs, and ideas.

However, when the ALA Council declared in the Library Bill of Rights that "libraries should provide books and other materials presenting all points of view concerning the problems and issues of our times," it moved quite a theoretical distance--from the classic liberal position on freedom of thought to a statement about the function of libraries. The ALA is here presupposing that the library ought to serve as society's soapbox, as an official guarantor of a Free Marketplace of Ideas.

Should the library function as such a soapbox? The ALA endorses the idea, but has never really made the case or even spelled out the consequences. Obviously, an astronomy library in a university is not under an obligation to stock astrology books just because astrologers promote a different point of view about stars. A medical library need not open its shelves to books by cancer-cure quacks. These institutions do not exist primarily to serve the cause of liberal democracy, but to provide materials for scientists working within the accepted parameters of their subject fields, as defined by them.

What ALA means, I take it, is that some libraries (probably public) ought to serve a democratic society by becoming a repository and distribution center for diverse written opinions, particularly in those areas touching on norms and values. Unfortunately, the ALA Committee on Intellectual Freedom, which defends the Freedom to Read and Library Bill of Rights statements, has simply repeated liberal doctrine designed for a different situation--that of Hands Off (no suppression or censorship) rather than Hands On (deliberate provision of materials reflecting many points of view). In so doing, it has contributed heavily to the selection-censorship muddle. The outcome is that those who oppose the Soapbox Function tend to think that they must simultaneously renounce the entire liberal doctrine of freedom of thought.

Look, for example, at a Library Journal article by Leo N. Flanagan: "Defending the Indefensible: The Limits of Intellectual Freedom" (Oct. 15, 1975, p. 1890). Flanagan is an ardent advocate of Tradition Two--the educational function of librarians:

> It is no accident that for 2,000 years librarians were priests very much aware that ideas, language, literature, information, and entertainment had definite moral influences on society. What is a professional librarian but one who holds such belief...? The Library Bill of Rights itself exhorts librarians to choose library materials 'for values of interest, information, and enlightenment,' and choice of those values certainly requires judgment. If it doesn't, chimpanzees might as well be doing it.

The Soapbox Function fills Flanagan with horror, for it not only--in his eyes--co-opts librarians into disseminating false and malicious doctrines, but it denigrates their status as well.

Why, however, should Flanagan's ardent advocacy of the educational tradition lead him to call for "limits" on intellectual freedom? It is in part because he, like the Committee on Intellectual Freedom, conflates the Soapbox Function with the classic liberal position on freedom of thought. Also, he fails to grasp that the Soapbox-Function position is, like his own, an intensely moral affair. Librarians who believe they ought to provide a diverse set of views on controversial subjects are taking a moral stand just as much as Flanagan: They are taking the position that in the long run, the publication and distribution of all views will be healthier for a free society than attempts by self-appointed guardians to keep supposedly harmful materials from the public. The Library Bill of Rights, though not well thought out and certainly not well argued, is a great deal more than, as Flanagan puts it, "a face-saving device to avoid responsible judgments on complex issues by librarians who lack the knowledge to make them."

The high road of moral guardianship is also taken by Dorothy Broderick, who always claims to know which books promote "the sanctity of life" and "growth," and which ones don't. Unlike Flanagan, Broderick is willing to grant that even professional librarians make mistakes. Attacking librarians who utilize the no-censorship principle by refusing to remove books from shelves in response to complaints, she asks:

> Did librarians suddenly and magically become infallible?
> ... Is the complainant always and automatically wrong?
> ... Somehow, to be self-righteous under the banner of intellectual freedom strikes me as the ultimate in absurdity. ("Censorship--Reevaluated," Library Journal, Nov. 15, 1971, p. 3816)

It is, I should like to suggest, not nearly so absurd as self-righteousness under the banner of "the sanctity of life."

Critics who, like Flanagan and Broderick, attack what they believe to be the liberal position, insist that true librarians know (or ought to know) which reading materials are good for others to read. They also hold that librarians who refuse, on libertarian grounds, to claim any authority superior to library patrons in selecting library materials, are acting unprofessionally.

True, the Committee on Intellectual Freedom was far too facile in moving from the classic liberal stand against censorship to the promotion of the Soapbox Function. As indicated earlier, this function is simply out of place in many kinds of libraries--it just isn't relevant. For very large research libraries, it is more or less built in because of the enormous range of materials collected. What self-respecting general research library would be without collections of Marxist materials, for example? Or of racist tracts?

It is in connection with public libraries that the question of the Soapbox Function becomes really interesting. (Also in connection with elementary and high school libraries--but here other factors enter the picture. The extension of liberal doctrine on freedom of thought to the world of children is still extremely controversial. Remember that John Stuart Mill himself excluded children and barbarians from the application of his concept of liberty.) Should public libraries attempt to "provide books and other materials presenting all points of view concerning the problems and issues of our times"? Even if they wanted to, could they? And if they wanted to and could, would attempts to carry out the Soapbox Function interfere with the traditional process of selection?

The Soapbox Function is, in my opinion, a legitimate one for public libraries, but it must be disentangled from "intellectual freedom" and discussed on its own merits. It is not doctrinally an integral part of the freedom of speech and press. By undertaking the Soapbox Function, however, public libraries could contribute in a very practical fashion to making generally available printed materials reflecting all shades of opinion, all manner of thought, and all levels of quality.

Again, it must be emphasized that public libraries could never in any case devote all their space and staff energies to the Soapbox Function. Their budgetary limitations alone would prevent them from acquiring all opinions "concerning the problems and issues of our times." In addition public libraries have other important goals--educational and cultural--that govern their choices of materials. The Soapbox Function is an additional consideration, one that necessarily lies outside the traditional selection process.

I see no gain in entangling the too-vague concept of "intellectual freedom" with the selection process. Somebody has to choose library materials. That somebody may be an advocate of Moral Guardianship or the Soapbox Function; he or she may be stupid or intelligent, knowledgeable or ignorant, conservative or liberal, cowardly or courageous; may be operating from good motives or bad. I can argue with that somebody on his or her ideas about libraries, philosophy of selection, or individual choices of materials, but I cannot stretch classic liberal doctrine to cover the selection process.

Selection policy must be argued in terms of library function; the "hands-off" doctrine of classic liberalism cannot be expanded to fit what must inevitably be a "hands-on" approach, designed to cover the acquisition of library materials. It may well be that the greatest accomplishment for a public library would be to fulfill the Soapbox Function. (I'm inclined to support that position, in fact.) The argument for it, however, cannot be fashioned from classic liberalism--not even when such terms as "freedom to read" and "intellectual freedom" are invented and mouthed. Let us abandon bad arguments and rhetorical overkill; let us discuss instead the functions of libraries and, in particular, The Public Library as Soapbox.

INTELLECTUAL FREEDOM AND
THE RIGHTS OF CHILDREN

By Judith F. Krug

In the controversy over the use of Slaughterhouse Five in the
Rochester Community Schools, all substantive actions and maneuver-
ings were initiated, developed, and resolved by adults. The students,
whose accessibility to the novel was at stake, never directly participated. This situation is not unusual. Almost all requests for removal of curriculum and library materials are generated by adults.
Attacks are based on the doctrine of in loco parentis, meaning, in
broad interpretation, that parents or other adults, such as teachers,
librarians, and clergy, designated by parents, have complete responsibility for--and control over--children, including their minds. The
in loco parentis concept, however, conflicts directly with the intellectual freedom concept, which provides for free choice, regardless
of age, in matters concerning the mind. This basic conflict has
reached new proportions in recent years because of the U.S. Supreme
Court's recognition of youths' rights in the First Amendment area.

The in loco parentis doctrine has been recognized in Western
civilization from about the sixteenth century, resulting in an unusual,
and in many ways incongruous, situation today. The term "children, "
in a legal sense, covers all individuals up to age twenty-one. In
general, but with a few exceptions, "children" can be drafted and
taxed, are subject to corporal punishment by the family, are subject to dictates of school authorities and to juvenile curfews, and
can be sent to adult prisons. But, again with a few exceptions,
children cannot sign a binding contract or hold and dispose of property, work in many occupations, represent themselves in divorce or
will proceedings, sit on a grand jury or jury, run for elected office,
be appointed to state agencies, marry or travel without parental consent, purchase liquor or cigarettes, attend certain movies, or read
certain books. It is, indeed, an incongruous situation.

The incongruity was accentuated by the Twenty-sixth Amendment to the United States Constitution granting a portion of the
"children, " the eighteen to twenty-one-year-olds, the right to vote.
Adoption of the Twenty-sixth Amendment made clear a new direction
for the nation in regard to children's rights, the advocacy of which
began nearly one hundred years ago. Over the years, other plateaus
such as Child Labor Laws and the juvenile court system were reached.

Reprinted by permission of the American Library Association from
"Intellectual Freedom and the Rights of Children, " School Media
Quarterly 1, No. 2 (Winter, 1973), pp. 132-135; copyright © 1973
by the American Library Association.

But, it was not until the 1967 in re Gault case that the courts recognized children's rights.

To understand the Gault decision, one must look at another milestone of juvenile rights--the juvenile court system. Created at the turn of the century, the juvenile court stresses that a child be examined and treated, not punished. This humane concept was verbalized by one of its original architects who, in 1909, wrote:

> Seated at a desk, with the child at his side, where he can
> on occasion put his arm around his shoulder and draw the
> lad to him, the judge ... will gain immensely in the ef-
> fectiveness of his work.

Unfortunately, the system didn't quite work that way. Among the juvenile court's more visible shortcomings was its rather blatant disregard for the concept of due process. To a large extent, juvenile courts seemed to believe that due process safeguards were irrelevant or unnecessary.

In 1967, however, the Gault case, focusing on due process in regard to juveniles, came before the U.S. Supreme Court. Fifteen-year-old Gerald Gault had been found guilty of making an obscene phone call. He was not notified of the charges against him, was not told of his rights against self-incrimination, was not represented by counsel, and, for an offense carrying a maximum sentence of two months for an adult, was declared a delinquent and subjected to institutionalization until age twenty-one--six years later. In its opinion, the Supreme Court asserted that a juvenile like Gerald Gault had a right to a timely notice of charges and that notice at the first hearing was not timely. It also said he had a right to counsel or appointed counsel if indigent, a right to be informed about self-incrimination, and a right to cross-examine the witnesses testifying against him. In the majority opinion, Mr. Justice Black wrote that children are entitled to these rights "because they are specifically and unequivocally granted by provisions of the Fifth and Sixth Amendments, which the Fourteenth Amendment makes applicable to the states." In other words, the Bill of Rights to the United States Constitution applies to all citizens regardless of age.

If the Gault case marked the turning point, the Tinker case of 1969 was not only a giant step in the right direction, but is even more pertinent to the conflict between adults and children. In Tinker vs. Des Moines Independent Community School District, the U.S. Supreme Court held, in February 1969, that the First Amendment protects the rights of public school children to express their political and social views during school hours. The decision held, further, that school officials may not place arbitrary curbs on student speech in the public schools. It is particularly interesting to note that, while many individuals had taken for granted that school children did have First Amendment rights of free speech, the Supreme Court had never directly said so prior to this case.

The Tinker case arose when a group of students decided to publicize their objection to the Vietnam war and their support for a truce by wearing black armbands in school during the 1967 holiday season. Principals of the Des Moines schools announced that any student refusing to remove the armband would be suspended.

A number of students, among them John and Mary Beth Tinker and Christopher Eckhardt (ages fifteen, thirteen, and sixteen, respectively) persisted in wearing the armbands to school. There was no disturbance or disruption of normal school activities but, nevertheless, the students were told to remove their armbands. When they refused, they were ordered to leave school. They returned two weeks later, without armbands but, in the meantime, had filed suit in federal court.

The students lost their case at both the district court level and in the U.S. Court of Appeals. The Supreme Court, however, reversed these decisions. In the majority opinion, Justice Abe Fortas pointed out that neither students nor teachers "shed their Constitutional right to freedom of speech or expression at the schoolhouse gate." He said:

> School officials do not possess absolute authority over their students. Students in school as well as out of school are 'persons' under our Constitution.... In our system, students may not be regarded as closed circuit recipients of only that which the state chooses to communicate. They may not be confined to the expression of those sentiments that are officially approved. In the absence of a specific showing of Constitutionally valid reasons to regulate their speech, students are entitled to freedom of expression of their views. [Emphasis added.]

As Justice Fortas saw it, the First Amendment was designed to insure toleration of dissent even where dissent may cause social discomfort or dispute. Accordingly, student expression in the schools may not be prohibited unless it "materially and substantially interfere[s] with the requirements of appropriate discipline in the operation of the school."

The Tinker case is a definite affirmation of students' or children's First Amendment rights. Also, upholding the right of the students to express their views by wearing armbands in school, the court said that such a form of expression "is exactly the type of symbolic act that is within the free speech clause of the First Amendment." Tinker thus makes it clear that symbolic forms of speech will continue to be protected by the court as long as the symbolic conduct does not interfere with legitimate and substantial state interests. Tinker has been tested several times in the last two years and it is now fairly evident that in order to curb students' First Amendment rights, disruption must have occurred. If disruption has not occurred, the courts have generally--but not always--found in favor of students' rights.

How, then, do these newly acknowledged rights of children
fit into the concept of intellectual freedom? To answer that question, one must first define "intellectual freedom." In its broadest
sense, it means that any person may believe what he wants to on any
subject and may express his beliefs orally or graphically, publicly or
privately, as he deems appropriate. The ability to express opinions,
however, through whatever mode of communication suits you, does
not mean much if there is no one to hear what you say, to read what
you write, or to view what you produce through other methods. The
definition of intellectual freedom, therefore, has a second integral
part--total and complete freedom of access to all information and
ideas regardless of the media of communication. This, in turn,
gives a man something to think about, to consider, and to weigh prior
to coming to his own opinions and decisions. Then he, too, is free
to express his beliefs. The definition is circular, and the circle
breaks if either the ability to produce or access to the productions
is stifled.

"It is in relation to access that librarians perform their
unique role on behalf of intellectual freedom. Through libraries, librarians have assumed a responsibility to provide materials presenting all points of view on all questions and issues of our times and,
in addition, to make these ideas and opinions available to all patrons
who need or want them, regardless of age, race, religion, national
origins or social or political views." These words, which probably
sound familiar, are taken from the Library Bill of Rights, the profession's interpretation of the First Amendment to the U.S. Constitution and its embodiment of the "intellectual freedom" concept. Articles II and V of the Library Bill of Rights specifically state:

> II. Libraries should provide books and other materials
> presenting all points of view concerning the problems and
> issues of our times; no library material should be pro-
> scribed or removed from libraries because of partisan or
> doctrinal disapproval.
>
> V. The rights of an individual to the use of a library
> should not be denied or abridged because of his age, race,
> religion, national origins or social or political views.

The word "age" was not always included in the Library Bill of
Rights, but was added to the document on June 27, 1967, about one-
and-a-half years before the Tinker case. The addition resulted from
a Preconference, sponsored jointly by the ALA Intellectual Freedom
Committee and the ALA Young Adult Services Division, entitled "Intellectual Freedom and the Teenager." The pertinent recommendation of the Preconference read: "... (3) that free access to all books
in a library collection be granted to young people." [Emphasis added.]

This revision of the Library Bill of Rights caused a few stir-
rings in 1967, but there was certainly no loud outcry, either pro or
con. Indeed, more debate has been engendered in the last two years

than in '67-'68. There was, however, some concern as to what exactly this addition to the Library Bill of Rights meant.

In mid-1968, ALA's stand was verbalized. Its position in regard to "protecting children" from materials that some individuals or groups may deem questionable is that it is the parents'--and only the parents'--right and responsibility to guide his child--and only his child--in appropriate reading materials. Once and for all, the general pervading concept of in loco parentis was cast aside, and responsibility placed solely and squarely on a parent for his child. This does not mean, however, that librarians are no longer to serve as librarians--to help individuals, regardless of age, to verbalize their needs or wants and to help them find appropriate fulfillment. It does mean that librarians should not tell patrons what they ought to want, the "ought" being based on some preconceived notions of age, or hair style, or height, or other equally unreasonable factors. It is a strong stand, but with two precedent-setting decisions by the U.S. Supreme Court, librarians cannot act in loco parentis.

During the last several hundred years of Western civilization, adults have made determinations as to what children may or may not read, listen to, and view. This is changing, and the change will continue. The U.S. Supreme Court has laid to rest the concept of in loco parentis as it relates to the mind. The Constitution and Bill of Rights apply to all citizens regardless of age. The conflict will continue only as long as adults force it to.

Notes

Civil Liberties, monthly publication of the American Civil Liberties Union, no. 261, April 1969, p. 1, 4.
Mark J. Green. "Growing Up In America: Subcitizenship of the Young, " The New Republic, September 18, 1971, p. 14-17.
"Juveniles and Justice, " Trial, September/October 1971.
Tinker v. Des Moines Community School District, 393 U.S. 503, 89 S. Ct. 733, 21 L. Ed. 2d 731, 737 (1969).

CENSORING THE CENSORS

By Tina Novaseda

Can anyone still doubt the extent to which films influence opinions, minds--lives? To those die-hard doubters, one can recount the true contemporary horror story of the young boy who joined the Marines and went to Vietnam because he'd "seen all the John Wayne movies and the Marines make you a man." This took place in the '60s; obviously, cinematic turkeys from World War II still served as effective pro-war propaganda. Whether the cause is inflammatory or pacific, a film can sell it to a mass audience and have an enduring effect.

Recognizing film as a powerful tool of influence, many educators, administrators, and parents are advocating censorship of media shown in schools and libraries in order to prevent the "wrong" ideas from reaching their young charges. A recent New York Times article listed dozens of communities across the nation where heated discourse and demonstrations have been generated over the use of "questionable" learning materials in the schools. Generally, the ferment centers around three areas: violence, sex, and radical departures from established norms.

It has recently become in vogue to ask the rhetorical question: how can people object to graphic portrayals of sex, and not object to the depiction of war, murder, beatings, and other variations on a violent theme. They point to the obvious relish children display when viewing the "good guy" do in the "bad guy," inferring that this may be a causative factor in the proliferation of violent crimes committed by the young.

Educators are looked to to spearhead a campaign banning media violence, i.e., to serve as censors. Teachers and librarians are often expected to screen from impressionable eyes any media acknowledging the existence of human sexuality. Frequently, educators have had to either combat, circumvent, or acquiesce to local mores that say that media showing the reproductive activities of any animal of a higher order than the paramecium were "dirty" and "immoral" and had to be dropped from the film collection. This attitude of denial has caused conflict between procensorship forces and sex education advocates. A case in point is Texture Films' About Sex, which deals with teenage sexual experiences as the teenagers themselves see them, including explanations of birth control. Many school districts

will not allow the film to be shown in the schools--even though many
of the teachers think it is a truly worthwhile film.

The third area that invites censorship is any radical departure
from established norms. Many people will not tolerate their children's exposure to ideas and values that differ from those they themselves hold. The vehemence with which parent groups often express
themselves causes local school boards to monitor media selection--
often in opposition to teachers who argue that education and all educational media should prepare the student for the world as it exists.
For example, removing scenes of violence from films merely denies
the existence of violence. The only way to establish that violence is
wrong is to show it that way in the media--as a fatal contest between
two parties with an equal right to live. Although it generated great
controversy, the Academy Award-winning Hearts and Minds (RBC
Films) provides a gripping, heart-rending portrayal of the real effects of war and violence.

Films used in schools have changed with the society they re-
flect--where once they were strictly information transmitting vehicles,
films now make statements or present questions about society, life-
styles, and values. Thus, a film like Wombat's controversial And
I Don't Mean Maybe presents a representative conflict between one
"have" and the "have-nots" that include scenes of vomiting, full-
frontal nudity, and defecation--yet it has received high critical ac-
claim from film librarians and teachers alike. We feel that the
change in emphasis is healthy--war, violence, sex, offensive and conflicting ideas are all things that will confront today's student. Carefully exposing young people to these things does not mean an educator
is advocating them, merely presenting the student with a picture of
the world as it exists. Censorship has no place in education. A
student is entitled to make his or her own decisions. The white-hat-
ted heroes of censorship are not cleanly killing off immorality, violence, and sex. What they are killing is freedom of choice. Just
as a barroom shoot-out does not in reality produce a tidy, bloodless
death, censorship does not produce morality, but instead the agoniz-
ing and untidy death of minds.

THE CHANGING CAPACITIES OF PRINT AND
THE VARYING UTILITIES OF LIBRARIES

By Kathleen Molz

We move today in a "world without walls." The phrase is
borrowed from the French critic and author André Malraux, who ex-
ternalized so brilliantly in his "museum without walls" the effect of
modern photography and facsimile reproduction in the field of the
fine arts. Today, because of the vastness of the art publishing industry, every man becomes his own curator, selecting for his home
or his office the foremost of those treasures that were once the sole
prerogative of the museum and gallery visitor. The phrase has been
extended so that we now speak of "schools without walls" or "universities without walls," and perhaps it is time to delineate that "world
without walls" in which we live.

Modern technology and contemporary transportation have
placed us in this world, and of it, even beyond it--into outer space
and on other planets. There is nothing particularly new about inno-
vation, exploration, and discovery; what the modern communications
media have done for us, however, is to make us witnesses to that
discovery and exploration. Technology, through some 225 million
television sets in a hundred nations of the world, permits us to sit
in our living rooms and watch mankind walking on the moon and soon
after to see the news clips showing us exactly how the Pope reacted
to the same event. Technology permits us not only instantaneous
awareness of natural calamity or historic happening but also simultaneous awareness, making of mankind one gigantic family in its perception of news and one very small and humbled household in its reaction to it. From this example, one might wonder if the truly
great event occasioned by the moonshot was the landing itself or our
permissive hobnobbing with the papacy--both occurrences are significant and unique to the twentieth century. "The whole world is watching," call out the youth of Chicago, and we watch them apprising us
of the fact itself.

In this changing configuration of communications media, the
place of print is being drastically altered. Let us consider, for example, the situation of the average American in the 1860s. The act
of writing and its subsequent transfer to print reigned supreme: the
social activism of the period was reflected in a significant novel that

triggered behavioral patterns in a war of two factions; the reportage of that war was the matter of the noted pictorial weeklies; its subsequent analysis through untold histories and commentaries was based upon its massive documentation--the lists of the war dead, the government reports dealing with the disabled and maimed, journals and memoirs, letters from parents to sons away from home, the speeches of politicians, the literature of emancipation and abolition. The period remains unexcelled in the transfer of human witness--the transfer of every sight and sound from the cannonball at Sumter through the cries of Andersonville to the silent burden of the slow-winding train from Washington to Springfield--into written document and printed record and, ultimately, into history. It was during such a period, a period of the unrivaled achievement of print in communicating the present and preserving the past, that the American public library was founded.

Compare the print-dominated scene of the America of 1860 or 1870 or even 1880 with the communications realities of our present-day society, with its recordings of famous voices, its documentaries of social problems, its news photos, its films, even its coinage of the phrase "oral history," and the difference, however much we seem to acknowledge it, is almost overwhelming. Such a contrast begs two questions: What relevance does that institution so singularly nourished by many of us, the library, now have? And, perhaps more significantly, what relevance has the medium of print in a multimedia world?

This latter question I shall take up first, and I should like to deal with three prevailing attitudes, or postures, (not necessarily constant with one another) concerning the medium of print and the act of reading that seem characteristic of our present culture.

The first attitude is posited on the theory that print has lost its primacy as the medium for the relay of news and for the analyses of affairs and has become instead the medium, not of public communication, but rather of introspection, the medium best guaranteed to gain for the reader privacy in this noisy, multimedia society. The second postulates that reading, at least serious reading, was and remains an elitist avocation, demanding leisure and education, an avocation that is gradually declining in a society of semiliterates. And the third, certainly the most vocal and emphatic, identifies reading and print orientation with basic education and entry into a society in which the obligations of citizenship, the choice of occupation, and the increase of income are all in part determined by the mastery of words. In brief, the first of these attitudes deals with reading as part of mass communication, the second with reading as art and high culture, and the third with reading as skill.

A massive amount of documentation would seem to validate the first of these postures. Not only have the theorists of mass communication attested to the rapid spread of audiovisual, in contrast to printed, devices, but the medium of print itself is also evincing changes. The mass circulating weeklies are still being published, yet their pages dwindle as their advertisers seek other and more popular means of displaying their wares. The daily newspaper, once the central source of national and international news, now liberally covers local affairs in a proliferation of "feature" pages, and the local press more and more picks up the nationally syndicated column of commentary and editorial assessment. Even Time magazine, ironically in view of its name, has succumbed to the posture that print is the conveyor of opinion and evaluation; thus, it now includes an "essay" of analysis on some national topic and for the first time in its history ascribes views to individuals by permitting the discreet use of initials in small type to inform us who is saying what about whom. And, finally, the academic community has been subjected to this changing attitude about print. Compare, for example, the biographies of Huey Long and John Keats, both published within the last few years and both notable prizewinners. The footnotes in the biography of Keats identify edition, memoir, letter, archive; the footnotes in the biography of Huey Long often refer to radio address, confidential communication, memoir in Oral History Project, and interview.

Print then, at least in terms of the popular press and to some degree of the academic press, is no longer a first source of public information; it is a source, rather, of informed opinion, this latter still a powerful force, for print not only has the capacity to review itself but also carries the authoritarian weight to review media unlike itself, and all of us look to print for our reviews of film, television, and recording. If print has lost its primacy as the chief agent of news about events, it has retained a role, perhaps even more important, of adjudicator of public opinion and taste, and it is obvious from any bibliography on the subject of mass communications that the theorists of the subject use print, and books, and ultimately reading, to expound their ideas.

The second postulate that reading, at least serious reading, is suffering a decline has been put forward by a number of aestheticians and critics, perhaps most notably George Steiner, whose essay on "The Retreat from the Word" appeared almost a decade ago in the Kenyon Review. Recently, Steiner contributed the lead article to the Times Literary Supplement on the "future of the book," and because his ideas have many implications for librarians, at least some of them should be detailed here. Steiner contends that the classical age of the book declined toward the close of the nineteenth century, for in his view reading demands a climate of privacy and leisure as well as an awareness of the literature of the past, an awareness that can be achieved only through privileged education. Steiner also believes that reading and the literate tradition have been "eroded" by the sense of impermanence, a sense of mortality characteristic of modern art forms that celebrate the ephemeral and transcendent. He writes,

Certain aspects of this suspicion of transcendence are gra-

phically present in the paperback book. The private library, with its leather spines and shadows, is all but obsolete; the hard-cover tome, the work in more than one volume, the collected oeuvre, may become so. The paperback revolution has obvious economic and sociological
sources, related to ever-increasing printing costs and the
image of a new mass audience.... But it also corresponds
to deeper, internal changes in the status of literacy. The
paperback is decidedly ephemeral; it does not make for a
library in the old sense. The book, as Montesquieu and
Mallarmé understood it, had a stability of format to which
the current paperback lays no claim. The threefold matrix
of literary creation, of reading and of time defeated or
transcended, found its expressive guise in the bound printed
work privately held, hedged with quiet. Today, the pact
with and against time, with and against the authority of the
individual ego, operative in the classic act of writing and
reading, is wholly under review. [1]

In contrast to this assignment of reading as an elitist and
private phenomenon is the third of the attitudes to which I referred:
reading as skill. Traditionally, at least in this country, this third
attitude dates back to the "three Rs" concept of the public schools.
It is typified in the well-known engraving of Lincoln as a child reading beside the fireplace in the log cabin; it is reflected today in the
recommendations of black psychologist Kenneth Clark, who calls for
a moratorium on the teaching of all subjects in the public schools
with the exception of reading and math; it is apparent to all those
who witness the persistent argumentation over the theories of the
teaching of reading evident in Jeanne Chall's classic study, Learning
to Read: The Great Debate; and it is climaxed in our day by the
enunciation of a national "right to read" effort, which has for the
first time received a presidential endorsement. Here reading is regarded as the keystone in the educational arch, the proverbial key to
unlock the storehouse of learning.

These three attitudes, or postures, then--reflecting, first, the
decline of print as a primary source of public information; second,
the decline of serious reading as a characteristic of lay culture; and
last, the renaissance of the populist and egalitarian belief that reading is and must be the bottom rung of the educational ladder--cast
their own unique shadows on the current and future course of the nation's libraries.

As has already been noted, the public library was founded during a period of print dominance. In essence, the printed word em-
braced during the nineteenth century all three major capacities of any
mode of communication: print was then the source of news and general information; it was the chief means for the exchange of serious
ideas; and last, it was the economical and therefore the primary
mechanism of the schooling experience. Emily Dickinson has expressed this power of the printed word perfectly:

> There is no Frigate like a Book
> To take us Lands away
> Nor any Coursers like a Page
> Of prancing Poetry--
> This Traverse may the poorest take
> Without oppress of Toll--
> How frugal is the Chariot
> That bears the Human soul.[2]

In this exquisite poem, now unfortunately so often relegated to children's anthologies, the poet has conveyed all three capacities: it was print that then transported the reader to new continents and to new experiences; it was print that allowed even the poorest person access to the literate experience; and finally, it was print, even within the confines of its frugality, that permitted the initiate admittance into the recesses of high culture. Reading was, then, indeed communication, skill, and art.

By the same token, it was the library, housing the current newspapers and periodicals, that functioned as a respectable source of information. It was the library, assembling the great retrospective collections of past writers of eminence, that served as the purveyor of the cultural and historic record. And it was the library, disseminating and circulating its materials to the ordinary household, that became the chief instrumentality for the free distribution of books in a democratic society. If the analogy can be drawn between the capacities of print and the functions of libraries, it can be said that print as a means of public communication refers to the general reference and informational function of libraries; print as the point of entry into high culture and serious scholarship relates to the library's role in acquisitions and collection building; and print as the instrument of equalized educational opportunity is closely attuned to the library's circulation and dissemination practices.

The question of print's sole utility in a multimedia world has been touched on; now it is time to examine the viability of this single instrumentality, the library, to maintain an efficient and satisfactory service in a society that no longer views print as its sole means of communication. I write this, not to suggest that libraries are no longer useful in modern society, but only to indicate that libraries will be forced to face new issues as they adapt to a multimedia world.

The library as a major source of public information will change. Generalized public information may, indeed, be of use to the student, but in an age geared to the data needs of the specialist, such information may be found wanting. Portents of the new discipline-oriented specialization in information transfer already exist in the network sponsored by the National Library of Medicine, in the proposed data aggregation of the National Agricultural Library with its land-grant college affiliates, and in the burgeoning lists of special collections and specific information demands for a whole host of topics, ranging from law to banking to industry,

Lowell Martin has suggested that one of the shortcomings of public libraries in handling general reference questions is "a concept of resources limited to the book or at most the book and the magazine rather than to the full range of communication media."[3] His point is well taken; the librarian who relies upon the latest edition of the World Almanac for data about the U.S. Secretary of Interior, Premier of France, or King of Jordan may find himself hopelessly obsolete in his iteration of anachronistic data. Poignant among the examples of a librarian's dependency on print is William Manchester's minor footnote to the assassination of President John F. Kennedy: "A petty functionary at the Library of Congress, clinging to a pet prejudice of librarians, refused to believe a word until it had been confirmed by the New York Times."[4]

The wresting away of the traditionally trained librarian from this symbolic dependency on the printed word is not a simple matter; education for the novice together with retraining for the initiated must cultivate in librarians a respect for sophisticated means of communication other than print. Otherwise, the general reference function of future libraries will be oriented totally toward bibliography: the checking of sources, identification of titles and authors, and verifications of imprints and signatures, primarily for the term paper writer and the dissertation candidate.

Even though the costs will be great and alterations slow, reference inquiries in libraries will ultimately be influenced by the whole range of communications media that libraries will assemble as well as the gamut of devices now under development that will permit the transfer of information with great speed and facility. Nascent experiments with telecommunications networking, telefacsimile transmission, and computerization of data presage a period in which questioners will receive their answers by means other than the traditional printed source. Indeed, the multimedia learning environment already evident in certain exemplary school libraries and media centers portends an adult agency with a variety of formats for educational materials designed to help the self-learner as well as to retrain the adult as employee in the changing technological society.

The utility of print and of libraries in providing an entry into high culture will not, on the contrary, be greatly challenged. Until the twentieth century, the written record had been man's chief means to interpret past cultures and civilizations. It is true that other arts--dance, music, architecture, painting, sculpture, and graphics-- have contributed to contemporary understanding of the past, yet our comprehension of these contributions has been largely a matter of interpretation and analysis. This scholarship, morever, has been conveyed to us through the written record in either manuscript or print form. Put another way, Schliemann rediscovered Troy because of Homer; Shakespeare celebrated Cleopatra because of Plutarch; and Freudian psychology identified the Oedipus complex because of Sophocles.

Libraries that have housed these records, whether they are in

research institutes, universities, or even large municipalities, will
continue to maintain that atmosphere of quiet and that climate of
leisure, signalized by George Steiner, as proper conduits to the pursuit of serious reading and scholarship. With their massive collections and their commitment to elaborate housing arrangements, the
great research libraries will continue their work of classification
and codification to make manifest the work of yesterday to the deni-
zens of today. Computers may indeed assist such libraries in record
keeping and circulation flow, but they are misapplied, in terms of information retrieval, to the files of centuries-old records in the entire
tissue of a civilization, running a historical gamut from hieroglyph to
computer-set type.

These last few paragraphs may appear to some as contradic-
tory or incongruent. The distinction should be made clear: Questions based on contemporary data will be rendered answerable by
multimedia means; in contrast, serious inquiries into the philosophical, literary, economic, or other elements that make the historic
past relevant to contemporary understanding will still be answerable
through the only means known to man, until the twentieth century:
the record of document and artifact.

If the changing capacity of print has any meaning, then the
most drastic change in libraries will occur, not in research libraries
nor even in reference libraries, but in neighborhood community libraries, which cope with the myriad of consumer demands, ranging
from the availability of the latest best seller to the need for information on moth control. Having neither monumental buildings nor retrospective collections, these community libraries will prove most
responsive to societal change, a variance in their case determined
by the changing capacities of print in the twentieth-century milieu.

Ironically, it is the attempts to cope with low-income readers, resulting from experiments with storefront facilities, that are
now influencing metropolitan area-wide service. Just as "Sesame
Street" has been adopted by middle-class as well as lower-class
children, so the concept of the rented ghetto library facility is being
extended to middle-class shopping centers. The factors involved are
these: an increased desire on the part of local communities to
govern their own institutions; the growing recognition that neighbor-
hoods need a facility where books, toys, films, and packaged instructional materials can be circulated (I might even suggest here that the
ephemeral nature of paperback books will lead to a free distribution
of printed materials); and the ultimate acceptance by librarians and
educators that in a populist culture such facilities need not take up
the majority of their floor space with stacks housing reissues of the
classics.

These facilities partake of many names: community learning
centers, library-learning centers, neighborhood learning centers,
etc. [5] They all have the following characteristics in common: the
initiation of multisensory education, in which the participants can
touch, manipulate, hear, watch, and respond as well as read; the

involvement of the community itself in determining the education of both adults and children; and the participation of the community through employment opportunities within the center as well as volunteer activities. What may be emerging is a new authority, based on coalition of school and public library interests, an authority that could be conceived as an alternative to the traditional institution.

The culture "happenings" of some innovative poverty projects, with their art shows, their children's games, their indigenous publishing programs, their sense of cultural life and identification--all these have given us a glimpse into a trend of tomorrow. These agencies reflect in part the transcendence, the impermanence, of contemporary life. Libraries will become part of the here and now, and at least some of them will bear little resemblance to those neat Carnegie branches once dedicated with marble plaques ensuring their usefulness "forever."

Because print has changing utilities, or perhaps because we are better able to articulate the varying usefulness of print, libraries will reflect these variables. Consequently, one library may indeed preserve the record of past achievement for the dedicated student and serious reader. Another may disseminate its wares to a very different group of users, who will in part determine the stock of libraries and may even help to create them.

The "library" then, and that word will have many connotations, both loses and gains from our changing concepts about print. In part, it loses its identity as physical plant and institution, for its location will be impermanent and its resources ever changing. Yet, it will gain in adaptability, since its clientele will become no longer readers but an audience (in the older meaning of that word), an audience of younger people attuned not only to reading but also to listening and watching.

There is something to be said in relation to this loss and to this gain. Buildings decorated with marble carvings honoring Dante, Shakespeare, and Homer smack only of the past; they do little to remind us that the future is yet to be explored. If the world without walls is a just notion, and I believe that it is, then those institutions that are to survive in it must partake of the flavor of that concept. A library where things do not always have to be brought back is an extremely attractive idea.

Notes

1. George Steiner. "The Future of the Book: I Classic Culture and Post-Culture," Times Literary Supplement (October 2, 1970): 1122.
2. Emily Dickinson. "There is no Frigate like a Book," The Complete Poems of Emily Dickinson, ed. Thomas H. Johnson (Boston and Toronto: Little, Brown and Company, 1960), p. 553.

3. Lowell Martin. Library Response to Urban Change (Chicago: American Library Association, 1969), p. 28.
4. William Manchester. The Death of a President (New York: Harper and Row, 1967), p. 211.
5. For descriptions of an innovative community learning center, see John Q. Benford, "The Philadelphia Project," Library Journal (June 15, 1971): 2041-2047; and Lynne and John Waugh, "Albuquerque's Free-Wheeling Library," American Education (August-September 1971): 33-35.

RECOMMENDED READINGS

Representing only a fraction of the literature available in the field of selection theory, the writings presented merely opened the discussion on themes of the selector's role, the issues of intellectual freedom and censorship, and implications of modern technology for library selection. The following citations were chosen to further develop those themes.

Also concerned with the concept of children's intellectual freedom rights is "Guardians of the Young" by Margaret Coughlan in Top of the News, 33, no. 2 (Winter, 1977), pages 137-148, in which she gives us the historical perspective from the seventeenth century to the present. Elaine Simpson invoked "Reason, Not Emotion" in her discussion of the contemporary realism in writing for young adults, and the reactions to it, Top of the News, 31, no. 3 (April, 1975), pages 301-4. The prominent Rochester (Michigan) school censorship case received thorough consideration in School Media Quarterly 1, no. 2 (Winter, 1973), which presented a history of the case and the viewpoint from different sectors: the school administration, Board of Education, the community and the courts. And in "Racism, Sexism, Intellectual Freedom, and Youth Librarians," Top of the News 33, no. 4 (Summer, 1977), pages 323-332, Dorothy Broderick examines a range of concerns and attitudes, relating to the American Library Association's Council resolution of July, 1976, which requested action to increase the awareness of librarians and library patrons to racism and sexism.

Continuing the theme of intellectual freedom, the study made for the Oklahoma Public Library Systems, published in the Oklahoma Librarian 26, no. 1 (Jan., 1976), "Limits to Freedom," included surveys, "Political Censorship" and "Obscenity/Pornography" among others by Sandra Martin. These discussed historical and contemporary aspects of the suppression of freedom of speech and of censorship of obscenity. Strongly-worded responses to Leo Flanagan's "Defending the Indefensible" appeared in the Library Journal issue of February 15, and March 1, 1976 "Letters" sections. An attempt to solve the dilemmas in the field of intellectual freedom was made by Patrick Williams and Joan Thornton Pearce in their "Censorship Redefined," Library Journal, v. 101, no. 13 (July, 1976) pages 1495-1496. They argue for a set of "controls" in libraries which would change the nature of the controversy, they believe.

Virtually a classic in the consideration of the selector's role is Lester Asheim's "Not Censorship but Selection," first published in Wilson Library Bulletin, September, 1953, and included in Building Library Collections, 4th ed., by Mary Duncan Carter, Wallace John Bonk, and Rose Mary Magrill (Scarecrow Press, 1974). His lucid explanation of the differences in these two activities stresses motivation and attitude as the aspects in which the difference becomes clear.

A collection of essays which explores the concept of freedom of expression in various settings is An Intellectual Freedom Primer (Littleton, Colorado: Libraries Unlimited, Inc., 1977). Besides giving a history of intellectual freedom in the 20th Century, the writers discuss the status of freedom of expression in the visual and performing arts and within an automated data system. A review of the research on the subject of intellectual freedom is provided.

Obviously, in this area of selection there is an almost limitless universe of materials and reading available. The person desiring to pursue the subject further would do well to secure a bibliography in the field, such as that published by A.L.A., "Libraries, Censorship, and Intellectual Freedom," 1970. The A.L.A. Office for Intellectual Freedom publication, Intellectual Freedom Manual, American Library Association, 1974, should be consulted for its official statements and the base documents included, as well as for its information on A.L.A. resources to aid the librarian.

Also from that office, the Newsletter on Intellectual Freedom provides an on-going record of the intellectual freedom scene--the current problems, developments in legislation, and judicial decisions.

CHAPTER 3

DEVELOPMENT OF SELECTION POLICY

Once the principles and philosophy of materials selection and collection development are comprehended, they must be transformed into policy before they can be realized effectively. Though it is possible to have a selection policy without formulation or adoption of the library's philosophy, such a policy would not reflect the professional attitudes that we expect of librarians.

Moving from the premise that there should be a selection policy, the next consideration is the form such a policy should take and the methods used in preparing one. The importance of a written selection policy is supported in library education texts, and is stressed in the standards for library service endorsed by various library associations. In practice, libraries may be building collections without having written policies, but such practice ignores the benefits derived from having formulated and written a policy statement.

Many different reasons are given for having written policies. Those formulated from the point of view of administration stress the functional advantages. This is illustrated by the reasons given in "Policy Statements" prepared by the Berrien County (Michigan) Library League. Though the rationale in the statement is not limited to a selection policy, many of the advantages listed could apply to such a policy. Two basic professional reasons are discussed by Le-Roy C. Merritt in "Writing a Selection Policy." The first is the importance of having a document on hand when a selection decision is challenged, which is probably the most frequently cited reason. The second reason he considers to be equally important and of more day-to-day value; that is, the need to define the scope of the selection activity in the library as a guide for selection decisions. He thoughtfully describes the process of preparing a written policy, giving strong emphasis to the public relations benefits, and how the completed policy can then be used to further good public relations.

The American Library Association provides guidance in the preparation of a policy in "Development of a Materials Selection Program" from the Association's Intellectual Freedom Manual. Responsibility for policy writing, the methods to be used, and considerations that must be made before a policy can be written are clearly defined and presented. The components which make up a well-thought-out policy are identified and explained.

Is there a difference between acquisition and selection policies? Calvin Boyer delineates the distinctions in his "Introduction" to Book Selection Policies in American Libraries. Librarians need to consider these distinctions as well as the need to have both types of policies in order to carry out thoughtful collection development.

The point of view of the librarian's partner, the library trustee, is represented in the article, "The Trustee and Intellectual Freedom," by Jane Cameron. She discusses not only the trustee's role in adopting a selection policy, but also other ways in which the trustee can help defend intellectual freedom.

The position of a library within a system or network is the special focus of Ruth Gregory and Lester Stoffel in the excerpts from "Collection Building and Maintenance." The effect of system membership upon the individual library's selection policy and its role in maintaining intellectual freedom is discussed. The authors present a realistic and well-reasoned consideration of the values of a materials selection policy.

An example of how a policy works at the specialized collection level is given by K. Linda Ward in "Collection Policy in College and University Libraries." In this case, the collection policy is discussed in terms of a music library, but the process of formulating such a policy could be applied to many academic library collections.

POLICY STATEMENTS

Why have a written policy statement?*

1. <u>Gives positive direction</u> to libraries and trustees who are charged with the direction of the public library program by defining their authority and discretion.

2. <u>Clarifies relationships</u> between the library board and the librarian, between the local governmental body and the board, between the librarian and the staff, and within the staff.

3. <u>Helps build public support</u>. The people served by the library can be provided with reassuring evidence of what the library board is attempting to do and why it is trying to do it.

4. <u>Saves time, effort and money</u>. Many questions arise in governing libraries that repeat themselves in various forms. Frees time for the librarian and board to plan for improvement in the library program. Written policy statements also facilitate an orderly review of board practices so that actions that are taken can (1) keep abreast of needs and (2) consider past decisions.

5. <u>Aids evaluation of services</u>. The board is able to appraise more intelligently the services provided when objectives are clear and responsibility is definitely fixed.

6. <u>Helps reduce criticism</u> by centering attention on clear-cut statements which people are more willing to accept than personal opinion.

7. <u>Assures greater uniformity and fairness of treatment</u>. Minor inconsistencies, which occur naturally and easily, can be eliminated and misunderstandings due to lack of information can be substantially reduced.

8. <u>Reduces pressures and irritations</u>. Individuals or groups wishing special consideration will know that their case is decided on the basis of established policy, <u>not</u> momentary nor personal considerations.

Reprinted by permission of Mr. J. Randy Peyser, Director, Berrien County Library.
*Adapted from <u>Written Policies for School Boards</u>, American Association of School Administrators and National School Boards Association, by the Berrien County Library League.

9. <u>Insures better informed boards and staff.</u> Acquaints them with policies and provides experience in formulating them, builds habits of thinking in terms of policy rather than immediate issues. Study of policies speeds orientation of new board and staff members.

WRITING A SELECTION POLICY

By LeRoy Charles Merritt

Although it is undoubtedly true that most public and school libraries have not prepared a written book selection policy, the fact that they ought to have written one can hardly have escaped the attention of their librarians. Documentation of this statement is abundant, and we need here refer only to Standard No. 87 in Public Library Service,[1] which reads as follows: "Every library should have a written statement of policy, covering the selection and maintenance of its collection of books and of nonbook materials."

For school libraries, the Board of Directors of the American Association of School Librarians have approved a statement of policy including this sentence:

> It is believed that such a policy should be formally adopted by each school district as a basis for consistent excellence in choice of materials and as a document that can be presented to parents and other citizens for their further understanding of the purposes and standards of selection of school library materials.[2]

Similar statements abound in the literature of the profession and in the official pronouncements of national, state, and local public and school library associations. The articulate members of the profession are unanimous in their support of the need for preparing a formal selection policy for every library, no matter how large or how small it may be. That more than a few libraries have not taken action may be laid to natural human procrastination rather than to disagreement or opposition, though some disagreement may indeed exist.

There are two major reasons for writing a book selection policy. The first, which may be said to have provided much greater impetus to librarians, is the importance of having a document in hand when a selection decision is challenged. Such policy statements have proved their value time and time again in minimizing both the possibility and the extent of the disturbance which a serious question about the presence or absence of a particular book might otherwise have caused. The very existence of the statement as evidence of the fact that a library staff has a selection policy which has been approved by the proper governing authority is likely to take the wind out of the sails of the would-be censor or propagandist.

Reprinted by permission of The H. W. Wilson Company from Book Selection and Intellectual Freedom by LeRoy Charles Merritt. Copyright © 1970 by LeRoy Charles Merritt.

The second reason for writing a book selection policy seems to be of equal importance and of much greater day-to-day usefulness, although it is infrequently cited by librarians and still less frequently utilized. This reason is simply the practical need to define the full scope of the selection activity in the library. Some definition is, of course, in the mind of every librarian as one book is chosen and another is not; otherwise he would be too undecided to act; but selection will be better and decisions can be made more consistently if a written selection policy guides the selector.

Most library selection policies are brief documents addressed too largely to the first objective only, that is, self-defense, and providing very little guidance to the library staff in the day-to-day selection process. A few are long enough to provide some guidance but only a handful are in sufficient detail to be really useful. It is possible that two documents are needed: first, a general statement of policy for the information of the public and for use in controversy; and second, a more detailed internal document for the day-to-day guidance of the library staff. The two could be bound together for some purposes and used separately for others.

The writing of a selection policy, if it is done seriously and deliberately, should produce other benefits besides the end product of a useful and workable policy statement. Among these is the intellectual stimulation afforded the staff in the process of thinking through an a priori statement of precisely what is to be in the library. Another is the public relations value of drawing the whole community into observing and participating in the process. The individual or organization which has participated in drafting the policy statement for the public library is much more likely to defend that statement and the library in any controversy that may arise and is much more likely to understand the entire scope of the library collection and its possible uses. In most communities the public has no conception at all of how books get into the library nor of the magnitude of the problems involved in selecting a maximum number of desirable titles from the wealth of material published each year, much of which has no place in any given library, not because it is bad, but because it is beyond the library's scope.

The actual writing of the policy statement should start with a meeting of the professional staff to discuss the need for writing a statement, the benefits to be gained from the process, and the anticipated usefulness of the statement once it has been written. The meeting should continue with some discussion of the technique to be used in the writing and particularly the need for making positive statements about the kinds of materials which are to be selected for the library, avoiding insofar as possible all statements negative or restrictive in character. It must be kept in mind that the concern is with a selection policy, not a rejection policy. Instructions on technique should include the concept of depth as well as breadth, so that the library staff would concern itself with the relative superficiality or exhaustiveness of selection in each literary form and subject area.

A division of the various subject areas among the professional staff would follow. The smaller the staff, the larger the areas would have to be; in very large libraries there might even be committees of the staff to work in each area. If possible these allocations, as well as the responsibility for selection itself, should take into account the subject background and interests of the staff members insofar as they are known. Some areas would need to be arbitrarily allocated; but such allocations can be considered a challenge rather than a disadvantage to the librarian who has not hitherto considered himself a specialist in typewriting or chess or eighteenth century poetry.

After some weeks, there might be a series of staff meetings to discuss and to edit the whole developing statement so that it meets with the approval and assent of the entire staff. A good deal of give-and-take discussion might occur during these meetings, as various members of the staff with varying intensities of exposure to the needs of the community argue both the extent and the depth to which the library ought to be selecting materials in various subject areas and literary forms. Remembering that the tone of the statement is to be positive rather than restrictive, a consensus should be possible in all cases; staff unanimity on the ultimate statement is not only desirable but attainable.

When there is general staff agreement that the best book selection policy possible for the time has been created, the librarian might well present a draft to the library board, the city manager, the city council, or other supervisory authority. Again the object would be to promote discussion, suggestions, possible revisions, additions, or better phrasing. These suggestions, all of which should be cordially and sincerely received, would then go back to another series of staff meetings for more discussion until the staff and supervisory authority are in substantial agreement.

If a properly positive attitude is maintained, disagreement is hardly expected. If a member of the board of trustees or the city council considers that the library ought to have a substantial collection in the field of public health for the use of the city health department, the library staff can have little reason for disagreement, at least in advance of the creation of such a collection. Conversely, if the library staff is firmly of the opinion that books in the field of medicine do not need to be collected in depth because of the excellent collection maintained by the county medical society across the street, no member of the city council is likely to disagree.

While this creative process is going on and the suggestions from the higher authority are being incorporated into the policy statement, the librarian or another qualified member of the staff ought to be presenting the draft of the policy statement to a wide variety of civic groups and organizations, such as service clubs, the PTA, the Garden Club, the Chess Club, and any other organization willing to schedule a librarian for a thirty- or forty-minute talk. The librarian would take along copies of the draft for distribution and would talk for fifteen or twenty minutes along lines somewhat like this:

We at the library are writing a selection policy for your
public library, and we need your help. We want this selection policy to be as broad and as representative of the
needs of this community as it can possibly be. Here is
a draft of what the staff of the library has written up to
now. We want your opinions, your suggestions, your ideas
of what you think ought to be in your public library. The
library staff, through its daily contact with the members
of your organization using the library, has a pretty good
idea of what you need and want; these needs have already
been incorporated into the policy statement before you; but
because it is possible that some areas in which you are
interested may have been overlooked, we would like to
have your help in filling any gaps inadvertently left by the
library staff.

In this talk the librarian might go over a few points to show
the kinds of materials the statement is concerned with and conclude
by asking for suggestions from the meeting; if there is no time he
might request that suggestions be made later, orally or in writing,
for careful consideration by the staff for inclusion in the policy statement. It may be anticipated that few good suggestions will be offered. But even if not very many usable suggestions are received in
the course of a series of meetings that might extend over a year's
time, the effort can still be considered to be worthwhile for getting
community participation in the writing of the selection policy. The
suggestions considered by the library staff and its supervisory authority to be useful and important are incorporated into the statement of
policy, which then can be said to be substantially the work of practically everybody in town, at least everybody who is represented by
one or more of the groups.

To gain the help, support, and participation of those patrons
of the library who are not members of local organizations, the librarian should make copies of the draft policy statement available at
various points of service throughout the library, along with a cor-
dial invitation to examine the draft and to make suggestions to the librarian or any member of the staff. Again, probably few new and
usable suggestions will be received. Nevertheless, it can reasonably
be assumed that virtually all the patrons of the library have the opportunity to participate in drafting the library's selection policy.
Even those who have made no suggestions will be aware of the fact
that they have had the opportunity.

The policy statement should incorporate all usable suggestions
from individuals and community organizations. After it has been
completed to the satisfaction of the library staff and approved by the
supervisory authority, it should be published as a separate document
for internal use by the library staff, for use by patrons as the occasion arises, and for general distribution to interested individuals
and organizations within the community. It would be desirable also
to publish the whole document or substantial portions of it in the local press along with a complete list of the organizations which have

participated in preparing the document. Before the use of the completed policy is discussed, it should be noted that the job, done once, is not likely to have been done for all time. Communities and their reading interests and needs change with the passage of time, as does the pattern of book production. Revisions of the basic policy statement will have to be made as conditions change, and the whole document ought to be reviewed at regular intervals, probably every five years.

The completed book selection policy, particularly if it has been prepared in considerable detail, can now be used by the library staff as a daily guide in the selection of materials for the library. With a firm statement in hand of the kinds of materials that belong in the library and, as a corollary, the kinds of materials that do not belong, the library staff will be able to do a more intelligent and more efficient job of selecting books for the library. The policy statement will be no substitute for knowing the collection or for knowing the clientele and the daily demands upon the collection, but it will be a useful guideline for deciding whether the next item in the current Publishers Weekly should be passed over as being beyond the library's scope or should be considered seriously for inclusion in the collection. With such a guide the library collection over the years should become intrinsically better and in greater accord with the demands and needs of the library's clientele. As those demands and needs change, the policy will need to be changed as well; but if all such changes become the subject of staff discussion, there will be much less danger that selection will be done capriciously or in response to a temporary fad.

The occurrence of questions raised by staff or clientele about the reasons why certain books are in the library or certain other books are not there will be less frequent than daily selection decisions. The library selector may even raise the question himself incredulously: "Now why on earth did I ever buy that?" When such questions do arise, the book selection policy statement will provide a guide or a standard against which to consider whether the book in question is in line with the policy. If it is, and in nearly all cases it will be, the book selection policy statement provides a ready means to assist in explaining to the questioner why the book he is concerned about belongs in the library or does not belong there. The very fact that the library can show that it has a selection policy and that books are not bought capriciously or at the whim of a particular librarian, goes far to mollify the anxious or exasperated reader. Furthermore, when the policy statement is placed in his hands, the burden is placed upon him to show how and why the book in question was purchased, or not purchased, in violation of the policy.

In all such discussions in the privacy of the librarian's office and in the absence of public controversy, the librarian must be careful to retain his perspective and realize that selection errors can be made. If upon reexamination of the book in the light of policy, an honest judgment is made that the book does not belong and that a mistake has been made in buying it, the librarian must be prepared to admit his mistake and withdraw the book. A decision on such a question becomes a point of no return. If upon reexamination the book's presence in the collection is substantiated as being in line with policy, the librarian is bound to reaffirm the earlier decision. Should the case then become a matter of public controversy, the librarian prepares to stand behind the book and the library's statement of policy. Back of him in that stance the librarian will find the library board and the city council, for they approved the policy under which the book was selected. Only a little farther back will be all the individuals and organizations in town who participated in the formulation of the policy and who are now moved to back up the librarian who can show that the book in question belongs in (or does not belong in) the library in accordance with a certain paragraph of the official policy statement.

Notes

1. American Library Association. Public Library Service (Chicago: The Association, 1956).
2. American Association of School Librarians. Policies and Procedures for Selection of School Library Materials (Chicago: The Association, 1961).

DEVELOPMENT OF A MATERIALS SELECTION PROGRAM

The primary purpose of a materials selection program is to promote the development of a collection based on institutional goals and user needs. A secondary purpose is service in defending the principles of intellectual freedom.

The basis of a sound selection program is a materials selection statement. Although a majority of professional librarians believe a materials selection statement is desirable, in too many instances the belief does not become reality. Many reasons for not writing such a statement are given, but often two unmentioned reasons are the most important: lack of knowledge about how to prepare one, and lack of confidence in one's abilities to do so. Regardless of past failures and existing difficulties, however, there is an absolute need for the firm foundation that a selection statement provides.

In virtually every case, it will be the librarian's task to prepare the materials selection statement. Although approval or official adoption of the statement rests with the institution's legally responsible governing body, it is the librarian who has the expertise and practical knowledge of the day-to-day activities of the library.

A materials selection statement must relate to concrete practices. It should, in effect, provide guidelines for strengthening and adding to the library's collection. Furthermore, if the statement is to fulfill its secondary purpose, that of defending intellectual freedom, it must be a viable, working document which relates to the library's day-to-day operations. In the case of very large libraries or even medium-sized institutions with highly sophisticated holdings, the librarian may prefer to separate the policy statement from procedural considerations. Thus, the materials selection statement would reflect institutional policies, while a separate procedures manual would deal with the day-to-day applications of those policies.

A strong collection and intellectual freedom go hand in hand. It is less likely that problems will remain unresolved if the collection reflects the logical, coherent, and explicit statement from which it grows. In developing a materials selection statement, four basic factors must be considered: (1) service policy, (2) environmental characteristics, (3) collection specifications, and (4) current selection needs.

Service Policy

A service policy will provide practical operational guidelines to govern future collection development in accordance with the needs of the library's users and the goals of the library. In order to establish a service policy, it is necessary to determine what groups the library is striving to serve and what purposes it is attempting to achieve. To do so will entail a study of user-group characteristics and institutional objectives.

I. User groups. A materials selection statement must reflect the needs of the people the library will serve in trying to fulfill its objectives. To establish guidelines for collection development and related library activities, it is necessary to gather detailed information on various user groups.

A questionnaire to establish basic data could be prepared and completed by each staff member working with the public. Or, such information could be compiled on the basis of institutional statistics and records. After the library staff has been surveyed, users can be given questionnaires on their purposes in using the library, their library activities, and the like. It should be noted that certain sections of the prepared form can be used to determine the desired state of affairs as well.

A. Population characteristics
    1. Age
    2. Education
    3. Employment level
    4. Etc.
B. Size of each user group
C. Primary purpose of each group in using the library
D. Kinds of material used in accomplishing these purposes
E. Kinds of activities engaged in during the accomplishment of these purposes.

II. Institutional objectives. The materials selection statement should define the library's goals and reason for existing. There are at least two sources from which institutional goals can be determined.

A. Statements of objectives are ideally available in a public document designed to inform all concerned persons.
    1. General need(s) the library is designated to fulfill
    2. Activities or standards most valued
    3. Distinction in some field of endeavor

B. Public documents and records, in lieu of a statement of objectives, may outline the institution's objectives and supplement statements of objectives.
    1. Annual reports of the institution
    2. Charter of the institution

3. Published history of the institution
4. Records of the governing body
5. Budget (Because preparation of a budget usually demands a resolution of difficult questions of priorities in order to allocate scarce resources, this item should not be overlooked.)

Environmental Characteristics

The librarian should determine all aspects of the environment surrounding the institution that could possibly influence the development of the library collection and the library's related activities. A few such environmental factors and their implications are the following:

Environmental Factors	Provisions Affected
Relative geographical isolation	Materials related to the cultural/recreational needs of users
Economic structure	Materials related to specific educational needs
Presence/absence of library resources external to the institutions	Degree of self-sufficiency or completeness of materials
Presence/absence of postsecondary learning institutions	Scholarly/technical works
Relationship to local industries	Technical reports and business materials
Relationship to local professional/cultural groups	Specialized subcollections

Collection Specifications

Specifications are to be established for each subject area or area of concern. (The data gathered to determine service policy and environmental characteristics will show, in large measure, what the library requires.) For this section of the selection statement, each subject area should be carefully reviewed in order to determine the types of materials to be acquired in each and the depth in which materials are to be sought. Such a review is especially important in smaller libraries where funds are severely limited and the needs of the users potentially great.

If possible, the following data should be collected for each area:

number of library materials currently held
total number of relevant materials available
percent of total materials held
distribution of current holdings by publication date

In addition, holdings should be rated by subject area in terms of specific user purposes:

recreation
self-help
continuing education
business

Finally, a desired acquisition level should be specified for each area.

The section of the selection statement dealing with collection specifications will no doubt be the largest and most detailed of all. It will specify the criteria to be used in selecting and reevaluating materials in terms of (1) users' age groups; (2) users' special needs by virtue of occupation, cultural interest, etc.; and (3) types of materials (books, periodicals, newspapers, government publications, maps, records, films, etc.). This section will also specify policies to be used in handling such matters as gifts and special bequests.

Current Selection Needs

Current selection needs can be determined by the difference between the present collection and the collection specifications. In deciding what is currently needed, the desired state of affairs that may have been detailed under service policy should also be consulted. Once current needs are determined, other considerations come into play. Most prominent among these is the library's budget. Regardless of the amount of money available, the selection statement should indicate in as clear a manner as possible which materials are to be bought and which are not.

After consideration of the above four factors: service policy, environmental characteristics, collection specifications, and current collection needs, the next step is preparing a final draft of the selection statement for the governing body of the library. This draft should contain an affirmation of the "Library Bill of Rights" (or if appropriate, the "School Library Bill of Rights") and "The Freedom to Read" as basic documents governing all library policies. The statement should also include the ALA "Policy on Confidentiality of Library Records," which states that circulation records and other records identifying the names of library users with specific materials should be considered confidential in nature.

The table of contents of the final draft of the materials selection statement might look like this:

I. General principles of selection
    A. "Library Bill of Rights," "The Freedom to Read," and "Policy on Confidentiality of Library Records"
    B. Institutional objectives
    C. Collection objectives
    D. Responsibility for selection
    E. Policies of selection
        1. Selection for user group A
        2. Selection for user group B
        3. Etc.

II. Special principles of selection
    A. User groups
    B. Form and nature of material
        1. Fiction
        2. Periodicals
        3. Audio-visuals
        4. Etc.
    C. Subject of material

It hardly needs to be said that preparation of a complete statement requires work--lots of it. And the work must be done before the censorship problem arises. Unfortunately, there are no shortcuts. It is impossible to borrow a statement based on another institution's goals and needs. Above all, the statement must be a working document, a handbook for daily activities reflecting the needs of those who are to use it.

INTRODUCTION TO SELECTION
POLICIES IN AMERICAN LIBRARIES

By Calvin J. Boyer

Purpose of the Book

Whether it is a public library trying to present a wide spectrum of materials and viewpoints on basic issues or a college or school library trying to support the educational objectives of its parent institution, a library is always vulnerable to criticism from persons or groups who are unhappy because certain materials were excluded. Thus, each public, school, or college library should put in writing its selection policies and have them approved by the governing authority. This measure will put the library in a clearly defined position if its holdings or selection practices are challenged.

Furthermore, a selection policy should aid collection development in a library by establishing guidelines for selection. Merely the existence or presence of a policy does not guarantee a good collection. However, a collection of quality is more likely to occur when a well formulated selection policy exists and is followed by the selection staff. The staff must be aware constantly of the policy and must follow it consistently when making selection decisions for it to be an effective aid. The more detailed the policy is, the more helpful it is likely to be, both in selection for the library collection and in defense of the collection's contents.

It is hoped that this book, by providing in convenient form policies from various types of libraries, will aid librarians in creating, reviewing, or revising the selection policies for their own libraries. These materials are not readily accessible to the individual librarian who wants guidance. The editors hope that the librarian or administrator using this book will turn to policies for other types of libraries than his own, since there is much to be gained from reviewing the contents of policies from all types of libraries.

This compilation is intended also as a source book for teachers and students studying selection in library education agencies. For example, it might be used to aid students in evaluating policies, in the exercise of writing policies based upon some selected community characteristics, or in comparing how policy content differs from the various types of libraries. The number of ways a teacher might utilize the policies in this book is directly proportional to his ingenuity.

Reprinted from Selection Policies in American Libraries (Armadillo Press, 1971; copyright © 1971 by Calvin J. Boyer), pp. iii-vi by permission of the author.

Scope of the Book

In choosing school, public, and college library selection policies for this volume, the editors interpreted "college" and "book" broadly. "College" library refers to a library for any institution of higher education. Whether the parent institution is a community college, four-year college, or an institution which includes graduate studies, the "college" library selection policies are applicable.

"Book" selection is common terminology, even though library collections include non-book materials. "Materials" selection policy is the more accurate terminology. Within a materials selection policy, a librarian may want to include acceptable technical specifications for the various non-book materials, just as many policies specify the physical requirements for a good book in terms of binding, margins, paper, type faces, and illustrations. The general policies concerning intellectual freedom and subject coverage are applicable to all materials, regardless of form.

When determining the scope of this book, the editors excluded "acquisitions" policies from the volume. The distinction being made is the following:

> A selection policy sets down general policies concerning (a) the intellectual framework within which decisions are made, such as intellectual freedom and the Library Bill of Rights; (b) final authority for selection decisions; (c) acceptable quality of materials, both physical and intellectual; (d) inclusion or exclusion of problem materials, such as gifts and controversial subjects; (e) maintenance of a high-quality collection by such means as weeding and discarding; and (f) the community served by the library.

> An acquisition policy is a detailed breakdown, subject by subject, of the depth in which a library expects to acquire materials in each subject area. The four levels of coverage often specified in acquisitions policies are (a) reference collection, (2) general collection, (3) comprehensive collection, and (4) research collection.

It is advisable that selection policies be accompanied by acquisitions policies for maximum effectiveness and consistency in building a good library collection.

A broad cross-section of policies was chosen for inclusion in this volume. In addition to presenting public, college, and school library selection policies, an effort was made to include policies from large and small institutions, religious and secular institutions, private and public institutions, as well as policies of varying lengths. Thus, many good policies were eliminated because one already illustrated that particular type of institution or that point of view or because another policy said essentially the same thing in a more concise way.

Even though many of the materials presented in the appendices are available elsewhere, the editors included them in this volume for the convenience of the reader. The objective was a self-contained book. Also, editorial decisions required that some of them be included. The Library Bill of Rights, Freedom to Read, the Statement on Labeling, and the School Library Bill appeared as part of many selection policies received. Rather than printing them in full each time they were included as part of the text, the decision was made to print them once as appendices and to refer to them in brackets when they appear as part of a selection policy.

The Library Bill of Rights was revised at the June, 1971, American Library Association Conference in Dallas. This newly-approved version has not had time to be widely circulated or printed. The editors considered it a convenience to the reader to include the original and revised texts for comparison, particularly since most libraries have not had time to revise their policies in accordance with the new version.

The American Library Association has permitted the editors to include its interpretations of the Library Bill of Rights in this volume. Presently these interpretations are not readily available elsewhere.

Creation and Utilization of
a Selection Policy

A well-written, board-approved materials selection policy will: (1) provide a statement of philosophy and objectives for the guidance of those involved in the procedures for selection, such as the ALA Library Bill of Rights, the AASL School Library Bill of Rights, and the ALA Freedom to Read Statement; (2) define the role of those who share in the responsibility for the selection of materials, including who is legally responsible for selection and to whom responsibility has been delegated; (3) set forth criteria for selection and evaluation of materials; (4) outline the techniques for the applications of the criteria; (5) clarify for the community the philosophy and procedure used in evaluating and selecting materials; and (6) provide a procedure for the consideration of objections to the use of particular materials.

The materials selection policy should be adopted officially by the governing board and communicated to library personnel and to the community. Several libraries which submitted policies for consideration by the editors had produced an effective public relations tool by printing their policies in an attractive, well-designed format. The Tucson Public Library, Berkeley Public Library, and Finkelstein Memorial Library (Spring Valley, N.Y.) are three such libraries. The policy that the library adopts should be reviewed periodically and revised if the nature of the library collection has changed.

The Council of the American Library Association, in its adopted censorship procedure for libraries, further suggests the following: (1) A file recording the basis for decision should be kept for titles likely to be questioned or apt to be considered controversial; (2) There should be a clearly defined method for handling complaints. Any complaint should be required to be in writing, and the complainant should be identified properly before the complaint is considered. Action should be deferred until full consideration by appropriate administrative authority; (3) There should be continuing efforts to establish lines of communication to assure mutual understanding with civic, religious, educational, and political bodies; (4) Newspapers of the community should be informed of policies governing book selection and use. Purposes and services of the library should be interpreted through a continuing public relations program, as should the use of books in the school.

Contents of a Materials Selection Policy

The librarian or administrator creating, reviewing, or revising his selection policy should consider for inclusion the items in the following outline. This outline reflects what authorities say a policy should contain and what has appeared in the many policies reviewed by the editors. Two items appear only in very recent policies; they reflect recent events in society and are due careful consideration by librarians today. These two items deal with the selection of materials on drugs and drug usage and on explosives and their construction.

I.   Community description and analysis

II. Responsibility for selection, legal and delegated

III. Intellectual freedom and procedures for complaints

IV. Policies by clientele served

    A. Adult
    B. Young Adult
    C. Children
    D. Readers of limited skill
    E. Students
    F. Blind, physically handicapped, shut-ins

V.   Policies by format of material

    A. Books
      1. Hardback books
      2. Paperbacks
      3. Textbooks and lab manuals
      4. Synopses and outlines
    B. Slides
    C. Films and filmstrips
    D. Newspapers
    E. Recorded sound--Records, tapes, cassettes

      F. Printed music
      G. Pictures
      H. Maps
      I. Pamphlets
      J. Periodicals
      K. Government documents
      L. Manuscripts and rare books
      M. Microforms

VI. Policies by subject of material

      A. Fiction
      B. Non-fiction
      C. Reference materials
      D. Foreign language materials
      E. Medicine
      F. Law
      G. Sex
      H. Drugs and drug usage
      I. Semi- and pseudo-scientific materials
      J. Religion
      K. Genealogy and heraldry
      L. Guns, explosives, jujutsu, etc.

VII. Gifts policy

VIII. Weeding, discarding, replacement, duplication policies

IX. Relationships to other libraries and library systems in collection development.

THE TRUSTEE AND INTELLECTUAL FREEDOM

By Jane Cameron

Often as a library trustee you can have a real sense of frustration as to your role. Endless hours of board meeting time can be spent on discussing leaky roofs, faulty furnaces, noisy air conditioners, and more importantly, salary schedules, budget needs, current legislation. You may wonder where is the excitement of books and the ideas they generate that has drawn you to the library since childhood. Certainly attractive surroundings, good professional staff, adequate financing are essential components of a popular library, but the heart of the library, the books, records, periodicals can come alive again for you when as a trustee you assume your role as an advocate of intellectual freedom. The first step is the articulation of a sound library materials selection policy which may one day help you defend some of the good companions you have enjoyed. For censorship as well as politics makes strange bedfellows. In looking over titles subject to attack the last couple of years I discovered old friends in my own library like Holden Caulfield and Billy Pilgrim and challenging books by black authors as Soul on Ice, Manchild in the Promised Land. Over the years the range of authors attacked have extended from Aristophanes to James Joyce, Walt Whitman to D. H. Lawrence, Shakespeare to Steinbeck. Our culture would indeed be barren if men and women had not fought for the freedom of expression, the right to read, the privilege of each individual to make his own choice.

The important first step for trustees of formulating a materials selection policy is a function of both board and staff. If you are sitting self-assured in the knowledge that you already have one, consider--have you or has anyone read it recently, much less reviewed it? Periodically, it should be subjected to critical scrutiny, at least every two years. Your board is apt to change as well as the times. From the American Library Association, from the State Library or from neighboring libraries you can obtain examples which may prove useful. The philosophy contained in the Library Bill of Rights and the Freedom to Read Statement is basic to the policy and should be appended to it.

With these two documents as your foundation, affirm in your policy the principles that freedom of expression means that materials shall represent divergent views on controversial issues and that an

Reprinted from Michigan Librarian, vol. 41, no. 2, Summer 1974, pp. 3-14, by permission of the Michigan Library Association. From a talk given at MLA (Michigan Library Association) Fall Conference, October 19, 1973.

individual may choose or reject a book according to his own taste but he cannot impose his judgment on others. A materials selection policy should clearly state who is responsible for selection. The ultimate responsibility is vested in you and the other members of your board through your power to determine policy. You delegate the day to day performance of choosing materials to your librarian and staff who have the professional competence and the selection tools to assist them in making good decisions. Policies treat at length or briefly on the quality of books, fiction, nonfiction, for adults, for children, the scope, emphasis, and limits of the collection, the criteria for selecting nonbook materials, the treatment of gifts, the handling of withdrawals and weeding the collection. Most important is the protection of the librarians and the staff if there is some library material which has been challenged. There should be a policy on removal of library materials which states that no materials will be removed except under the order of a court of competent jurisdiction.

Beside the policy, procedures should be established to handle a complaint on library material if it occurs. There is a form based on recommendations of the National Council of Teachers of English. Having one available which will make the complainant organize his thinking as to the basis of his objection may even be a deterrent to his pursuing it. Remain calm. In our family we have a favorite verse, "When in danger or in doubt, run in circles, yell and shout." Don't do that. Keep calm, secure in the knowledge that your library materials have been chosen by professionals using the best selection tools available. The question of enlisting the support of other groups or news media will depend on the circumstances of the case. If possible don't get involved in the merits or the minutiae of the specific item challenged but stand on the broad principle of the right of all people to have access to different types of materials so they can freely make choices according to their individual tastes. Above all, remember that it is up to the courts to interpret what is to be removed from the library.

Sometimes a form of censorship can exist in a library by the way some materials are handled. The Library Bill of Rights has been interpreted periodically and one such statement relates to restricted access to certain library materials. It is not uncommon for libraries in the case of rare books or books subject to theft or mutilation as certain motor car manuals, sex manuals, Jane's Fighting Ships, books on heraldry, etcetera to have a locked case or closed or inaccessible shelf. The decision to segregate should not be colored by any fear that the material is so controversial that its exposure on the open shelves would invite criticism. From time to time the restricted list should be reviewed to be sure that the materials are not so overprotected that no one knows about them or asks for them even though the titles are in the card catalog. Also the need for separating them from the regular collection may have passed.

Trustees should keep informed about legislation, judicial deci-

sions, and acts of individuals or groups which effect intellectual freedom. Of immediate concern is the Supreme Court decision on five obscenity cases, June 21, 1973. The defense that a book has some re-
deeming social value is no longer valid. The test will be whether
"the work taken as a whole, lacks serious literary, artistic, political, or scientific value." There will be no national standard but the
question of fact will be whether "the average person, applying contemporary community standards, would find that the work, taken as
a whole, appeals to the prurient interest." Having standards which
vary from community to community creates a nightmare for booksellers, publishers, motion picture producers, as well as librarians.
How would interlibrary loan be effected? The work must depict or
describe in "a patently offensive way" sexual conduct specifically defined by the applicable state law. At present many state laws are
very vague in their definitions of obscenity, as is Michigan. Another
effect of the decision is that there is no need for expert testimony
to reinforce the charge that a work is obscene, just the presentation
of the work. The burden is placed on the defendant not the prosecu-
tor. The obscenity of a book is an issue of fact for the jury and
hence not appealable. An interesting result is that what a person
possesses in his home cannot be deemed obscene but he cannot purchase, import or acquire it. Apparently he must write it.

The role of the trustee as an advocate of intellectual freedom
includes formulating a materials selection policy, establishing procedures for handling complaints, supporting MLA and ALA, keeping
informed on legislation and judicial decisions. Finally, a good public relations program is essential to promote an understanding of
the library's function in the community and its importance in preserving our individual liberties. It is indeed a warm and friendly
place with staff and board members who are responsive and helpful.
In addition, the library nurtures our democracy by giving access to
divergent ideas so that citizens will be stimulated to find innovative
and creative solutions to the many problems which beset us. If you
are secure in your conviction of what the library represents and have
projected a positive image of the service it performs in maintaining
the vitality of our free society, you need never fear attacks on intellectual freedom.

COLLECTION BUILDING AND MAINTENANCE (Excerpts)

By Ruth Gregory and Lester Stoffel

Selection Policy Statement

One of the major administrative responsibilities in collection building is the local library's selection policy statement. In 1962 James F. Fixx observed:

> Although all libraries, from the very best to the very worst, have their share of failings and misjudgments, each of them tries, sometimes clumsily, sometimes with a skill approximating art, to provide its public with a reliable and useful collection of books. In this task they are ordinarily guided by formal statements of policy that have been thoughtfully worked out to explain to themselves, to their readers, and to potential book-banners why they choose the books they do. [1]

The pertinent words in this quotation are "to explain to themselves, to their readers ... why they choose the books they do." This is the prime purpose of a book and library materials policy statement. It is an instrument of communication. It gives evidence that the policy planners are able to answer basic questions: Where will the library concentrate its strength? What does it expect to be able to offer its patrons in ten years? What redirections in collection building may be taken on the basis of system development? A materials selection policy statement indicates an awareness of necessary steps to move into a world that, as Robert Oppenheimer said, "alters as we walk in it." [2]

System affiliation changes neither the character nor the content of a local library's selection policy statement. System encouragement to develop local selection policy statements is based on the wisdom derived from years of experience within the profession and documented in library literature. The responsibility for the preparation of a selection policy statement in a local library is a joint responsibility of the librarian, the staff, and the board. It may begin with background readings suggested by the librarian and frequently obtained from the system's professional collection. These readings will bring out a number of important points helpful in understanding the need for such statements.

One basic point brought out by the literature is that the right to read or to listen is not one which can be passively accepted; it is one which is subject to constant vigorous defense. A materials selection policy statement in the local library will not solve all problems connected with intellectual freedom for all time. It will, however, help to solve problems more intelligently. Another frequently repeated professional observation is that the average American citizen has the capacity to judge library materials without the help of labels or warning signs. Many social commentators have noted that the nation has made remarkable progress on the assumption that there are extraordinary possibilities in ordinary people. The intelligence of the average library patron must not be underestimated. The literature continuously restates the obligation of modern libraries to make certain that citizens are given a chance to become aware of the pros and cons of the issues in their communities, the nation, and the world. One of the most vital assignments undertaken by the public library is to provide attractive factual material on all sides of contemporary problems so that citizens may get their mental exercise not by jumping at conclusions but through the process of thinking about information, ideas, and opinions.

The selection statement must fit the specific needs of the library and the community concerned. There is little value in merely adopting the policy of another library, although the statement of another library may well serve as an index to the subject areas to be covered. The process of developing a sound selection policy for any library involves analysis of existing resources, sensitivity to continually shifting trends and interests, and alertness to the types of materials required by current conditions and foreseeable changes.

The materials policy statement must be built on established objectives of the library. It may bring out supporting objectives such as the planned guidance of purposeful individual readers or the long-term strengthening of a specific part of the collection. Whatever the goals, they must be the library's own. They must have significance for a particular library at a particular time.

A materials policy statement should recognize the distinction between the use of books by children and the use of books by adults. It has been said that children want a good book and adults want the latest book. There frequently is a difference. The policy statement should indicate an awareness of suitability without limiting book opportunities for any age group. The policy should serve as a reminder of the importance of equity in the allocation of funds to meet the book or nonbook needs of skilled and unskilled library users of every generation. It also must acknowledge the importance of objectivity in the choice of materials in order to save the collection from the unconscious personal prejudices or the ungoverned bibliographical enthusiasms of the librarian and staff.

The statement should give evidence of high standards of selection, with particular concern that a library item be judged as a whole rather than by sections to which there may be objections.

It should reflect the library's appreciation of one of the fundamental American traits, that of fairness in judgment. A book or a film must be assessed by what it is rather than by physical appearance or the racial, political, or religious affiliations of the author or producer.

The materials policy statement should cover the disposition of free material that comes unsolicited from many sources and is outright propaganda. The basis for decision is use. The best use may be to add weight for a wastepaper sale. The material may, on the other hand, be a good example of its kind and thus be valuable for students or citizens interested in the methods of practitioners of the art of propaganda. Directions should be given for proper identification of the source of propaganda as a gift to the library so that there is no possibility of inferences that tax funds have been used for its purchase. The materials statement must further point to local decisions on the acquisition of pseudoscience, textbooks, duplicate copies, withdrawals, or any other problem area.

The selection policy statement may be used in many ways. It is most useful for clarification and guidance and for the stimulation of those who are actually engaged in the practice of book selection. It is designed as a tool for information and interpretation. Librarians work in a communications field, and it behooves them to become experts in interpreting in words their objectives and concepts of standards and service. The University of Wisconsin Library School once had an instructor who said that no one should accept the responsibility for book selection unless he were willing to speak up as an expert. Selection of books and related communications materials is the librarian's specialty. No one else in the community has the opportunity or the desire to apply positive criteria to the evaluation of materials or has the awareness of possible choices related to fulfillment of the objectives of the library.

For many librarians the book selection policy statement is a tool in the defense of intellectual freedom. Granted, this is a more critical issue in some types of libraries than in others and in some parts of the country than in others. However, a selection policy provides a positive approach to the acquisition of controversial materials. It puts the focus on selection rather than on censorship. It is a tool that reminds librarians that "freedom of book selection and fears for book selection"[3] cannot operate simultaneously in a climate productive of intelligent collection building for a well-defined purpose.

The selection policy statement is also a device for in-service training. It can give direction to the handling of situations which occur and recur in collection problem areas. Public libraries are besieged with problems, sometimes called pressures; the consequences can sometimes be circumvented by well-considered and well-expressed principles. Many times librarians tend to think their most distressing problems are related to books with four-letter words and realistic bedroom scenes, but there are others. To take just one example, the field of popular medicine all too often offers half-baked theories about diet, arthritis, or the use of hypnosis. What does the library's policy statement have to say about this type of material? Then, too, there is the question of student use of library resources under the impetus of highly accelerated educational programs. What does the selection statement indicate about the responsibility of the library to adults in a youth-oriented society?

A materials policy statement, like the library itself, is never finished. It is subject to frequent revision. Without continued vigilance, policies become outdated. They lose their power to stimulate. To be of real value, a materials selection policy statement must be revised often, and constant attention paid to the rate of change in technological advances, social attitudes, patron interests, and expanding system services.

Every library has complete autonomy in the development of its book and library materials policy statement. The points recommended for inclusion are:

1. Simple explanation of the way in which selection relates to objectives
2. Description of the library's clientele: a statement that reflects sensitivity to the materials needed by the served and the unserved in the total population
3. Statement of accountability: who in the last analysis is responsible for the materials chosen?
4. Interpretation of the scope of the collection: what it is to include and what it will exclude, not in the sense of self-censorship, but on the basis of a planned program of local collection building that recognizes other collections in the community and wider access through system resources
5. Short commentary of the principles of evaluation, indicating an alertness to criteria that will maintain high standards of acquisition and control of obsolescence
6. General policies on subjects such as gift books and magazine subscriptions, textbooks, and duplications
7. And last, but perhaps most important of all, the library's stand on intellectual freedom.

Supplements to the local library's materials policy statement may include the Library Bill of Rights, the Freedom to Read Statement, and other pertinent releases from the American Library Association, which may have been studied and adopted by the local library board. These statements are of great value as supporting documents for the local library, but they are not substitutes for the library's own statement.

A system may participate in discussions on the development of a member's materials policy statement, but only on request. The system may collect policy statements from many libraries, in and outside the system, for reference by local policy planners. It may help the local library in fact-finding as a basis for policy-making. It will provide professional literature on policy-making and stand by to give advice through its consultant service. The local materials policy statement, however, is not the system's responsibility.

System Materials Policy Statement

The cooperative system's policy statement on the selection of library materials should explain to member library administrators and trustees the responsibility the system assumes in collection development. The statement should also indicate what the system collection is not designed to provide, thereby defining the distinct responsibilities of the system and the local library in collection building. The responsibility for definition of roles rests with the member libraries. The responsibility for developing collections in accordance with the definitions rests with the system administrator, for the system collection, and with the local administrator, for the local collection.

Obviously, membership understanding of the cooperative system's policy is essential. This seems to be particularly true in systems that have been unable to contract with strong existing libraries and have been required to build and house separate collections to fulfill their function. The system policy statement should be discussed in open forum meetings and reinterpreted with reasonable frequency so that old and new members of the system know exactly what to expect from the implementation of system selection and collection building policies. The total librarian who is familiar with the system's selection policy will be better able to tailor the local library's collection to the community's more frequent demands and will know what less frequent local needs can be satisfied from the system collection.

The system materials policy statement should be based on the system's unique objectives, as outlined in its plan of service, and on its role in developing a collection of communications materials as the second-level resource for the library patron. Included will be recognition of the broad geographical area and the wider, more diversified clientele than that of the local library. The system's intention of avoiding unnecessary duplication of local holdings will be included. The role of the system in developing and maintaining an up-to-date professional library will be clearly stated. Standards and quality, the importance of bibliographies and indexes as selection tools, and selection in accordance with the Library Bill of Rights should be emphasized in the system statement, a model to be emulated by member libraries.

Intellectual Freedom

Intellectual freedom cannot be divorced from selection policies. Safeguarding a climate of intellectual freedom is an obligation shared by the local library with all types of libraries and all kinds of systems and information networks. The library by its very nature is hospitable to continual change in ideas and opinions. Librarians as professionals are advocates of mankind's right to create, to write, to read, to listen, to look, to accept or reject ideas and opinions. The library as an institution has been a symbol of intellectual freedom through the ages. The librarian's and the trustee's acceptance of this heritage involves responsibilities.

The local library is on the firing line where professional theories and the courage of librarians and trustees are tested by community standards and customs. The exploration of once-taboo subjects in creative literature and the arts arouses the protesters in the average community. Worries about taxes, street gangs, dissenters, national defense, poverty, and hunger practically disappear with the news that the library is circulating a novel filled with four-letter words and vivid bedroom scenes.

The frustrated middle-class adult, usually the parent of a teenage daughter, needs a target. There is little he can do about the overall state of morals in American society. The closest target, and the easiest to attack, is the local library, which is allegedly packed with realistic novels, frank social studies, and sex instruction books for children. The Supreme Court has not been able to define pornography, but the citizen thinks he can. The librarian in the small community often is caught between the commitment to the principle of freedom to read and community outrage. The adult revolt against vulgarity and other forms of expression that diminish the dignity of the human being is understandable. A deliberate citizen hunt for offensive words and scenes to safeguard the morals of others may be explainable even though it is not acceptable in a free society.

To many librarians, there is more of a challenge in fighting attempted censorship of opinions and ideologies than in defending four-letter words. Arguing over vulgarity becomes as boring as the words are. There is some incongruity when a library with an avowed educational objective and a concern for excellence must become overly concerned with the defense of the cheap and the tawdry in popular publications. Nevertheless, the basic right of the adult to choose his own reading remains a constant in the philosophy of librarians.

The librarian in the small community comes closer to the disaster area in censorship conflicts than does the librarian in metropolitan centers. The large library with adequate funding is justified in claiming its responsibility to collect highly controversial materials for the use of specialists and for the historical record. The larger library can justify the collection of the near-pornography, which according to some librarians must have social significance because there is so much of it. The departmentalization of large libraries is a shield against the censor's most persuasive piece of ammunition: that the offending item will fall into the hands of a child.

Recognition of the vulnerable position of the librarian in the small library does not imply less need for dedication to the principles of intellectual freedom. It simply acknowledges that the individual librarian can be helped by system exploration of problems, techniques, and experiences. One of the benefits of the system is that the librarians and trustees of the small library no longer have to stand alone in resolving censorship problems unless they choose to do so.

The cooperative system has a stake in maintaining an environment of intellectual freedom in the communities within its jurisdiction. The maintenance of such an environment requires more than a universal adoption of the Library Bill of Rights by member libraries, helpful as that is. It involves more than making available a collection of material on intellectual freedom for the use of member libraries. The system must actively assist member libraries to develop the skills necessary for the defense of intellectual freedom.

The system has the capacity for direct assistance to its member libraries troubled by problems in intellectual freedom. One avenue for this assistance is the establishment and training of an intellectual freedom committee composed of member librarians, trustees, a representative of the system staff, or any combination of interested system people. The first assignment for the committee might be to define intellectual freedom as it applies to the circumstances and interests of the members of the system. "Intellectual freedom" in libraries is a phrase that stands for freedom of the press and the right to read. Interpretations of intellectual freedom in the early 1970s introduced other concepts involving elements such as civil rights and the insistence on strong institutional positions on social problems of national concern.

Intellectual freedom, regardless of interpretations, relates selection and collection building to the Library Bill of Rights, which focuses on the rights and needs of the user. At the same time the personal convictions and professional zeal of the book selector may overemphasize some aspects of collection building, and trouble may arise in the name of intellectual freedom. A system committee must be prepared to establish policies that determine the conditions under which it is proper for a system committee to engage in membership controversies involving the rights of the library, the rights of the librarian, or both.

Specific charges to a system's intellectual freedom committee will naturally vary from system to system. There may be a charge to determine what types of educational programs the system will sponsor. There may be a directive to examine the degree of need for system action in critical cases, in view of the specialized assistance available through the American Library Association. It may be the committee's responsibility to monitor and disseminate information on legislation affecting intellectual freedom being proposed on both state and federal levels. A system's intellectual freedom committee would be a logical liaison between the system and the profes-

sional associations, the state library, and the other systems active
in the defense of intellectual freedom.

A prime function of a system's intellectual freedom committee
is education. The framework of the system lends itself to the establishment of a forum through which librarians and trustees may become familiar with the literature, the case studies, and the defense
techniques of the 1970s. An intellectual freedom forum offered by the
system and its committee to member libraries can do more than
channel information and build up a background of strategies. It can
help the individual clarify his own convictions, which influence selection. The librarian, after all, is as human as the censor. The librarian as a person is not always free of qualms about strange political opinions or free of prejudice against extreme realism in literary
forms. There is a certain amount of ambivalence in practice even
among some of the staunchest defenders of intellectual freedom.
This is not necessarily a form of self-censorship. It is more often
a failure to think through the human elements in matching philosophy
and practice.

The system forum can serve as a continuing reminder that
freedom to read cannot be taken for granted as a gift from the
authors of the federal constitution. The profession rightly assumes
responsibility to protect this basic right of a free people. It is a
freedom that each generation of librarians must defend anew. To
paraphrase Somerset Maugham: If the library values anything more
than its freedom, it will lose that freedom; and the irony is that if
it is security and peace of mind that the library values more than
freedom, it will lose that, too.

The advisory function of an intellectual freedom committee or
of the system itself requires carefully developed policies. Advice
may be requested by a member library to prevent trouble. An appeal for help may follow an attack on a book or a film. The problem
may originate with the leadership of an irate community organization.
It may rise because of philosophic differences between the librarian
and the trustees. The system must differentiate between types of
problems related to intellectual freedom. There are community-
generated problems, for which system fact-finding and the counsel of
experienced librarians and system consultants will provide the answers. There are internal problems, in which the system may best
assist the local library through counsel on the best use of the services of specialists in library organizations or legal firms. There
are also occasions when the local library and its system advisers
may be asked to participate in the formulation of policies for academic freedom in area schools and colleges.

Notes

1. James F. Fixx. "The Library Goes to Market," Saturday Review 45:14-15 (7 April 1962).
2. Robert Oppenheimer. "Prospects in the Arts and Sciences,"

Perspectives USA 11:10-11 (Spring 1955).
3. See Freedom of Book Selection (Chicago: ALA, 1954), 132p.,
   and Robert B. Downs, ed., The First Freedom (Chicago:
   ALA, 1960), p. 469.

COLLECTION POLICY IN COLLEGE
AND UNIVERSITY LIBRARIES

By K. Linda Ward

I

A major project of the Music Library of the University of
Western Ontario this past year has been the development of a formal
collection policy[1] for music materials.

Before the writing of the collection policy was begun, it was
decided that a search of the literature on collection policies and a
comparison of collection policies from other university libraries
would be both practical and informative. The literature search revealed very little other than vague generalities. There were numerous articles which described the reasons certain materials are acquired by different types of libraries. Several articles suggested
where and how to acquire the materials. No article, however, discussed the purposes and the formulation of collection policies.

For comparison, copies of existing collection policies for
music materials were requested from ten music libraries--both
Canadian and American. These ten libraries were chosen because
of their stature as music libraries or because of their similarity in
size, curriculum, or state of development to the Music Library of
the University of Western Ontario. Nine libraries responded.
Three of these had formal collection policies, two had informal policies, and the other four were either in the process of developing
such policies or dod not believe that they were necessary.

This apparent lack of information on the purposes and the
formulation of music collection policies led me to believe that some
of the insights gained in formulating our collection policy might be
of interest to the readers of Notes. It is the intent of this paper to
discuss collection policies in general and music collection policies
of university libraries in specific.

II

A collection policy is a statement indicating in what direction
the collection is headed; it is not a description of an existing collection. Consequently, the primary purpose of a collection policy is to
state the principal collection objectives of a library. It ensures that

Reprinted from Notes, vol. 29, no. 3, March 1973, pp. 432-440, by
permission of the Music Library Association.

the collection is developed in a rational and systematic manner and that the budget available for acquisitions is spent on materials most needed by the library's users. A document of this nature is an essential guide for the people responsible for the selection of music materials.

A collection policy also functions as an informational document which presents an overview of the library and its collection. For example, from the "Subject and Collection Levels" section of Western's music collection policy, [2] one has a general idea of where the major strengths and weaknesses in the collection lie.

If it is assumed that a collection policy reflects the focal points for collection development, it is logical to use it as a basis for appraising the present collection. At Western an appraisal of the collection using the collection policy has just been completed. The most difficult part of the task was to find an accurate and appropriate bibliography for each subject area being appraised. Once a bibliography was found, it was a simple matter of comparing the library's holdings with the items listed in the bibliography. In a like manner, the weeding of a collection may also be based on the collection policy.

A collection policy is used in preparing the budget for acquisitions. For instance, when the appraisal of a subject is completed, the number of items which are to be acquired for the collection is calculated. The average cost of these is then determined, and this figure is multiplied by the total number of items. The resulting figure is an approximation of the total amount of money required for a subject area.

A collection policy is also used to justify the budget requested. Such a policy justifies the budget by indicating that the money requested is to be used in developing those areas of the library's collection which both the faculty[3] and the library feel need to be improved.

Finally, a collection policy is used as the justification for the rejection of requests for items to be acquired and for the presence of items already in the collection. For example, if someone at Western questioned the validity of purchasing a piece of music by an obscure Canadian composer, it would be easy to justify the purchase since our collection policy states that Canadian music is to be collected intensively. By this I do not mean to imply that the collection policy is the "last word"; on the contrary, it is essential that there be other recourses open to both patron and librarian. A collection policy is similar to any other document in that it functions well in most situations but not in all.

For any or all of the above objectives to be meaningful and valid, the collection policy must be recognized as a legitimate document itself. Consequently, it is essential that the policy be a joint document of the library and the faculty and that it be approved by both.

Since a collection policy is basically a library document (that
is, the functions of a collection policy as outlined above are basically
library functions), it is natural that the library should take the initiative in the drafting. To what degree the faculty should participate
in the drafting would depend on the "political" situation. Who does
the selecting is not an important factor in formulating such policy.
What is important is that the people directly involved in selection--
be they faculty or librarians--agree with the selection criteria as
outlined in the policy.

III

In order to discuss the contents and formulation of collection
policies, I thought it would be best to use a model. For this
reason, the music collection policy of the University of Western On-
terio is appended to this paper.

The first major problem encountered when developing a collection policy is the choice of a format which would be most suitable
for the type of document desired. In making our choice, we examined the collection policies of several academic libraries and decided
that the basic formats of the policies for the Stanford University Libraries[4] and for Northwestern University[5] would serve as our models.
We also felt that in our situation (that is, all materials pertinent to
music are housed in the Music Library), it was most logical to have
one collection policy for all music materials. The decision to have
more than one policy for a subject depends basically on where the
pertinent materials are actually housed.

In most universities, the music library is not an independent
unit, but rather an integral part of the total library system which
serves a campus. Consequently, a collection policy for music materials is usually a section of a total collection policy. This is the
situation at Western. [6] However, we felt that our collection policy
should be as complete in itself as possible for the benefit of our
users. Therefore, the first section of our collection policy is simply an introduction, a short paragraph in which we try to explain in
general terms the purpose of the policy. Moreover, in this section
we have emphasized the fact that the policy is based upon the curriculum of the Faculty of Music and consequently, the policy will have
to be revised periodically so that it will be current with the changes
in the curriculum.

Since the collecting aims of a library can only be perceived
from within the context of its own particular situation, an understanding of this situation must be reached before collecting objectives
can be established. The purpose of the next section of our policy is
to define, in broad terms, the context within which the Music Library functions. To define the context, we derived from the documents
indicated what we considered to be the general purpose of the Music
Library. Based on this definition, we then developed a list of the
principal collection objectives of the Music Library.

There are at least six general factors which determine the scope of music materials collected. They are: language, geographic area, chronological periods, price, types of material collected, and the types of material not collected.

The first category, language, is not really applicable to music, either in print or in sound, since music is collected for its intrinsic value. Works on music (that is, books), however, are subject to language restrictions. These restrictions depend on such local factors as the size of the library and of the user group serviced.

The geographical areas from which music materials are collected is also a factor in selection. The limitations in this category again depend on the individual library.

For music and works on music there are really no chronological restrictions; however, each library will probably place special emphasis on certain music periods.

The price of an item is usually assumed to be a selection factor, but it is not always listed with the "regular" factors. A collection policy should be as complete as possible; consequently, there should be a statement concerning price as a selection factor. In our policy, we also felt it necessary to indicate the two major considerations which determine whether an item is to be bought when the price is considered high.

The types of materials collected and not collected are two very important factors for both collection and selection purposes. A simple, complete listing of the types of materials collected is desirable in a collection policy. Such a specific list, although essential, is very constricting. To try to overcome this difficulty in our policy, a footnote to the section provides that materials not listed above may be purchased as the occasion arises. We also felt it necessary to explain that phonodiscs have additional collection criteria; they were to be collected with the aim of complementing the music collection and with an emphasis on a variety of performances of a composition. This is the only situation in which phonodiscs needed to be treated separately.

One of the most important parts of the collection policy is the section, "Subject and Collecting Levels";[7] it is also the most difficult to define. Its purpose is to indicate which subject areas are to be collected at what levels of intensity. The purpose and contents of collecting levels can best be explained by actual example (please see the definitions of our collecting levels contained in our collection policy). Once the collecting levels have been defined, it is necessary that the subject areas be placed in the appropriate levels. The collecting levels of the subjects for our library were determined through analysis of the academic calendar of the Faculty of Music and of the remarks made by the department chairmen concerning the future direction of their departments. The subjects in the two highest collecting levels should be defined as specifically as possible in order to avoid any misunderstanding.

Since not all materials which are added to the collection are purchased, a statement concerning the acceptance of gifts should be made. As can be seen from our policy, the statement is very broad, but it does indicate that the library does not accept all gifts simply because they are free.

If money must be spent to replace materials already in the collection, the amount of money available for new materials is thereby reduced; consequently, the replacement of materials becomes a factor in selection. For this reason, there should be a statement to indicate this in the collection policy.

The actual method of formulating a collection policy is different for each library; however, to demonstrate what might be involved, I would like to explain the method we used. First, I would like to say that this method worked very well; we attribute this to the effective communication, both formal and informal, which existed among all parties involved.

The music librarians as a committee made the initial draft of the collection policy; it was then circulated to the department chairmen, who were asked for their comments. Their comments were then incorporated into the policy and a second draft was prepared. This draft was distributed to the Associate Dean of the Faculty of Music and to the appropriate administrative personnel in the Library System for their comments. When their approval had been received, the music collection policy was considered official.

Upon completion, it is necessary to decide to whom copies of the collection policy will be distributed. Naturally, all persons involved in the actual formulation will receive a copy; however, not all people who will be affected by the collection policy (that is, faculty members other than department chairmen, students, etc.), were involved in its formulation. Consequently, the library might choose to distribute the policy to these people also.

IV

In conclusion I would like to emphasize the two most important aspects of a collection policy:

(1) A collection policy is an official document which gives formal recognition to the criteria which probably have always been tacitly followed by a library. This recognition, however, is becoming more and more important in an age when university spending is receiving so much scrutiny.

(2) A collection policy as the basis for the rational and systematic development of a collection ensures that the needs of the library users are met.

Notes

1. The three terms, acquisition policy, selection policy, and collection policy are often used interchangeably. For the purpose of this paper (and for clarity in general), I have arbitrarily made a distinction among the three terms. An acquisition policy could be defined as a list of sources and agents from whom materials are purchased, while a selection policy could be defined as a description of criteria to be used in selecting individual items. A collection policy, on the other hand, could be defined as a general statement concerning the principles directing the development of the collection. A single document may contain any or all aspects of the above terms.
2. The collection policy of the Music Library of the University of Western Ontario is appended to this paper. Also, the term "Western" is used throughout this paper to refer to the University of Western Ontario.
3. There may be some confusion with the word "faculty." In most cases it is probably synonymous with the words "school," "department," or "college" in the U.S.
4. Stanford University. Libraries. Book Selection Policies of the Libraries of Stanford University.
5. Northwestern University. Music Library. Music Library Acquisition Policy.
6. The Music Library is one of the seven divisional/professional libraries which, with the General Library, comprise The Libraries of the University of Western Ontario. The Music Library is located near the faculty of Music.
7. We have just encountered a problem in this section; no where is there mention of reference materials. We had assumed that reference works for each of the subjects listed would be collected in accordance with the collecting level of the subject. This however, does not take into consideration the need for an academic music library to have a majority of the most important music reference works no matter to which area of music they pertain.

Bibliography

Benton, Rita. "The Music Library of the University of Iowa." Fontes Artis Musicae, XVI (1969), 124-129.

Bradley, Carol June. Manual of Music Librarianship. Ann Arbor: Music Library Association, 1966.

Hall, Mary M. "Theoretical Considerations of Selection Policies for University Libraries: Their relevance to Canadian University Libraries," Canadian Library, XXIII (Summer, 1966), 89-98.

Lane, David O. "The Selection of Academic Library Materials, a Literature Survey," College and Research Libraries, XXIV (Summer, 1968), 364-72.

Maley, George E. "On University Libraries in the United Kingdom,"
Fontes Artis Musicae, IV (1957), 3-6.

Murphy, Richard M. "The Library in a Music School," Notes, X
(September, 1953), 537-45.

Northwestern University. Music Library. Music Library Acquisition Policy.

Stanford University. Libraries. Book Selection Policies of the Libraries of Stanford University.

Stevenson, Gordon. "Music in Medium-Sized Libraries," Book Selection and Censorship in the Sixties. Edited by Eric Moon.
New York: Bowker, 1969.

Taggart, W. R. "Preparing a Collections Policy for the Academic
Library," Canadian Association of College and University
Libraries Newsletter, IV (September, 1972), 53-56.

Collection Policy

The Library, Faculty of Music
University of Western Ontario

I. Introduction:

This collection policy was developed to establish formal
guidelines in order to ensure consistency in the selection of materials to be acquired for the Music Library. It is not a descriptive
statement of the existing collection; it merely sets forth the collecting aims of this Library. From time to time this policy will be
reviewed and brought up to date with the changes in the curricula
of the University.

II. General Purpose:

The general purpose of this Library is to make available material which will support the University's aims, goals, and functions
in the field of music.

The three documents consulted in the preparation of this collection policy were:

A. Report to the Senate Committee on University Development
by the Subcommittee on Music: "the Trueman Report".
1967;
B. University Library System Objectives. 1971;
C. University of Western Ontario Faculty of Music Calendar
for 1971-72.

The following principal collection objectives were derived from
these documents. They are, in order of importance:

    A. To collect material which will support the curricular needs of the library users.

    B. To collect material which will, in general, support research and advanced study.

    C. To collect material which will assist the library users' intellectual and recreational interests which may or may not be directly related to the curricula.

III. <u>General Guidelines</u>

    A. Languages:

    Music, both in print and in sound, is collected for its intrinsic value, regardless of the language of its texts or notes. Works on music, however, are primarily collected in Western languages, and in particular, in English, German, French and Italian.

    B. Geographical Areas:

    Music, both in print and in sound, and works on music are acquired on a world-wide basis, with emphasis on Europe and North America.

    C. Chronological Periods:

    There are no chronological restrictions in the collecting of music materials. As the post-graduate programmes are further delineated, areas of specialization will be developed.

    D. Price:

    There are, of course, price restrictions in the collecting of music materials. These restrictions are dependent upon the budget and the importance of an item to the collection. Therefore, each item is considered individually.

    E. Types of Materials Collected:[1]

Books
Clippings
Facsimiles of manuscripts, music scores and treatises
Manuscripts[2]
Microforms
Music scores and/or parts[3]
Pamphlets
Periodicals
Program notes
Catalogues of publishers, agents and dealers
Sound recordings[4]
Theses and dissertations
University calendars
Visual materials

F. Types of Materials Excluded:

Multiple copies of method books.

More than five copies of any one title, multiple copies of choral music excluded, will not be purchased except where long-range use is anticipated.

IV. Subject and Collecting Levels:

The collecting levels, A-D, are defined in Appendix I.

A Level Subjects:
   Canadian music
   opera and instrumental forms between 1750-1850
   performance practices
   standard repertoire

B Level Subjects:
   curriculum development[5]
   development of
      a) instrumental forms
      b) operas
      c) orchestras
      d) art song
   history of music theory
   performance materials for large ensembles
   programmed instruction
   twentieth century music

C Level Subjects:
   all other areas of
      a) applied music
      b) music education
      c) music history
      d) theory and composition

D Level Subjects:[6]
   aesthetics
   art
   dance
   education
   ethnomusicology
   theatre
   other subjects related to music

V. Gifts:

Gifts are accepted at the discretion of the Library.

VI. Replacement of Materials:

Inasmuch as disc and tape recordings are fragile and as

damage often renders them unplayable, these materials must be replaced frequently on a systematic basis.

To a lesser extent, scores and/or parts must likewise be replaced on a systematic basis.

Other materials are replaced as required.

Notes

1. From time to time materials may be acquired which are not
   specifically mentioned in this section.
2. When items of a manuscript nature are acquired, either through
   purchase or through gift, a statement concerning their use
   will be required of the appropriate person(s).
3. Music scores and/or parts are collected primarily for the purpose of research: it is assumed that applied music majors
   will develop their own libraries of performing materials.
4. As far as possible, sound recordings are collected with the aim
   of complementing the collection of music. In addition, there
   is emphasis on collecting a variety of performances of a
   work.
5. Curriculum development here is considered as a section of music education.
6. In view of the curricula of the Faculty of Music such related
   areas as mentioned here should only be represented in the
   collection.

Appendix I

University of Western Ontario Libraries
Collection Development Policy

Collection Levels

A. Comprehensive Level

   At this level, the collection policy is designed to support
doctoral and post-doctoral programs with limited resort to interlibrary loan. Materials are collected in the necessary languages and
from the appropriate geographical areas in a variety of formats:
monographs, serials, microforms, maps, newspapers, manuscripts,
and audio-visual materials. Expensive and esoteric materials (mainly primary sources) are procured in the light of clearly established
library requirements, the provisions for provincial co-operation in
university academic policy, and the availability of financial resources.

B. Beginning Research Level

   The purchase of materials at this level consists primarily of
printed sources (books and periodicals) in the appropriate languages

for the support of teaching and research to the level of the Masters Degree. Included are all basic works of scholarship and other relevant secondary sources, but not necessarily all printed materials at the primary source level. Aspects of particular subjects classified in this category may be developed further in response to demonstrated needs, but not with a view to a major expansion of research.

C. Teaching Level

This collection policy is designed to provide effective support for undergraduate teaching to the level of 4th year Honours Programs, but excludes research activity. Materials collected include monographs in the appropriate languages, serial literature, and all types of basic reference material including subject indexes and bibliographies.

D. Reference Level

This level includes those subject areas not specifically covered by the academic curriculum or the research programs of the University. Materials are collected mainly in the English language to serve general needs, and on account of the relationship of a subject not formally offered to those currently covered. Generally, this level is inadequate to support extensive undergraduate instruction. Subjects in this category may be developed to higher levels in response to specific or anticipated needs; collected include basic monographs, significant periodical titles, key reference works, and important subject bibliographies.

Appendix II

Music Programmes

I. Bachelor of Music with Honors in:
   A. Music Education
   B. Music History
   C. Performance-organ and church music, orchestral instrument, piano or voice
   D. Theory and composition

II. Bachelor of Arts with Honors Music

III. Bachelor of Arts with Music Options

IV. Bachelor of Musical Arts

V. Master of Music in:
   A. Composition
   B. Music Education
   C. Music Literature and Performance
   D. Music Theory

VI.   Master of Arts in Musicology

VII. Music Courses for Arts and Science Students

VIII. Music Courses for the Department of Summer School and Extension

IX.   Doctoral Programmes (projected for 1975)

RECOMMENDED READINGS

Collections of actual policies provide a source for further
reading. Chapter three of LeRoy C. Merritt's Book Selection and
Intellectual Freedom (New York: Wilson, 1970) contains several
sample policies. Book Selection Policies in American Libraries by
Calvin J. Boyer (Austin: Armadillo Press, 1971) is a compilation
of selection policies from different types of libraries. Library Acquisition Policies and Procedures, edited by Elizabeth Futas (Phoe-
nix: Oryx Press, 1977) reports the results of a survey of acquisition and selection policies found in public and academic libraries
and includes many complete policies and significant excerpts from
others. The Systems and Procedures Exchange Center, Association
of Research Libraries, Washington, D. C., has devoted Number 38
of its series of collected materials to collection development policies. The policies included illustrate the practice of determining
collection development levels according to the needs and objectives
of the various institutions.

To aid libraries in carrying out collection development activities, the Resources Section, Resources and Technical Services Division, A. L. A., Collection Development Committee prepared a set of
guidelines which were published in Library Resources and Technical
Services, 21, no. 1 (Winter, 1977) 40-45. "Guidelines for the Formulation of Collection Development Policies" provides much useful
information, including definitions of levels, principles to be observed,
and elements of a collection development policy statement.

An example of selection policies within one university setting
is provided by Stanford University Libraries' Book Selection Policies
of the Libraries (Stanford, Calif.: The Libraries, 1970). The introductory material defines five levels of collection development and
also the limitations established.

A complete but concise handbook on the writing of selection
policies has been prepared by the Michigan Association for Media in
Education Intellectual Freedom Committee. Selection Policies: A
Guide to Updating and Writing (Ann Arbor: The Association, 1977)
includes rationale and other information on selection policies along
with several bibliographies. Also included in this compilation is the
"Students' Right to Read," an excellent statement on intellectual freedom for students issued by the National Council of Teachers of English.

Discussion of the usefulness of selection policies in all types
of libraries is included in Building Library Collections by Mary Dun-

can Carter, Wallace Bonk, and Rose Mary Magrill (4th ed. New York: Scarecrow Press, 1974). Some complete policies and many excerpts are also presented.

A cautionary note on selection policies is provided by Marion Crush in "Policy for De-selection," Wilson Library Bulletin, v. 45 (Oct., 1970) 180-1. She points out how statements in a policy can be used to eliminate many materials from consideration for purchase.

The library preparing a selection policy would certainly want to examine the various policy statements prepared by the American Library Association, such as the "Resolution on Challenged Materials," "Statement on Labelling," and others pertaining to particular kinds of library work, with children, in schools, etc. Many of these statements appear in the Intellectual Freedom Manual (Chicago: A.L.A. 1974). Revisions of these documents and related new ones are presented regularly in the journals.

CHAPTER 4

THE SELECTION ENVIRONMENT:
THE COMMUNITY AND THE COLLECTION

One of the traditional principles of selecting materials for libraries has been the "know your community" concept. Helen Haines[1]
stated it thus: Study your community and know its general character,
special characteristics, cultural and racial elements, chief activities,
and leading interests.

That principle is given almost universal endorsement. "Of
course different communities have different needs," and "The librarian selects for her (or his) own community" are often-expressed
views. In many cases, this principle may be given more lip-service
than actual observance, if no attempt is made to learn how the librarian can "know the community." Does one depend upon casual, first
impressions, statistical reports of the community, user reports only,
annual reports of the administration of whatever kind, or are there
ways in which we can systematically appraise and investigate the environment of the community in which we serve?

This chapter includes discussions of the reasons for and the
methods of making a community study or analysis. By this term is
meant an organized, thoughtfully planned attempt to determine the
factors, such as population characteristics, cultural and educational
facilities, occupational patterns, community goals and attitudes, and
administrative structures that relate to the library. These factors,
and many others, create the environment within which the theory of
selection, the philosophy of a library, and the evaluation process for
materials operate, forming a matrix on which actual selection decisions are made.

The term community can be applied to any of those situations
in which a library is expected to give service, the school, college
or university, the diverse organizations with special libraries, as
well as the public library community. Thus, community analysis
can and should be done in any of these settings.

A broad overview of the growth of American academic libraries and the changing patterns of selecting materials is presented in
Robert Downs' "Collection Development for Academic Librarians:
An Overview." He relates how academic libraries, particularly
those concerned with research, have sought new ways to cope with

the great increases in materials available and in the needs of their clientele. All of these are factors in the academic library environment which affect selection.

Continuing the consideration of the academic library community, Edward Holley, in "Multimedia and the Information Requirements of Researchers," provides effective examples of the various forms of media that would enhance the quality and range of present-day research. He also considers the expense of such materials, the principles of evaluation to be applied, and then concludes that libraries are the logical places to gather and organize these other informational materials.

Turning to another one of our library communities, the case for analysis of the public library's environment is effectively made in "Studying the Community: An Overview," by Allie Beth Martin. The groups and agencies concerned with public policy planning and their dependence upon solid community analysis are given as evidence of the need. Martin identifies the previous roles of libraries in such studies and their increasing opportunities to participate in such studies.

An important element to the community analysis is a study of the library's own resources--its collection and services, and their ability to meet the needs already known of and those disclosed by the study. Demonstrating the thinking and methods followed in one such study is Lolly Eggers' article, "More Effective Management of the Public Library's Book Collection." The methods described could be used in many libraries to establish a more rational basis for selection decisions.

The attempt of a specific university library to arrive at a similar basis is described in the article, "A Method for Quantitatively Evaluating a University Library Collection," by Barbara Golden. The evaluation was made to determine how well the library's collection was meeting the curricular needs of the university. The methodology and results are explained and evaluated.

Taking a look at one type of special library, the hospital library, Eleanor Phinney, in "Library Materials for Patients," carefully delineates the various factors that govern selection in that setting. Included are the policy, budgetary considerations, criteria used, special considerations for special patrons, and collection appraisal. This discussion could serve as a model for other libraries in "special" situations.

Another type of library and another situation are discussed in Frances Dean's article, "Design of Initial Media Collections for New Libraries." The process of selecting an initial collection is described and explained, from philosophy to practical guidelines. Many of the factors mentioned are applicable in an established school media center too.

A further important factor in the library environment is that of the standards set by various associations and accreditating agencies. They cover, of course, a broad range of concerns, but the status of the collection is a significant one in most of them. Such standards for library collections have to be considered in any collection/selection policy and process. Some of them, particularly those of accrediting agencies, carry semi-official weight, but all of them can be used as goals and guidelines in collection development. Because of the multiplicity and the changing character of the standards, none is included in this collection, but specific references to some are given in the recommended readings.

Note

1. Helen Haines. <u>Living with Books</u>, 2nd ed. (N. Y. : Columbia University Press, 1950), p. 41.

COLLECTION DEVELOPMENT FOR ACADEMIC LIBRARIES:
AN OVERVIEW

By Robert B. Downs

     The rapid growth of American college and university libraries, especially in state-supported institutions, is one of the most remarkable changes that has occurred in higher education during the present century. No region of the country is an exception to this phenomenon.

     Why this emphasis on strong libraries? The best explanation, I believe, is a statement included in a report issued by the American Council on Education, entitled An Assessment of Quality in Graduate Education. The statement reads: "The library is the heart of the university; no other single nonhuman factor is as obviously related to the quality of graduate education. A few universities with poor library resources," the report continues, "have achieved considerable strength in several departments, in some cases because the universities are located close to other great library collections such as the Library of Congress and the New York Public Library. But institutions that are strong in all areas invariably have major national research libraries."

     The reasons for what may rightly be described as an explosion of academic library collections in all the American states are complex. Among the important factors are the establishment of hundreds of new institutions of higher education and the enrollment of millions of additional students in colleges and universities across the land. Changing methods of instruction are sending students to their libraries in increasing numbers. Also, there is constantly growing emphasis on faculty research and scholarly productivity. Book budgets expanded steadily during the fifties and sixties, including a limited amount of federal aid to libraries. Extensive new foreign acquisition programs developed following World War II. Finally, the rate of publication of books and journals has been expanded year by year, and libraries have responded by stepped-up acquisition activities. I suspect that institutional rivalries are also a not insignificant factor, for a strong library has become a status symbol which lends prestige to a college or university--something to point to with pride-- while a weak one requires a lot of explanation to faculty, students, and accrediting associations.

An address delivered March 6th, 1975 in Durham, North Carolina at the Banquet during the Spring Tutorial on Collection Development for Academic Libraries sponsored by the College and University Section of NCLA. Reprinted from North Carolina Libraries, vol. 34, no. 3, Fall 1976, pp. 31-38, by permission of the publisher.

According to U.S. Office of Education statistics, the libraries of the United States contained 45,000,000 volumes in 1900, 75 years ago. By 1970, the number had risen to more than 800,000,000, an 18 fold increase. Of the total, about 350,000,000 volumes are held by college and university libraries.

Another important aspect of the study of library resources is their geographic distribution. In his Geography of Reading, published in 1938, Louis Round Wilson found that there were 77 library centers in the United States containing 500,000 volumes or more. All except 19 of the centers were concentrated in the Northeast. Only a half-dozen were located in the Southeast. In a follow-up study published in College & Research Libraries last March, it was discovered that the number of centers holding in excess of 500,000 volumes each had jumped from 77 to 265, 80 of them in the South. There were 9 such centers in North Carolina alone: Asheville, Boone, Chapel Hill-Durham, Charlotte, Fayetteville, Greensboro, Greenville, Raleigh, and Winston-Salem. Among the 6 principal regions of the country, the Southeast ranked third in total volume holdings.

In 1960, Publishers Weekly reported that 15,000 new books or new editions of books were published in the United States. Last year, the total had risen to more than 40,000, nearly tripling in 15 years. World-wide, according to UNESCO annual compilation, the number of book titles published is now up to about 600,000, more than doubling in the past 20 years. That gives one some conception of a research library's acquisition problems.

Actually, separately-printed books have become a lesser part of a library's current accessions, especially in universities. The Library of Congress and the Harvard University Library, the nation's two largest libraries, report that about three-fourths, 75 percent of their current acquisitions are in serial form. As anyone who has dealt with them is well aware, serial publications present problems of immense scope and complexity. Nevertheless, serial literature has assumed an increasingly important place in libraries. The learned and technical journals, transactions of academies, museums, observatories, universities, and institutions of all sorts, and the serial publications of governments demand more and more library funds, space, and staff.

Then there is the huge field of nonpublished or nonbook materials. Even more complex than books and serials are such types of material as manuscripts, archives, maps, sound recordings, motion pictures, slides, prints, and photographs. Many institutions are building up extensive collections in these categories.

The dilemma of our academic libraries, particularly those concerned with research, is worsened by the fact that no practicable limit can be set on the number of books and other materials needed even by a single department, or for that matter, perhaps by a single research worker.

It is this situation which has caused research libraries in recent years to search for ways and means to hold in check the mounting flood of printed materials. Thus we have the creation of national, regional, and local union catalogs to locate books in other libraries, saving the necessity for every library to acquire them. We have cooperative purchasing agreements; there are no programs for the centralized housing of little-used books, a plan now under consideration for North Carolina; we have ambitious projects for microfilming large masses of material for preservation and to reduce their bulk for storage purposes.

We also have agreements for subject specialization among libraries, limiting the number of fields each has to cover in depth, an area in which Duke University and the University of North Caroline were pioneers; and a widespread system of inter-library loans has grown up.

Viewing this complex state of affairs, prophets of gloom are predicting that we have reached the twilight of the printed book, and that the book as we know it will be replaced by newer media of communication. Lest this prospect unduly depress you, let me hasten to point out that the end of the printed book has been regularly predicted for the past several centuries. Proponents of the manuscript codex were certain that the invention of printing spelled the end of the book. The doom-sayers saw the coming of the bicycle, of the automobile, and of the moving picture as the book's finish, and now we have Marshall McLuhan telling us that television is driving the last nail in the coffin. Still, as indicated, the book's numbers increase yearly, and I am convinced it will still be with us long after such false prophets as McLuhan are mere footnotes in history.

Turning to the specific theme of this tutorial on academic library collection development, a retrospective note may be in order. Pioneer American college and university librarians were strongly addicted to rugged individualism in their methods of book procurement. Funds were limited and collections grew at a snail's pace. Nevertheless, each library was regarded as a completely independent entity, its development proceeding with little or no consideration of its neighbors. It was reliant upon its own resources except for an occasional interlibrary loan.

The first major evidence of a change of direction came with the establishment of the National Union Catalog in 1900 and publication of the Union List of Serials in the United States and Canada in 1927. Thereafter, librarians began to view their holdings within a larger frame of reference, as elements of a national resource, the sharing of which could be of immense mutual benefit. The coming of the Great Depression in the nineteen-thirties expedited the process, when such cooperative enterprises were born as the regional bibliographic centers in Denver, Philadelphia, and Seattle, along with numerous local and state union catalogs.

Not until after World War II was there any major effort undertaken toward joint or coordinated acquisition. The first was the Cooperative Acquisition Project for Wartime Publications, sponsored by the Library of Congress. This program demonstrated several points: (1) American libraries could look to their national library for leadership in large cooperative activities; (2) research libraries were able and willing to support a broad program for the improvement of library resources; (3) the idea of libraries combining for the acquisition of research materials was feasible and desirable; (4) and the research resources of American libraries were a matter of national concern.

Profiting from the experience gained in the project for wartime publications, other large foreign acquisition programs followed, notably the Farmington Plan, the Latin American Cooperative Acquisition Project, and the Public Law 480 program for acquiring multiple copies of publications in certain countries where counterpart funds or blocked currencies had accumulated.

These various enterprises culminated in 1965 with passage by Congress of enabling legislation for the National Program for Acquisition and Cataloging, centering in the Library of Congress. The plan places upon the Library of Congress responsibility for acquiring, as far as possible, all library materials currently published throughout the world of potential value to scholarship and of providing catalog information for these materials to other libraries promptly after receipt. Within their respective spheres, the National Agricultural Library and the National Library of Medicine are active participants in the over-all program. It is apparent that when this undertaking is fully implemented, the world's publishing output will reach the United States soon after it comes off the press, fully cataloged and ready for use.

The concept of collecting in the national interest is being furthered by another type of institution, exemplified by the Center for Research Libraries in Chicago, which now serves a membership of nearly 200 libraries in the United States and Canada. The Center has two main functions: to house and service little-used research materials for member libraries and to acquire selected materials for cooperative use.

From the point of view of the acquisition policies and programs of the individual member libraries, the principal value of such an organization as the Center for Research Libraries is to relieve them of responsibility for collecting a variety of fringe materials, expensive to acquire, seldom needed, and filling valuable space, but perhaps important when needed.

One aspect of the Center's program being rapidly developed is subscriptions for some 10,000 current periodicals, with emphasis on the scientific, for lending to member libraries.

A similar, though much smaller operation is sponsored by an organization known as the Associated Colleges of the Midwest, which maintains a periodical bank in the Newberry Library in Chicago. Some 2, 500 journals are currently received and 25, 000 bound volumes and over 30, 000 microforms are held for lending to the members, mainly college libraries, scattered through the Midwest. The reasoning back of such cooperative schemes is that they make available a considerably wider range of periodical literature than the smaller libraries could afford individually.

On the other hand, the idea has certain limitations. As Fremont Rider pointed out some years ago, "On one matter, our scholars all seem to be amazingly unanimous; they all seem to have a desire--to the layman a sometimes quite incomprehensible desire--to have their materials available, not in New York or California, but under their own fingertips wherever they may happen to be working." Some academic administrators, however, are welcoming the periodical bank plan with enthusiasm, seeing it as a device for economizing on their libraries. Faculty members and students who may have to wait a minimum of 24 hours every time they wish to consult a periodical article are likely to be less happy.

It should be recognized that programs of library cooperation, especially in universities, must depend principally upon institutional attitudes, specifically on the willingness to rationalize graduate and research activities. Libraries can hardly move faster or farther in inter-institutional agreements than their parent universities are willing to go.

Every state in the union has seen the mushrooming of its institutions of higher education in recent years. Former agricultural and engineering colleges and teachers colleges have been transformed, in many cases overnight by legislative fiat, to the status of general universities. The financial implications for the states are staggering, if all these institutions are to become universities in fact as well as in name. A major item of cost is library expansion, including the building of university-level collections. Can the states allow each library to grow separately and independently? Is it realistic to expect that state legislatures will provide the generous support required for building strong libraries? Is it feasible for state-supported university libraries to work together to bring maximum library service to their users at costs somewhere within reason? These are questions that will be confronting librarians increasingly if the current economic crisis persists into the indefinite future.

Let me turn now to another topic, the library staff's responsibility for collection development. In the past, book selection in college and university libraries was regarded as a faculty prerogative on the assumption that as experts in their field faculty members were best qualified to determine what publications were important and desirable. The result was that the library acquisition department staff was often reduced to mere order clerks. A radical change in attitudes and practices has occurred in recent years, especially in university libraries. Collections are being built in large part by subject specialists on the library staff. In some institutions, the entire professional staff may be involved to some extent in book selection.

The reasons for the change are reasonably clear. Professors nowadays are a different breed of cats from those of a generation or so ago. In these times, professors are occupied with their own research and writing, with governmental and industrial contracts, with foreign travel, with consulting and lecturing, and committee assignments, because of which a majority have no time for or interest in the building of library collections. They simply have too many other concerns to do a conscientious and thorough job, though they expect the books to be there when they need them.

In an ACRL conference talk several years ago, Robert Miller, Director of the Indiana University Library, looking back on 25 years' experience as a university librarian, commented that he had "known only a handful of faculty men who were bookmen in the sense that they used judgment in submitting recommendations in their own fields and who had some knowledge of key books and journals in related fields." Dr. Miller added that he had known only two faculty members whose book knowledge extended into other areas and who approximated the knowledge of antiquarian book dealers.

My own experience, based on 40 years as a university library director, closely parallels Dr. Miller's. The number of faculty members who are eager and willing to participate in building library resources is always limited. In retrospect, the leading figures in collection development in the University of North Carolina, New York University, and University of Illinois during my administration were a small but highly potent group of faculty members, representing a variety of disciplines. Their advice and guidance in the building up of resources were invaluable. These individuals possessed an extensive knowledge of their own fields, past and present, and usually of related areas; they checked new and antiquarian catalogs as fast as they appeared; they were aware of the state of the book market; they were familiar with the library's collections, what was there and what was lacking; and they maintained constant pressure on the librarian and the university administration for more book funds.

On the other hand, I have never believed that the faculty should have sole responsibility for building a strong library. The departmental librarians, the personnel of the acquisition and serials divisions, the reference and circulation librarians, and catalogers should all contribute in varying degrees to the total acquisition program. There is no question in my mind that librarians must do more selection than in the past if the quality and usefulness of our collections are to meet the future needs of students and faculties. In short, we must take over full supervision and responsibility for selection.

In this connection, Rogers and Weber, in their University Library Administration, conclude that "one type of book fund, the departmental allotment, is passing from the scene in most universities," because book funds are more affluent and library staffs are more competent. The authors added that: "Blanket order arrangements have contributed to the relinquishment of the allotment system also because many books are acquired across the whole range of disciplines."

Not everyone agrees with that point of view. Another experienced university library administrator maintains that in his institution the library has excellent support from the faculty because it has a voice in how funds are spent. A happy middle-ground solution to this question is for the librarian to draw upon faculty advice, guidance, and participation to whatever extent they are available.

Reference was made to blanket or standing orders. This increasingly popular device gives a new dimension to problems of book selection. What effect the collapse of the Richard Abel empire may have remains to be seen, though there are probably enough other firms in the field, such as Blackwell's and Baker & Taylor, to carry on. For university libraries, especially, the standing order scheme has numerous advantages, if dealers, publishers, and categories of material are chosen with care.

The reasons for the growing popularity of standing orders and approval plans are complex. Several particular factors appear to have influenced librarians in their acceptance of such plans. The proverbial rate of increase of printed materials has made new selection mechanisms imperative. The volume of publication and the rise in staff costs have forced libraries to seek methods of selecting the most books in the quickest way. So has a trend towards larger book budgets in academic libraries. University libraries moving into approval-plan buying have often acted at a time when large amounts of new money were added to their book budgets, permitting approval purchases to be added on top of the regular acquisition program. Also, the sudden expansion of a college into a full-fledged university or the creation of an entirely new institution places heavy responsibility on librarians.

Paramount to many librarians is the saving in time and clerical labor in acquisition procedures. To have the books ordered with minimum clerical and routine work, perhaps with catalog cards provided, saves time for other, more important activities. A further advantage may be a saving in time for the user, for an efficient standing order plan should insure the prompt receipt of the most current materials. As foreign acquisition programs have expanded, there is a need to acquire materials from areas of the world for which no adequate bibliographic tools exist. The national bibliographies and reviews on which our traditional selection system depends are simply lacking for most countries.

Once the librarian has been freed from the routine ordering of current materials, new and more challenging areas in book selection open up. The faculty and library staff will have more time to spend on antiquarian and backfile ordering, with opportunities to appraise and correct the weaknesses and gaps in their collections.

Nevertheless, despite these obvious, at least theoretical, advantages of standing orders and approval plans, there are problems and certain dangers risked by a library in their extensive use. For example, serial publications present problems. Many duplicates may be received as a result of exchanges, blanket orders, and simultaneous publication in more than one country. Too many ephemeral and marginal materials may be sent, while pertinent books may be overlooked in a blanket order shipment. Furthermore, there is a question of complete coverage. How can a library be assured that its jobber is supplying it with all worthwhile publications? The same problem is posed, perhaps in more acute form, in the case of foreign publications. Can librarians trust their European dealers, for instance, to send all important books on blanket orders?

More serious than the omission of an occasional single title is the fact that jobbers not infrequently overlook certain types of publications central to an academic library, for example, publications emanating from various departments of universities, art museums, learned societies, and private membership organizations. Such publications may not get into the regular book trade and there is little or no profit for dealers in handling them.

Still another objection voiced by critics of standing order plans is that the major academic libraries of North America, by utilizing the services of a small number of jobbers and dealers, are building book collections that are too similar in both strengths and weaknesses.

What all this boils down to is that librarians should not and cannot rely solely on dealers for book selection. Final responsibility for book selection is something that librarians cannot afford to abdicate. The entire book selection procurement is one of the most fundamental and challenging functions of the professional librarian. The significance of the librarians' role comes out in research studies which show that on the basis of actual use by library readers, most used books are those selected by librarians; second, from the point of view of demand, are the books selected by the faculty, and the least used are the titles chosen by book jobbers.

Incidentally, it may be noted, the larger a university library becomes, the less selection is involved in its growth. Not all fields are covered comprehensively, of course, but in areas of primary concern to the institution, the library is likely to be engaged in collecting, not selecting. Completeness becomes the main goal.

In measuring quality in college and to some extent in university libraries, there is a tendency to think in terms of standard lists. There are values as well as dangers in the practice. Standard lists naturally make all libraries alike, they discriminate against good books not fortunate enough to be listed, and soon get out of date. The hazards may be illustrated by Choice, the most common tool for book selection in college libraries. Choice uses hundreds of reviewers, many of them amateurs, ill-informed, and

biased. Such a guide should be used with caution, but if one recognizes their limitations, standard lists selected and recommended by
experts and specialists are helpful in the development of library collections. They help to insure against serious omissions.

One other aspect of collection development on which I would
like to expound briefly is the role of microforms. One of the most
useful devices that modern technology has provided libraries is microform reproduction. Since the microform roll came along in the
nineteen-thirties, a variety of other forms have been invented: mi-
crocards, microprint, microfiche, and most recently ultramicro-
fiche. Microreproduction projects have proliferated, miniaturizing
large bodies of newspapers, manuscripts, archives, journals, early
printed books, and other types of specialized research materials.

The reasons for the microform revolution are diverse. Some
promoters are convinced that the traditional book is obsolete, as
noted previously, and they want the whole great world of literary materials turned into a microcosm. Better-informed persons, however,
have recognized the potentialities and limitations of the new media.
They have seen the value of micro-reproductions in preserving fragile
records, in saving war-endangered materials from possible destruction, in increasing the availability of unique and rare items, in saving storage space, and in the case of works of highly specialized interest, for original publication. At the same time, they realize that
by no means all library collections are as useful in micro-reproduc-
tion as in their original formats. In short, we have here an extraordinarily important and versatile device for strengthening library
resources and services but we should view it as only one weapon in
our varied arsenal, a means to an end.

From the point of view of colleges and the smaller universities, the answer to the microform question, as with any other library materials, is selection. Exactly the same principles should
govern the purchase of micro-reproductions as standard books and
periodicals. Almost without exception, originals are preferable to
microtexts, because they are nearly always easier to use. Frequently, however, it is a microtext or nothing.

Reproduction of material in full size is also having a dramatic effect on library acquisition activities, that is, publication in
near-print form by photo-offset and similar processes. Since the
coming of these processes, it has been stated that no books should
be considered out of print, assuming that somewhere copies are
available for reproduction. The importance of the fact is accentuated by the requirements of the many new "instant" university and
college libraries. In the past, it would have been virtually impossible for such libraries to have acquired the numerous basic periodical files, collections of historical sources, and reference works
needed by a research library. The material had gone out of print
and was simply unprocurable. The latest edition of Guide to Reprints lists about 200 firms engaged in reprint publishing, in the
United States and abroad. Their productions include complete runs

of general and special journals, society publications, bibliographical and other reference works, series dealing with special subjects, and innumerable individual book titles.

The advisability of buying current publications, such as much used periodicals, in anything except the original paper form is questionable. Some space and binding costs may be saved, but at the expense of satisfactory service. There is a temptation, which has to be resisted, to be swept off one's feet by the inspiring thought that here is an opportunity to provide one's library clientele with rare books and journals and great masses of primary sources hitherto unavailable to it. If these little-used materials are to be bought with funds more urgently needed for current publications, on the other hand, librarians have to use their best judgments in deciding which should come first.

In summary, the task of developing a strong college or university library collection is never completed. It calls for the best efforts of the faculty and library staff, working together. Subject specialists on the library staff can supplement and complement faculty experts to insure thorough coverage of field of interest. Each library should clarify its goals by adoption of an acquisition policy statement.

Beautiful buildings, well-trained staffs, and the most modern cataloging and classification, circulation, and reference systems can compensate only to a limited degree for the absence of strong collections. The first essential in an academic library is to possess the books, periodicals, government publications, newspapers, pamphlets, maps, and other materials required to meet the institution's objectives in instruction and research. Future generations will doubtless praise us or condemn us mainly on the basis of what we preserve and pass on to them.

MULTIMEDIA AND THE INFORMATION
REQUIREMENTS OF RESEARCHERS

By Ed Holley

Recently, when she appeared on the campus of the University
of North Carolina at Chapel Hill to talk about the changing needs of
public libraries, Allie Beth Martin, Tulsa City-County librarian,
commented upon a just-completed study of the aging in her city. A
number of the elderly were asked what they considered their major
needs. The first, not unexpectedly, was access to food, including
not just the payment of it but also convenience in obtaining it. Secondly, to the surprise of many people, was access to information.
Because many of the aging are less mobile than their younger coun-
terparts, the normal ability to go places and do things is simply not
one of their options.

At about the same time I had had a letter from Ernest J.
Reece, Melvil Dewey Professor Emeritus at Columbia, in which he
lamented that one of their problems was not having access to the
marvelous library facilities available in Boulder, Colorado, since
he and Mrs. Reece were fairly well confined to their rooms in a
senior citizens apartment building. That seemed to me particularly
unfortunate since Mr. Reece always kept up with the library profession after his retirement in the early fifties, and one of the joys of
his longtime residence in Urbana, Illinois, was his access to a car-
rel in the University of Illinois Library.

In preparing this lecture, with its emphasis upon multimedia,
I was also reminded of the anxiety all of us in my family felt when
my father was forced to retire early when advanced diabetes caused
him to lose his sight. We were fortunate, though, in his case to
have the marvelous Library of Congress Talking Books program.
The weekly phono records kept him fully informed about political
matters through provision of news magazines and kept him enter-
tained by the works of fiction and other materials provided regularly
through the mails.

Each of these three examples seems to me appropriate for
the topic we address ... though they may well be on a more elementary level than we will discuss later. Access to information,
especially on the part of those who both need it and want it, whether
or not they are researchers, is a fundamental need which government

Speech given May 14, 1974, at the Seventh Annual Congress of Trustees of the Reference and Research Library Resources Systems held
in Sandborn. Reprinted from The Bookmark, vol. 33, no. 6 (July/
August, 1974), pp. 178-182, by permission of the editor.

must meet. This is nothing new for tax-supported public libraries, which have served as centers for providing information and recreation for many citizens for well over 100 years. What may well be new is the format in which such materials can be packaged and the better technology available for distributing them. The need to use non-print and sometimes unconventional sources has by now been amply demonstrated in many communities, and there are some notable experiments going on in a variety of libraries--school, public, and academic--across the country to provide services appropriate to the needs of all citizens.

What may be imperfectly understood in this context are three rather important principles on which I solicit your discussion: the importance of convenience of access, the expense usually associated with newer formats for information, and the necessity to apply the same measures of evaluation to the information received as one applies with any other format for information, whether it be a manuscript, a book, a tape, or a film.

First let me address the problem of access. Despite a long history of saying the right things, the evidence is still very clear that most libraries are not heavily involved with information other than that contained in books or magazines. Academic libraries are especially vulnerable to the charge that they have not responded well to users' needs which involve more than the printed word. There are, of course, some notable exceptions, but they generally tend to be the newly emerging institutions rather than the older ones, and even Title II-A of the Higher Education Act did not do a great deal to remedy this situation. Public libraries have fared somewhat better, thanks chiefly to LSCA (Library Services and Construction Act), as Ralph Folcarelli's recent study of audiovisual services shows, but even here development has been slow. Yet, we all know very well that we are now dealing with a generation reared on television, where films have long been a part of their upbringing, and where the photo, the cassette, and the phonorecord are very much a part of early learning.

Within the past couple of years most students have been among the millions who watched the funeral services of two Presidents on television or subsequent tape, as well as the marriage of an English princess. When the historian of our contemporary period begins his analysis and evaluation of the two Presidents, if he expects to be successful in presenting his data on Mr. Truman or Mr. Johnson, he cannot do so merely upon reading the official documents relating to either man. He will certainly want to see the television interviews which were used as television specials so that he can catch some of the flavor of their personalities, and the historian will also want to see the actual filmed record of the funeral services: the great and near great proceeding into National City Christian Church for that moving eulogy by Dr. Davis for Mr. Johnson and the spartan simplicity of the Episcopal service in the Truman Library for Mr. Truman. James Reston of the New York Times could capture the latter with his interpretive article "A Lovely Farewell for

Our Harry," in that superb English of which he is capable, but one would not want to depend upon that alone. Both sight and sound reveal more to us, with all their imperfections, than words by themselves.

Recently, at a meeting of the Virginia school librarians, I was much taken by several of the media exhibits which are now becoming available to schools. One which particularly impressed me was an exhibitor's special 12 audio cassettes recording major documents of the Cold War. Here in one case can be found such major documents as Winston Churchill's "iron curtain" speech delivered at Fulton, Missouri, General MacArthur's address to a joint meeting of Congress, and other similar items. There are booklets to go with the cassettes, outlined in good chronological fashion and put together by distinguished historians. For the relatively small sum of $99.50, this material could be made available to your library and its users. To which I promptly raised the question, "When are you all going to put it on video tape?" The response to this was, "You are a dreamer!"

That leads me to my second point, that such material is expensive. Librarians have been chided for their insensitivity to the multimedia, for their obtuseness in not being more innovative and creative in their approach to the information problem, and they have flagellated themselves for not doing more in this area. Some of the criticisms are deserved, but many of them are not. The recent Report of the Advisory Committee on Planning for the Academic Libraries of New York State (1973) notes that

> libraries are no longer able to fulfill their responsibilities
> without a fairly extensive range of audiovisual services and
> to recommend that delivery capability in the audiovisual
> area hereafter be considered almost a required library activity. (page 9)

Moreover, a subcommittee suggests that a possible model to be considered in fulfilling this need is the Regional Media Center, which would be a comprehensive library of nonbook materials and technical support equipment for teaching and learning purposes (pages 15-16). This might work reasonably well for some materials, especially the more expensive materials, but it would probably work only if one assumed that certain basic materials and equipment were available on campus just as is true of printed materials. No one claims that any college or university can support its basic program using somebody else's collections, either in print or nonprint form.

Nowhere is this more true than in the area of the more sophisticated data bases now becoming available for information purposes. The 1970 census tapes are one notable example. The Midwest Consortium for Political Science Research with its extensive computer tapes on various elections held in this country, including precinct by precinct comparisons, is yet another. Certain abstracting and indexing services like Chemical Abstracts and Psychological

Abstracts are now available for literature search services. On most campuses these computer tapes are not housed in or serviced by the library, usually because of expense, but whether they should be is a question to which libraries must address themselves in the very near future. My own particular bias on this point is that libraries are in the information business on a multimedia basis and that they are the logical and inevitable location for such services. Let me digress for a moment to say that librarians too often get overlooked as individuals with expertise in the information area, and I have often seen new government agencies paying phenomenal prices to set up what are essentially libraries and repeating mistakes in this area that libraries long ago learned not to make. But, the introduction of such new materials as audio and video tapes, computer data bases, films, and so forth will all call for greater support if the library as an information research center is to provide for the needs of its users.

That leads me to the next point which deserves attention: the necessity to apply the same principles of evaluation to the information received regardless of the format in which it originates. Let me add that one does not need to apply more stringent standards to non-book materials than he does to book materials, but he must at least recognize the level at which the request comes.

Let me cite two examples to illustrate my point. When my children were young, one of the privileges of being a father was reading to them. Among our favorites was Robert McCloskey's book about the hatching of ducklings on an island in the Charles River in Boston, Make Way for Ducklings. The text and illustration of that book go together, and one would want to be sure that a filmstrip and record of the book were faithful to the original, though one might use an audio cassette in the place of reading the story to the youngsters. The problem here is to assure that the author's creativity is not violated, whatever the medium.

Another example might be that old favorite of many growing boys, Huckleberry Finn. Huck Finn can be read on many levels and its format can be varied indeed. For just good reading, one could buy a standard paperback edition, ignoring the textual and other problems, and perhaps giving some illustrations not a part of the original. Depending upon one's taste, a film, filmstrip, or record of portions of Huckleberry Finn could provide information for students. These serve useful purposes for a large majority of citizens. To illustrate Mark Twain's style, one could anthologize portions of Huckleberry Finn for a survey course in American literature where the aim of the course is merely to introduce the student to some major American authors and samples of their work. But none of this would satisfy the textual critic. To do that one would have to depend upon the critical apparatus provided by the Modern Language Association's American Authors Project. where each volume will include exhaustive analyses of all manuscripts and related materials in an attempt to determine just exactly what Samuel Langhorne Clemens did write and how he wished it to be presented to the public. This is the same level of accuracy at which we expect scientific and technical information to be available. It must conform to certain rigid specifications, and any other approach will not be acceptable.

This, it appears to me, is at the heart of the controversy between the President and the Judiciary Committee of the House of Representatives. According to the rules of evidence, an individual making a judgment on a basic question of fact wants a complete record, or at least as close to it as he can possibly come. Most of us as historians learned this principle from such basic textbooks as Allan Nevins' Gateway to History and Louis Gottschalk's Understanding History. The researcher at this level must have not only a piece of information, but all other kinds of material relating to that information. A text can be established as accurate and complete only when it has been examined for its credibility, preferably by objective witnesses. In an age of the multimedia, can one do this from the written text alone? A good many historians would say no, and they are probably right.

Let me cite another case of a friend of mine who did a critical edition of the wartime speeches of Cordell Hull, Franklin Roosevelt's longtime Secretary of State, as his doctoral dissertation. When Cordell Hull addressed a joint session of the U.S. Congress, he had with him a copy of his speech. Likely this speech had already been mimeographed and given to the press with an official release, and may even have been set in type by such an authoritative source as the New York Times. But Mr. Hull may well have made corrections to his speech just prior to delivering it (many of us do), or he may actually have omitted some sentences when he gave it to Congress. How did the Congress react? What were Mr. Hull's intonations as he delivered the address? Did he use some inflections more than others? What kind of information was he trying to convey? This is available, of course, in the National Archives in the filmed or record copy of the address, and will provide the researcher with information which he could scarcely glean any other way. Not many documents will call for this kind of intensive analysis, but where they do, one cannot ignore documents other than printed ones.

In the late sixties the Texas legislature passed a bill authorizing the State Library to film significant state occasions and also to provide photographs of such events. While the motive for this act was stated as preserving the historical record, there were some of us who thought its more pragmatic intention was simply to supply free publicity for some of the honorables who occupied seats in the legislature. Whatever the real motive, the intention was a noble one, and I could spend time demonstrating again the value of such a record for the researcher. However, I will not do that, which would seem to be spelling out the obvious: that the researcher needs access to a vast quantity of material, often in a nonprint format, that this information is frequently expensive, and that he must be assured that he has access to the maximum amount of information to accomplish his task.

Now let me try to pull it all together. I have not mentioned the problems of control, that is, who is to have access to this information? Such a matter had better be weighed carefully in view of our long commitment to the principle of equal access for all citizens in the tax-supported library. Nor have I addressed the problem of ownership, particularly as this is reflected in copyright. Vanderbilt University's suit with CBS over the Walter Cronkite newscasts certainly will be watched with interest by the library community as we try to sort out two conflicting interests: the public's right to know and the copyright owner's right to a reasonable fee for his product. These are matters which certainly concern us, and the scare stories being spread by the media coalition are obviously matters with which we will have to deal. Ultimately, however, they will be settled in either the courts, e.g., Williams and Wilkins, or in the Congress through new legislation. So I doubt that it is worthwhile for us to spend our time on those problems ... [here]. I mention them merely so you will be aware that they should not be overlooked.

Let us in closing, though, focus on those requirements of the researcher we can do something about. I would state as a fundamental premise that libraries are the logical place to satisfy the informational needs of researchers outside of the laboratory. They have been handling problems of selecting, organizing, and disseminating information for centuries. Now that it comes in a different form does not mitigate the fact that libraries exist and have the experience to deal with the multimedia. The problems are the expense and the different equipment needed. I believe the user of information is likely to get a better break for his money if we try to pull together the multimedia, whether microform, film, video and computer tapes, or whatever in a library, and provide the kind of expert staff assistance needed to exploit such media. Here in New York State there already is a network which is the envy of those of us in less favored states. New York State is already sharing resources in printed formats. What would seem to make sense would be not to create a whole series of new and duplicative centers, but to use the ones we have in an expansive way. According to one of the State Education Department's recent reports, NYSILL's "... raison d'être is to provide New York State's research community a means of access to advanced level library materials." In my view, the kinds of multimedia we have been discussing ought to be included in any reasonable definition of "library materials." That would be in line with the recent report of the National Commission on Libraries and Information Science which urged a national network and would accord with the findings of a recent report of the Urban Library Trustees Council which cited the need for a variety of nonprint materials and a capable staff. Moreover, the Urban Library Trustees Report reminded us of yet another fact: that the professional managerial category represents the largest user group in urban libraries. To meet these needs of researchers will require not only supplying the local libraries with some basic materials but also strengthening the library networks so that the multimedia materials at a more advanced level are available to the user.

One of the truly encouraging signs in recent years is a new

public awareness of the citizen's right to know. For some of us, in the history field, this is a welcome trend, for it is fully in accord with our basic traditions. Thomas Jefferson said that we could not expect to have a citizenry both ignorant and free. In a complex technological world this is more true than ever. But to remain free, the citizen will need more than the newspapers and pamphlet speeches of Thomas Jefferson's day; he will require a broad range of materials in different formats. To meet modern needs his deliberations, as he makes his choices, must be informed by the most accurate and the most reliable sources we can provide.

STUDYING THE COMMUNITY: An Overview

By Allie Beth Martin

The importance of community analysis, which serves as the
foundation for governmental planning at all levels, cannot be overestimated as today's societal problems multiply and become increasingly complex. "The more fateful the problem grows of how daily life
is experienced where one lives and labors," Roland Warren observes,
"the more important it becomes to seek a valid understanding of why
things are as they are, so that we may go on to consider how they
may become worthy of the best that is in us."[1]

Ironically, libraries have been little concerned with their potentially important role in community analysis, nor have they effectively utilized the products of community analysis in their own planning. Too often the library has not even been considered an element
of the community worthy of study by professional planners. Browse
the shelves of richly varied books about the American community in
any library of more than modest size. Study the analytical documents proliferating from planning and development agencies which
abound in every state. How many references can be found dealing
with libraries? When libraries are mentioned, how many reflect an
understanding of their potentially active and important roles in the
community? How much of the substance of these publications has
been used in the process of determining the objectives for individual
libraries?

The Importance of Community Analysis

The full understanding of the communities in which our libraries operate, be they urban, suburban, or rural, is no longer solely
the province of professional planners. In addition to demographic factors, an understanding of social and physical indicators and the complexity of community structures is involved. Similarly, public policy
is not determined independently by the elected officials, the planners,
or the heads of individual agencies working in isolation. In recent
years ordinary citizens have begun to participate more actively in the
planning processes. Articulate local groups are influencing community
decisions as well as the expenditure of funds necessary to implement
the community's goals and objectives. As a result, analyzing the
community is not a simple process of determining the numbers of
people, their gross characteristics, educational levels, economic
levels, and racial composition. This information is basic, but ef-

Reprinted from Library Trends, vol. 24, no. 3, January 1976, pp.
433-40, by permission of the publisher.

fective community analysis involves more. Developing a useful profile of a community now requires a complex range of information.
An accurate picture should be drawn to serve as the basis for decisions on goals and objectives. Available funds can then be allocated
within a framework of priorities undergirded by substantive information.

In this process, public services such as libraries must justify
their financial support on the basis of their ability to fulfill community needs. Funds will no longer be distributed on the strength of
what was allocated the previous year, but on the basis of priorities
of services to be performed. John Gardner suggests that this process of problem solving will require the research of social structures, the renewal of institutions and the incentive of new human arrangements, and that familiar ways of doing things will be endan-
gered.[2] A writer from the field of public administration states:
"Policy, performance, impact and feedback are all products of local
administration. From the perspective of the client, they are the
real meaning of government and public service. If they are not
right, or cannot be changed to suit the citizen's desires, then the
faults may challenge his sense of satisfaction with the government
and his sense of control over its activities."[3]

Today we see evidence of these processes at work at various
governmental levels and from differing societal viewpoints. Citizens
are newly aware that something can be done about their most pressing problems. Local neighborhood improvement groups form and
seek new or improved services. City and town governments attempt
to deal with conflicts of interest, to set priorities, and to cope with
financial shortages. States establish required planning districts in
order to resolve interjurisdictional problems. Community analysis
is recognized as essential in governmental management and has contributed to better response to the real needs of individuals and their
communities.

Individual agencies and institutions, including libraries, are
also being told repeatedly that they, too, must meet the needs of
their users. Indeed, their survival will depend on meeting those
needs. If they are not met, other, more responsive agencies will
be created to do the job. Individual communities can threaten to
withdraw from or refuse to join library systems lest their needs be
ignored. Urban and suburban libraries are sometimes in conflict,
each claiming a lack of understanding by the other of their particular problems.

State library agencies are also involved in community analysis. They must analyze the patchwork for which they are responsi-
ble--a complexity of dense urban, suburban, small city, small town,
and unincorporated rural areas. Coherent and acceptable statewide
plans which meet the greatest possible diversity of needs are essential. Moreover, these needs are continually changing at all levels.
For example, public libraries have historically been most successful
in serving children. Today this population is declining and libraries

are acutely aware that in the future the need will be to serve an
ever-increasing older population. In the past, libraries have served
older citizens poorly or not at all. Will senior citizens in the future
be served with imaginative creative programs as successfully as
children have been traditionally? Would libraries have responded
more readily and more effectively to this new need if a continuing
process of sound community analysis had been practiced? Would
they have anticipated earlier the necessity to refocus if they had
been active in the community-wide analysis and planning process?

The Importance of Community
Analysis for Libraries

For some time, critics of public libraries have emphasized
the necessity for clearly defined goals, and have deplored the vagueness and haphazard formulation of presently existing objectives.
Others have said that universally adopted goals are not practical except in the most general sense; instead, each library must develop
its own goals, determined by the uniqueness of each community or
institution. Assuming the latter to be true, community analysis on
the part of the library is critical, and must be a constant process.

The first considerations in attempting to establish library
goals usually relate to the people who are now unserved as well as
to those who are presently served, and to increasing the population
to be reached in the future. It is a cause for concern that many
segments of the population are not served by the library. Groups
heretofore relatively unserved and unresponsive include the disadvantaged, ethnic minorities, the illiterate and semiliterate, residents
of institutions, and the aging. In an attempt to reach these groups,
numerous experiments have been undertaken. These experiences have
been extensively described and reported, but little thorough analysis
has been involved. The nineteen studies of various aspects of library service in Indiana under the sponsorship of the Indiana State Library do, however, comprise a valuable body of research at the state
level.[4] Lipsman's analysis of library service to the disadvantaged in
fifteen cities provides a starting point for the collection of data on
service to the deprived which will answer questions about the disadvantaged to be served by libraries in the future.[5]

Banfield asserts that many of our library services are already obsolete and are the business of some other public or private
agency.[6] If he is right, libraries which fail to reevaluate objectives
in terms of current demands may find their support dwindling relative to that of other services.

Again, many questions must be answered. Are services which
are thought to be obsolete in libraries now performed better or more
efficiently by other agencies? If so, the transfer is reasonable.
Are there other library services which should replace those becoming obsolete? For example, public libraries are currently examining
their roles as suppliers of information and referral services. Infor-

mation services are springing up daily. Is the library at fault for
not anticipating the need for these services? Would better community analysis have helped libraries revamp traditional reference functions so that they could become information and referral services in
the broadest sense? How much would such a change cost in terms
of staff retraining, added materials and other out-of-pocket expenses? How much use of the new services could be anticipated in
comparison to those traditionally provided? Numerous libraries are
now initiating community information services, some are modifying
existing departments, and others are starting new information and
referral centers separate from traditional reference departments.
In any case, no one knows the volume of use to expect or what the
costs will be. Can the information needs of the community be
served more effectively through the library than through new agencies? Within each library the decision must be made whether to expand present services or to set up a new department, or whether the
service should be centralized or decentralized through branches.

New adult education services are also being considered by libraries as the forces of change emphasize the importance of continuing education for large segments of the population. Recent studies have found that less than one-third of the people desiring continuing education have an opportunity to engage in adult education.[7]
Most of these do not want to or cannot return to school. They are
potential "adult independent learners." Can libraries satisfy the
needs of these people? What segments of the population would avail
themselves of such services? Again, what would be the cost to libraries? In this case, the College Entrance Examination Board is
conducting such an analysis as a pilot project so that individual libraries will have a basis for determining the practicality of providing
such a service if the community analysis reveals that this is an un-
met need. Data are being collected which will help the libraries;
however, better methods of measuring the effectiveness of library
services are urgently needed. A beginning has been made by De-
Prospo and others at Rutgers.[8] The process of planning, programming and evaluation promises to insure better financial control and
to provide the data so necessary in this era of accountability.

The Extent of Library Participation
in Community Analysis

A survey of the general literature on community analysis indicates that almost no attention has been paid to libraries. A
search of the literature yielded only one chapter in one book in the
entire field of community studies and planning which deals specifically with libraries.[9]

In the past ten years, federal library funds (LSCA grants)
have been variously used for surveys and plans at the state level.[10]
These have been library surveys rather than analyses of communities
which provided the rationale for the service's existence. Every
state but one has had either a statewide survey, state plan, or sur-

veys of individual regions, counties and cities. Until recently, most surveys tended to analyze the services of the library. Limited analysis of the communities being served was included. In the early 1970s, many of these surveys were conducted by library consultants and by professional research firms. Most surveys described the level of library development at the time. There was little provision for continuous updating.

More recently, concentration has been on the techniques of planning and evaluation, including community analysis. Self-studies have been conducted in some libraries. State libraries have been encouraged to adopt the CIPP (Context-Input-Planning-Program) model for planning and some have adopted the process as a result. Widespread adoption of this process is significant since it does originate with the "context" or environment in which the service is to be rendered.

A few of the large urban libraries have commissioned surveys and studies yielding a body of library planning information which has had an influence on other libraries. All of these recognize the necessity of beginning any evaluation of libraries with a study of the communities they serve. These include: Lowell Martin's studies of the Enoch Pratt Free Library in Baltimore,[11] the Chicago Public Library,[12] and Tucson Public Library;[13] John Frantz's study of the Brooklyn Public Library;[14] and the Arthur D. Little study of the San Francisco Public Library.[15] The Indiana studies mentioned earlier comprise the major work done at the state level. More recently, some new techniques for systematic analysis of libraries at the local level have been demonstrated. The Rutgers study by DeProspo and others mentioned earlier promises to provide a methodology applicable to various types of libraries and useful in libraries of all sizes. Unfortunately, only the early phases of the original project were funded. These techniques are now being further applied in statewide demonstrations. In addition, Newhouse's in-depth analysis of library use in Beverly Hills[16] will be useful to other libraries; the study done for the Denver Urban Observatory on public library use in Denver may also prove of interest.[17] Robbins examines the relationship between the library and the community from another angle.[18]

Opportunities for Libraries to
Engage in Community Analysis

There are three avenues which a library may take to realize the benefits of community analysis. First, it can hire a consultant. With a competent consultant, this approach will produce results most quickly. It may also be productive in the long run if part of the project serves to educate the staff to continue the process of analysis on an ongoing basis. A second alternative is to conduct a self-study. This approach may take longer and even be more costly if a thorough job is done and the project includes staff training by an expert. It strengthens staff competency which will be a continuing

advantage. Finally, a library can participate in community analysis
with other community agencies, including governmental planning units
and citizen planning groups. Regional planning agencies now serve
almost all standard metropolitan statistical areas. These are logical
agencies for libraries to approach for assistance and to join as members. Marilyn Gell, a library planner with the Metropolitan Washington Council of Governments, reports: "It is time for libraries to see
themselves in this role, to think about cooperating with non-library
officials and to affiliate themselves with these regional councils.
While other forms of library cooperation have been extensive, and at
times effective, it is this political element which has been overlooked.
It is significant that of the over 300 regional councils in the country,
only three (Denver, Baltimore, and Washington) have any involvement with libraries."[19]

In summary, libraries involved in community analysis will
realize both direct and indirect benefits. Planning and goal setting
will be based on total community needs from the widest perspective--
not from the tunnel vision of the library. Change can be managed
more responsibly; that is, the need for change can be better anticipated in time to make positive adjustments. The library will acquire
new advocates among planners, governmental representatives and citizens in the process of the community analysis. A broader understanding of financial needs will result. The library will also gain a
better understanding of the activities and problems of other agencies
and organizations. Cooperation will thus be more natural and practical.

The importance of community analysis and libraries cannot be
overestimated. The papers in this issue of Library Trends provide
a substantial introduction to the topic by experts from librarianship
and other disciplines. It is hoped that this will provide every library administration with the simulation and information necessary
to get started.

References

1. Warren, Roland L., ed. Perspectives on the American Commu-
    nity. 2d ed. Chicago: Rand McNally, 1973, p. v.
2. Gardner, John W. No Easy Victories. New York: Harper and
    Row, 1968, p. 27.
3. Sharkansky, Ira. "Basic Concepts in Public Administration,"
    in Raymond Holt, ed. Local Public Library Administration.
    Chicago: ALA. (In progress.)
4. Hiatt, Peter, ed. Indiana Library Studies; Reports. Blooming-
    ton: Indiana State Library, 1970-71.
5. Lipsman, Claire K. The Disadvantaged and Library Effective-
    ness. Chicago: ALA, 1972.
6. Banfield, Edward C. "Needed: A Public Purpose," in Ralph
    W. Conant, ed. The Public Library and the City. Cam-
    bridge, Mass.: MIT Press, 1965, pp. 102-13.
7. Commission on Non-Traditional Study. Diversity by Design.
    San Francisco: Jossey-Bass, 1973.

8. DeProspo, Ernest R. et al. Performance Measures for Public
    Libraries. Chicago: ALA, 1973.
9. Gans, Herbert J. People and Plans: Essays on Urban Pro-
    blems and Solutions. New York: Basic Books, 1968, Chap-
    ter 8: "Supplier-Oriented and Use-Oriented Planning for the
    Public Library," pp. 95-107.
10. Rike, Galen E. Statewide Library Surveys and Development
    Plans; An Annotated Bibliography 1956-1967. Springfield:
    Illinois State Library, 1968.
11. Martin, Lowell A. Deiches Fund Studies of Public Library
    Service. Nos. 1-4. Baltimore: Enoch Pratt Free Library,
    1963-74.
12. _____. Library Response to Urban Change; A Study of the
    Chicago Public Library. Chicago: ALA, 1969.
13. _____. Survey of the Library. Tucson: Tucson Public Li-
    brary, 1974.
14. Frantz, John C. "Big City Libraries: Strategy and Tactics
    for Change," Library Journal 93:1968-70, May 15, 1968.
15. Arthur D. Little, Inc. The Urban Central Library: Develop-
    ment Alternatives for San Francisco. Cambridge, Mass. :
    Little, Inc. , 1970.
16. Newhouse, Joseph D. , and Alexander, Arthur J. An Economic
    Analysis of Public Library Services. Lexington, Mass. :
    Lexington Books, 1972.
17. Freeman, James E. , et al. Public Library Use in Denver:
    An Analysis of Denver Citizen, Business, and Government
    Use of a Community Information Resource. Denver: Denver
    Urban Observatory, 1974.
18. Robbins, Jane B. Citizen Participation and Public Library Po-
    licy. Metuchen, N.J.: Scarecrow Press, 1975.
19. Gell, Marilyn. "The Politics of Cooperation," Library Jour-
    nal 98:3228-29, Nov. 1, 1973.

MORE EFFECTIVE MANAGEMENT OF THE
PUBLIC LIBRARY'S BOOK COLLECTION

By Lolly Eggers

In order to more adequately serve the complete information needs of our users and potential users, the public library has turned much of its attention in recent years to exploring new formats, new types of library services, and new methods of delivering traditional services, and has used much of its energy and resources to provide these newer services.

Despite these developments, book lending is still seen as our most important function by the public. The study recently completed by the Gallup Organization, The Role of Libraries in America, is only the most recent survey to confirm that in the minds of the general public--users and non-users alike--books to borrowers is the public library's principal product.

My purpose here is not to question the value of the public library's other services, but to ask how effectively are we providing this most basic function. Do we move into the future adding services to satisfy perceived needs and to attract a public who is then frustrated at our shelves because a copy of For Whom the Bell Tolls is never there?

If a basic goal of the public library is assuring that materials needed by a user of the library is available to that user within a reasonable time, do we get caught up in the more glamorous and technical aspects of this goal--networking for interlibrary loans, special collections of rare and unusual materials, complete cataloging data, larger and larger collections--and fail to provide basic material in a minimum time?

Do we know enough about how our collections are used? What percentage of total titles held account for the majority of use? What basic titles (or subjects) should a user have a reasonable chance of always finding on the shelf? How many copies of core titles would be needed to adequately meet this demand? How much of the traffic in and out of our buildings is caused by people unable to find a copy of a special title? Typical patron: "I wonder if your copy of this book could be lost. I've been looking for it for several weeks (months)?" What percentage of this type of shelf failure is identified through those who place a reserve for titles not found?

Reprinted from "More Effective Management of the Public Library's Book Collection," The Aardvark (July 1976), pp. 3, 7, by permission of the editor.

How often do users settle for an inferior title because it's there and the best titles on the subject are not? If at least 25 to 30 percent of our collection is always in circulation, how do we correct for the "collection bias" that results--that the best and most useful titles are the ones most apt to be checked out? How many titles (not volumes) do we really need to serve a community of 10,000? 50,000? 100,000? What are the chances of finding on the shelf a title that is listed in the card catalog? 50% 60%? 85%? What is a satisfactory availability rate?

What is the relationship between the length of loan periods and availability? Would variable loan periods increase effective use of the collection? Do shorter loan periods necessarily make more titles available?

What correlation is there between subjects on which we spend our book dollars and the subjects most heavily used or requested? Do we allow our collections to grow generally in all directions without some analysis on where growth is needed and where a modest but well-chosen collection would suffice? Which types of books get the most use per dollar spent? Is there a case for considering this kind of cost-effectiveness in allocating book dollars?

We've been trying to deal with some of these kinds of questions at Iowa City Public Library in recent years. Faced with very limited space and resources for the number of users and potential users in our university community, we're experimenting with a number of ideas and techniques to measure and improve the use of a relatively small but carefully chosen book collection. We think effectiveness in this area is the base on which other library services are built and public support is strengthened.

Briefly, here are some of the techniques we are using to gather data on which to make decisions about collection management. Few are unique to our library but in combination they are beginning to provide a base for intelligent planning.

1) Every book is stamp-dated each time it circulates. This is a natural by-product of some circulation systems but not on a photocharging system used by Iowa City Public Library and most medium-sized or large libraries. A complete history of a book's use is invaluable in collection analysis and weeding.

2) Circulation records are sampled and analyzed four to six times a year to look for trends and seasonal variations.

3) Each year's purchases are analyzed by class number and cost and correlated to the circulation analysis. All staff members who participate in the selection process are given a breakdown of what was spent in their assigned areas, the average unit costs by class number and the opportunity to review all processing slips for titles and copies added. This is used as a basis for next year's budget allocations with changes made for

those areas needing more or less dollars in order to meet the collection building goals for that budget year.

4) All reserves and books lost through circulation and/or inventory are routed across the subject specialists desk to keep them informed about activity in their areas. New titles, shelved separately for about six months at ICPL, are removed from the new book area by the subject specialist--again in order to get some feedback on how much the book was used. If a book appears to be more useful as a browsing title than by a subject approach through the catalog it may stay in the "new books" area for two or three years.

5) Core titles are being established for each subject area and for fiction. Shelves are checked monthly and additional copies are ordered until at least one copy is on the shelf most of the time.

6) A statistically valid sample of the shelf list was drawn in 1973 and taken to the shelves to establish a title availability rate. Only 58 per cent of those titles selected were found on the shelf at that time. A repeat of this procedure soon will be one way to determine if some of our other techniques are helping to improve our title availability rate.

7) A statistically valid sample of books returned from circulation was analyzed to determine the date of last circulation and to establish a potential use rate formula for assistance in making weeding decisions. (Ninety-three per cent of all returned books have previously circulated at least once in the last 12 months.)

8) Security and book retrieval procedures were strengthened to decrease loss and increase the chances of finding titles listed in the card catalog.

9) We are still looking for a method to accurately record shelf-failure. For a survey period how can we get users to write down the title and author of the book they failed to find on the shelf? This would be a gold mine of information about core titles, collection bias, user satisfaction and perhaps, the amount of shelf failure caused by the public's inability to use the card catalog and or search out class numbers correctly.

We are just getting started at ICPL. The ultimate usefulness of any one procedure has not yet been determined. We are not substituting an objective, statistical method for the skills of the book selector but rather are providing information which will help the librarian make effective decisions.

Much of what we're doing can be eliminated when we have access to a computer-assisted acquisitions and circulation control system. The computer will gather the data about collection use for

us and be able to print it out in a variety of forms. Until then--
and it is still a long way away for smaller libraries--I believe we
need to devise methods to fine tune the collection to most effectively
serve the needs of our users.

There will never be enough book dollars now or in the future
unless we devise a rational method for choosing titles, the number
of duplicates and the loan periods most suited for getting maximum
use from the resources provided. One way to increase the public's
satisfaction with library service is to increase their expectancy
rate--their hope for success at our shelves.

The following titles would be especially helpful to anyone interested in reading more about some of the ideas and techniques discussed:

Buckland, Michael K. Book Availability and the Library User.
Pergamon Press, Inc., 1975.

De Prospo, Ernest R., Ellen Altman and Kenneth E. Beasley.
Performance Measures for Public Libraries. Public Library
Association, ALA, 1973.

Measuring the Quality of Library Service: A Handbook. Scarecrow Press, 1974.

Newhouse, Joseph P. and Arthur J. Alexander. An Economic
Analysis of Public Library Service. Lexington Books, 1972.

Slote, Stanley J. Weeding Library Collections. Libraries Unlimited, Inc., 1975.

A METHOD FOR QUANTITATIVELY EVALUATING
A UNIVERSITY LIBRARY COLLECTION

By Barbara Golden

The Acquisitions Department of the Gene Eppley Library of the University of Nebraska at Omaha (UNO) was created in July 1971. The acquisitions function, as performed by the four professional librarians in the department, encompasses materials selection, faculty liaison, and collection evaluation. Collection evaluation has been of prime importance from the inception of the department; shortly after the formation of the department, library director John M. Christ emphasized the importance of collection development in a memorandum which charged the department "to thoroughly evaluate the library collection and prepare a comprehensive review of our holdings as they compare with the curriculum structure to determine our ability to support the academic programs of this university." What follows is an account of the first steps in carrying out this directive and an analysis of the results.

How is an academic library collection evaluated? A literature search revealed that the standard qualitative procedure followed by libraries is to check their holdings against subject bibliographies or major library catalogs of a specialized nature, e.g., the catalog of the Baker Library for business and economics.[1] Often a library uses the Choice opening day collection or Books for College Libraries as a tool for evaluation. One value of the qualitative method for acquisitions is that it combines evaluation with selection.

The question may be raised, however, are the bibliographies checked relevant to the library collection being evaluated? For instance, must every library that serves students of business and economics emulate the Baker Library at Harvard? Doubtless, inadequate budgets will refute the possibility of such emulation; but, if there are no budgetary restrictions, allowances must be made for differences in university programs. The undergraduate program in economics probably will need fewer research materials than a graduate program; concentration on the various aspects of business will differ from college to college; and, within a geographic area, other

Reprinted by permission of the American Library Association from "A Method for Quantitatively Evaluating a University Library Collection," Library Resources and Technical Services, 18, no. 3 (Summer, 1974), pp. 268-274; copyright © 1974 by the American Library Association. The author acknowledges with appreciation the contributions of Jon A. Boone, Christopher P. Eichhorn, Karen Powell, and John M. Christ, who offered constructive criticisms and encouragement during the writing of this paper.

resources available to the library user may reduce the immediate
need for the library to purchase many materials. It must be decided, therefore, what percentage of the Baker Library's catalog and/or
acquisitions lists the library should have. In effect, we must evaluate our evaluative tool. To accomplish this, one requires thorough
knowledge of the university's curriculum, a necessity which often
leads librarians to consult faculty or other specialists in the fields
being evaluated for assistance in determining the adequacy of the
measuring tool.

To summarize, the merits of bibliographic checking include
faculty interaction, the creation of lists of titles for future collection building, and the gathering of statistics to be used for collection evaluation. Such a qualitative evaluation, however, does not
assess fully the current collection's actual support of the existing
university program. We concluded that we could obtain this assessment only through a two-part study covering both qualitative and
quantitative collection evaluation. Believing that knowledge of what
was in the collection was necessary before we could begin to evaluate
the collection qualitatively, we decided to conduct the quantitative
study first.

Our first step in the collection of quantitative information was
to divide the collection into segments by format, i.e., books (monographs), serials, audiovisual materials, microforms, and government documents. We reasoned that the format of the material
would affect the method of evaluation; therefore, each format was to
be studied individually. The initial study was limited to books, primarily because the core of the collection is in this format.

If the purpose of a quantitative study is to assess the actual
support provided by the current book collection for the courses offered by the university, then the key to the evaluation is knowledge
of the university's programs. To collect information about programs,
we used the university catalog which contains concise descriptions of
the courses in each department. Each course description was read
carefully, and, when available, faculty and class outlines were consulted. To index the subject coverage of a course, we assigned Library of Congress (LC) classification numbers to the description.
A background subject or a topic of interest to, but not specifically
included in, the course content was considered peripheral, and no
LC number was assigned to it. The basic rule for assigning entries
was termed the "principle of primary support."

After LC numbers were assigned to the course descriptions,
student assistants used the shelflist to count the number of books
giving support to each course. And, to gain an idea of the demand
for that support, course enrollment statistics for the year just ended
were included. With this information we thought that a satisfactory
quantitative evaluation of the book collection in relation to the university's programs could be made. Table 1 illustrates an example
of the data collected.

TABLE 1

EXAMPLE OF QUANTITATIVE DATA COLLECTED FOR COURSES

RELIGION

Course Number	Course Title	LC Class Numbers	Total Number of UNO Books	Course Credit Hours	Enrollment 1971/1972			
					Fall Semester		Spring Semester	
					Under-graduate	Grad-uate	Under-graduate	Grad-uate
211	African and American Indian Religion	BL2400-2499 E59.R38 E98.R3	38	3	37	0	32	0
215	Old Testament	BS1-1830	676	3	111	0	-	-
216	New Testament	BS1-680, 1901-2970	817	3	-	-	124	0

The methodology used at UNO is similar to that of William E. McGrath, who has classified college catalog information for many uses, including collection assessment. [2] We believe that, although UNO's methodology for collection evaluation is similar to McGrath's, sufficient dissimilarities in philosophy and procedure exist between UNO's work and McGrath's work to warrant comment.

McGrath did not allow an LC classification number to be assigned to more than one department, and, at most, three numbers were assigned to a course. To produce unique ranges of LC classification numbers representing the support profile for a department, McGrath integrated the numbers assigned to courses. Therefore, although LC classifies mathematics in QA, McGrath's study found that at the University of Southwestern Louisiana mathematics is supported by materials classified in HF5691-5761; QA11, 39, 135-263, 266, 269-699; QC851-999; and TA329-347. [3] In this manner McGrath is provided with unique statistics, that is, a classification number or range supports one, and only one, department. We believed, however, that to show the actual collection support for a field, overlap must be allowed. We assigned, therefore, all pertinent LC classification numbers to a course, without regard to previous assignments of the classification number to another course. UNO set no limit to the number of LC classification numbers that could be assigned to a course--following the principle of primary support, we assigned as many classification numbers as necessary. Furthermore, because we desired to prepare a detailed analysis of program support, we presented our figures without editing. We included enrollment figures at the course level while McGrath took the departmental approach.

Basically, the procedural differences result from the reasons for collection assessment. McGrath's primary purpose was to provide data to aid in budget allocation; he also desired to collect other data (e. g., statistics on collection use, for directions in weeding, as a shelving and storage aid, as a guide to the collection). [4] For McGrath, collection evaluation was an added benefit. Our procedure was directed toward a single purpose: collection evaluation in regard to the university's programs with its implications for collection development. Thus, our method was more detailed and included more analysis of actual collection support of the curriculum.

The data collected at UNO appears in Quantitative Evaluation of the Gene Eppley Library Book Collections in Relation to the Courses Offered at the University of Nebraska at Omaha. [5] The report is arranged by department and grouped by college, and for each department three major sections appear:

1. introduction, in which the department is discussed and analyzed in terms of number of faculty, undergraduate and graduate programs, subfields in the department, new programs, orientations or emphases, interdisciplinary influences, and departmental demands on the library;
2. statistics, in which data are presented in the format illustrated in Table 1; and

3. data interpretation, in which data are analyzed in light of
the information gathered about the department, and judgments
are made about the strengths and weaknesses of the collection
in each area.

Throughout the course of the study, problems in the methodology were discovered. These problems arose from two sources:
the LC classification and the university catalog. In many cases, the
LC schedules did not contain specific classification numbers for the
subject treated in UNO courses. In such cases, broader classification assignments than preferred were allowed, and sometimes no distinction in collection support between two very different courses
could be discerned because both courses drew support from the materials classified in the same LC classification range. Thus, it
was almost impossible to state the actual amount of collection support for these courses or make comparative judgments. Inadequate
(or, we sometimes believed, inaccurate) course description was the
major problem presented by the university catalog. Nevertheless,
the catalog descriptions were taken as authority in all cases.

The UNO study does not include all courses listed in the current university catalog, but uses 1971/72 as the base year because
the most recent enrollment statistics available were from this year.
Courses not included in the 1971/72 catalog were ignored unless enrollment statistics were available (this occurred when courses that
for one reason or another were not included in the catalog were offered during 1971/72). Courses excluded from the 1972/73 catalog
were marked "discontinued" in the study and not analyzed because
we reasoned that they were considered obsolete for the current university program and, as such, did not need their collection support
evaluated.

Knowledge of the university's programs and their correlation
with the LC classification is an important result of the study. Librarians found that their ability to understand and assist faculty
members in locating resources increased as the study progressed.
Prior to the study, librarians were acquainted only with those needs
expressed by the library-oriented faculty. Librarians found that, as
the study progressed, they gained a more detailed and comprehensive
picture of the university's programs and needs and were better able
to understand and assist faculty members in locating resources. Faculty liaison greatly increased during the study, and with completion
of the report even more faculty became involved in meetings established to discuss the study. At these meetings, faculty assessed the
report, added their insights on collection evaluation and improvement,
and indicated changes in program emphases, the importance of other
types of resources besides books (in some fields), and the lack of
publishing in some areas. Information obtained in these meetings
has been recorded for possible use in future evaluations.

Better understanding of the relationship of the collection to
the university's programs and increased faculty liaison are important and beneficial to the acquisitions program, but did the study

evaluate collection support of the university's programs successfully?
In the estimation of the UNO Acquisitions Department, the answer
is a qualified "yes." The limitations of the study are apparent. It
is a quantitative evaluation and, as expected, additional research,
both quantitative and qualitative, is necessary. This was merely the
first step. We have gathered data about the number of books available to the student on a certain subject, but this study does not, nor
was it designed to, estimate the exact pertinence of these books to a
course. Such factors as collection age, condition, variety, and duplication are not measured. For example, we have no figures on the
number of titles, as distinct from the number of volumes, and we
have no information concerning date of publication. The study does
not measure whether library use is stressed in a course. Circulation statistics and patterns could be studied profitably to ascertain if
they support our findings. In interpreting the data, we made some
generalizations (which may not hold in all cases) about library use,
e.g., freshman-sophomore science courses usually concentrate on
textbook study instead of library research. In other words, the statistics may be misleading if not interpreted in light of the subject
and situation. (This was the major reason for adding the sections
on data interpretation to the report.)

Although we could not evaluate fully the collection support of
the university's programs with only a quantitative study, we are confident that we determined collection weaknesses and strengths. For
example, less than ten books (assuming more than ten books have
been published) on a subject about which a course is taught is probably weak support. On the other hand, a collection of 10,000 books
probably may be considered strong support. It was, however, virtually impossible to assess areas of average support. What is an
adequate level of support? Ten books per student? Twenty books
per student? Knowledge of quantity alone is not sufficient to determine whether an area is well supported, even with the added information on enrollment. A qualitative study is needed.

The LC schedules also made evaluation difficult. If a subject
area was well developed by LC, evaluation was aided greatly. But
when the classification is relatively undeveloped, as in the case of
computer science, evaluation of collection support becomes virtually
impossible. Other methods of evaluation will have to be devised for
such fields. Assigning an LC number to more than one course
assesses properly the collection support for each course, but the
immediate demand on the books is not the enrollment for one course
but the enrollment for all courses covered by that classification number. Within one department common subject coverage is readily apparent, but it is difficult to know which other departments may also
be drawing on the same resources. This is particularly a problem
with strongly interdisciplinary departments such as the Speech-Com-
munication Department.

Finally, the study needs continuous updating. Enrollment
statistics change each semester, materials are constantly being added to and withdrawn from the collection, and course offerings are

continually changing, frequently at a rate not reflected in the university catalog.

The limitations mentioned were, in most cases, known to the department and carefully considered before the study was conducted. The methodology was developed for the specific purpose of assessing the current collection's support of the current university program, and we believe the results to be significant. A more comprehensive understanding of the collection related specifically to the curriculum and course enrollments was gained. Problem areas and areas supported well by the collection were identified. University program emphases and de-emphases were discovered. An important incidental benefit was the gathering of information useful for analysis of budget allocations, that is, given university programs and related collection statistics, is the acquisitions budget properly allocated? Most importantly, the study encouraged librarians to meet the faculty on an equal informational level and effective working relationships developed in many cases.

Currently, the UNO Acquisitions Department is conducting the next phase of collection evaluation, i.e., a qualitative evaluation of the book collection. Using the quantitative evaluation as a starting point, major bibliographies in the fields designated particularly weak or strong, or those fields emphasized by the departments, are being checked against the catalog. In addition, a study of the bibliographic structure of each field is in progress in order to discern which format of resources material best serves the field. For example, the importance of serials in the sciences may reduce the need for much further study of the book collection in these areas. Finally, some specific studies will be conducted for each field deemed appropriate by the previous study and the discussion of the study with the academic departments. These studies include a study of the age of the books in the business collection and a study of the amount of publishing available for certain subjects such as kinesiology.

Each new study will bring added knowledge and raise further questions that must be explored, as all studies have limitations. The UNO staff is convinced, however, that quantitative research can provide the library with a sound basis for communication with the administration and faculty concerning collection evaluation and development.

References

1. Signe Ottersen. "A Bibliography on Standards for Evaluating Libraries," College & Research Libraries 32:127-44 (March 1971), contains an excellent annotated bibliography of articles discussing evaluation.
2. William E. McGrath. "Determining and Allocating Book Funds for Current Domestic Buying," College & Research Libraries 28:268-72 (July 1967).
   William E. McGrath. "Measuring Classified Circulation Ac-

cording to Curriculum," College & Research Libraries 29:347-
50 (Sept. 1968).
William E. McGrath, Ralph C. Huntsinger, and Gary R.
Barber. "An Allocation Formula Derived from a Factor
Analysis of Academic Departments," College & Research Libraries 30:51-62 (Jan. 1969).
William E. McGrath and Norma Durand. "Classifying Courses
in the University Catalog," College & Research Libraries
30:533-39 (Nov. 1969).
3. McGrath and Durand, "Classifying Courses," p. 536.
4. McGrath and Durand, "Classifying Courses," p. 534-5.
5. Nebraska. University at Omaha. Gene Eppley Library. Acqui-
    sitions Department, Quantitative Evaluation of the Gene Eppley
    Library Book Collections in Relation to the Courses Offered
    at the University of Nebraska at Omaha (Omaha: 1972), 362p.

LIBRARY MATERIALS FOR PATIENTS (Excerpts)

By Eleanor Phinney

Steps in the Development of the Library Collection

Preparing a Written Selection Policy

In chapter 4, the importance of a written policy statement, adopted by the library advisory committee and approved by the administration, was stressed. Part of that overall policy will be the statement of the library's position, on the basis of which materials are to be chosen for the collection. The whole is intended to express the goals and purposes of the patients' library and to show the ways in which they are geared to those of the institution and to the goals and characteristics of the patients. The relationship to the other departments and the library's purpose of providing materials which will aid and supplement the work of each will also come into play in both the formulation of policy and the choice of materials. The advisory committee can make a contribution here by assisting in the preparation of a materials selection policy for the guidance of the library staff and, after its adoption, by acting as a source of expertise and advice in special areas of selection, while leaving the professional aspects of materials selection to the qualified librarian.

Those preparing the policy statement need to strive to make clear their realization that the institution's clientele and staff will need a library which maintains its own special atmosphere as a place of many uses--to relax and browse, to enjoy and explore, or to do serious research--while not infringing on the role of the medical library. Developing a collection which is attractive to reader and nonreader alike, meeting a variety of tastes, interests, and levels of reading and physical abilities, is one of the ways in which this atmosphere is created.

A statement of objectives and policy, brief but sufficient for its purpose and exemplary in the way it relates objectives and policy, is given here with the permission of the Mayo Clinic Library. It should be noted, however, that any statement of policy should include, although not necessarily in the section on materials selection, the library's recognition of its need to know and utilize all the avail-

able resources of the area to supplement its collection.   Other
chapters detail the rapidly increasing and developing possibilities of
cooperation and aid for the patients' library.

Objectives and Materials Selection Policy of the
Mayo Clinic Library Program for Patients

Objectives:

The objective of the Library Service for Patients is to assist in
raising the level of patient care by providing, for all hospitalized
Clinic patients, recreational, therapeutic, educational reading materials and audiovisual aids, including recommended patient health
education information.   The purpose of the program is to contribute to the recovery and welfare of the individual patient and to
promote reading as a satisfying experience.

Reading is one of the activities which is coordinated with other
activities in the rehabilitative, occupational, recreational therapeutic programs.   In choosing books for the patient, it is essential the librarian select those titles which will divert, entertain,
and in some measure, act as a bridge to the outside world, by
directing his interest and perspective outward.   In a planned program, regulated by a physician, reading activities may be used
as a part of the treatment of the patient, i. e. , bibliotherapy.

Selection Policy:

Reading materials, both print and nonprint, and audiovisual aids
and equipment shall be chosen to fit the needs and abilities of all
hospitalized Clinic patients, adults and children, whatever the
background, culture, education or race.

Interest shall take precedence over literary quality; however, the
collection shall be broad in scope and well-rounded, including popular and classical literature, in English and foreign languages
and shall be kept up to date.   Overall and predictable use in fur-
thering the objectives of the program (recreational, educational,
therapeutic) shall be the basic criteria in the selection of all materials, including appropriate audiovisual aids and equipment.
Additional criteria are colorful bindings, pleasing typography,
format, size, and fine editions.

Gifts are accepted with the understanding that they are included
in the collection only as they meet the standards and needs of
the Department and that they are available for use with all patients.

Some further statements on the formulation of objectives for
the patients' library collection should also be given consideration before leaving the subject.   The National Commission on Libraries
and Information Science (NCLIS) has studied the problem of providing

adequate information services to all segments of society, and has proposed eight objectives which would insure a nationwide system of networks from the federal to the local community level. Broad in scope, these objectives reach from the highest academic levels to those persons presently unserved or even unaware of their needs. Its recent report includes this statement: "Users' needs can be described from several perspectives. For example, the retarded, the illiterate, the blind, the visually handicapped, the physically handicapped, and the institutionalized require highly specialized resources and services" (pp. 10-11).

This broad statement developed from the strong demand from librarians that the ill and handicapped, in or out of the institution, be identified among those unserved. Basic to this demand was the Standards for Library Service in Health Care Institutions, which has been frequently referred to in this text. These needs are again emphasized from a slightly different point of view in the pamphlet Materials Selection for Hospital and Institution Libraries. Relating these needs to a specific clientele, this pamphlet states: "Books and other materials are selected primarily from the standpoint of readers' needs and abilities; for example, in selecting materials for patients, interest takes precedence over prestige or literary quality" (p. 5). As stressed in chapter 3, before admission to the institution the individual may not have been a library user, and yet intellectual curiosity about some subject is latent in every person. The problem is thus to match the level of comprehension and understanding with material which will adequately satisfy the patient's curiosity. For instance, this does not mean that the patient whose reading has been limited to movie or detective magazines will not develop other interests when there is an opportunity and encouragement to do so. There are many worthwhile pictorial histories of Hollywood, biographies of stars and other theatrical figures, etc., which can lead to the introduction of new subjects. Again, it must be emphasized that no hint of criticism or condescension on the part of the librarian can be allowed to creep in; there can be only a willingness to enlarge upon existing interests and create new ones.

Determining the Selection Policy

The scope, size, and character of the collection will depend on many of the same factors as those governing the development of the program of service which will bring the collection into active use. These factors include the size and type of institution, especially whether it has a short-term or long-term program, the emphasis made in its care and rehabilitation program, and the characteristics of the patients, their age range, nature of illness or handicap or both, and how many are readers or nonreaders. All these factors will be analyzed here in much the same way as they are in chapter 5.

That the tenets expressed in the policy will incorporate the ALA Library Bill of Rights should go without saying, as the Standards suggests, stating further that the policy should emphasize the responsibility of the library to support the total institution program (p. 13)--an approach consistently followed throughout this text. For a further succinct summary of what should be included in a selection policy, consult the section on "Collections" in the Standards, a portion of which has just been quoted. Another excellent source of assistance in formulating a policy for an individual patients' library is the pamphlet Materials Selection for Hospitals and Institution Libraries, which contains considerably more detail than the Standards.

In some manuals and similar sources, the suggested size of the collection is based on the number of beds in the institution. The size and mobility of the collection will determine the estimate of current shelving needed, while the type and characteristics of the patients will indicate how much growth, if any, must be allowed for. In the case of service provided by the outside agency, the book storage or library rooms are likely to be small, especially in hospitals, where space is at a premium. [1] The liberal use of a request and reserve system, as described in chapter 6, must compensate for an adequate permanent collection; a statement to this effect should be included in the portion of the agency's policy concerned with its service to institutions. Chapter 9 further covers these aspects of collection size, while the budgetary considerations of wear-and-tear, rising prices of materials, and providing sufficient copies of current favorites are found in chapter 10.

The scope of the collection needs to be considered from the viewpoint of form and format and the areas of service where the materials are to be used. Among the categories included by the Standards are: Books, including those in large type and paperback; periodicals; newspapers; pamphlets, and similar materials. These are usually grouped under the heading of print materials. Pictures may be both print and nonprint. Among the increasingly understood and utilized kinds of nonprint or audiovisual materials, those most frequently found are 8mm and 16mm films and filmstrips, recordings of books, now almost universally referred to as "talking books"--a term originating with the then head of the American Foundation for the Blind, Robert B. Irwin, and adopted by the Library of Congress Division for the Blind and Physically Handicapped (DBPH)--and recordings of other types, commercially or individually produced, especially music for all tastes, on discs, cartridge and cassette tapes, television, and radio. [2] The equipment to use these materials is an important, in fact indispensable, item. More on equipment will be found in chapter 9, and further mention of audiovisual materials later in this chapter.

Materials Selection for Hospital and Institution Libraries tends to define the scope of the collection primarily in terms of function or areas of service. Beside the above mentioned audiovisual materials are found information and reference services; recreational reading services; inspirational reading; educational reading, including that for informal self-education and self-improvement, as well as materials designed to meet the needs of other departments carrying on educational and training programs; and materials for such uses as those made by discussion and therapy groups, remotivation programs, etc. --all are included among those functions listed and enlarged upon.[3] To those areas of service should be added patient education, discussed in chapters 5 and 6.

In addition to developing the collection to meet the general needs of both the individual patient and staff member in the institution, and of the library's program of service (also, of course, geared to those needs), the materials selection policy statement may need to include some reference to the principles to be followed in determining the appropriateness of given items in the collection. For instance, is the collection designed for the non-reader as well as for the reader? The incoming patient may never have been a library user, may not be able to read English, or may be illiterate. All these possibilities must be taken into account and anticipated if a study of the institution's usual clientele reveals the likelihood of their occurring. Such commonly held interests as sports, model cars and planes, postage stamps, home decoration and cooking can be used as a basis for developing wider reading than that offered by the sports page, for example. Biographies of famous athletes, or accounts of colonial and pioneer days and ways, with old recipes and attractive illustrations, can provide good introductions.

The question of criteria to be applied to specific areas of interest is also well handled in the pamphlet Materials Selection. These criteria will be helpful for the development of a selection policy and for judging titles under consideration in the actual process of materials selection.

Criteria for Selection

With the librarian's frequent reliance on lists or specially chosen selection aids thus minimized, the use of reliable criteria is the best recourse. Materials Selection places strong emphasis on giving well-expressed criteria for a number of subject areas and types of materials, and will be drawn on extensively in what follows.

The choice of fiction has been mentioned, but some further comment is needed. In general it is agreed that emphasis should be placed on selection rather than censorship, the only exception being the exclusion of materials that would undermine confidence or respect for the treatment programs or skill of the personnel. Quoting directly from Materials Selection, among the useful questions to be asked about each title are:

> Does the librarian have first-hand acquaintance with a reader who would enjoy it? Is there opportunity for discussion and reading guidance to clear up the distorted response or misunderstandings that may arise from this material?[4]

Although written a number of years ago, Dorothy Canfield Fisher's statement on truth in fiction retains its value:

> Whether we are aware of it or not, we look, in every self-respecting work of fiction, for a 'bulletin from the front,' the front being human life. Other things being equal, the more truthful such a report on reality, the more valuable. And to make one's little narrative honestly a part of truth is a big undertaking, rather beyond the ability of many authors. Yet I maintain that the first thing to say about a novel is whether the writer has been able to do just this.

With nonfiction, coordination with the activity therapy staff, as previously stressed, requires the library to be a dependable resource for the many kinds of material needed to strengthen that department's program; a good poetry collection; as much material as possible on games, parties, and holidays; and books on arts, crafts, hobbies, and music that supplement those found on the department's reference shelf. Reference books should be limited, if the library is adequate, to just those items usually in daily use; all others are likely to be just as necessary and desirable for other departmental programs and for the general reader.

There has been a concerted effort to develop a wide range of high interest-low reading level materials for the disadvantaged and below average reader. It is advisable to make selections only after seeing these books to determine their suitability for general reading and adaptability to a variety of programs and activities. This is where the question of the use of abridgments, simplified versions, and comic books arises.

> When considering the abilities and needs of the clientele of adult hospitals and institutions, it is both practical and realistic to include materials not traditionally accepted for library use. Light, uncomplicated material, reasonably well-written and illustrated that will hold the attention of a near-illiterate or a sick or disturbed individual may be found helpful for therapeutic use. [5]

If an extensive educational program is carried out in the institution the library will be deeply involved as an integral part of that program. Special education departments in some states have compiled detailed curricula which coordinate print and nonprint materials. These are excellent guides for general selection as well as for special groups. [6]

Health education materials are also likely to be centered in the library. Here the advice and direction of the physician and the extensive availability of multimedia on all aspects of this field are factors which enter strongly into the selection of these materials. Medicine and psychiatry are also included in this area; Materials Selection makes the following distinction between what is and is not suitable for the patients' library:

> Authoritative, up-to-date books on health, hygiene, diet, common diseases, medical dictionaries and physiologies may be selected for the library. Clinical texts, books on diagnosis and treatment, textbooks for students and practitioners in medicine, surgery, psychiatry, etc., should not be included in the general library collection. (p. 7)

Inclusion of the subject area of human relations is increasingly necessary for all ages and levels of library users. Reading Ladder, prepared by Virginia Reid, is the type of classified and annotated list useful for programming and as the librarian's reference and reminder; it is helpful not only in the selection of materials, but also for the planning of therapy and discussion programs. Materials Selection states:

> Materials which promote mutual respect and sound understanding of the common characteristics and needs of people of many different national, religious and ethnic backgrounds should be provided. (p. 7)

One caution may be necessary. In the matter of racial and national origins and the problems of minorities, it is better to choose background material that is informative and which will help the person to a feeling of self-worth and cultural pride. The need for foreign language books can also be considered in this context, as Materials Selection points out:

> Books in a native language can have a marked therapeutic effect on patients or inmates; therapy and personal interest may also include the study of foreign languages. Effort should be made to acquire foreign language materials that match [the level of reading ability and] the needs of the clientele. (p. 8)

Being able to draw on a large public, regional, or state library will be useful in keeping this section of the collection fresh, especially in a long-term institution.

Books of inspiration and religious reading are usually in demand. According to Materials Selection, the criteria for the selection of these materials, which need to be handled with tact, circumspection, and evenhandedness, are:

> Materials on religious customs and traditions, stories from the Bible, several versions of the Bible, lives of religious heroes, religious holidays, etc., should be selected. Libraries in hospitals and institutions operated by one religious group contain the teachings of that faith and also materials to serve the needs of the population outside of that faith. (p. 7)

Earlier in Materials Selection, under the heading "Inspirational reading," the statement is made that books, periodicals, and pamphlets of religious sectarian content are distributed by chaplains--another area, it might be added, in which close collaboration and mutual understanding of specific roles are necessary to accomplish the goals set for the patient's care and rehabilitation.

Great care should be exercised in the selection of reference materials, particularly the choice of an encyclopedia, so that the choice will be consistent with its level of use. The various other types of materials which may be needed--certainly a good dictionary and the World Almanac or a similar title--are covered in chapter 5. The vertical file fits into this area, and here free and inexpensive materials have their uses; but to collect indiscriminately is poor economy, since the cost in time and space for processing, storing, circulating, and finally discarding these is the same as for other items. Pamphlets are, however, often the only means by which divergent opinions may be expressed; much up-to-date material on health education can be found only in pamphlets or magazines. The federal government offers a variety of pamphlets on every conceivable subject at nominal cost. A number of popular and consumer-oriented magazines, in addition to the professional journals, list new offerings of this type of material. The librarian needs to take care to select only those topics which will be useful to that institution's patients and staff, and to exercise a good deal of judgment in the matter of quality control. This collection can easily get out of hand and out of date. Pamphlets form the basis of the vertical file collection, and although not mentioned, should form an integral part of the reference services described in chapter 5. Clippings, too, should constitute part of the vertical file--another reason for weeding frequently to keep the file fresh. Bibliotherapy: Methods and Materials suggests that maintenance of these files may be the work of a volunteer or patient assistant in the library.

Poetry is a good item to clip, since much of what is published in periodicals never finds its way into books. It should carry a clear message that is easily read and understood; to be useful in therapy it should be imaginative or emotional in content.

All of the above holds true for a picture file, which should have relevance to specific programs, such as remotivation groups. The activity therapy staff should be consulted as to which categories need to be collected. Some patients require pictures containing one concept only, so that there will be no blurring of the message conveyed. This applies to patients with aphasia and also to some of the developmentally disabled. A carefully chosen picture collection is worth having mounted and laminated. This will preserve the material, keeping it fresh even with much handling, and there will be less likelihood of loss. Duplicate copies of magazines received as gifts or from the Post Office (see chapter 10) are a good source for both pictures and articles for the vertical file.

Criteria for the selection of paperbacks, whether purchased or received as gifts, should be the same as for all library materials added to the patients' library collection. In recent years, the variety and extent of material in paperback form is nearly endless, as are their possible uses. Chapter 10 mentions the advantages of a special contract with a dealer; it will be an added convenience if the dealer carries both the popular and so-called "quality" paperback titles. Acquiring paperbacks with the binding already reinforced, in titles of permanent value, can be a good investment when the quality of paper and clarity of typeface warrant as well, but many titles will serve their purpose as they are. The librarian should, in fact, watch for suitable format on all acquisitions, avoiding those with overtight bindings, which are difficult for many patients to hold, and seeking those with the qualities already mentioned in regard to paperbacks. The large print book, while it may be of temporary use for a number of patients, will be discussed later, in the sections on appraisal of the collection and specialized materials for specialized needs.

Periodicals

A good magazine list provides current awareness to the library user in an institution, as well as filling recreational and specialized and general information needs. Patients look for the familiar popular magazines they are accustomed to seeing regularly. The list should be broad in scope, with some out of the ordinary titles which will stimulate interest in new subjects. A few examples of titles useful in specific situations are suggested in chapter 3. The list should be reviewed from time to time to see that it reflects current needs and interests. General policies regarding serials are discussed in Melcher on Acquisitions, and both sides of the periodical situation are presented in the July 1972 issue of Special Libraries, featuring one article by a serials librarian and one by a subscription agent.

Appraisal of the Collection

The logical time to weed the collection is when an inventory or, more properly, an appraisal of the collection is made, since each book is examined at that time. Worn and out-of-date books are removed from the collection. This is also the time to dispose of copies of books which are beyond their popularity, possibly in a book sale or by exchange. (See chapter 10 for more on maintenance of the collection, especially the steps leading up to, and following, appraisals.) When a rebound book is again in need of repair it should be discarded and replaced if the title is still needed. Old volumes of the classics having fine print should be replaced with new editions which have a typeface legible both as to size and design, opaque paper, and lines of type neither too closely printed nor too long for the eye to follow comfortably--a difficulty some visually handicapped readers encounter in large print books. Good illustrations add to the appeal of many books. Books which have not circulated within a given time, but which the library judges to be of value to the collection, may either be stored or transferred to a regionally maintained central storage, depending on the size of the collection and the avail-

ability of central storage from which the title may be readily re-
trieved when needed. If the demand for a standard item is not heavy,
a paperback edition will be adequate as a replacement. Here, also,
the specifications given above as to typeface and paper should be observed. It is important that the collection look fresh and inviting,
while retaining its central integrity and balance as dictated by the
demands and needs of the library's clientele.

The reference collection will, of course, be subject to appraisal as well. Replacement of an encyclopedia, for instance, or
addition of one in braille or large type, are matters for long-range
budget planning, while other items, which quickly lose their timeli-
ness and are inexpensive, such as The World Almanac, should be
replaced as frequently as possible.

The same considerations as those suggested for books--con-
dition, continuing usefulness and suitability, and possible obsolescence
of content--are also applicable to nonprint materials. Items held on
long or indefinite loan, whether print or nonprint, should also be
checked to insure that they are still useful and usable and that they
actually remain in the library's collection. If a search of shelves,
circulation records, and a check of patients' rooms, discreetly made,
fails to turn up an item which has been loaned to the library, such
losses should be covered by previously agreed-upon arrangements
with the loaning agency.

The assistance of the regional or state institution library consultant, particularly to the librarian who does not have access to a
wide range of materials selection tools, should be called into play
throughout the selection, weeding, and replacement process.

Notes

1. Fleak, Public Library Services..., p. 5.
2. Dickman, Living with Blindness, p. 22; Standards for Library
   Service in Health Care Institutions, p. 14.
3. Paraphrased from pp. 6-7.
4. p. 7. Some of the preceding material is quoted or paraphrased
   from pp. 7-8 of Materials Selection.
5. ALA Materials Selection, p. 8.
6. Selection of materials for specialized needs is considered in a
   later section of this chapter.

DESIGN OF INITIAL MEDIA COLLECTIONS
FOR NEW FACILITIES

By Frances Dean

If, in the opening days of a new school, the members of the media staff are able to cope effectively with 90 per cent of users' needs and questions by direct referral to the collection, the goal of the Division of Evaluation and Selection of the Montgomery County (Maryland) Public Schools has been reached and an appropriate initial collection is accessible to students and faculty. A major responsibility of this division is the selection of initial collections for new schools. It is the purpose of this article to share with others our experiences, basic principles, and what we believe are important considerations when initial collections are selected.

The first and most important responsibility of the coordinator of the Division of Evaluation and Selection is to interpret and implement the philosophy of the Department of Educational Media and Technology to the professional staff of the new school. The major aspect of this philosophy is that there be a unified media program within each school as a positive and effective force for leadership in curriculum change and instructional design within the school.

Thus, materials are selected that will support and vitalize a unified media program within a particular school, not just a collection of nonrelated items. In addition, bibliographic access is provided through book catalogs to a much broader range of media available throughout the system: 16mm films, audio and videotapes, and professional materials.

The second responsibility is the actual selection of the initial collection which is to be accessible to students and faculty on the first day of school. New collections are not considered an additional responsibility for this division but rather a continuing operation with high priority.

Planning Design

As soon as feasible, an appointment is made with the principal of each proposed school to discuss specifics: budget, curriculum, special needs of the student body, the design of the center, and implications of this design on the collection. Later, the same topics are reviewed with subject supervisors and area office professional staff in order to gain the benefit of their expertise as well as the assurance that the total system is considered.

Ideally none of the budget would be encumbered until the professional media staff of the new facility could be involved. From a practical standpoint this is impossible. Materials selection must begin in December, whereas the appointment of the media specialist often is delayed until July. In actuality, the initial collection budget is expended in phases as follows:

Phase I: One-third of the budget is expended solely by the Division of Evaluation and Selection for basic materials prior to the appointment of school staff in order to meet processing center deadlines and to insure materials on the shelves and ready for use on that first day of school.

Phase II: The next third of the budget is expended by the Division of Evaluation and Selection based on recommendations and advice of the principal and other professional staff members directly concerned with the opening of the school.

Phase III: The final third of the budget is expended by the media specialist of the school in conjunction with teachers and students. The specialist may expend the money any time after her appointment, but our experience has been that specialists elect to make final selections after they meet their students.

Our entire evaluation and selection program is based on the principle that

Materials should be evaluated by those who are to use them. Group evaluations are generally preferable to individual evaluations. Evaluations are best when they are based upon the actual experience of using the materials in a teaching-learning situation. Therefore, materials must be evaluated and selected cooperatively by teachers, principals, librarians, and students, using standard, uniform criteria to be supplemented by school-adopted policies. [1]

Although there is a general "Program of Studies" for the Montgomery County Public Schools, it is the special adaptation of the curriculum offerings in this program as they relate to the new school that is the primary concern in building its media collection. Some specifics which are considered include: (1) In an elementary school, is open education the policy? Are the classes to be graded or nongraded? What degree of structure is to be presented? (2) In the secondary school, what specialized courses will be taught? Are special time factors a part of the restructured curriculum? (3) In both levels, what are the spans of grade units housed in a given building: K-4, K-6, 5-6-7, junior high and senior high or any combination of the above?

If the school opens with a different alignment of grade levels than is ultimately planned for the building this will have an impact on the design of the initial collection. Each situation is unique, but there are at least two options. The first is to select materials for the students actually enrolled and work out an agreement with the appropriate administrators for future collection exchange. The second option is to select materials for the student levels as they ultimately will be constructed, meeting the needs of temporary grades with paperbacks. Variations of these two options may be used, but it is important to have a clear written statement of the plans for the collection including any future exchanges.

Although the phrase "to meet the special needs of children" can be a tired cliché, the action it connotes is still vital and necessary. The Montgomery County Public Schools have staff members who know the needs of students in their administrative areas. We ask these staff members the following questions. Are there non-English speaking students? Can the school qualify as a Title I school? Will there be classes for students with specific learning disabilities? And, finally, the question with many implications for the collection, what is the over-all reading level of the students who will attend the new school? The answer, by necessity, must be based on the reading level of the school the students are presently attending. We have found the professional judgment of these staff members to be extremely accurate. However, we continue to relearn that each school acquires its own distinct personality.

The physical structure of the new media center raises additional questions that must be considered in the collection building stages. Will there be satellite collections? Will there be storage facilities for microfiche? What kinds of production spaces and studio facilities will be provided? Will the center be wired for sound retrieval with wireless headsets? The converse is also true--are there items selected for the collection that would require any specialized physical arrangements?

Practical Guidelines
for Selection of Collections

Theoretically, if one plans well and executes properly, there will be few mistakes in an initial collection in a new school. However, when one meshes the practical demands of the Processing Center, the philosophy of the unified media program, the educational needs as espoused by the principal and his staff, plus the over-all standards and budget of the total school system, a selector of media will find some mistakes have been duly made. Noticeable omissions can be corrected through the use of the unencumbered funds in the last third of the budget.

The following practical guidelines for selection of initial collections are offered:

1. Be systematic. Have a plan of action, in writing, by date. Keep in mind that the school will open in September.
2. Identify the unique characteristics of the proposed school requiring special consideration in the collection design.
3. In selecting those materials which fall in the Phase I category of the budget, do not be overly concerned with numbers and standards. Attempt to cover areas of information on different literacy levels in the most appropriate formats. Keep in mind what a student wants to know.
4. Plan for and seek input from potential users but do not wait for titles to be handed in on three-by-five-inch cards.
5. Rely on standard tools and reviewing journals. Do not proceed to reinvent the wheel through complex systems of evaluation.
6. Search the literature of allied fields and subject categories for recent trends and developments which have implications for collections. Identify and use reputable new bibliographies as sources that deal with current concerns: sex-stereotyping, ethnic and minority groups, drug education, human development, and family life.
7. Do not be afraid to trust your own professional judgment and good sense. For example, order paperbacks for elementary schools, maps on transparencies, puzzles and games for social studies curriculum, and microfiche periodicals for back issues.

Evaluation

Any effort as encompassing as selecting initial collections must be carefully evaluated. Key questions should be answered, such as the following:

1. Were appropriate materials available for use on the first day of school?
2. Are varied and appropriate reading levels, diversity of format, balance of collection, curriculum relationship, relevancy, and ethnic and minority group representation reflected in the items contained in the collection?
3. Does the total collection meet the needs of users? Adequacy of a collection can not be evaluated in a vacuum, so a paramount consideration must be: Does the initial collection designed for this new school enable the media program to become vital and vibrant?

Reference

1. Evaluation and Selection of Instructional Materials and Equipment (Montgomery County Public Schools, Aug. 1971).

RECOMMENDED READINGS

Further reading in the area of the library environment follows closely the themes represented by the preceding articles. The
following are selected from an extensive literature base.

College and university libraries and their surrounding circumstances are thoroughly and lucidly discussed by Louis Round Wilson
in his books: The Library in College Instruction (New York: H. W.
Wilson Co. , 1951) and The University Library (2nd ed. , New York:
Columbia Univ. Press, 1956). Though not recent, much of this information remains basic to an understanding of the ways in which we
should look at an academic service area.

The topic of surveys in college libraries is dealt with in
Guy Lyle's "Book Selection and Acquisition," in his The Administration of the College Library (New York: H. W. Wilson Co. , 1974),
pages 170-175. He discusses factors that affect the development of
the collection for a college library. Important among these are the
curriculum, which should reflect the purpose of the institution; the
faculty, their specializations and teaching methods; the budget, and
size of the collection as evaluative criterion. In this context, the
Clapp-Jordan formula's application is illustrated.

The community college learning resources center environment
is surveyed by Kenneth and Loren Allen in Organization and Administration of the Learning Resource Center in the Community College
(Hamden, Conn.: Shoe String, 1973). They mention the different
methods for measuring the adequacy of a collection and indicate questions that must be answered in developing a collection policy.

Additional reading on the attempts of academic libraries to
measure the effectiveness of their collections is provided in the article, "Library Collections and Academic Curricula: Quantitative
Relationships, " by John J. Knightly in College and Research Libraries 36, No. 4 (July 1975), pages 295-301. In this study, twenty-
two Texas college and university library collections were compared,
and their coverage of various curricular areas was analyzed.

The preparation of an allocation formula for book fund distribution is described by William E. McGrath, Ralph C. Huntsinger,
and Gary R. Barber in "An Allocation Formula Derived from a Factor Analysis of Academic Departments, " College and Research Libraries 30, no. 1 (Jan. , 1969), pages 51-62. They determine three
main factors out of twenty-two variables and use those in their formula. McGrath's study of the use of library materials as indicated

by circulated items is reported in the article, "Correlating the Subjects of Books Taken out of and Books Used within an Open-Stack Library," College and Research Libraries 32, no. 4 (July, 1971), pages 280-285. He concludes that out-of-library circulation is a reliable indicator and gives methods for using it.

A different role for the academic librarian is discussed in the article by Howard W. Dillon, "Organizing the Academic Library for Instruction" in Journal of Academic Librarianship 1, No. 4 (September, 1975), pages 4-7. In this instance, a different organization of library facilities and duties was set up that emphasized the concept of the "teaching library," along the lines of the library college. Such an organizational pattern has definite impact on the library collection and its development.

All types of libraries and various aspects of analyzing the community are covered in "Community Analysis and Libraries," the Library Trends issue of January, 1976. Articles range from the historical aspects, through methods used, to the teaching of community analysis. An extensive annotated bibliography is included.

Studying the public library community is the focus of Ruth Warncke's "Analyzing Your Community: Basis for Building Library Service." Published in 1974 by the Illinois Library Association and the Illinois State Library, this booklet would serve well as an introduction to the concepts and methods of community studies. Her earlier Studying the Community (Chicago: A. L. A., 1960) is a more comprehensive, detailed work on this subject.

The situation of a public library in a cooperative system and the effects on collection development is given comprehensive and informative treatment in Ruth Gregory's and Lester Stoffel's "Collection Building and Maintenance," chapter five of Public Libraries in Cooperative Systems (Chicago: A. L. A., 1971). Different levels of collection building are defined and illustrated, and the whole selection function carefully described.

Concerned with selection of materials in the school media center are a number of articles from the theme issue entitled "Marketing, Selection, and Acquisition of Materials for School Media Programs. Part I," in School Media Quarterly 6, No. 2 (Winter, 1978). Including in their scope acquisition as well as selection procedures, the authors point out a number of factors, both internal and external, that bear on selection decisions and collection building.

The variety of materials that a media center should consider to supplement and enrich the curriculum are discussed in "Action Activities," by Mildred Laughlin in Learning Today 10, No. 3 (Summer, 1977), pages 57-60. The importance of consultation between the teacher and the media specialist to insure the best selection is stressed.

Written from a British point of view, the book, Children Are

People: The Librarian in the Community (New York: Crowell, 1974) by Janet Hill, gives the reader an enlarged perspective on the children's library field as well as excellent, constructive guidelines on selection and its relationship to programming, the community situation, and other factors.

The Special Child in the Library, edited by Barbara H. Baskin and Karen H. Harris (Chicago: A.L.A., 1976), is a collection of essays dealing with all needs of the exceptional child in the library, but particularly with the range and variety of materials that are appropriate and desirable for many kinds of "special" children.

Collection evaluation is examined in the chapter "Evaluation of the Book Collection," by Rudolph Hirsch, in Wayne S. Yenawine's Library Evaluation (Syracuse Univ. Press, 1959), pages 7-20. Hirsch provides an overview of traditional evaluation methods and general guidelines. Building Library Collections (4th ed., Metuchen, N.J.: Scarecrow Press, 1974) by Mary D. Carter, Wallace J. Bonk, and Rose Mary Magill also includes descriptions of the various methods for surveying collections (Chapter VI, pages 163-167).

A comprehensive review of collection survey methods and of particular surveys is included in F. W. Lancaster's The Measurement and Evaluation of Library Services (Washington, D.C.: Information Resources Press, 1977), Chapter 5, pages 165-206. A practical, informative introduction to conducting a library survey is provided by Maurice B. Line's Library Surveys (Hamden, Conn.: Archon Books, 1967). Material on the actual construction of questionnaires is included.

A component of the total process of collection surveying and development is weeding. Though there is not a wealth of material on this subject, texts such as Building Library Collections include sections on weeding. Stanley J. Slote, in Weeding Library Collections (Littleton, Colo.: Libraries Unlimited, 1975) devotes a volume to it, providing background information and a survey of methods. State library agencies are often sources of weeding guidelines or manuals that define responsibility, point out the likely materials for weeding, and give guidance for weeding in particular subject areas. An example, noteworthy for its concise, clear, informative content and attractive format is the one published by the Library Services Division, Michigan Dept. of Education.

As we mentioned in the introductory materials, the various standards that apply in different situations are a factor of the library environment. Several of the existing standards are listed here. Many of these are not officially adopted or applied standards, but are statements of desirable levels of service expressed by groups within the American Library Association, active in the different kinds of library service.

American Association of School Librarians. Media Programs: District and School. Prepared by the American Association of School Librarians, American Library Association, and Association of Educational Communication and Technology. Chicago: A. L. A., 1975.

American Library Association. Audio-Visual Committee. Guidelines for Audiovisual Materials and Services for Public Libraries. Chicago: A. L. A., 1970.

Association of Hospital and Institution Libraries. Hospital Library Standards Committee. Standards for Library Services in Health Care Institutions. Chicago: A. L. A., 1970.

Canadian School Library Association. Standards of Library Service for Canadian Schools Recommended by the Canadian School Library Association. Toronto: Ryerson Press, 1967.

Public Library Association Audiovisual Committee. Recommendations for Audiovisual Materials and Services for Small and Medium-sized Public Libraries. Chicago: A. L. A., 1975.

Public Library Association. Committee on Standards. Subcommittee on Standards for Children's Services. Standards for Children's Services in Public Libraries. Chicago: A. L. A., 1960.

Public Library Association. Committee on Standards. Subcommittee for Work with Young Adults in Public Libraries. Young Adult Services in the Public Library. Chicago: A. L. A., 1960.

Public Library Association. Standards Committee. Minimum Standards for Public Library Systems, 1966. Chicago: A. L. A., 1967.

North Central Association Quarterly and other publications by that association and similar groups provide information on existing and contemplated standards for academic institutions. Comparative information on library collections is often included in such publications.

CHAPTER 5

THE SELECTION PROCESS

Earlier chapters have presented information about developing
selection policies and procedures, as well as examining the significance of a library's environment upon the development of its collection. In the literature "selection process" and "evaluation process"
are frequently discussed as related and simultaneous activities. The
editors view them as separate activities of the total process. The
articles in this chapter focus on the broad aspects; that is, attention
is given to general concerns in selection, who should be involved in
the process, and resources used in the process. In chapter 6,
"The Evaluation Process," the articles deal with specific criteria
used to examine specific materials. Arguments can be made that
evaluation does not occur until the material is actually used and
assessed. This point is worth remembering when reading these two
chapters that approach the processes from the angle of what occurs
when one is making the decision whether or not to purchase materials.

The first two articles deal with problems faced by those responsible for selection. Writing on "Media Selection: Six Concerns,"
Mary Frances K. Johnson identifies areas of concern to school librarians which have application to other library settings. Specifically,
she identifies six areas that need improvement. These needs are:
(1) broader provision and use of selection tools; (2) improved bibliographic control; (3) widespread examination centers; (4) broader preparation of school media specialists, at both preservice and continuing education levels, in media selection; (5) active participation by
teachers in collection building; and (6) a broader view of what should
be represented in a school media collection.

Additional concerns are raised in "Focus: Recent Developments in Materials Selection," from the Division of Library Development and Services of the Maryland State Department of Education.
Among the questions raised in this feature are: "If user demands
are important, how are they to be identified and evaluated and then
applied to selection procedure?" Examples are given as to how
school and public libraries are responding to this challenge.

Both of the above articles speak about the role and value of
examination centers in the selection process. For readers unfamiliar with this concept, Mary Virginia Gaver traces the work and

thinking of the Educational Media Selection Centers Project in "A Report in Progress: Dreamers and Educational Media Selection Centers." Unfortunately, for many librarians such examination centers are still at the dream stage.

Another means of obtaining books for personal examination is found in the system of "approval plans." The advantages, disadvantages, and possible misuse of such a program are described by Margaret Dobbyn in "Approval Plan Purchasing in Perspective." Her narrative footnotes add further insight into the concerns of academic and research libraries about these programs. Approval plans can provide a means for involving college faculty members in the selection process, as George M. Jenks points out in his article, "Book Selection: An Approach for Small and Medium-Sized Libraries." Jenks also describes how librarians and faculty members can work together at the "weeding" stage of collection work.

Another means of being able to personally see an item before deciding to purchase it is found in the process known as "previewing." This term is used to describe the library's obtaining of a nonprint item for a limited time in order to examine it prior to a commitment to purchase. This practice also provides an opportunity to involve more than librarians in the selection process. Emily Jones, in "Forming the Committee" (Educational Film Library Association Manual), describes the role of such a committee whose membership includes: chairman, film specialist, subject area specialist, and utilization specialist. Each individual has a distinct responsibility in the process. But "previewing" is not without its problems when considered from the viewpoints of producers, distributors, or librarians. Misuses of this process are described by Phyllis Levy in her editorial entitled "The Preview Privilege." A further plea for responsible use of this privilege is presented by Diana L. Spirt in her editorial, "Practice What You Preach: Help Stop Pyramiding Prices."

This situation, where opportunities to personally examine materials prior to purchase are limited, if indeed they are available, leads one to understand why librarians rely heavily upon the reviewing tools. To use selection tools intelligently, one must understand how such tools are generated and the types of decisions that editors and reviewers face. Information collected from twenty-two editors of social science journals serves as the basis for the information presented in "A Note on the Role of the Book Review Editor as Decision Maker," by Rita James Simon and Linda Mahan. Three questions examined in this study are: what types of books are reviewed, how are reviewers selected, and how are reviews placed in the issue.

In "To Review or Not to Review," Richard K. Gardner enumerates the myriad activities connected with the publishing of Choice and describes the complexities faced by a reviewing journal. Gardner points out that reviewers are an important factor in creating such a journal. The requisites for a reviewer are delineated by Zena

Bailey Sutherland in "Book Reviews: Before & After." She elaborates on problems that reviewers face, which in turn become problems for the users of selection tools. One such dilemma is how much reviewers should tell their reader, especially when such descriptions relate to aspects of a work which may be considered controversial. Lillian Gerhardt, in her editorial "Booby-Trapped-Books--and Reviewer Responsibility," addresses the problems for selectors when reviewers remain silent about potential problem passages.

The articles in this chapter focus on many concerns faced in the selection process. Additional readings, recommended at the end of the chapter, direct the reader to further views on this topic and to ways libraries are meeting the challenges involved in the selection process.

MEDIA SELECTION: SIX CONCERNS

By Mary Frances K. Johnson

In these times of shrinking budgets and rising costs of materials, with increased competition for scarce resources, the need
seems greater than ever for competence in selection of school library materials.

The issue theme, "Media Selection and Ordering," calls to
mind several concerns that deserve further consideration by individual school librarians, consultants and administrators working at
system levels, library educators, and representatives of professional
library associations.

The need for broader provision and use of available selection
tools. For years we have deplored the gaps in availability of reliable retrospective lists of recommended materials, and in the coverage given new materials, especially those in nonprint media formats, by current reviewing media. For some years now these gaps
have been narrowing--although they are not yet closed--with publication of more of the "comprehensive" recommended lists and with increased coverage of new materials in audiovisual media formats by
reviewing journals. In spite of these gains, a real gap continues to
exist: the gap in the purchase of available selection tools at individual school and/or school system levels, and the limited extent of
their use if and when they are purchased. Too often the selection
tools and review journals purchased by the school are viewed as the
librarian's property, to be shelved in office or workroom shelves
rather than to be housed and publicized for maximum accessibility
to all users. Demands made on the bibliography collection in our
Center for Instructional Media at the University of North Carolina
at Greensboro, by practicing school media specialists and classroom
teachers enrolled in my courses, continue to reinforce my conviction that we need to invest more of our available budgets in reliable
selection tools that can support not only the selection of materials
but also, often, fuller utilization of materials once they are acquired.

The need for improved bibliographic control of nonprint media.
While great strides have been made in reviewing new audiovisual materials, in their inclusion in evaluative lists, and in the availability
of commercial cataloging and processing services for these materials,
we continue to be plagued by the lack of adequate item identification.
A particular filmstrip may be repackaged with other materials, re-
issued with changes in title or captions but not in frames (without

Reprinted by permission from Catholic Library World vol. 47, no.
10, May 1976, pp. 416-417.

identification of its origins), or made available for distribution through a film whose catalogs omit producer and copyright information. We need a standard means for identification of the item. Meanwhile, the recommendation for "preview before purchase" assumes added importance--which leads to my next point.

The need for widespread development of materials examination centers as advocated by the Educational Media Selection Centers (EMSC) Program sponsored by the National Book Committee, Inc., with funding from the U.S. Office of Education's Bureau of Research. Such centers, often serving a significant geographic area and users from many types of institutions, offer a viable means by which new (as well as retrospective) materials and related equipment can be acquired, organized, and made available for examination and evaluation. They represent, potentially, an important avenue for cooperation among many types and levels of agencies, for the good of all. The guidelines provided in the EMSC Program's two published reports[1] deserve renewed attention and increased support.

The need for broader preparation of school media specialists, at both preservice and continuing education levels, in media selection. Although library education programs are probably doing more about this concern than ever before, examples can be found almost daily of the need for fuller understanding of the characteristics of various presentation forms, as they are described by Tosti and Ball,[2] and for more closely defined criteria by which to evaluate the quality of visual representations and auditory materials. Similarly, we need to give more attention, in materials evaluation work, to the evaluation of textbooks and instructional systems, accepting the responsibility of school media specialists for participation in selection of these materials as recommended in Media Programs: District and School.[3] Effective participation in this role requires knowledge and application of "systems" approaches to appraisal of instructional materials in terms of their learning objectives, their target audiences, the consistency of approach and methodology to intent, and other such considerations. The pioneering efforts of the Educational Products Information Exchange (EPIE) in its Report series provide a useful model, and basic guidelines are developed in Report No. 54: "Improving Materials Selection Procedures: A Basic 'How To' Handbook."[4]

The need for active participation by teachers in collection building, a concern that follows from the preceding statements. The idea is far from new but it is also, in my observation, far from being realized in many situations. Teachers may be hesitant to make requests for materials because they feel inadequate in knowledge of materials or do not view the media center as a source of "teaching" materials or "don't have time"--another way of expressing the same problems. Or, they may make questionable suggestions or place demands far exceeding present budget capabilities. Whatever the particular situation, most of the media specialists with whom I work recognize the need to work further with teachers in the cooperative selection of materials. The most promising avenue, they report,

is the establishment of a media advisory committee whose membership includes representative teachers, principal, and media specialist.
Together they identify needs in the present collection, establish priorities for expenditure of funds to improve the collection, and plan
for the reevaluation of existing materials. Achievement of joint responsibility of this order, coupled with opportunities for inservice
education of teachers in materials evaluation, can lead to the development of media center collections that serve as the backbone, rather
than an enrichment source, for the instructional program. Such a
view of the collection is the subject of my final comment.

The need for a broader view of what should be represented
in a school media collection, taking into account the changing demands of the instructional program and the changing levels of maturity, awareness, and interest on the part of students. As one example, a shift to elective courses rather than a single required
course in a given subject area can mean dramatic shifts in the demands on materials. Duplicate titles once needed to support assigned
readings may now gather dust. So may materials selected from outmoded perceptions of students' need to know, or current interests,
or preferences among media formats. Continuous "audience research," to borrow Father Culkin's term, is needed to connect to
the concerns of students now. Protectionism is an unrealistic approach. So is the old notion of the "balanced" collection, in the
sense of holdings neatly distributed over classification areas, or in
the sense of prescribed ratios of different media formats. Betty
Fast discussed "unbalanced" ideas in collection development in a recent issue of Wilson Library Bulletin, presenting alternatives by
which to achieve saturation coverage for particular topics or units,
thereby demonstrating the potential contribution of the media center
collection to teaching and learning--and generating the demand for
increased budgetary provisions for essential resources. [5] Further
support for flexibility in collections is found in the 1975 standards,
Media Programs: District and School, in which the chapter on collections groups related presentation forms, including the various
types of materials and related equipment in each such category, and
presents recommendations that encourage each school to develop the
"mix" of formats most appropriate to the needs and purposes of its
user group.

References

1. Rowell, John, and Heidbreder, M. Ann. Educational Media Se-
    lection Centers; Identification and Analysis of Current Prac-
    tices. Chicago: American Library Association, 1971.
    (ALA Studies in Librarianship, No. 1).
    Bomar, Cora Paul, Heidbreder, M. Ann, and Nemeyer,
    Carol. Guide to the Development of Educational Media Selec-
    tion Centers. Chicago: American Library Association,
    1973. (ALA Studies in Librarianship, No. 4).
2. Tosti, Donald T., and Ball, John R. "A Behavioral Approach
    to Instructional Design and Media Selection," AV Communica-

tion Review 17 (Spring 1969): 5-25.
3. American Association of School Librarians and Association for Educational Communications and Technology. Media Programs: District and School. Chicago: American Library Association; Washington, D.C.: Association for Educational Communications and Technology, 1975.
4. "Improving Materials Selection Procedures: A Basic 'How to' Approach, " EPIE Educational Product Report, No. 54 (June 1973).
5. Fast, Betty. "Mediacentric, " Wilson Library Bulletin 50 (January 1976): 370-71.

FOCUS: RECENT DEVELOPMENTS
IN MATERIALS SELECTION

By Division of Library Development and Services,
Maryland State Department of Education

Writing in Metropolitan Public Library Users, page 102, Mary
Lee Bundy said in 1968, "Book selection policies and practices, in
particular, need review in terms of subject orientation, type of reading fare, and level of reading." The need for such review is under-
scored by the proposed public library goals-feasibility study coordinated by Allie Beth Martin. The section on page 34 on selection policies in "A Strategy for Public Library Change" states, "The concepts of selecting what is 'best,' of relying on time-worn book selection policies, of pre-selection for all libraries in a system by co-
ordinators or by committees, of selection from so-called 'standard'
selection aids and lists--all are in question."

Some of the questions relating to materials selection that are
relevant to libraries in Maryland are:

How does the selection policy reflect the objectives of the library or parent institution?

How does value influence selection and how is value determined?

What effect do user demands have upon selection policy?

If user demands are important, how are they to be identified
and evaluated and then applied to selection procedure?

What levels and types of materials are appropriate for Network
borrowing, and how does this relate to local selection policies?

The selection of materials in Maryland's Public Libraries and
School Library Media Centers is a complex process that involves librarians in a consideration of not just the materials, themselves,
but also the specific communities, curriculums, or users that the
materials are intended to serve.

Economic factors have compounded the problem of developing
library collections. Book, periodical, and audiovisual prices have
risen dramatically and, along with expenditures for salaries, materials expenditures are subject to the pressures of economizing re-

Reprinted from Library Keynotes, vol. 7, no. 6, October 1977, pp.
1-3, by permission of the Division of Library Development and Services, Maryland State Department of Education.

sulting from increasingly stringent budget allocations. Library systems may find it difficult to justify the costly expenditure of time and staff required by an elaborate and thoroughgoing evaluation procedure.

School systems generally need a series of careful evaluation procedures because they must assure that the materials which they select correspond to the local curriculum, the needs of students, and the needs of the local community.

The job of rethinking the subject of materials selection is more than can be undertaken in a single issue of the Newsletter. What will be attempted is to describe present approaches to materials selection and highlight the development of the selection process in both public library and school library media center settings.

Public Libraries

How should a public library determine which materials to buy?

Many librarians have held to the ideal of the well-rounded collection. Robert N. Broadus, in Selecting Materials for Libraries, pages 24 and 25, has stated:

> The real goal is to build an optimum collection for a given community of users or ought-to-be users. In such a library, it would be the part of common sense to have a few books which appeal to each interest, rather than to fatten up one area too fast.... In order to be fair and to insure the presentation of as much truth as possible, there should be some materials on all sides of controversial issues.

The increasing cost of maintaining such a collection has led to the development of additional ways to satisfy interests. One such way involves developing a profile of actual user behavior that will help identify a user's ability to get a book when it is wanted and focus on the results of library activities.

Recent surveys have indicated that most requests for library books are concentrated in a small percentage of the collection. Richard L. Trueswell has observed in academic libraries that about 20 per cent of the collection accounted for 80 per cent of the use. Stanley J. Slote in studies of public libraries in New Jersey and New York showed that 20 per cent of the collection accounted for 70 per cent of book usage. Some of Maryland's libraries are trying to grapple with the implications of such findings.

Baltimore County Public Library

During the fifties and sixties, the Baltimore County Public Li-

brary operated under a traditional materials selection policy--sub-
scribing to the Greenaway plan and having examination copies of books
and other materials for staff review and evaluation. There was fairly strong branch autonomy in ordering, and materials were divided into three age level categories--children, young adult, and adult.
(Staff specialists existed for each age level and the selection process
might be further refined by assigning materials to persons specializ-
ing in fiction, 200's, 600's, and so on.)

By the end of the sixties and during the early seventies, preparation of staff reviews had been primarily reduced to controversial
materials and centralized ordering of high demand materials, as well
as standing orders was being practiced. By 1975-76 prepublication
expenditures accounted for about six per cent of the adult book budget.

Fiscal Year 1976 marked the planning stage for a change in
the system's approach to the selection of materials. Thinking about
its relationship to the community clarified Baltimore County Public
Library's perception of itself as a public service agency. The more
often library users can be served the better the chance that the library is performing its public service role satisfactorily.

In order to serve people better, BCPL has chosen to concentrate on what people are actually reading. By Fiscal Year 1977, 50
per cent of all adult titles were being centrally purchased. Selection
was based on a formula that considered predictions of what users
would actually be reading and the experience of the system's branch
libraries. By Fiscal Year 1978 the system hopes to have all new
hardbacks centrally purchased, with 85 per cent of its adult material
determined by formula. They are also working to insure that 80 per
cent of the paperback books will be centrally selected.

The implications of such a policy for selection are that purchasing decisions are being based upon a buying formula and actual
use as reflected by circulation. The wide-ranging interests of the
users are reflected in the 7,400 new adult titles added during Fiscal
Year 1976. An average patron in Baltimore County has a 33 per
cent chance of getting a specific title immediately, and 92 per cent
of all identified requests for specific adult titles are owned by the
system.

As the system is refined, the chance of immediately getting a
specific title will improve. Instead of being overwhelmed by user
demand for an everbroadening range of titles, BCPL has actually seen
fewer titles purchased and an increase in the number of copies of a
given title.

Economic factors of the new approach to selection include economy in book purchasing because of the ability to predict the order
for a given title, a reduction in travel and personnel costs, and a
reduction in other behind-the-scenes costs. In short, for BCPL the
changes in the selection procedure have provided the means to continue to provide an adequate level of public service.

Charles County Public Library

The Charles County Public Library system in Southern Maryland has undertaken a shelf list survey to identify what parts of its collection are being used; and it has also conducted a user survey to determine what people are coming to the library to find, if they found it, and their degree of satisfaction with the library's services. As a result of the survey, requests that usually go unidentified (people who walk in the library, do not find what they are looking for, and walk out without alerting library staff to the request) were uncovered, and it was determined that about 93 per cent of all specific book titles sought were owned by the tri-county system. A user's chance of immediately getting a particular title was 44 per cent. Of specified requests, about 44 per cent were filled immediately, 12 per cent were placed on reserve, 15 per cent were requested through interlibrary loan. Of special concern to the system were the approximately 30 per cent of requests that remain unfilled.

Now that present library performance has been determined, the Charles County Public Library will apply techniques of book selection that have been shown by researchers to improve library performance without increasing costs. Special attention will be given to the increased purchase of duplicate materials, as well as to the purchase of paperbacks. Library users will be resurveyed to discover the actual effects of the selection techniques.

Regional Library Resource Centers

As addressed in the Master Plan, "By 1976, the specific needs of each region will have been determined, and subsequent allocations should be made on a need-and-use basis rather than on a pre-determined formula."

Since 1976, the regional libraries have set about to discover the information needs of people in their service areas and the users' behavior in using the regional libraries' services. The regional libraries' service programs emphasize the interlibrary loan (ILL) function because: (1) the household surveys showed that people are interested more in borrowing materials than in other existing library services; (2) the local library administrators have given the function the highest priority; and (3) the regional libraries play an important role in the statewide interlibrary loan network.

An analysis of specific book requests received showed that the requests through interlibrary loan are mostly for current popular materials. The majority of requests are in 10 categories and 50 per cent of the requests are for materials published within the past five years. (See accompanying table, "Regional Library Resource Center...")

An analysis of unfilled requests at the regional level indicated that 50 per cent of the unfilled requests were for materials owned by

Regional Library Resource Center
Author/Title Requests Grouped by Subject Category

Fiscal Year 1976

Eastern Shore		Southern Maryland		Western Maryland	
Fiction	29%	Fiction	23%	Fiction	21%
Philology and		Philology and		Social Sciences	9%
Literature	7%	Literature	8%	Technology	6%
Social Sciences	6%	Social Sciences	7%	Religion	5%
Religion	5%	Medicine	5%	Medicine	5%
Fine Arts	5%	Education	5%	Psychology	5%
Medicine	5%	Science	5%	Philology and	
Biography	4%	Technology	5%	Literature	5%
History, World	4%	History, American	4%	Agriculture	4%
History, American	3%	Fine Arts	4%	Geography and	
Technology	3%	Recreation	4%	Recreation	4%
				Fine Arts	4%

the regional library. The unavailable materials already were in circulation. Also, analysis showed that a significant per cent of the
books placed on reserve eventually are canceled, resulting in unfilled
requests. The canceled reserve problem is particularly pernicious
because it is probable that most canceled reserves might have been
filled by another library in the network or by purchase at the regional
level if the requests had not been reserved.

An analysis of the use of the Western Maryland Regional Library collection in meeting ILL requests for specific titles showed
that the regional collection of 20,000 volumes filled more requests
than the host library collection of more than 100,000 volumes.

Using the data gathered for the analyses mentioned above, the
regional libraries have tried to improve their performance and provide better service. After only a few months of applying some different techniques for book selection, performance levels have improved
by as much as 40 per cent without an increase in expenditures.

School Library Media Centers

The Office of School Library Media Services has been working
with local school systems to develop selection policies and procedures.
Staff members of the Office have stressed the responsibility of each
local education agency in developing and adopting a written policy statement covering the selection and adoption of textbooks and instructional
materials. According to the Guidelines for the Evaluation and Selection of Instructional Materials, the following elements should be included in the policy statement:

The nature and scope of collections

The governing body legally responsible for the operation of the
review and selection program

The specific role(s) of the person(s) responsible for the coordination of the selection of materials

The objectives of the selection of materials

The types of materials for consideration

The criteria for the evaluation and selection of materials

The selection sources for use as guides in the selection of materials

The procedure for the selection of textbooks and instructional
materials

The procedure for handling gifts, loans, rentals, and free materials

The procedure for handling challenged materials

The process for the reevaluation of materials in existing collections

To date, 23 of the systems have adopted selection policy statements.

The local education agencies in the metropolitan area have developed the most extensive approaches to selection. Montgomery County has been chosen as an example of a complex metropolitan system. Other local systems or private schools have an opportunity to expand their selection capability by using the services provided by the Review and Evaluation Center in the Anne Arundel County Department of Education

Montgomery County Public Schools

The Montgomery County Public Schools have developed a highly organized and sophisticated system of materials selection whose primary function as stated on page six of Evaluation and Selection of Instructional Materials and Equipment "... is to support the curriculum and to meet the individual needs of students as encompassed in the Educational Goals for the Montgomery County Public Schools. "

All books are evaluated and approved prior to their addition to the collection. The criteria reflect current cultural values, as interpreted by the education profession, by considering the material's relevance, its coverage of women and minority groups, and its consideration of controversial issues.

A significant aspect of the service provided by the Department of Educational Media and Technology are annotated bibliographies such as People, an annotated multiethnic bibliography K-12, Being Black in America, and Sexism. During the past school year (1976-1977) a series of programs highlighting various ethnic groups was conducted for school personnel. The programs represent an attempt at consciousness raising and also serve to make users aware of materials which exist on a particular ethnic group.

Montgomery County attends the student needs in the selection process by stressing on page five of Evaluation and Selection, "materials should be evaluated by those who are to use them ... (and) materials must be evaluated and selected cooperatively by teachers, principals, librarians, and students, using standard, uniform criteria ... to be supplemented by school-adopted policies. " They do more than pay lip service to student involvement as indicated on page seven of Evaluation and Selection by providing "An allotment of 15 per cent of these funds for new materials will be designated for student requested materials. "

Review and Evaluation Center

The Review and Evaluation Center in the Anne Arundel County
Board of Education building was established by agreement of the Media Services Division of the Anne Arundel County School System and
the Maryland State Department of Education, Division of Library Development and Services, on June 30, 1975. It is an example of a
"shop before you buy" approach to materials selection and concentrates on current materials, including:

— Curriculum-related books,
— Textbooks,
— Trade books,
— 16mm films,
— Kits.

The Center provides a setting where education personnel and
others can evaluate materials, and it also has available a "placemat"
with selection criteria. Copies of reviews are provided for individual items that have been reviewed by Anne Arundel County staff or
by the professional review media.

Because the Center concentrates on providing current materials and because it does not include a circulating collection, it functions as an aid to the selection process. It exemplifies a coordinated
warehousing of materials that may require more thorough evaluation
than is possible by means of a review.

An on-site review committee which evaluated the operation of
the Center during January of this year complimented the Center for
the way it handles materials:

> The Review and Evaluation Center is to be commended for
> the excellent quantity and apparent high quality of the media
> that are available for review and evaluation. Materials
> are openly displayed, organized into curriculum support
> areas, and intershelved to promote their examination.

The Committee went on to suggest changes that might be made
in the handling of material and the Center has taken the following action:

Shelving of material by the producer.

Labeling of shelves to permit quicker and more efficient retrieval of individual items.

Using pressure sensitive labels to provide clearer identification
of materials. (One color denotes materials appropriate to
levels K-8, another color denotes those items that have been
evaluated by an Anne Arundel County evaluation committee, and
another color denotes the date items must leave the Center.)

The range of materials represented in the Center puts severe strain on the limited physical resources, but Rose Cardamone, the Center's director, and the Center staff manage to perform admirably despite the limitations. Over 250 publishers are represented and there are currently more than 2,000 nonprint items and 700 textbooks in the collection. In addition to these materials, users of the Center have access to trade books from over 60 publishers.

Conclusion

In addition to arranging for the direct inspection of materials, the Office of School Library Media Services is working to assist media personnel throughout the state to develop and use sound selection procedures. The Office accomplishes this through the provision of Statewide Workshops on the Selection and Evaluation of Materials (See Keynotes, August 1977) and by working with individual county systems.

DREAMERS AND EDUCATIONAL MEDIA SELECTION CENTERS:
A REPORT IN PROGRESS

By Mary Virginia Gaver

A real skeptic, in describing the work of the "Educational
Media Selection Centers Project," might well begin by stating that
the two publications issued to date describe the notions of a bunch
of educational dreamers, since the first publication[1] proved that almost nothing really exists that exemplifies their dream and the second
publication[2] describes a network that is still a gleam in the eye of
Russell Shank, Frances Henne, and the rest of the EMSC staff and
advisers. As time passes, the likelihood that the dream will ever
become reality fades as the National Book Committee, sponsor of the
project, reorganizes its office and takes on other priorities, President Nixon and Congress continue to squabble over funding of education and libraries, and budgets for the National Institute of Education,
the U.S. Office of Education, and local and State library agencies become ever more restricted.

However, educational reality also demonstrates again and again
that the existence of a real need felt by enough people will eventually
result in some kind of an agency to meet the need, despite administrative intransigence or financial limitations. If, for the moment at
least, this last assumption is accepted, then let us consider the objectives of an EMSC and what the two publications (particularly the
latest one) have to say to the profession. For, be assured, the need
is real and some sort of an EMSC will be provided; the question is
will it really meet the need and be as effectively set up as it ought to
be?

As evidence of the widely recognized need for an EMSC agency, examine the list of advisory committee members and the associations they represented. These members faithfully contributed their
best thinking and active participation to numerous meetings over a
considerable period of time in order to bring about the Guide to the
Development of Educational Media Selection Centers. A broad range
of educational associations were included, from the Rural Education
Association to the National Science Teachers Association, and outstanding individual representatives such as Alexander Frazier for the Association for Supervision and Curriculum Development and Joseph Becker
for the American Society for Information Sciences participated, to select only a few examples. Representation of the American Library
Association was provided by the author; Frances Henne served as vice-
chairman of the advisory committee with Mason Gross (then President

of Rutgers) as chairman, for the National Book Committee. Evidence of the need is shown further by the proliferation, during the period of heavy federal funding, of a variety of kinds of educational laboratories, curriculum study centers, and centers for special education programs (the handicapped, the exceptional, vocational, regional and intermediate units, and the like), many of which incorporate in varying degrees specific aspects of the "educational media selection centers" concept.

It is well-known that the EMSC Project was set up in four phases: 1) to find out what existed; 2) to set guidelines for what ought to exist; 3) to strengthen or establish several agencies to the level of the guidelines, for demonstration purposes; and 4) to evaluate the demonstrations and reassess the job to be done. Originally, it was anticipated that the publication of the report on the second phase would be the signal for establishing one or more demonstration projects and continuing the four-phase plan of action. Instead, since the second report was issued in the spring of 1973, only one real review has appeared, [3] and the staff at the National Book Committee which had taken the most interest in and responsibility for the project is now absorbed in other activities and responsibilities.

Exactly what is an Educational Media Selection Center? The first 1971 report described it as: "1) a comprehensive collection of teaching and learning resources which serves as a depository for examination and selection, and 2) a place where in-service training programs are conducted."[4] Key words in this statement are "collection of ... resources," "depository," and "in-service training." Their full meaning needs to be understood for real comprehension of the difference between what the Guide describes and the reality that many librarians and educators see.

Who are or who will be the potential users of an EMSC as described by the Guide? There is no one nice neat list, but the text of both reports indicates that users fall into two categories:

Professional:

educators of all kinds and specialties, including adult educators;
librarians of all types of libraries;
library school faculty and students;
classroom teachers;
administrators of many kinds of agencies--local, State, national, public and private;
publishers, especially editors;
authors;
social workers, etc.

Community workers:

adults working with civic, religious, labor, or other private or volunteer agencies;
organizations and clubs which sponsor youth-serving, informal educational activities and projects;

adult educators;
public officials, etc.

Perhaps a further sense of what an EMSC is or can be will be made clear by stating what it is not intended to be:

It is not a source for borrowing or circulation for any of the groups listed above (note the key word depository).

It is not a district selection center to be used as a central distribution source for the district (an agency with a different purpose entirely).

It is not a collection of books or other materials donated by publishers. (Note the chapter in the Guide on the collection, indicating the importance of a policy for selection of what needs to be evaluated.)

Its "parent agency" is not limited to school or public libraries but can be a college or State library agency or any two or more such agencies.

Since Cox in his review has described thoroughly the contents of the 1973 report on the EMSC Guide, those details will not be repeated here except to point out that this report describes "a logically sequenced collection of data beginning with the rationale for the development of educational media selection centers and concluding with the networking of centers into a national system." Each chapter carefully outlines the main points of the respective aspects of operation and function and can only be understood in the "light of its predecessors and the final culmination in a national network."[5] It should be pointed out, too, that although specific chapters are not credited to a particular author, areas of responsibility are noted in the "List of Contributors and Topics" and include some of the most important names in education and librarianship. The most significant chapters, for this reviewer, are those on collections, program and network.

Many present agencies which call themselves "selection centers" exist primarily on the philanthropy of publishers, or are geared to provide a selection service in a highly specialized subject field such as vocations or special education, or are limited to current publications only, or have few facets of in-service education, called an essential throughout both publications. Collections are frequently not supported by continuing budgets sufficient to insure that those media which need to be studied and evaluated are in fact provided, or they have been haphazardly gathered without a systematic policy. Therefore, the section on "Media Collections" lists factors which must be considered in developing a policy, an adequate budget, and in stating the purposes and parameters of the center's collection. Policies are suggested for a retrospective collection, a current collection, the needed reference and periodical collections, and for acquisition, organization and housing of materials. Noting the broad range of possibilities, the point of view is expressed that a center must do more than "simply 'recognize' both print and audiovisual materials"; directors "who embrace both print and audiovisual concepts" will therefore be essential.

Perhaps one of the most revolutionary concepts of the document lies in this chapter: the principle that such collections must be acquired primarily by purchase. This principle may prove traumatic to many librarians if it means their source of free copies of books is to dry up suddenly, with publishers requiring that all books be paid for! It is well known that free copies of audiovisual media are practically impossible to obtain, particularly the more expensive formats. The expectation that publishers, producers, and (indirectly) authors will subsidize a network of educational media selection centers around the country (in every State? within 30 minutes driving time for each teacher? for Girl Scout leaders?) is as unrealistic as the current practice of free copying of recordings and cassettes--also a totally unrealistic (and in this case, illegal) infringement of the rights of both publishers and authors. Many publishers, however, are loath to take the necessary steps to bring this practice to a halt, and in only a few cases (and then with much difficulty, as in the State of Pennsylvania) have budgets been established for purchase of the needed collections of media.

In the section on program, a number of disparate elements are brought together, all, however, geared to bringing the resources of the center to focus on a wide variety of users, all emphasizing and illustrating the strong element of in-service education to which the Guide frequently refers. Reference and consultant service is considered to be an important element, and examples are given of the kinds and levels of such service in different situations. The obligation for evaluation of media is obvious, and the discussion shows the considerable attention paid to a definition of evaluation and its differentiation from selection by the authors, consultants, and advisory committee members for the Guide. The instructional program as an essential element in in-service education is discussed in considerable detail, as are its components; identification of needs significant to the users, involvement of users in planning the training program, and identification of objectives. Possibilities for research, program review and evaluation, and communications and public relations--aspects in which existing centers are very weak--are also considered essential to the program of a media selection center and are specified in some detail, in relation to the peculiar characteristics of selection centers.

Throughout this section, constant reference is made to the role of the professional and supporting staff. As selection centers are presently set up, this role is too frequently ignored or provision for it is totally inadequate. The program of an EMSC is an area of potential impact in which most existing centers still have a long way to go. It is, however, essential to the basic justification for such centers.

The truly original concept which this report presents is in the

section on networks. While the committee owes a great debt to
Russell Shank, director of libraries for the Smithsonian Institution,
for his role in developing this chapter, the concept as it relates to
educational media selection centers is one which has been cherished
and espoused for years by Frances Henne, now of Columbia University. Her work in helping to establish the Children's Book Center
and its evaluation program at the University of Chicago is an example of her foresight in developing one unit which can play a significant role in a future network. While this valuable center does not
embody all the concepts outlined in the Guide, it has vital poten-
tiality for contributing to the kind of network described by Shank in
the closing chapter. He describes levels of a network graphically
and in text, details network operations, and differentiates the roles
and functions of a national center and of regional, State and local
centers. The figures provided in this chapter (of which one example
is shown on page 656) are especially helpful in visualizing the national network concept and its relation to a National Laboratory System.

This network chapter and the supporting sections of the Guide
which lead up to it are indeed no "pie in the sky" reveries. Many
of the elements of a network already exist and could feasibly be
brought together, although not overnight, of course. That such a
network could make a major contribution to the improvement of education in the 1970s and 1980s should be evident to anyone who has
kept up with developing educational thought. Such differing sources
as Shane's study on The Educational Significance of the Future[6] and
Keppel's report on The Mohonk Conference[7] attest to the necessity
of incorporating into programs of educational development effective
consideration of instructional materials centers and their contribution to the continuing education of teachers (and other youth-serving
occupational groups). The funding of Phases III and IV of the EMSC
Project and other steps in the development of the recommended network of centers appear to be essential elements in the educational
establishment of the future. However, funding of the next two phases
of the EMSC Project is at a crucial stage. Guidelines or standards
seldom are implemented without an active and aggressive program
of action for such implementation, and indeed unless there is some
source of reasonably adequate funding available to motivate such implementation. There are skeptics who question whether the Guide
describes an agency which is feasible, or indeed possible to realize.
An evaluation in the State of Pennsylvania by staff members of the
State Department of Education of the three "branches" of the State
school library agency illustrated both the problems and the possibilities. [8]

The State of Pennsylvania in 1966, under the leadership of
John Rowell, then director of school libraries in Pennsylvania, established three branches of its State agency designed to serve as educational media selection centers for the three major regions of the
State--in suburban Upper Darby for the east, in Harrisburg for the
center of the State, and in Pittsburgh for the west. The western
branch is the only one with its own building; the central branch is
housed in an office building near the Statehouse, and the eastern

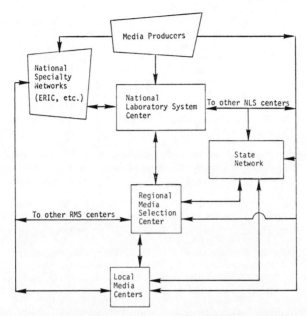

Model of a national media selection network with paths of communication combined and integrated. (From Guide to the Development of Educational Media Selection Centers.)

branch is in a large office building shared with other agencies, close to the end of the Philadelphia subway line. Collections are purchased annually with, since fiscal 1970, a modest allocation added to the book appropriations for the acquisition of non-print media. A model budget for this kind of operation is illustrated in an Appendix to the Guide. 9 Staff at present consists of at least one professional in each branch, with Elizabeth Hoffman, the present State director, Division of School Library Services, having to carry direct responsibility for the branch in Harrisburg. In the announcement brochure for the branches it is stated that:

> Professional consultatives ... will include assistance to local education agencies in: evaluation of current instructional materials collections; short and long-range planning for acquisitions of instructional materials consistent with the educational programs of the local education agencies; administration, organization, and use of instructional materials; selection of instructional materials, effective planning of quarters, staff utilization, and scheduling of libraries. 10

A fourth branch is to open soon in Wilkes-Barre, with quarters and staff provided by Intermediate School Unit XVIII. Materials, however, will be provided by the State, under Mrs. Hoffman's supervision. Intermediate Unit XVIII represents a combination of twelve school districts. Use of the center in Wilkes-Barre has been made mandatory for school personnel within these districts, but services will be offered to other interested units in that region as desired. These four branches can provide only very thin coverage for a State the size of Pennsylvania. The eastern branch (in Upper Darby) is about to be moved to one of two Philadelphia institutions of higher education which, it is expected, will assume responsibility for personnel and quarters while the State, through Mrs. Hoffman, provides the materials collection and supervision. This tie to the State will provide essential funding for purchase of materials and assurance of in-service education programs for education personnel.

Briefly summarized, the "Cost and Service Study" was carried out as the result of a recommendation by The Governor's Review of Government Management Report "to determine if the present arrangement should be terminated or replaced and also [to evaluate] the program's total effectiveness and alternative approaches." Data from sign-in logs, a survey instrument, and financial reports were analyzed. The authors of the report summarized their findings as follows:

The number of visits from a school district's geographic proximity to the center.

At least 5,980 people visited the centers from January to December 1971, and 3,292 of these were from public schools in assigned areas.

The survey indicated that over half the school districts send representatives to the centers; only about 30 per cent would use a central facility; most are satisfied with current center operation related to Title II funds; very few visits were made by an employee of the center; and the school districts would like more service.

The cost of operating a center is between $33,000 and $45,000 (includes salaries but not cost of collections) annually.[11]

Some implications of the findings may be of interest. Distance is not the only geographic factor affecting use: access to parking facilities or easy public transportation, convenient eating facilities, and the character of the neighborhood all have some influence in determining accessibility--and the Pennsylvania branches are all affected negatively to some extent by these concerns. Of course, some use by non-school personnel occurred at the branches; 2,698 were either non-school, public library users and/or out-of-State visitors. Also the voluntary character of the use is perhaps a factor, although one would like to think that a strong public information program could do more than mandate use. Among the findings of the survey noted above, a particularly interesting implication is the assump-

tion by the surveyors that visitation to the schools by the center
staff was important; however, such activity could hardly be expected
with no more than one professional to a branch.

Alternatives considered by the surveyors were to 1) increase
service, 2) decrease service, or 3) maintain service at its present
level, with costs being increased, decreased or achieving some level
of stability respectively. Under increase of service the report identified sixteen intermediate units in the State which need more service,
some of them possibly by a mobile unit. Other intermediate units
could be encouraged to develop and support their own examination centers; this action is currently underway in Wilkes-Barre. The surveyors also noted that a third way to increase service would be
through an increase of staff and size of the current operation, allowing State employees more time to work in the field--an alternative,
however, which would not benefit remote schools. The cost of the
fourth alternative--to increase the number of branches--can be estimated by data provided in the report.

Any consideration of decrease in service would have to be
based on the assumption that a school can make good use of Title II
allocations without examination centers--an alternative which few
among either education or library groups would defend. A decrease
might also be effected by maintaining one large central center with
enough staff to provide in-service activities for the whole State.
However, this might not effect a cost reduction and certainly would
not promote accessibility.

No recommendation for action is made in this report. It
simply provides data for making a sound decision. The State would
appear at present to be moving ahead on the basis of maintaining
present operations in the three branches, plus encouraging development of centers by intermediate units. However, this whole operation, including its budget for materials, is based on the availability
of federal funds under ESEA Title II, which can be allocated under
the State plan for the materials budgets of the centers. The Pennsylvania experience so far demonstrates the need for careful and
long-range planning, the problems of geographical access, the need
for regular funding of collections, and the problems and difficulties
of building up a program of in-service education. The fact that
funding has persisted for so long has undoubtedly been due to the un-
tiring work of the State Director of School Library Services and the
availability of federal funds. There must also be, although this was
not measured by the surveyors, a sizable base of public and professional support which has maintained the centers through many ups
and downs in a very political State.

A number of questions, not within the purview of the Pennsylvania study, remain to be asked and answered:

Why is it so consistently difficult to have centers used by non-
school groups? Even the level of impact reported by the Pennsylvania study is relatively low and high in cost on a per user/visitor
basis.

How can use by individuals be motivated rather than use almost entirely by groups, workshops or institutes?

How can use be motivated by non-school personnel such as social workers, Girl Scout leaders, religious education personnel, and the like?

How far will people travel to make use of an EMSC? Some research has been carried out to determine the distance factor in relation to public library use; to what extent do the findings of this research apply to the EMSC, a somewhat different kind of agency?[12]

How can the need for adequate staff be demonstrated--professional, technician, and other kinds of supportive personnel--especially in the absence of special funds for staff? Most centers established to date have been so limited in staff that they have not only been handicapped in program-impact (as is true in Pennsylvania) but also have in other cases been criticized for tying up skilled consultant staff in duties more properly assigned to bibliographic assistants.

How can the value of evaluation of materials be demonstrated? Evaluation, which is peculiar to the selection center concept, is not a function which has the kind of face validity that can with ease be objectively justified, yet the flood of material demands some kind of screening before effective use can take place in schools and other institutions and agencies. Plans for district centers which serve other functions similar to a selection center--but not the full role of evaluation--have been prevalent in the literature for at least a decade and in some cases have already been successfully implemented.[13] For these and other reasons, it may be that the most needed or feasible next step is the implementation of the "National Laboratory Systems Center" as depicted and recommended in the Guide.

To conclude, the Guide to the Development of Educational Media Selection Centers describes a well thought out plan for a network of agencies still largely at the innovative stage, amenable to implementation by a variety of library agencies--centers essential, in my opinion, to the achievement of a high level of education for the next generation of young people. The funding of Phase III of the project, so that the concept can be demonstrated at an effective level and tested by further evaluation is essential.

References

1. John Rowell and M. Ann Heidbreder. Educational Media Selection Centers: Identification and analysis of current practices. Chicago: American Library Association, 1971. (ALA Studies in Librarianship, Number 1.)
2. Cora Paul Bomar, M. Ann Heidbreder and Carol A. Nemeyer. Guide to the Development of Educational Media Selection Cen-

ters. Chicago: American Library Association, 1973. (ALA Studies in Librarianship, Number 4.)

3. Carl T. Cox. "Current Research," School Media Quarterly, 2 (Fall 1973), pp. 60-63.

4. Rowell, op. cit., p. 4.

5. Cox, op. cit., p. 61.

6. Harold G. Shane. The Educational Significance of the Future: A Report prepared for Sydney P. Marland (Contract No. OEC-0-0354). Washington, D.C.: World Future Society. (Box 30369, Bethesda Station 22014. $3.)

7. Francis Keppel, ed. The Mohonk Conference: A Report on an International Symposium on the Role of Books and Other Educational Materials in Meeting the Educational and Economic Goals of Developed and Developing Countries. N.Y.: National Book Committee, 1973.

8. Pennsylvania. State Department of Education. "Cost and Service Study/Eastern, Central and Western Branches/Division of School Library Services/Bureau of Instructional Support Services." January 1973, 32p. mimeo.

9. Bomar, op. cit., p. 95-97.

10. Pennsylvania. Department of Public Instruction. "Central Area Branch." (One was issued for each area.)

11. Pennsylvania, "Cost and Service Study....," op. cit., p. vi.

12. Thomas Shaughnessy. "The Influence of Distance and Travel Time on Central Library Use." Ph.D. thesis, Rutgers University, New Brunswick, N.J., 1970.

13. See, for example, Jack L. Tanzman and others, "A Study to Explore the Role and Feasibility of a Regional Educational Communications Center." Plainview, N.Y., Plainview-Old Bethpage Public Schools, June 1964. (Report No. NDEA VIIB-353. Office of Education. Contract OEC3-16-D42.)

APPROVAL PLAN PURCHASING IN PERSPECTIVE

By Margaret Dobbyn

Approval plan purchasing of domestic current publications is dynamic evidence of the conditions which have developed in academic libraries during a period of affluence, conditions which have made this method of purchasing possible. In evaluating approval plan purchasing the questions to consider are whether it is economical compared to other methods, and whether it supplies the library with needed materials. Although the purposes behind purchasing books for libraries should be clearly defined on the basis of needs or goals, the goals are often described as "stated educational objectives" and "established program goals,"[1] or "maintaining current research strength,"[2] or "most academic librarians today agree...."[3] It has become an assumption without attempts at explanation (indeed, who can explain it) among research librarians that the goals are to acquire everything possible of a "scholarly nature." Even "scholarly" is often defined only nebulously due to the assumption that everyone knows what scholarly is. Another rationalization is reflected in the attitude that anything in print can be discerned or distorted to have some measure of research value to someone at sometime for some unknown reason which the future alone will disclose. In this way actions and explanations are based on remote possibilities removing the librarian further from the reality of decision-making.

As goals become more difficult to define, needs impossible to assess, and criteria for scholarship deteriorate into being exemplified by what is published or printed, advances in understanding approval plan purchasing are not evident although this simple method of purchasing came about due to stress situations which developed in academic libraries' acquisitions departments.[4] The most specific cause of this stress was, of course, the rapid increase in book funds which had placed heavy burdens on many acquisition departments. Although staffs had increased somewhat as the book funds had grown, the staff increases were often viewed to be insufficient compared to the book fund increases. Others attribute the growth of approval plans to the pressures caused by poor business techniques and technical services procedures.[5] Whatever the causes for the stress, approval plan purchasing of current domestic publications gave promise of relieving this pressure on acquisition departments.

Along with the immediate stress situation, other factors contributing to the increase of funds can be traced to increases in expectations, all stemming from growth of population and affluence. Colleges expanded to include graduate programs and universities expanded to include more and more subject areas of research and graduate programs. Standards of criteria based on numbers of volumes per student and faculty were developed.[6] University administrations frequently assigned prestige and salary according to research and number of publications, thus creating a climate in which graduates and faculty pressure the library to have everything they might want immediately available in order to publish before they perish. Ironically, the tremendous influx of material in print is partly due to the pressures to publish (along with an available market!) spurred on by an exaggerated reverence toward research, and competition among scholars to get the papers and books into print.

The attitudes of the accrediting agencies have been sympathetic to the goal of supplying scholars with all needed materials. They produced systems of counting numbers and volumes and numbers of subscriptions (and gaps in periodical runs!) for each individual library. In short, these agencies have exerted their own unique pressure on the academic system.[7]

As the various pressures operate throughout the system, the library has become the machine for adding as many volumes and subscriptions to each library as book funds will allow. Initiating orders in such quantities became impossible for the busy faculty; consequently, the teaching faculty released more and more of the responsibility for selection to the librarian and thereby shifted this burden to another desk. The librarian in turn, as noted above, has generally centered the problem in the acquisitions department.

From the agents' view, a plan to supply books for libraries had to be based on the expectation of broad comprehensive coverage in order to justify a library adopting the approval concept and discontinuing the former procedure of placing bids or scattered orders among many suppliers. The book agent surveying the above conditions in academic libraries in 1966 logically reached the conclusion that he would be able to capture the bulk of the domestic book market and make a profit by capitalizing on the librarian's goals of comprehensiveness, inefficient procedures, and a lowering of criteria toward judgment and selectivity. So he sold his approval plan package to librarians who were also anxious to move the problem onto another desk, thereby eliminating some of the pressures exerted on the acquisitions department.[8]

The approval plan contract, once entered into, needs to be defended because an acquisition program geared to an approval plan can no longer be based on needs or values. Discussions of approval plan purchasing of domestic current publications generally center on the questions of economy, selection of materials, and speed of availability of materials. While some insist that it is an economically efficient way of procuring books, others insist that it is not.[9] Those who advocate that selection is more valuable with the book in hand, know that very little selection takes place after the books arrive, and that redundancy, duplication, and an increasing rate of obsolescence are evident in the mass of print so purchased. The fact is ignored that the percentage of unscholarly material that is added during the process clutters the catalogs and shelves and is available to the unsuspecting student.[10] The literature even presents various justifications for turning over the selection of what is needed by the university library to a businessman, whose primary interest in the academic community is profit.

Those who argue that the speed of availability is an important benefit of approval plan purchasing neglect the fact that this is actually not important for the great majority of books so purchased. Then too, after receipt many volumes are held up for cataloging and processing, negating in most instances the supposed value of speedy receipt.

As economy and speed become the focal points on which to judge approval plan purchasing, the assumption that every academic library needs all of this material is difficult to bring to the forefront and relate to goals, unless, of course, the goals of academic libraries have become truly broad, comprehensive coverage insofar as funds will permit with a deterioration of criteria on scholarship. In other words, the goals seem to have become, in reality, "add volumes" and hope that if enough volumes are added, broad, comprehensive coverage will result.

It is interesting to view Price's logistics curve as related to the future additions of vast quantities of volumes in libraries. Price states that "In the real world nothing grows and grows until it reaches infinity. Rather, exponential growth eventually reaches some limit, at which the process must slacken and stop before reaching absurdity."[11] Hope may exist that something will happen in libraries to prevent the continuous addition of volumes toward absurdity.[12] Leveling off may occur, but for a time the logistics curve will show signs of fluctuation due to efforts to preserve the status quo. Indications are that recent decreases in funds may have already affected the curve.[13] If Mason is correct in regard to economics, attitudes toward approval plan purchasing will change as librarians begin to experience less affluence.[14] Perhaps then we can get down to the business of examining more intelligently Urquhart's first law: The library exists to meet the needs of the user as economically as possible, and find more economical ways to serve the scholar.[15]

It is well known that problems proliferate as college libraries become research libraries. The undergraduate library's needs can be more explicitly defined and provided for.[16] Suggestions are available for alternate systems of providing research materials but they will be difficult to initiate due to the present system of expectations which has been created. Not to be overlooked is the competition which exists between libraries, and the difficulty of organizing and implementing alternative patterns of organization and service.[17]

In the meantime, while we wait for changes in values, attitudes, and behavior in order to effect institutional changes, [18] approval plans will continue to be a means of purchasing books for libraries; library volume counts will continue to escalate even though 50 to 75 per cent of the books so purchased will be little or never used items. [19] Approval plan purchasing is a simple, easy, expensive method used by some acquisitions departments to purchase materials, many of which prove to be unnecessary and thus create a drain on other aspects of library operations.

References

1. H. William Axford. "The Economics of a Domestic Approval Plan," CRL 32:368, 370 (Sept. 1971).
2. E. M. Grieder. "Letters to the Editor," CRL 31:344 (Sept. 1970).
3. Jasper G. Schad, Ibid., p. 346. While Schad states that "Most academic librarians agree ... thirty acquisitions librarians at an Institute on Acquisitions Procedures in Academic Libraries in San Diego, Aug./Sept. 1969, from thirty different libraries throughout the country did not have acquisitions policies and could reach no agreement on how to set up such an animal. While one staff member recommended "Collection Development Policies" another staff member discredited the idea. One participant stated that the only selection policy evident in his library was reflected in the distribution of funds, while another admitted that since funds were no longer assigned to departments in his library, he "just spent it" as requests came in. Others were more or less silent about their practices, presumably in an effort to gain some guidance toward more meaningful procedures of expenditures. No guidance was given and no consensus arrived at except, "It depends on your library," which became a standard Institute quote.
4. Carol Schaafsman, "Reviews," Library Resources & Technical Services 15:557-58 (Fall 1971). Schaafsman reviews Advances in Understanding Approval and Gathering Plans in Academic Libraries, edited by Peter Spyers-Duran and Daniel Gore. Kalamazoo, Michigan: Western Michigan University, 1970, in which she indicates that there are more prejudices than understandings.
5. Much of the information used to summarize the present state of the art in this paper can be found in detail in the literature and needs no repetition here. For more information concerning these statements see: (in chronological order). Perry D. Morrison, "A Symposium on Approval Order Plans and the Book Selection Responsibilities of Librarians," with reactions by LeRoy C. Merritt, Joseph P. Browne, Stanley A. Shepard, Library Resources & Technical Services 12:133-45 (Spring 1968). Ian W. Thom, "Some Administrative Aspects of Blanket Ordering," Library Resources & Technical Services 13:338-46 (Summer 1969). Norman Dudley, "The Blanket Order," Library Trends 18:318-27 (January 1970). Roscoe Rouse,

"Automation Stops Here: A Case for Man-Made Book Collections," CRL 31:147-54 (May 1970). Marion Wilden-Hart, "The Long-Term Effects of Approval Plans," Library Resources & Technical Services 14:400-06 (Summer 1970). "Letters to the Editor," Comments and Rejoinders to Roscoe Rouse, by Grieder, Rebuldela, Schad, Schnaitter, CRL 31: 341-48 (Sept. 1970). Colin Steele, "Blanket Orders and the Bibliographer in the Large Research Library," Journal of Librarianship 2:272-80 (Oct. 1970). Axford, "Economics of," p. 368-75.

6. While continuing attention is on standards for evaluating libraries (see Signe Otterson, "A Bibliography on Standards for Evaluating Libraries," CRL 32:127-44 [March 1971]), the National Advisory Commission on Libraries in 1968 found it impossible to evaluate existing standards adopted by the American Library Association which are based on numbers of volumes, and they also point out that "sweeping generalizations with respect to user needs are likely to be misleading through incompleteness and inaccuracy." See the Report of the National Advisory Commission on Libraries, "Library Services for the Nation's Needs: Toward Fulfillment of a National Policy, October 1968," in ALA Bulletin 63:74, 72 (Jan. 1969).

7. It is presently a matter of fact that the university community has available to it on request through interlibrary loan facilities much more than is presently in the individual library locally. The complete list of holdings of all of the libraries from which any library may request material is the actual fact of the number of volumes and titles available. Accrediting agencies must be aware of this. Nevertheless, in May 1971 I was approached to assist in the purchase of $10,000 worth of "gaps" in runs of mathematical journals. The government funds had to be spent in a short time and the "gaps" were chosen for purchase to gain "points" (Brownie points?) with the accreditation agency which, as the mathematics professor stated, "counts each gap as a point against the department with graduate programs." One issue may be a "gap" or many volumes may be a "gap"! And too, the "gaps" up for purchase represented titles which had just been proven to be little used or never used titles in this library by a use study of mathematical periodicals completed three weeks earlier by this reviewer.

8. If ninety academic libraries were currently participating in one or more of one agent's approval plans in 1968 (see Morrison, "Symposium on Approval"), it might be estimated that sales amounted to over $7,200,000. What are the facts?

9. Again I refer you to the articles listed in footnote 5. However my figures do not agree with Axford's 7.16 per cent average discount. Using a sample of invoice slips for science books here, the average discount was determined to be 3.07 per cent; and a random sample of social science books gave an average discount of 5.62 per cent. The stated percentage rates on the invoice slips did not check out to be mathematically correct. When this was discovered, a call to the agent verified an extra charge of 2 per cent for each invoice.

10. On looking through 150 invoice slips for current approval plan purchases in H to HX category, a sociology professor on this campus remarked that he would estimate about 25 per cent of these titles as "junk," and also that he hoped his students did not get hold of any of it. See also Henry Voos, "The Information Explosion; or, Redundancy Reduces the Charge!" 32:7-14 (Jan. 1971).

11. Derek J. DeSolla Price. Little Science Big Science. (New York: Columbia University Press, 1963), p. 20.

12. It is interesting to note that the current Bowker Annual has rounded off volume counts to the millions of volumes since 1964-65.

13. In 1966 it was predicted that upper limits of growth of research libraries were unlikely to be approached during the "fifteen years immediately ahead.... All would agree that such growth cannot continue indefinitely. Nevertheless, no clues appear (1966) which adequately suggest an early deceleration of growth. If deceleration occurs, it can hardly be expected before 1980 and perhaps not for many years thereafter." O. C. Dunn, W. F. Seibert, and Janice A. Scheuneman, The Past and Likely Future of 58 Research Libraries, 1951-1980: A Statistical Study of Growth and Change. Lafayette, Indiana: Purdue University, University Libraries and Audio Visual Center. Second Printing, March 1966, p. 76.

14. Ellsworth Mason. "The Great Gas Bubble Prick't; or, Computers Revealed--by a Gentleman of Quality," CRL 32:193 (May 1971).

15. D. J. Urquhart. "The Library User and His Needs," Research into Library Services in Higher Education. London: Society for Research into Higher Education Ltd., February 1968, p. 2.

16. Virgil F. Massman and David R. Olson. "Book Selection: A National Plan for Small Academic Libraries," CRL 32:271-79 (July 1971). A promising design if cooperation were possible!

17. Many writers come to mind. Pings, Kraft, Rose, Boutry, Voos, Ralston--to name a few. I found the most encouraging and yet the most discouraging to be Mason's "Libraries and Change," PLA Bulletin (May 1971), p. 141-50.

18. Vern M. Pings. "The Library as a Social Agency, Response to Social Change," CRL 31:177 (May 1970).

19. No hard data has been found to prove or disprove these statements; however three years experience in two university libraries in acquisitions and in reference handling approval plan books gives one some insights to accompany review of the literature. Axford's tables ("Economics of," p. 375) could easily be interpreted to indicate that four of the five libraries did not need one-half of the material that Library 1 was accumulating. He gives no indication of how much the material is used or how much of the unacquired 50 per cent is missed in Libraries 2 to 5.

In a library with simple automation procedures which correlate the acquisition of books with circulation records it would not be impossible to actually measure the use, over five or even ten years, of 13,000 volumes received in one year on a domestic approval plan contract. The expense and tedium of such a use study probably do not seem practical in view of signs which indicate that the results will yield evidence of waste and who wants to be shown up as wasteful? Besides, at this time it may be impossible to get a government grant to finance such a study.

BOOK SELECTION: AN APPROACH FOR
SMALL AND MEDIUM-SIZED LIBRARIES

By George M. Jenks

   With the growing acceptance of approval plans, libraries will
have to try a different approach to their book selection policies.
The receipt of books on a regular basis forces the small and medium-
sized library to reconsider some time-honored practices, such as allocation of funds to departments and selection by classroom faculty.

   I start with the premise that an approval plan is a desirable
means of acquiring books. There are those who would take issue
with this, but I think the problem is in the mechanics of particular
plans, not the principle.[1] An approval plan enables a library to acquire a large part of current book production for inspection, a very
useful first step in book selection.

   The question of who selects the books and how much money is
allocated to a department often raises problems of power and status
and causes conflict between departments and the library and departments. Formulas for allocation of funds to departments are based
on a variety of factors, but the overriding factor should be the need
that the college or university has for a particular book in order to
satisfy curriculum requirements. The number of students and the
number of faculty are minor considerations. If a university offers a
degree in biology, the books that are necessary are necessary whether
there is one student or forty. Fortunately at my own institution we do
not allocate the book budget by department. We do keep a record of
expenditures by subject, partly as an insurance policy against the
time when a department may feel it is being done out of its fair share
of the book budget. For obvious reasons, when money is tight, this
problem worsens.

   The question of who selects is a touchy problem when the faculty member feels that any delegation of book selection to a librarian involves a loss of status and/or admission that he is not competent to select material in his field. The only way to resolve this
problem is to have librarians who are competent and can work with
departments. One can ask each department to appoint one member of
its faculty as a "library representative" to serve as departmental liaison with the library. Each librarian is assigned a section of the
Library of Congress classification as his responsibility for book se-

Reprinted by permission of the American Library Association from
"Book Selection: An Approach for Small and Medium-Sized Libraries,"
College and Research Libraries, 33, no. 1 (January, 1972), pp. 28-
30; copyright © 1972 by the American Library Association.

lection and weeding. It is necessary for a librarian to cover several departments, since there are not as many librarians as departments. This has obvious drawbacks since a library usually cannot provide specialists in every field, and in some cases there is no one interested in a particular subject. Science specialists are difficult to come by. Those people assigned a field in which they have no expertise must depend on good communication with the departments concerned.

In the area of current book selection our library receives books weekly on approval. These are placed on shelves in the acquisitions department by rough LC classification (supplied by the vendor) and every two weeks library representatives are sent notices of the display and asked to come to the library to make selections during a five-day period. Selections are made by signature on the multiple-order form placed in each book. The books are left on the shelves one more day so that the librarians may make additional selections and also see what books have been chosen. This provides an additional guide to departmental interests.

This system works, and its ideal of two-way communication between library and departments is good, but it does not function as smoothly as it sounds. There are two principal reasons for this. First, not all library representatives take their responsibilities seriously. Some departments appoint the junior member of the department as library representative. This can mean the representative changes each year and continuity and sometimes ability is lost. On the other hand, in some cases the young faculty member is well acquainted with the literature of his field and indeed is even more current than senior members. In some cases the department head doesn't trust book selection to anyone else and tries to do it all himself, with the result that it may not get done, the chairman's duties being what they are. Some departments encourage all members to make selections. This, we feel, is good because one man may not be interested in or know the literature outside his own narrow field.

The other reason that the selection procedure does not always measure up to the ideal is that, sad to say, some librarians are not concerned. My feeling is that book selection touches the essence of librarianship and all librarians should be involved in it. There is an understandable tendency for some to place other duties first and book selection last, especially when there is much to be done. Also many academic librarians have never been involved in book selection, since it has usually been a faculty prerogative or limited to bibliographers or acquisitions librarians.

The question of retrospective purchases is somewhat more difficult because the range of possibilities is much greater, and there are not nearly enough funds to buy everything wanted. At the moment our approach has not been systematized to the point necessary for a thorough review of every classification. We have used Books for College Libraries as a basic minimum guide, and each librarian has ordered the books thought necessary to our collection. Beyond this we accept requests from the faculty and distribute them to the staff for review. This is necessary, of course, if the librarian is to know what is being requested and what is being purchased in his area of responsibility.

"Deselection," or weeding of the collection, is often difficult. The faculty may not see the need to discard books that are not used or are superseded. We consider weeding important if we are to have a vital, useful, and used collection. Since we are not a research library we should not attempt to keep forever everything we have acquired. We will leave that to Harvard. We have to guard against building for the faculty alone. The students come first. However, we have had some success in weeding. We have asked library representatives to examine the books in their subject area and recommend ones for discard. In some cases the librarians have made preliminary selections for discard and asked the representative to make recommendations from these. This is more effective because the initiative is in the library and psychologically, the faculty member feels relieved of the responsibility of discarding a book.

When we receive a large number of gifts, we arrange them by subject and ask the library representatives to select those for retention. For the small number of day-to-day gifts, the order librarian asks the librarian concerned to decide what to keep. The librarian may in turn consult with the library representative. Since no expenditure is involved, and the titles will appear in the monthly accessions list, the main reason for consulting the library representative is to keep him informed.

This method perhaps approaches the point whereby the reference function, the book selection function, and the cataloging function are combined, with one person doing all three. [2] We have not attempted to go this far. I think the combination of functions is not always desirable, although I believe that all librarians should at some time in their careers have the experience of cataloging.

Involving all librarians in book selection has two worthwhile side effects. It broadens a person's view of the library, and it provides a means of contact with the faculty. This latter effect may be important where faculty status is still an issue. It may seem as if the library representatives are doing a great deal of work and making most of the decisions, but it is a case of a shift of decision-making from one group to a sharing by two groups for the library's benefit.

References

1. For a contrary view see Roscoe Rouse, "Automation Stops Here: A Case for Man-Made Book Collections," CRL 31:147-54 (May 1970).
2. See Frank A. Lundy, Kathryn R. Renfro, and Esther M. Shubert, "The Dual Assignment: Cataloging and Reference: A Four-Year Review of Cataloging in the Divisional Plan," Library Resources & Technical Services 3:167-88 (Summer 1959).

FORMING THE COMMITTEE

By Emily S. Jones

There are a number of ways in which an evaluation committee can be formed and organized, and committees evaluating films for a particular purpose will operate somewhat differently from committees which screen films in a large general subject area. The format given below is based on that used by EFLA in its Evaluating and Festival Pre-Screening Committees, and has been tested by long use. It is suggested as a guide, and should of course be modified to fit particular circumstances.

Chairman. A few of the Chairman's duties are outlined in Section VI. However, he has many other duties, some of which may be delegated. He must select the films to be evaluated, send for preview prints, arrange for a screening place and date, notify the committee members, round up a projectionist, and check to make sure the films have arrived on the day of the session. He should have the details mentioned in Section VI made available to the committee members, possibly on a single sheet of paper for all the films, or by filling in the top part of the evaluation form being used for each title. When the committee members arrive, he should make sure they understand just what the procedure will be, and that they are familiar with the form to be used and the objectives of the group. He must keep the session moving along, without wasting time in unrelated conversation or fruitless argument, but at the same time allowing scope for real discussion of the films. Many people don't know what they think about a film until they have talked about it with others; others prefer to write down their own comments first and then engage in discussion. The Chairman must work out the system to be used by the committee, and if possible develop a pattern of procedure which will be followed at subsequent screenings, thus giving a continuity to the evaluation program.

Committee Members. EFLA requires that its committees have representatives of the three groups described below. Sometimes one person may be qualified under two or even all three headings, but the committee should still have a minimum of three people, to insure a balance of opinion.

Film Specialist--Must know enough about film technique to judge the quality of the photography, sound, and editing. This committee member is particularly responsible for the section of the report dealing with technical quality, and should be able to tell whether

Reprinted from Manual on Film Evaluation, revised edition, Educational Film Library Association, p. 10, by permission of author.

the fuzziness of the image is due to artistic photography, poor camera handling, or an out-of-focus projector. The specialist's knowledge
of the film medium and of other films of the same type should help
the committee in appraising the value of the film under discussion.

Subject Area Specialist--Selected according to the subject area
of the films to be screened. Often a different Subject Specialist is
needed for each film, particularly in highly technical aspects of
science or technology. The Subject Specialist should be able to say
whether the content is accurate and up-to-date; whether it is presented logically and correctly; and what its importance is in the subject field. He or she does not need to be experienced in film technique, but should have a sympathy for the visual medium. Teachers,
supervisors, department heads, specialized librarians, or experts
from the community may be used. Inviting someone to act as a Subject Specialist is a good way to get people outside the AV department
interested in films.

Utilization Specialist--Someone familiar with the audience who
might use the film. A teacher or librarian, a minister, a community mental health worker, a Scout leader--anyone who can predict with
some degree of accuracy what the audience reaction of a specific
group would be. Would they find it dull, or exciting? Is it over
their heads, or much too simplified? Is it highly pertinent to their
interests, or not worth spending much time on? The best Utilization
Specialist is a person who has used films with a variety of groups,
of various ages and types, and different educational and cultural
backgrounds. However, really experienced utilizers may be hard to
find, and anyone with practical experience of the particular audience
for which the film is designed, or of the group which the evaluation
committee is set up to serve, will be helpful.

THE REVIEW PRIVILEGE

By Phyllis Levy

It has been brought to our attention recently that the privilege granted to consumers of audiovisual items to preview the material prior to purchase is being abused. Producers and distributors of non-print items have permitted educators to examine films, filmstrips, slide programs, and other items to determine whether or not this material will be useful to enrich their school curricula. Previewing these items is extended to prospective purchasers only. And it is, indeed, a privilege and a responsibility.

Several firms have informed us that, in many instances, they are receiving preview requests for the same item from several persons within a given school. This is unnecessary duplication. These firms have also determined that items being sent to many teachers for preview are being used within a classroom situation to supplement a lesson and then being returned to the producer or distributor with the notation that the film, filmstrip, or other item is not satisfactory for the educator's purposes. If the item is really not satisfactory, then the return of the material is perfectly understandable. However, many producers believe that the item is being requested with the explicit intention of using it during a class period and then returning it.

It is understandable that educators with severe limitations imposed upon their budgets still wish to supplement their programs with some of the excellent audiovisual items on the market. Many may feel that, while they are being dishonest to the producer of the item, they are benefiting the students by permitting them to view these media during a class lesson. However, in the long run, this dishonesty might force producers and distributors to curtail the preview privilege. Producers and distributors might, in fact, be forced by the sheer economics of the situation to discontinue their previewing policy or charge a substantial fee for this privilege. This preview charge might then be applied to purchase (if the previewer does decide to purchase the item) or not refunded in the cases where the item is returned to the producer.

Since there are only a limited number of preview copies available to send to educators, when someone requests a preview copy with the prior knowledge that budget limitations will certainly not permit the eventual purchase of the item, this individual is depriving others who do have the intention of purchasing the item of receiving a preview print as quickly as possible. The producer or distributor who is sending out the item for preview incurs a good deal of expense--even if the individual to whom the preview print is being sent pays for postage. There is a good deal of office paperwork and record keeping which must be done for each item which is sent to a prospective purchaser for preview.

It is true that there really is no way that a producer or distributor can determine whether the requests they are receiving for preview prints are legitimate. However, the increasing rate of returns on items being sent to educators for previewing purposes is forcing these firms to re-evaluate their previewing procedures. So far, it has not come to our attention that any firm has halted their previewing policy, but we are afraid that, in time, this might become necessary. Since 16mm films are available for rental, it might become necessary for firms to charge the present rental fee in place of the gratis previewing privilege.

If these reports of widespread previewing abuse are, in fact, true, we are afraid that producers and distributors will find it economically infeasible to continue their present previewing practices. We call upon all those involved in the selection, purchase, and utilization of audiovisual items to examine their present policies and determine whether they are being fair to all those concerned. Previewing is more than a privilege--it is a responsibility which should not be taken lightly or abused. We would welcome your reaction to these charges by producers and distributors.

PRACTICE WHAT YOU PREACH: HELP
STOP PYRAMIDING PRICES

By Diana L. Spirt

Filmstrips are stellar performers in a school audiovisual
market that still hopes to reach parity with print in the next decade.
Not always tops in sales by dollar volume, filmstrips nevertheless
have grown rapidly in sales volume during the early seventies, and
in spite of hard times remain steady sellers. In fact, if kits (which
usually contain filmstrips) and filmstrips were lumped together for
reporting purposes, the combination would account for the lion's
share of the audiovisual market. A relatively affordable price, an
adaptability to group or individual use, and other sensible reasons
too numerous to mention assure the popularity of this format.

From the beginning, filmstrips have been easily absorbed by
the educational market. Even companies that were once solely print
producers or solely 16mm producers and distributors have taken note
and today are marketing filmstrips or stripfilms. There is good
news and bad news in all this activity, and media specialists can
help to wipe out the bad aspects.

One of the benefits that can be traced to the increase of interest in filmstrips is the appearance of some superior strips over
the last few years. At one time only a few producers accounted for
a few exceptional filmstrips; more recently many companies are producing more quality filmstrip programs. The improvements in the
synchronization of sound, the smoother automatic advance in the cassette projector, the technical aspects of film production, and especially the artistic and imaginative quality of the scripts have contributed to the appeal and usefulness of this medium.

The number of filmstrips available is large and the selection
is difficult, dependent as it is finally on the purpose for which the
acquisition is made. Admittedly, the task is troublesome.

Nevertheless, it seems that the historical audiovisual precedent of "previewing" a filmstrip, stoutly demanded by media specialists because of the cost of the materials, aggravates one of the standard and real complaints that media specialists repeatedly make--
high prices. The paradox is easy to grasp and easier to explain.
The "previewing" privilege can be easily abused. Each time a filmstrip is returned the mailing, inspection, and replacement costs auto-

matically become part of the firm's operating expense and will very likely be reflected in a future price increase. Previewing and pricing are closely related.

Another plaint often heard among media specialists is a commonsense request to reduce the price of filmstrips by using less expensive packaging. It could and has been done; however, the packaging appeal is lessened and so are the sales. Who would believe it? Previewing and Packaging and Pricing. Somehow, even media specialists--or a majority of them--do not practice what they preach.

To hold the line on filmstrip prices and do a more professional job, one simply has to borrow two techniques that have proved their worth over the years in the educational world of print:

Rely more on retrospective and current authoritative evaluative sources in order to limit previewing only to those filmstrips that require it.

Demand plain packaging in sizes comparable to books (with appropriate lettering) that can be intershelved with the print material in a media center.

Both ideas should have been adopted universally long before this. Eliminate Previewing Privileges/Pretty Packaging/Pyramiding Prices!

A NOTE ON THE ROLE OF THE BOOK REVIEW EDITOR AS DECISION MAKER

By Rita James Simon and Linda Mahon

For professional or technical audiences, a good review has been defined as "one prepared by an expert in the particular field. It contains essential specific information; it evaluates the author with his book; it classifies and summarizes the book; it places it in its proper frame of reference; and it presents an accurate, trustworthy, critical examination in an acceptable style" [1, p. iv]. The reviewer for professional journals is selected on the basis of "his ability, experience and training. ... He is expected to present his interpretation and criticism in carefully chosen statements" [2, p. v].

The purpose of our study was to find out how decisions are made about who will review which book at what length, at which location in the journal. To get this information, we went directly to the men whose job it is to make those decisions: the editors of the book review sections of professional journals; in other words, from persons who occupy the most sensitive position vis-à-vis the three leading protagonists--the author, the reviewer, and the audience.

What we most wanted to know from the editors were (1) how they decided who should review what book; (2) how prominent a review it ought to be as determined by location, length, and date; and (3) the types of books that are most and least likely to be reviewed in their journal.

We obtained this information by sending a questionnaire to the book review editors of all the major social science journals.[1] The fields represented in this study are cultural anthropology, economics, geography, American history, political science, psychology, and sociology. In all but one instance, the book review editor of the official journal of the society responded; and in total, twenty-two out of the thirty-five editors contacted completed the questionnaire and returned it. In addition to this more than respectable rate of return for a mail questionnaire (we did reimburse our respondents, but as some of them indicated, at rates much below their market value), a further indication of the respondents' interest in the study was shown by the fact that almost all of them asked for a copy of the results. In only one field, political science, did less than half of the respon-

Reprinted from Library Quarterly vol. 39, no. 4 (October, 1969), pp. 353-356, by permission of the University of Chicago Press as publisher and Rita James Simon as senior author.
[1]Major was defined as the official journal of the professional or learned society; or journals with large circulations; and/or reputations in the profession.

dents complete the questionnaire. But, here again, the editors of the more important journals did cooperate.

The editors were almost unanimous in the criteria they applied for establishing priorities. Almost all agreed that texts, anthologies (collections of essays, reprints or originals), and reissues of earlier works have the lowest priority, and new books which the editor believes (1) are most relevant to the field or the more narrowly defined interests of the journal; (2) are written by an author who is well known and well thought of; and (3) are scholarly or serious works as determined by the editor's own brief perusal of the volume, are most likely to get reviewed.

For the purposes of our study, the most crucial questions were:

> How do you decide on a particular reviewer for any given book? What influences your decision on this matter? After you have mentioned the factors that you think are pertinent, please rank them in the order of their importance to you.

"Competence or expertise in the field or in the subject matter of the book" was ranked first by all but two of the respondents. After that, the following considerations were mentioned: "I have a file system or inventory of review and I go through the cards, trying to match fields of interest between potential reviewer and content of book"; others said essentially the same thing, but instead of an impersonal inventory, they call upon a network of friends or personal contacts to find the "right man. " In both instances, the "right" match is determined by similarity of substantive interests between reviewer and author. Six editors emphasized their bias in favor of "younger, less established scholars over well-known men" because the former take the job more seriously and are more likely to meet the deadline, and "it makes me feel good because I have given someone a publication. "[2] A few others said that their strategy is to match the status of the reviewer to that of the author of the volume. To quote one, "an important book needs a reviewer of maturity and stature. " A few emphasized the importance of adequate geographic representation. One or two others said they try to avoid asking the same people over and over again. [3] Two respondents commented that

---

[2]In a second survey that we conducted of book review editors for major journals in education and selected fields in the humanities (English, philosophy, art, classics) the quality of their responses, with one exception, was very similar to those made by the social science editors. The exception was that the editors in the second sample believed reviewers must be men who are well established in their fields. None of them made any mention of the desirability of selecting younger scholars.
[3]Once every two years was the rule of thumb offered by one editor.

they are especially concerned about avoiding "internecine wars among schools or cliques."

At the end of the questionnaire, when we asked the respondents for "any other observations or comments about the selection of reviewers," several said that they "try to keep the reviewing process as objective as possible" and to the best of their knowledge, avoid having former students review their teachers' works and vice versa; or members of the same faculty; or faculty members at a university whose press has published the volume in question. Two others commented that occupying the position of book review editor makes one vulnerable to all sorts of attacks by disgruntled authors who feel they received unfair treatment by a particular reviewer or by the journal in its choice of reviewer or its failure to review; and by reviewers who feel they have been unduly chastised for tardiness in completing the review or who feel that their work has been "harshly" edited. Two or three referred again to the opportunities it provides for giving less established members of the profession "a publication."

These responses are both consistent with and opposed to the advice Richard Kluger (former editor of Book Week) offered in an article entitled "What I Did to Books and Vice Versa" [3]. Kluger agrees with our respondents in their preference for younger reviewers. He wrote: "There is a good deal to be said for young reviewers. Those who understand the burdens of integrity and scholarship in passing judgment on someone else's life blood may make the best reviewers, for they are willing to do the necessary homework and to say where their elders may not be that the emperor's clothes are pretty threadbare or missing altogether." But, he added: "Indeed, I almost came to feel that one should not be eligible to review a book until one had learned firsthand the torment and craft that go into the process of writing one." He is wary about the desirability of having one expert review another's work: "Experts often know a lot about their subject--sometimes too much to write a book review.... Experts ... are subconsciously or even consciously defending their own scholarly point of view; they may be disinclined to respond sympathetically to works of conflicting testimony. Thus, the fairest review of a specialized book is likely to be written by an authority who knows the literature in the field but is not working the very same vineyard."

In answer to the question "How do you decide which review will be published first in any given issue of the journal?" three out of four editors answered: "by my estimate of the importance of the book to the field." A few added, "and by the reputation of the reviewer or the quality of the review." In only three instances did the latter consideration supersede the content or subject of the book as the most salient consideration. Five respondents said, "on a first-in, first-published basis"; "alphabetically by author"; or "chronologically by subject matter."

Other than the first, the order of the remaining reviews is determined most often by similarity of fields and chronologically with-

in subfields. But six editors claimed that they try to rank each review so that the first is, in their opinion, the most important or the
best from point of view of subject matter, relevance to the field, or
quality of review, and the last is the least significant or least well
done. One respondent said he tries to hide reviews that are stupidly
done by putting them "near, but not at the very end of the section."

The length of the review is closely tied to the editor's perception of its importance. Three out of four said that they recommend different lengths depending on their estimate of the importance
of the book to the field and the reputation of the reviewer. The
others said they leave it completely up to the reviewer, or they have
a standard length and all books and reviewers are treated equally.

Book reviewing is a competitive business. When we asked
"Do you send some books out for review more quickly than others,
after you have received them from the publishers? If you do, how
do you decide on the order in which you send the books out?" eight
of the respondents said they sent those books out first that they
thought would be widely reviewed in other journals. These were also
books that they thought were more important in terms of their contribution to the field. The practice followed by the others was either
to send books out "en masse" every few weeks or to send a book out
as soon as a reviewer could be located. A few editors commented
that their biggest headache was getting reviews "back on time" or,
in a smaller number of instances, "back at all."

Some books are much more difficult to find reviewers for than
others; and there is consensus about the kinds of books they are:
highly specialized works or topics of very limited or narrow interests; books of readings or symposia; books written in foreign languages. A couple of editors wrote that they have more trouble finding reviewers for books in fields that they know less about because
the names of prospective reviewers are less likely to come to mind.

Only four respondents claimed that they were unable to use as
many as 5 per cent of the reviews they received over a period of
about a year. But, with two exceptions, all of the editors complained
that many of the reviews they received were poorly done and in need
of extensive editing, which in most instances is done by the editor
or his staff at the journal. Many were critical of the quality of the
reviews but added, "even the exceptionally stupid ones are published."
More than half commented that many of the reviews they receive lack
any real critical element and are little more than "elaborate tables
of contents."

When the respondents were given a chance to make any comments they wanted to about reviewers, books selected for reviewing,
etc., all but four took advantage of the opportunity. Most of them
described the problems they have with tardy and/or poor reviews and
with the failure of about 10 per cent of the reviewers to complete
their assignments at all. Some took the opportunity to emphasize
that they are pleased to be able to "help out" younger scholars or
persons at small colleges get a chance to publish.

212 / The Selection Process

On the whole, however, those editors who spent more time on the questionnaire used that time to criticize the quality, style, and reliability of the materials they received from their colleagues. They said that many of their reviewers did not take "their responsibilities seriously enough--a mere survey of a table of contents will not do. They should come to grips with the substance of the book in a critical and significant way." One editor suggested a rating system. After commenting that "We are in a public relations climate and book reviewing has become a matter of summarizing point of view, data and conclusions," he made this suggestion: "Since reviewers are not critical enough, no one in the profession really feels that the works are being evaluated. We need some kind of rating system--this is an 'A' book, this one a 'C' and finally this book failed. Instead, a look at most reviews will indicate that most of their reviewers gave their books 'C' grades. There must be some 'A's' and 'B's' but it will be difficult to spot them by the language used."

References

1. Borchers, Gladys. "What We Expect of a Book Review," Quarterly Journal of Speech 37 (February 1951):81-86. Cited by Maurice F. Tauber in the Foreword to Reviews in Library Book Selection by LeRoy C. Merritt, Martha Boaz, and Kenneth S. Tisdel. Detroit: Wayne State University Press, 1958.
2. Tauber, Maurice F. Foreword to Reviews in Library Book Selection, by LeRoy C. Merritt, Martha Boaz, and Kenneth S. Tisdel. Detroit: Wayne State University Press, 1958.
3. Kluger, Richard. "What I Did to Books and Vice Versa," Harper's (December 1966), pp. 69-74.

TO REVIEW OR NOT TO REVIEW

By Richard K. Gardner

All those beautiful new books! You get to see all those wonderful new publications before anybody else!" And that is certainly
true. One of the great excitements of being editor of Choice is the
fact that one does get to see all of the important and interesting new
books long before they get to any library or book store.

But there is also a frustration that goes along with the job in
that there are so many new books coming into the editorial office
(1200-1500 a month!) that one cannot possibly read or even browse
through all of those that attract one.

The editor of Choice does have the responsibility of looking
carefully at everything that comes into the office, but that is a lot
different from reading for pleasure. Even so, there are many
nights and weekends when he ends up at home on a bookman's holiday, busily devouring some splendid new tome!

Another great pleasure in being associated with Choice lies in
the very interesting contacts that one has daily with the publishing
world. Over the years many friends have been made among this interesting group, particularly among the promotion and publicity
people--contacts that have been broadening as well as fascinating.

Then there are the contacts with faculty members--not at just
one institution but nation-wide--with some of the finest minds active
in our academic institutions today. Just to read every review (and
that is another of the editor's duties) provides exciting access to a
continually changing world of ideas. One sits at the crossroads and
watches as the world of ideas parades by.

Finally, there is the immensely rewarding feeling that Choice
is really helping others; that it is contributing to the upgrading of library collections around the world--for Choice goes to every corner
of the globe, bringing news of what is best in American publishing
to libraries abroad as well as to those at home. There is also the
satisfaction of being able to reward good work in the publishing industry through praise and commendation.

Our annual list of "Outstanding Academic Books" is a very
time-consuming undertaking but it is satisfying at the same time.
When one sees so much that is mediocre on the weekly "best-seller"

Reprinted from OLA Bulletin, vol. 44, no. 1, January 1974, pp.
4-7, by permission of the Ohio Library Association.

lists, it is good to be able to call attention to some really outstanding publications and thereby perhaps help increase their sales.

People often wonder how I came to shift from being a college librarian and, more recently, a library school director and professor to being a book review editor. It was originally quite by accident. My qualifications for a job as an editor were quite nil but in the beginning it was felt that, since the product had not yet been created, a knowledge of the potential market for which the magazine was being designed was more necessary than a technical knowledge of daily editorial routines.

But just what kind of expertise or training or experience is needed in running a book review journal such as Choice? Library training and experience help in judging what should go into the magazine, but they are of little help with the day-to-day routine of editing, publishing, advertising or promotion.

Obviously an editor needs a sound foundation in the English language--in grammar, punctuation and style. He also needs to learn the signs and symbols used in communicating with printers, a technical vocabulary that is not usually taught in library schools. Ideally one should know the University of Chicago Press Manual of Style practically by heart. Then there is the necessity of knowing in great detail all of the processes which go into the printing of a magazine or a book.

It is also necessary to have an understanding of the financial and business end of publishing--how to get a quality job done for the least amount of money, where corners can be cut without hurting the final product. One of the greatest differences in running an operation like Choice rather than a college library is that Choice is really like a commercial enterprise despite its nonprofit status. The books must balance or there will soon be no magazine. This means that Choice must constantly go after advertising and promote subscriptions.

What I knew when I first came to this job about Madison Avenue could have been put in a thimble but fortunately I had hired a knowledgeable advertising and promotion assistant and I quickly picked up the necessary know-how from her. The world of book advertising is a distinct corner of its own within the world of advertising. Each individual book title must be marketed separately unlike untold quanties of the same brand of soap. The agencies that handle book advertising are relatively few in number and tend to be less commercially-oriented than the rest of Madison Avenue. Naturally very few librarians have had any experience in this world at all.

In fact, as I indicated, I knew little or nothing about any of the myriad aspects of editing, publishing, advertising, or promotion when I took on the job. I had the good sense, however, to go out and hire people who did. Another difference in running a magazine rather than a library, even though the magazine may be a library-oriented publication, is that one cannot find within the library profession much of the expertise one needs for the staff. The recruiting must be done elsewhere.

Even for the editorial staff subject expertise is more important than a knowledge of cataloging rules, for we are primarily dealing in the world of ideas rather than with furnishing technical data. We must perforce have closer links with publishers and with the academic community than with the Library of Congress Descriptive Cataloging Division. Some of our readers would like us to achieve 100 per cent agreement with LC in our bibliographic entries but this will never happen--at least not until the use of "Cataloging-in-Publication" becomes universal within the publishing community.

The difficulty in outguessing LC's Cataloging Division leads me to other difficulties that we face. The primary one is keeping current. Some days we feel like building a wall around the office to keep the flow of books out--now running at 12,000 to 15,000 books a year--and there have been periods in the history of the magazine when we were clearly inundated by the avalanche of materials. The secret to maintaining currency seems to me to be in insisting upon drastic selection. We cannot possibly review all the books which come in to us. In point of fact, we reject about half of them for one reason or another, but what we decide to review we must review promptly or we are of little service to our readers. (This is the area in which I have sought to make some decided improvements since my return to the magazine a little over a year ago and I hope these are now beginning to show up.)

Books that are rejected must be disposed of promptly or we would soon face a warehousing problem of mammoth proportions. Our present system is to sell our rejects en bloc to a secondhand book dealer who will take everything--the dregs as well as the good stuff--so there is a constant flow of materials in and out of our offices.

The second greatest problem is undoubtedly that of facing the ever-present deadlines. One has to learn to live with them since with three issues always in the works (one being written and edited, one in the early galley stages, and one in the page proof or final stage of printing) they cannot be avoided. The copy must go to the printer on a certain date, galley proof must be read by a certain date, the advertising mechanicals must be in by a certain date, the magazine has to be dummied by a certain date, the page proofs have to be returned by a certain date, or the magazine will just not come out when it is supposed to and 6,500 irate subscribers will write in to find out where their copies are.

In the early days of the magazine we did not have the work force adequate to cope with all of these deadlines without monthly crises, but this is no longer true and we only have to cope now with certain periods of what is undoubtedly inevitable tension and rush.

Then there is the problem of the bad reviewer. Usually a reviewer's lack of knowledge of his field is not in question, although this does come up from time to time and leads to the immediate "retirement" of the reviewer. It is rather a problem of the reviewer who knows his field but who does not write very well or who goes on at too great length or who uses professional jargon. Then there are those who like to ride their own hobby horses or who show religious, political or social bias, and even those who seem to be taking revenge on their colleagues.

All of these types are quite readily handled, even the last few. There are various remedies at our disposal. We can obtain another copy of the book and get someone else to review it if we feel that bias or unfairness is involved. As for those who know their field but do not write well, there is always the remedy of some good hard editing. Whether we want to spend the time doing this depends on how hard-pressed we are for a good reviewer in that particular subject field. The ideal reviewer is one who knows his subject and who also writes well. We have more of these paragons of virtue on tap than you might imagine!

Besides the problems of deadlines and bad reviewers the editor is faced with certain dangers. The first of these is pressure from publishers--pressure which can be very subtle but which is ever-present nevertheless. There is a constant struggle on the part of publishing houses to gain attention for the titles they are issuing. No review medium in the United States is able to review all that it would like and constant choices have to be made. In the eyes of many publishers a bad review is better than no review at all. At least someone will have heard about the book and he might be intrigued enough to buy a copy!

So the editor of a review journal is constantly bombarded with publicity releases and sometimes even telephone calls to bring certain books to his attention. Unintentionally, it would be very easy to start to play favorites with certain publishing houses--showing preference to their publications rather than to those of another publisher. The physical presentation of a book can also influence decisions as to whether it is reviewed or not. Good ideas in plain packages may not get as much attention as something beautifully gift-wrapped. All this must be constantly guarded against.

Then there is also the danger of forgetting the audience for whom the magazine is produced. Choice was founded to assist undergraduate college libraries but as time went on there was a tendency toward the inclusion of too many graduate-level materials in proportion to those at the lower end of the spectrum. Little account seemed to be taken of the great proliferation of community colleges and of their specific needs. Hopefully, we are now rectifying these errors and are striking a more equitable balance.

A constant effort must be made to keep abreast of the latest curriculum developments on our nation's campuses. Who could have foreseen just a few years ago the proliferation of courses on the film or on women's studies? The fact that Choice is located in a small academic community rather than at ALA headquarters helps in this respect. We are in daily contact with Wesleyan University's faculty, as well as with those of other academic institutions in the area. A local community college is gaining strength with which we hope to have close contact in the future. All of this is in an effort not to become lost in an ivory tower.

Undoubtedly the most frightening part of the job as editor of Choice comes with the realization of how much power Choice wields. Publishers are not loathe to remind the editor from time to time that a negative review in Choice can pretty well kill the sales of certain types of books--those aimed specifically at the library market and which are not reviewed extensively elsewhere.

One of the reasons for the success of Choice over the past decade seems to be due to the fact that it has not been afraid to speak its mind and to condemn shoddy merchandise when it appeared on the market. This is a very difficult task, for we must attempt to remain scrupulously honest and avoid any feeling of partisanship. There is often room for difference of opinion and if so, it is necessary that the reasons behind a particular opinion be clearly stated.

Choice has been involved in a few disagreeable situations with authors and publishers over the years. Some authors and publishers may feel that Choice reviewers hide behind the policy of anonymous reviewing that the magazine practices. A word of explanation is probably therefore in order concerning this policy. It is, of course, one with an honorable history--witness the Times Literary Supplement. But that does not make it any more acceptable to some of our critics.

However, there are enough instances each year of professors who would not be able to review a book as candidly or as honestly as they have done if they had to sign their name to it, simply because they are faced with reviewing the works of colleagues whom they know well or of senior persons in the field to whom they will be beholden for the furtherance of their careers.

The editorial staff of Choice naturally go to great lengths to avoid sending a book to a reviewer who appears to have any association with the author. Thus we scrutinize where each got his Ph.D., where each has taught, and in the case of university presses, we will avoid sending a book published by the press to anyone at that university.

We have made mistakes over the years, but we do attempt to make amends through corrections. There are also books which we should have reviewed, but which slipped through the net. We do have the possibility of remedy in this case through our monthly bibliographic essays. Hopefully in the future we will also have the updated supplements to Books for College Libraries as a possible place to remedy our mistakes and omissions. But all in all I think our track record has been pretty good.

Finally, everything considered, the rewards of this job are far greater than any of the difficulties that I have faced. There is an excitement about this work and a feeling for its importance that drew me back last year after a number of years away. It is very gratifying to see something I helped start come to such fruition, and at the present moment I would not want to be in any other job in the world.

BOOK REVIEWS: BEFORE & AFTER

By Zena Bailey Sutherland

On Reviewers

I think it is very important to realize that what goes into a review depends in part on the time in which the review is written as well as on the policies of the publication and the audience for whom it's published. Reviewers change in response to the times. I doubt that any reviewers achieve perfection. If we are honest, we can assess our strengths and weaknesses in much the same way we assess the strengths and weaknesses of a book.

On Requisites

A reviewer should have, I think:

a wide acquaintance with children's literature

the stability to remain objective

the ability to see each book as a whole and report its balance of strengths and weaknesses

the capacity to understand the uses to which a book will be put without becoming preoccupied with potential usage at the expense of consideration for literary quality. To me, literary quality is the most important aspect of a book.

On Content

You describe the book. You say whether or not you like it and why. You point out the strengths and weaknesses you see. You analyze it critically. That's it. Then, the librarian decides.

On Criticism vs. Reviewing

There has been a great deal of discussion, in print and wher-

Reprinted by permission from School Library Journal, vol. 21, no. 6, February, 1975, pp. 22-23; published by R. R. Bowker Company/ A Xerox Corporation. "These general observations on book reviewing were extracted from the author's keynote speech for Book Discussion Day sponsored by the Velma Varner Memorial Fund at Columbia University School of Library Service, December 14, 1974" (p. 22).

ever reviewing is talked about, on the difference between reviewing and criticism. I think there are some differences and some overlap. A critic is more concerned with an intensive personal examination of a book (or an aspect of a book) as literature. A reviewer is more concerned with telling the audience for his or her reviews what a given book is about, what factors make the book good or bad.

On Objectivity

A question I'm often asked is "Doesn't it make it difficult to review a book objectively if the author or the editor is a friend?" It sure does. But, I think it is incumbent on the reviewer to be perfectly honest about every book. You don't need to review with your nails sharpened. You may be misguided, but you must always be honest.

On Bias

Reviewers have to watch themselves for bias toward a favored cause. For instance, if we are militantly feminist or espouse any other philosophy, we must sit back from our reviews and ask, "Is this book really good or is it because it promotes one of my pet causes that I think it is so good?"

On Censoring

Reviewers censor consciously or unconsciously in several ways. The most obvious form of censorship--although we prefer to call it "selection"--can be in what we do not choose for review.

Obviously, Horn Book, Booklist, and The Bulletin of the Center for Children's Books (for which I write the reviews) cannot review every book that's published. Therefore, there are a lot of books we don't review. As a result, I do a great deal of nail-biting about whether or not the omission of those books I haven't reviewed will be construed as censorship.

For instance, a new shipment of books comes in and I see that among ten titles, one of them is a book about new frontiers in medicine. Well, O.K., I know I'm going to do that one, not only because I like the subject, but because I feel I know something about it. (I started out as a premedical student, but the Depression killed that. I went to library school to become a medical librarian and I took a course in children's books and was hooked on books permanently.) If the rest of the shipment includes nonfiction on subjects on which I have varying amounts of knowledge, my choice of the one on medicine nevertheless has an element of censorship in the choosing.

There can be censorship involved in the way we review controversial books. I'll illustrate this with a story on myself. You know

Freddy's Book (J. Neufeld, Random, 1973). You cannot read Freddy's Book without seeing the word "fuck" 500 times. Now how can
you honestly write a review about this book--whether you are going
to praise it, take the middle road and simply comment, or scathing-
ly object to it--without using the word the book is all about? Well,
I did. O.K., I weaseled in the review. Later that year, I was
speaking at the University of Arizona and the program chairman
asked me if I would talk about Freddy's Book since she was using
it with her class in children's literature. I said I would.

Well, I was very conscious of the fact that I had weaseled in
the review, but faced with an audience, I still felt sort of hesitant
about using the word. The program chairman wanted me to, but I
decided next morning to ask some older person. Male. (If that
makes any difference.) He patted me reassuringly and said, "I'm
sure you can find some way around it." So I found some way around
it, again. In the question period, one young man rose and asked,
"How do you people [meaning people of my age] expect to understand
us and the kids who follow us, to whom the word "fuck" means even
less, if you can't bring yourself to put it in a review or mention it
when you're talking about it?" So, called on to defend the honor of
my generation, I said, wording it perhaps too hastily, 'Oh! I say
'fuck' all the time!" Guess who got in the papers.

Actually, when I wrote that review, when I weaseled, I was
aware of the fact that I was being a censor. The self-awareness
has to be there before you can start the process of stopping yourself.

On Prejudicial Reviewing

A reviewer can prejudice review users and throw the wrong
light on a book by including one fact certain to attract attention.
For example, at the 1974 National Council of Teachers of English
Conference, an author told me she was very disappointed because
she had written what she thought was the first children's book in
which the mother of the child protagonist had a lesbian relationship;
that is, the mother had separated from her husband and was living
with another woman. The author said nobody got it, I said, "Yeah,
somebody got it." I had thought seriously about whether or not to
put my adult conclusions about this living arrangement in my review.
I decided not to because it really wasn't what the book was about.
Mentioning it would merely mislead users of the review, leading
them possibly to talk about this suspected aspect exclusively.

Another form of prejudicial review statement is discussing a
book's merit in terms of its price. I never say, and most reviewers won't say, "This used to be $3.95, but now at a higher price,
it isn't worth it." Readers can judge what their budgets can bear.

Then, there is the prejudicial review commentary urged on
reviewers by librarians. I've talked to other review editors over

the last year and found that we've all experienced an increase in the
sort of correspondence that begins, "I have always read and trusted
your reviews, but ..." and on to a request to note the presence of
any profanity. This is one of those cases where I think you can
give, in a review, a wrong impression of the book and throw the
review off balance.

The first such letter I ever got complained of blasphemy I'd
failed to mention in my review of Ellen Grae (Vera & Bill Cleaver,
Lippincott, 1967). Well, it just goes to show what a low character
I am, but I couldn't remember any and I had to look it up. What I
found was that an older girl, boarding in the same house as Ellen
Grae, is just old enough to have become conscious of her sex role
in the old-fashioned way--sending off for cold cream samples, making up, trying to be sophisticated. One of her attempts at sophistication is to say, "Oh, God!" whenever she can. In this book the
phrase contributes to characterization. I thought the characterization
among the strengths of this book. To label this use of dialogue blasphemy would have skewed the review. I simply had to disagree with
the librarian who wrote the letter about this sort of labeling as the
function of the reviewer.

Each of us--editor, reviewer, librarian, teacher, or parent--
has a different idea of what "protecting" children means. Each of
us has a point at which we may say a book has gone too far; what
we differ about is where that point is. And as long as each of us
must make a judgment, whether the decision is to mention or not,
to publish or not, to buy or not, it is incumbent on us to be aware
that we are susceptible to playing a censorious or prejudicial role.

On Coverage

In 1967, I analyzed four children's book review sources used
by most librarians--Booklist, The Horn Book, The Bulletin of the
Center for Children's Books and SLJ. I turned up one statistic that
interested me then and does still. Of the close to 3000 new children's books that had been published during the previous year, only
94 titles had been reviewed by all these review publications. It's a
statistic better described as appalling rather than interesting. Although I can see all the problems attached to it even as I suggest
it, I say that we need some sort of cooperative distribution of reviewing among the review sources. It really seems a shame that
so many books get so little coverage.

There was a study done at the Graduate Library School of the
University of Chicago by Judy Goldberger in which librarians were
asked to talk about what they felt were the gaps in review coverage.
Here's what they came up with:

inadequate reviewing of foreign language books
not enough reviews of new books about minority groups--espe-
    cially Spanish surname, American Indian, and European-

American ethnic groups
scanty reviewing of books from new or alternative presses
too few reviews of books considered for their potential use by
  the visually handicapped
not enough identification of high-interest, low-reading level books
too few reviews of books not recommended for purchase
too few suggestions for and too little comment on use of books
  in the home
the time lag between the publication of books and the appearance
  of reviews.

All review agencies are concerned all the time about this lag.
I must admit that I know many people in publishing and in library
service who feel very strongly about it and I know why they do. I've
never been able to see what the rush is. Children's books stay in
print a long time and are read by succeeding waves of new children
to whom the books are new. However, most of us try very hard to
make our reviews as current as possible.

Since there is a clamor from publishers for current reviews,
I wonder why it takes them so long to get new books to the libraries
that order them. Since there is also a clamor from librarians for
current reviews, I wonder why it takes them so long to get new
books they've received to the shelves. All of the procedures--re-
view scheduling, book ordering, shelf preparation--are very complicated. But, it's not just review scheduling procedures that cause
the lag.

On Self-Perception

I guess, when I look at all of the problems of the children's
book reviewer and all of the pleasures (because it is a pleasure to
see the new books), I think the advice I have for all who review,
for all who select, is: We had better take our work seriously; we
had better not take ourselves too seriously.

BOOBY-TRAPPED BOOKS--
AND REVIEWER RESPONSIBILITY

By Lillian N. Gerhardt

A booby trap is a hidden bomb that can only go off after some unsuspecting soul moves the harmless objects surrounding it. Volunteer boobies are hard to find.

A booby-trapped book is a generally well-written entertainment with one brief passage, often unrelated to the main course of the story, sure to offend many readers on moral or ethical grounds and to raise questions about the book's suitability for recommendation to young readers. Reviewers are expected to be the willing, even eager, boobies in evaluating such books--to either defuse the bombs through persuasive justification for their contribution to the stories that surround them or to set them off by condemning them for their irrelevancy or inappropriateness to surrounding plots, character development, or readers' information needs.

Any library that maintains a costly file of staff reviews, any members of oral evaluation sessions expensively transcribed, and any regular readers of SLJ's Book Review "Letters" column discover when complaints arise that some librarian-reviewers decide to skip discussion of the brief passages that can bring organized censorship groups in full cry after a juvenile novel. They have not told of the one or two blasphemous sentences in a "suspenseful science fiction novel" that can blow up into charges of irreverence or irreligious collection intent. They've ignored the snatches of profanity or the racial slurs in the dialogue of an otherwise "warm family story. " Or, they've failed to mention that an interlude of sexual dalliance is tacked into "a rugged adventure of wilderness survival. "

Everyone in library service is aware that our textbook controversies and demands for the withdrawal of books from library collections erupt from excerpts that feature the use of four-letter words, employ blasphemies in dialogues, or describe some form of sexual behavior. It is therefore difficult to defend any reviewer or librarian who refuses to critically confront these factors when they are present, however briefly, in a new book under evaluation for younger readers.

The only reasonable defense never convinces. This centers

Reprinted with permission from School Library Journal, vol. 22, no. 9, May 1976, p. 9; published by R. R. Bowker Company/A Xerox Corporation.

in the unwillingness of responsible reviewers to inflate one perceived flaw to the point where it overrides many perceived and demonstratable virtues in an evaluation of an author's writing skills and total fictional concept. The defense is weak because censors do their damage with excerpts, not full context concerns. It follows that reviewers are expected to deal with these easily excerpted passages before the censors find them.

There are also some unreasonable defenses that are offered against charges of reviewer copout:

Those words are in constant use by, and before, children. I thought nobody would notice them anymore.

The sexual implications are written between the lines. No sense calling attention to it.

I don't like to feed information to those librarians who would reject any book, however great, if it mentioned sex, or employed obscenities or profanities.

Nobody wants to buy a pig in a poke. Every librarian urged to buy a book on some reviewer's say-so deserves to know if the recommended book should be read before it's shelved. No amount of information is going to change the practices of the willing censors in library service and neither will any amount of information withheld.

We are fortunate to practice and influence book buying in a time when reviewers and librarians are not expected to automatically recoil with horror at every mention of a bodily function or every vulgarism in ordinary speech that may be part of a new book for youngsters. However, until such time as the wider community agrees that concern for literary merit in books for children and young adults equals concern for the manners and morals of the young, reviewers will be held responsible for providing full information on content and sound backup advice on purchase or rejection of new fiction.

Reviewer silence on potential problem passages in books is only golden to their publishers and authors; it serves library selectors not at all.

RECOMMENDED READINGS

Certain aspects about the selection process have received greater attention in the literature than have others. Two such topics are the reviewing of books and approval plans.

The amount of attention given to the reviewing of books may be a reflection of the broad audience that is affected and influenced by this activity. Indeed, authors, librarians, publishers, and reviewers are all concerned with the activity. One example of how this concern is shared is found in the report of meetings such as that sponsored by the Resources and Technical Services Division/ Association of American Publishers Joint Committee in "Program on Reviews Dares to Ask: Who Needs Them?" American Libraries 7, no. 8 (September, 1976), page 515. The relationship of publishers/reviewers and the role of reviews in the mass media are highlighted in "Such Good Friends" by Richard Kluger in American Libraries 4, no. 1 (January, 1973), pages 20-25. An examination of our professional reviewing journals, of their selection policies, editorials, and letters to the editors provides a fascinating and revealing glimpse into contemporary concerns. Studying the letters and replies found in journals such as Library Journal, Booklist, Previews, and School Library Journal provides the reader with a sense of the attitudes and opinions held across the country. One might even say that such exchanges provide a social commentary on the library and its environment.

The topic of approval plans has also received considerable attention in the literature. Arthur L. De Volder, in "Approval Plans--Bounty or Bedlam?" Publishers Weekly 202, no. 1 (July 3, 1972), pages 18-20, traces the concept of approval plans from the 1930s, compares the early concerns of librarians with those of contemporary ones, and then discusses the problems encountered at the Zimmerman Library of the University of New Mexico. In "The Long-Term Effects of Approval Plans," Library Resources and Technical Services 14, no. 3 (Summer, 1970), pages 400-406, Marion Wilden-Hart describes the types of approval plans and how they change the work of the bibliographer. A study conducted to determine the effectiveness of approval plans is reported by G. Edward Evans and Claudia White Argyres in "Approval Plans and Collection

Development in Academic Libraries," Library Resources and Technical Services 18, no. 1 (Winter, 1974), pages 35-50. The findings of this study, which focused on "use," indicate that approval plans may bring into a collection materials that are not used. Evans and Argyres enumerate advantages/disadvantages of approval plans and offer practical advice about the use of such plans.

Libraries, wherever their setting, have been encouraged to involve their patrons in the selection process. An interesting approach that involved senior citizens is described by Jewel Drickamer in "Rhode Island Project: Book Reviews by Older Citizens," Library Journal 96, no. 16 (September 15, 1971), pages 2737-2743. Another approach is found in the EPIE Institute, Educational Products Report; An In-Depth Report, Number 54, Improvising Materials Selection Procedures: A Basic "How to" Handbook, New York: Educational Products Information Exchange Institute, 1973. Although directed to teachers, curriculum specialists and administrators, this is a useful guide for those working in an educational setting. The handbook offers practical advice on how to set up a committee, write criteria, and prepare scientific evaluation of materials.

The readings in this chapter and the recommendations made above represent only a fraction of the literature on the selection process.

CHAPTER 6

THE EVALUATION PROCESS

In earlier chapters the environmental factors in which library collections are developed and the selection process were discussed, setting the stage for this chapter on the evaluation of materials. This evaluation process is closely related to and influenced by the environmental factors and the selection process, for a collection consists of specific items which, regardless of format, must be evaluated in terms of their unique worth and their contribution to the value of the entire collection and its users. A specific item may meet all the criteria, but without consideration of the total collection, the purchase of such an item may be unwise. As an example, an art book limited to one artist, with beautiful reproductions and a lucid text, may be inappropriate for the collection in terms of the needs of the community the library serves, the size and budget of the collection, or the desired level of treatment of the subject if either a more scholarly or more popular coverage is preferred. Thus, the librarian needs to be able to evaluate the individual item and at the same time consider the factors discussed in the preceding chapters.

The writings in this chapter discuss general criteria applicable to all forms of materials, as well as criteria dealing with specific formats. Other aspects of evaluation beyond the scope of this collection of readings are: (1) special criteria relating to the needs of specific audiences, (2) criteria for content in specific disciplines, and (3) criteria used with specific genres. These are important, but the selected articles were chosen to identify more general criteria used in evaluating materials (both print and nonprint) found in a wide range of library collections. The criteria identified may apply to more than one form of media, although composite criteria for multi-forms of media are seldom found in the literature.

The first three articles discuss general criteria which can be applied to the evaluation of a variety of media formats. Using the approach that the quality of library service is dependent upon the quality of the materials in a collection, Carolyn Field in "The Librarian as Selector" identifies and discusses general factors which require the librarian's professional judgment in selecting all types of materials. These factors are: (1) authoritativeness of publisher or producer, (2) significance of subject matter, (3) importance of author or film maker, (4) accuracy of information and data, (5) literary merit of artistic quality, (6) potential or known use by patrons, (7) importance to total collection, (8) current and/or permanent values, (9) scarcity of materials on the subject, and (10) price and format. Field goes on to point out that the evaluation of the collection includes not only consideration of new materials but consideration of materials which need replacing or have become obsolete.

Some of the above criteria also appear in the article by Robert N. Broadus entitled "Selection and Acquisition" from Nonprint Media in Academic Libraries. Broadus focuses on the academic librarian's responsibility for evaluation of nonprint items as a part of collection development. He discusses general considerations of the relative values of different media, such as durability of the physical item, durability of information, effectiveness in communication, convenience of use, and cost factors. Indeed, these are matters that all libraries need to consider about nonprint materials.

Addressing the question of evaluating materials to meet needs of learners and the objectives of the school, Namu Olaolorum Orderinde presents an evaluation instrument in "Instructional Material Assessment Tool." The eight points of assessment, which overlap some of the criteria noted earlier, include: (1) goal and objective oriented, (2) objectivity, (3) promotes understanding, (4) level of sophistication, (5) validation, (6) design variable, and (7) personal assessment. Although the focus in this article is on the instructional use of materials, the factors covered are similar to those covered in articles by Spirt and Limbacher.

Diana L. Spirt in "Criteria, Choices, and Other Concerns about Filmstrips" discusses two basic criteria: (1) idea (intellectual content), and (2) use of the most suitable medium for the treatment of the intellectual content. Using specific examples of children's materials, Spirt compares their treatment as found in books, filmstrips, and films. The effectiveness of one format over another varies from example to example, emphasizing the need to evaluate each medium's suitability for the presentation of each unique idea.

A broader approach is used by James Limbacher in "Hints for Film Evaluation." This list of questions to be considered in evaluating films is arranged according to the following headings: content values, psychological values, artistic and technical values, social and ethical values, entertainment values, and audience reactions. Although generated by an audiovisual librarian in a public library, these questions have applicability in many other library settings.

The unique physical characteristics of many materials in library collections mean that special criteria must be used in evaluating these formats. Common criteria for materials, regardless of format, are content, suitability of treatment, appeal to audience, potential worth to the collection, and durability. The articles selected to illustrate this point provide criteria for evaluating (1) realia, which includes toys, articles, and other three dimensional objects, (2) maps, (3) microforms, (4) pamphlets, and (5) recordings.

A new format in libraries, that of realia, has resulted from the concern of librarians that young children be provided an opportunity to develop through play. The physical nature of this format and the characteristics of their users, aged 3 and 4 years, call for special criteria to be used in evaluating such materials. In "Criteria for Selecting Realia" from Toys to Go: A Guide to the Use of Realia in Public Libraries, Jean Rustici lists questions that are intended to serve as guidelines for establishing criteria. The questions cover such factors as design, durability, and safety.

Maps, as another unique format found in collections, call for specific criteria, which are presented in "The Acquisition of Maps for Schools and Other Small Libraries" by Charles E. Current. Specific criteria mentioned for such evaluation are: (1) visibility, (2) size, (3) amount of detail and suitability for grade level, (4) color, (5) durability, and (6) accuracy.

For microforms libraries are dependent on the micropublishers for the technical qualities of image reproductions, as is pointed out by Ralph J. Folcarelli and Ralph C. Ferragamo in the excerpt from "Microform Publications: Hardware and Supplies." However, the authors do identify additional criteria that librarians need to consider, such as existing equipment, packaging, and microformat. This excerpt also identifies additional sources of information to assist librarians in their evaluation of microforms.

Another unique format commonly found in library collections is that of pamphlets. In an excerpt from "Supplementary Pamphlet File in an Academic Library," Doris Snyder identifies the following contributions of a pamphlet collection: (1) currency, (2) uniqueness, (3) multiplication of sources, (4) compactness and accessibility, (5) extension, (6) authority, and (7) reference. These contributions can serve as criteria to be used in evaluating pamphlets.

Trying to establish and maintain a record collection, especially one dealing with popular music, involves other considerations for librarians. The role of libraries in providing such collections and the range of concerns are discussed by Frank Hoffman in "Popular Music Collections and Public Libraries." Hoffman's call for libraries to become depositories for the "preservation and documentation of popular phonorecords for future generations" need not be limited to public libraries.

In summary, these readings provide an overview of criteria commonly used for the evaluation of materials in a library's collection. The examples of the unique criteria applied in evaluating specific formats point out the increasing range of knowledge needed if sound professional evaluations are to occur. Additional sources identified at the end of the chapter provide further guidance in this important process in the building of a collection.

THE LIBRARIAN AS SELECTOR

By Carolyn W. Field

In this age of emphasis on technological equipment and services to the non-reader, there has been a tendency to overlook the
importance of the materials to be used and the place of the librarian in selecting these materials. The key to quality service is the
librarian but the key to the quality of the librarian's work is the
material used--whether it be a book, a film or a recording. Today,
the librarian may use a variety of materials to service his clientele
but the basic tool is still the book and I will discuss it although
many of the statements made can be related to audiovisual materials.

What is book selection? In Practical Administration of Public
Libraries by Joseph L. Wheeler and Herbert Goldhor, the following
statement is made: "Book selection is an art, involving personal
knowledge of many factors and professional judgment. "

Book selection includes much more than the decision to accept or reject an individual book. It includes the policies for acquisition for review, reviewing, selecting, maintaining and withdrawal
of each book in the collection. It includes personal knowledge of the
needs and interests of the community to be served--school, college,
public or special. It includes personal knowledge of the collections
in other agencies in the community and the policies and procedures
for the use of those materials. It includes personal knowledge of
the budget and space for materials as well as staffing to acquire,
prepare and service the materials. And above all, it includes a
written selection policy, endorsed by the managing body of the institution, that is specific not only in what is to be accepted but in what
is to be excluded.

The most important factor in the book selection procedure is
the selector himself who should have an extensive background in the
subject for which he is responsible and should be an avid and speedy
reader. I am afraid that there are too many people in the library
profession today who are not readers. The argument I have heard
in defense of these people is two-fold--one, that technological processes are taking over and the technician is more important than the
bookman, and two, that reading has declined to the point that community workers and audiovisual materials are more vital to library
service than print. Well, I disagree with both arguments and firmly believe that the librarian who works with or for the public served
must be a reader and have a consuming desire to serve as an inter-

Reprinted by permission from Catholic Library World, vol. 46, no.
1, July-August 1974, pp. 4-7.

mediary between the writer and the reader in the communication of knowledge and information.

Selection Policy

Let us talk briefly about a selection policy and what it should include. First, there should be a statement of the general objectives relating to the institution and the community it serves. Since I work in Philadelphia, let me quote the opening paragraph from the Free Library of Philadelphia's General Library Objectives: "The Free Library's policies and objectives in the selection of library materials seek to carry out its functions as the public library resource and information center for the people of the Philadelphia area. Its primary role is both educational and cultural; its secondary role is recreational. It serves both individuals and groups. Recognition is given in the acquisition of library materials to the total composition of the community, including such factors as age levels, racial makeup, religious affiliations, educational, economic, recreational and cultural characteristics, national origins and political viewpoints. "

The Free Library's policy explains its relationship to other libraries and institutions and lists general factors influencing selection. More details are given in the separate policies for the selection of materials for children, young adults and adults. Many of the factors require professional judgment on the part of the librarian. What are these general factors?

1.   Authoritativeness of publisher or producer:

Approximately 30,000 books are published every year and no librarian could read them all. In fact, even though a small percentage of the total output is reviewed in professional publications, few librarians would have the time to read all the reviews. So it is essential for the librarian to have knowledge of the dependability of the publisher for books and producer for films. One of my favorite film producers is Robert Radnitz. He believes in producing quality films for children from children's books. Among his successes are Island of the Blue Dolphins, My Side of the Mountain, Sounder, The Little Ark and Where the Lilies Bloom. Mr. Radnitz has impeccable judgment in his choice of books and produces films of the highest quality. If his name is on a film, I know that I can trust to his good taste.

2.   Significance of subject matter:

Anyone who just glances at the titles published each year will be overwhelmed at the variety and superficiality of material being published. There are many non-books published, many cut and paste jobs, and many titles on subjects that contribute little or nothing to information or knowledge. Each librarian has to use judgment in deciding when a particular subject is necessary for his collection.

3. Importance of author or film maker:

One of the most difficult aspects of selection comes when the item in question is in contradiction to the current mores of the selector and/or the community. And yet the work in question may be an important part of the literary and cultural arena due to the place of the author or film maker in it. For example, for many years Henry Miller's books were banned in the United States. Just a few years ago, libraries which circulated the books were involved in cases of censorship. And yet, the work of Henry Miller influenced many of our current writers and represented a new direction in the literary world.

4. Accuracy of information and data:

It hardly seems necessary to mention this factor but carelessness or dishonesty on the part of the author and/or publisher or simple typographical errors can lead to inaccurate information. False information could be a matter of life and death, such as, an antidote to poison or the proportion of chemicals in a mixture or it can just spoil a cake if the proportion for specific ingredients is wrong. In the children's area I have found that the tendency to inaccuracy is more prevalent in fiction than in non-fiction.

In 1955, I reviewed two books that came out the same year on the history of Sault Ste. Marie. The first one, called The Mighty Soo: Five Hundred Years at Sault Ste. Marie, was written by Clara Ingram Judson, known as a careful researcher who wrote in a semifictionalized style that would appeal to children. The second book emphasized the early history of the region and told the story of Henry Schoolcraft's journey to find the source of the Mississippi in 1820. Henry Schoolcraft was a geologist and kept a detailed diary of his life and experiences in that region. The same incident was used by both authors but the facts were quite different. Which author was accurate?

I felt sure that the Free Library had a reprint of Henry Schoolcraft's Journal which would include the incident concerned. Mrs. Judson was right. I wrote to the editor of the 'nameless' author expressing my concern at the carelessness of the author and the publisher. Her reply was to the effect that since it was a children's book what difference did it make. Well, it made a lot of difference to me and I have never trusted our nameless author or the publisher since that time.

5. Literary merit or artistic quality:

   With limited budgets, limited time for people to read, watch TV, go to the movies and take part in cultural activities, it seems sensible to provide the best when a choice has to be made. Some years ago, a research study was made on the number of books an average student was exposed to during his school years. 700 books, including readers, primers, textbooks and books for pleasure and information was the average read. Today, television and programmed teaching has cut sharply into this and the average will be much lower. Therefore, it behooves us, at least with children, to provide for them the best during these formative years.

6. Potential or known use by patrons:

   Any book that fulfills all the factors mentioned up to now is a waste of money and a shelf sitter if there is no current demand for the subject or a potential demand. Interlibrary loan should be used to fill the unusual and rare request for a particular title. Or the patron could be referred to the neighboring agency or library where the title would be available. This factor points up the importance of knowing the resources in your community.

7. Importance to total collection:

   Basically this factor would relate to a large public library or academic library where serious reference and research is carried on. I grew up on the philosophy that every library, no matter how small, should have a "balanced collection." But this was before the days of networks and systems and the flood of print materials. Today, one has to consider the use of a particular item.

8. Current and/or permanent values:

   Professional judgment is the key to adding to the collection items that may be of current interest but of ephemeral value, such as the underground newspapers, and in the early sixties slight superficial books on the black. For an academic library the underground newspapers could be of permanent value for research purposes.

9. Scarcity of materials on the subject:

   We live in an "instant communication" age and the majority of people want information on a subject immediately. When John F. Kennedy became president of the United States, primary grade children wanted a book on his life and there was nothing suitable. Books were rushed through the presses that related to few factors in quality book selection and yet were bought in quantity by librarians because nothing else was available. Early books on the Black and

the American Indian were poorly written but bought widely because
there was little choice. Today, there is an adequate supply of well
written books so there is no need to buy or leave on the shelves
books on the Black or the American Indian that do not meet our
criteria.

10. Price and format:

Price and format are low men on the totem pole except to
libraries with meager budgets. Paperbacks are a boon to those libraries with small or inadequate budgets. In general, format is
more important in the children's area than in the adult because older
boys and girls will not accept a book that looks "childish" in size,
print or illustration no matter how well written or important in subject matter it is.

For the benefit of the school librarians, I will quote from the
Philadelphia Board of Education's Policy: "The philosophy of the
school library, whether central or classroom, is one of service to
teachers and pupils. Its object is to provide informational and recreational materials selected to meet the needs of the school community. It seeks to enrich all areas of the curriculum and to select
material of good taste at all levels of reading ability represented in
the school. The long range goal of the school library program is
to develop lifetime reading habits and the ability to evaluate intelligently what has been read."

The policy quotes Lester Asheim in differentiating between
selection and censorship: "Selection begins with a presumption in
favor of liberty of thought; censorship, with a presumption in favor
of thought control. Selection's approach to the book is positive,
seeking its values in the book as a book, and in the book as a
whole. Censorship's approach seeks to protect--not the right--but
the reader himself from the fancied effects of his reading. The
selector has faith in the intelligence of the reader, the censor has
faith only in his own. "[1]

Selection Technique

Earlier I mentioned that approximately 30,000 titles are published each year of which approximately 2,500 are children's books.
Although a number of the titles published are reprints, there are
still a great many new books. The best reviewing technique for
considering a title for your collection is to read the book yourself.
With so many titles published each year this is an impossible task
even where the librarian devotes full time to "book selection. "
Thus, the critical use of the reviewing media is essential for all
librarians. Reviews done by an individual should be considered in
the knowledge of the reviewer's experience, background and bias.
Reviews done by a committee should be considered, as with many
committee reports, as a compromise.

Not least as an influence in the selection of books is the traveling salesman. Some publishing houses have a large sales staff of their own and some publishers join together to send salesmen into the hinterlands to promote their books. The librarian will be delighted to see the actual books, can be wooed by the salesman with a pleasant personality and will not discover until too late that the budget is spent and the books bought are mediocre or poor. Of course, there are honest salesmen but there are also those who care only for the quick buck. The only solution I can see is for the librarian in a small library to join with other librarians in the area for cooperative reviewing and guidance in selection. There are other ways to get help if it is not essential to have a publication hot off the press.

The Collection

Up to this point, I have emphasized the selection and acquisition of new titles. But the replacement of worn out books and the discarding of the ephemeral and obsolete is just as important and requires even more expert professional judgment. Again, the librarian needs to know the community and its needs. Books in the collection need to be compared for content and format with new titles being published. The ideal would be for the librarian to have read personally all the books but this would not be humanly possible. Most large library systems, school and public, have a continuous process of reevaluating books and assign a specific portion of the budget for this replacement of older titles.

Although the copyright date on a book of nonfiction can be a guide to the up-to-dateness of the information, and can be used for discard, it means nothing for a book of fiction. Treasure Island, Little Women, Alice's Adventures in Wonderland are as popular today and necessary in a collection as when they were published. However, the copy on the library shelf might be discarded for a more attractive edition.

For the librarian who does not have the extensive reading background necessary for careful weeding, the H. W. Wilson publications are invaluable: Children's Catalog, a basic volume with four annual supplements, Senior High School Catalog, a basic volume with five annual supplements, the Fiction Catalog and the Standard Catalog for Public Libraries which is for non-fiction. Since the Junior High School Catalog duplicates many titles that are in the Children's catalog and the Senior High School Catalog most libraries would not need to buy it.

Earlier when I mentioned the selection policy of the Philadelphia Board of Education, I quoted Lester Asheim and his definition of selection and censorship. Every librarian must select and not censor.

One of the most devastating actions of the Supreme Court is

last June's ruling giving communities the right of censorship. Over 78,000 units of government exist in the United States and the book world can be thrown into complete chaos with each political unit determining what shall and shall not be considered pornographic or obscene. An effort is being made by the American Library Association, publishers and writers to have the state be considered the "local community." Even though this could mean 50 different interpretations of a book, it would be more practical than 78,000 different opinions.

Another serious aspect to the decision is that librarians, teachers and booksellers are presumed to have knowledge that a book is obscene and can be arrested on a criminal charge with no redress to the Supreme Court. Carried to an extreme, the librarian would dare to provide for the reading public only the saccharine, mediocre book that contributed nothing to the reader intellectually, socially or morally or the "classics," such as Little Women, Robinson Crusoe, Silas Marner and The Water Babies.

The great danger of censorship is that people tend to let emotions determine what is or is not obscene and no individual or book would be free from censorship.

Helen E. Haines in her introduction to Living with Books; The Art of Book Selection has expressed the librarian as bookman and selector far better than I can. She said "Librarianship is the only calling that devotes itself to bringing books into the common life of the world. The materials librarians work with are the materials which furnish the understanding, knowledge, and reason that can inform the mind and direct the will to meet the challenge of the time, to fit ourselves to its compulsions, to discern and guide the forces that are shaping the future.... The spirit of delight and confidence in books, the receptive and adventurous attitude toward new and experimental, the catholicity of life-long friendship and understanding for literature, are attributes of librarianship more than any other calling. And those attributes must be fused in a dynamic of social consciousness, of confidence and purpose, if librarians are to rise to their potential leadership in welding public understanding and unity for the building of a safer and better world."[2]

References

1. American Library Association. Proceedings of the Second Conference on Intellectual Freedom. Chicago: 1954. p. 98.
2. Haines, Helen E. Living with Books: The Art of Book Selection; second ed., Columbia University Press, 1950. p. 10.

SELECTION AND ACQUISITION (Excerpts)

By Robert N. Broadus

A great deal has been written about the selection of audiovisual material by teachers for use in classrooms; considerable attention has been given the task of choosing media for learning resource centers in elementary and secondary schools; but
little advice has been offered for the selection of these
intellectual, inspirational, and entertaining forms of information by academic librarians. Those facts and theories
used by the teacher, as he or she chooses materials
for achieving some specific goal in the classroom, have
some relationship to the building of a library collection
as a whole. The differences are also significant.

Responsibility

In planning a collection for the college or university library,
one of the first questions to be settled is the role to be played by
the classroom faculty in the selection process. Their contribution
may vary with the difference in intended use of the materials. If it
is assumed that motion picture films, for instance, will be shown
before assembled classes only, and not viewed by students as individuals, then the faculty should have primary authority for their selection. If, however, the items are to be integrated with the
library's book and periodical resources, so that students may
use them according to individual interests as well as class
assignments, then the librarian must take primary responsibility for their selection, as is done in the case of printed
materials.

Lane has documented the growth in the influence of the librarian, as opposed to that of the teaching and research faculty, in
building collections.[1] This movement away from faculty dominated
selection is a phenomenon of the twentieth century academic library.
Felix Reichmann, in a recent survey of research libraries, found
evidence confirming the assumption that faculty participation in selection is declining.[2] It makes sense that the librarian, skilled in
evaluating materials, should, as Pringle suggests, take the leadership in collecting audiovisual and similar materials.[3] The librarian

alone is in a position to see the collection as a whole and also comprehend the vast array of items available for acquisition. Few persons limited to a particular subject field can have such a comprehensive view.

Perhaps it goes without saying that choices should be made with the advice (and probably consent) of the classroom faculty. The librarian, and those on the staff to whom authority for selection is delegated seek guidance wherever it can be found--whether in periodicals, books, computer data banks, or from knowledgeable persons. Those faculty who are interested enough to make thoughtful suggestions for the library collection are to be treasured and cultivated. They are more likely to use the materials and to recommend them to their students. The librarian should, therefore, encourage faculty members to offer suggestions by making catalogs and other aids available, routing announcements to instructors, and providing opportunities for them to preview possible purchases. [4] Teamwork is required, although the librarian must make the final decisions.

The fact that the librarian takes primary responsibility for building the collection does not necessarily preclude the allotment of some portion of funds to departments of instruction, provided these allocations are kept fluid. It should be made clear to all faculty that this money is not being given to the departments; it still belongs to the library or, rather, to the institution as a whole. Departmental allotments thus can be treated as an administrative convenience to facilitate a spread in expenditure so that no units of instruction are slighted. If a significant portion of the budget is divided among departments, there is an advantage in placing all forms of material in these allotments. Not only does this procedure provide a fairer distribution, it will also stimulate the departments, their faculties, and perhaps their students to become more aware of and concerned with nonprint media.

If a department then advises buying several color motion pictures, the point can be made that such a purchase may reduce the number of books, periodicals, and other materials which may be obtained in the field. It is very important, though, that a film or other expensive item useful to more than one department, not be rejected because a single department is not willing to have the entire price taken from its own allocated fund.

The Field from Which to Collect

When the librarian, with his or her staff, assumes responsibility for the collection of nonprint along with the usual library materials, it becomes necessary for certain broad assumptions to be made as to which ones will be best for the particular library. The librarian is then forced to come to terms with the stubborn question of what constitutes the specific library. Strangely enough, there is no satisfactory answer, for definitions of the library are woefully inadequate. Is it a service organization? If so, what is the precise nature and limit of that service? Is it a collection? If so, what specific kinds of material does it collect?

So far the answers to these questions are not entirely rational. The academic library does not collect and distribute things such as animals (as some public libraries do proudly), nor does it collect vials of odors from which the clientele may identify chemical compositions (as at least one special library does). How, then, shall the limits of a library's resources be described? Some people, trying to define policy, say that the library collects the materials of communication, but this province also is too broad. Ogden and Richards, in their Meaning of Meaning, say that all experience is either "enjoyed or interpreted ... or both," and that very little experience fails to be interpreted in some way. [5] And everyone knows that the campus will have many materials of communication--materials which are to be "interpreted" but which are not under the jurisdiction of the library.

In the present state of the art it should be admitted that each director of an academic library has to decide how large an empire to build, bearing in mind that conquered territory sometimes has to be defended. [6] It is important, though, that each college or university work out a policy which contains a clear statement of what resources are to be the responsibility of the librarian.

Once the general boundaries are established in terms of the kinds or forms of materials to be gathered, the objectives of the institution should be taken into consideration, and the collections built accordingly. These objectives are not always well defined, but differ slightly from one institution to another. Although it may seem that they are chosen more for appearance than for purposes of practical guidance, they must be an integral part of the selector's thought process. As Robert Haywood suggests, the librarian by rights should get together with deans and academic departments, establishing the goals each part of the institution intends to pursue and setting up priorities for courses and library needs. [7] Then yearly changes in faculty will be less likely to disrupt the building of the collection. Resources which support the curriculum are of first importance. However, there is both precedent and reason for obtaining so-called recreational materials for they too can have significant value.

As a general proposition, the library should collect those items which convey the most important information and the knowledge most worth having--materials which stimulate thought on the gravest problems of life, which build acceptable attitudes, which develop desirable skills, which entertain constructively. Within this framework, the utilitarian philosophy of the best (most useful, most valuable) materials obtainable for the money would seem most sensible. Its application is not simple. Those responsible for decisions do not know what materials are going to be published and have to make judgments, based largely on the production of previous years. They are aware of some gaps to be filled, but do not know how long certain items now available will remain so. At the end of the year, is it possible to know how much has been spent for each type of media, such as books, periodicals, transparencies, maps, filmstrips, photograph records, motion pictures, tapes, cassettes, and slides? Twyford's estimate that the number of new films, filmstrips, tapes, recordings, models, and graphic materials produced each year totals about five thousand is undoubtedly low. [8] In 1967, the National Information Center for Educational Media (NICEM) surveyed seven forms of materials (16mm motion pictures, 35mm filmstrips, 8mm motion cartridges, overhead transparencies, video tapes, phonodiscs, and audio tapes) and concluded that their annual production totaled thirty thousand. [9] The number of obtainable nonprint items surely approaches that for books, periodicals, and pamphlets published in the English language. To purchase all print and nonprint materials (of the types commonly collected by academic institutions) offered each year in English would require something over $1 million. This statement should not, of course, be interpreted to mean that older items or those in foreign languages should be neglected.

Relative Values of Different Media

If the selection process is to be intelligent, that is something other than random, haphazard, and opportunist, the librarian must have some overall assumptions about the relative values of different media. If a color motion picture film is purchased, it means some thirty books or twenty filmstrips must be rejected. Even free materials are an expense, for time and money are required to obtain each item and then to catalog, store, service, and discard. With a budget of $100,000, less than one-tenth of the relevant, current, English language materials can be obtained. Assumptions as to value have to be made in spite of the fact that no one has enough information to make decisions with a great degree of assurance.

Nonprint media are highly diversified. Their capabilities and psychological implications vary widely. Some are appropriate for groups, others for individuals. Some convey messages through the eye, others through the ear, and many utilize both. There are materials for presenting specific concrete facts, others for creating moods or emotional tones. How shall one judge these types? C. J. Duncan of the University of Newcastle-upon-Tyne, has said that the real dilemma in the use of audiovisual materials in higher education is the interaction between cost and appositeness. [10] The simpler, cheaper aids tend to be more specific for a selected audience. Those which are more expensive to produce are usually planned to appeal to larger audiences (in order that costs may be recovered) and unfortunately their messages are often too diluted or blunted for specific classwork. With reference to art education, William H. Allen has a chart showing the relationships of particular kinds of institutional media to learning objectives, estimating the relative effectiveness (high, medium, low) of nine forms or combinations, vis-à-vis given purposes. [11] More analyses of this kind are needed, but in the meantime, some general considerations involved in getting the most useful materials for the cost will be discussed.

Durability of the Physical Item

Ordinarily the longest-lasting form is preferable to the fragile. Books normally are damaged very little by reading, while films in clumsy hands are particularly vulnerable. Recordings may be scratched, but have no pages to be torn out. The durability of each form may be increased by improved technology; e.g., phono-records are less subject to breakage than they were only a few years ago.

Durability of Information

Some fields of thought change rapidly. Facts on such subjects as political boundaries, manufacturing processes, dress fashions, and hair styles are quickly outdated while other information remains stable over a long period of time. The atom, the tree, and the hyena have about the same nature in 1971 as they had a few thousand years ago. There is, however, another dimension to the problem of change. The object studied may remain stable, while information about it increases rapidly: the moon presumably has changed little for millenia but informational materials describing it are constantly becoming outdated.

The general rule is that for rapidly changing subjects the less expensive media is to be preferred for purchase while the more expensive item may be rented. Thus replacement can be made as required. For concepts that change slowly, expensive items are favored for purchase.

A similar problem is pointed out by Frank Johnson of the University of Leeds. [12] He feels that professors in higher education are close enough to the frontiers of knowledge that they tend to present in their lectures a distinctively individual view. While the substance taught in a history course in one high school may be quite similar to the content of the same course taught in another school, at the university level each professor is more likely to prefer his own interpretation. Hence, a film, which is useful for modern history in one college, may not satisfy the faculty responsible for the same course in another institution.

Effectiveness in Communication

It is extremely difficult to get reliable information on the relative effectiveness of communicative media. Numerous experiments in classrooms have proven disappointingly little with regard to the relative effectiveness of various presentation formats.[13] Individual differences among users are important but difficult to measure without isolated factors that reveal reliable data from which to base generalizations. One student seems to get more from a book, another from a film. Motion pictures obviously are better for objects which need to be shown in motion, especially scientific subjects, while they may be less effective for other topics. Though it would seem that a medium presenting its information through two sensory channels, e.g., eye and ear, would be more instructive than a medium using only one such channel, recent studies seem to demonstrate this assumption is not necessarily true.

People are taught how to read, but spend far less time learning to look at pictures. If we were instructed more thoroughly in extracting information from pictorial matter, nonprint media would undoubtedly be more useful. To some, films have the advantage of novelty, but as the novelty wears off, effectiveness may be reduced. In television, color seems to show little if any learning advantage, at least for some subjects, over black and white, though it may bring more pleasure and satisfaction to the user.[14] This conclusion does not necessarily imply that it is valid for libraries to save money by obtaining other formats in black and white rather than color. Indeed, a great deal is yet to be learned about these matters, requiring the librarian to refine his views as more results of research studies become available.[15]

Convenience of Use

Other things being equal, a format which is fast and easy to use should be preferred to one which is inconvenient. Mere portability is a factor. A book ranks high in this respect, since it is easy to carry about, and may be used for relatively long periods of time, several hours on the average. Since 1948, the use of phonorecords outside the library has become more convenient due to long playing discs. A student is willing to carry a bulky package home to get more music or spoken time. Tape cartridges add to this advantage. Video recordings and players appear to have a promising future as equipment for them is standardized.

The requirement of a projector or other machine reduces for most people the satisfaction with which materials can be used. Pocket and lap-size viewers for microforms now in research stages may well increase the relative value of these materials. Since few people today have microform readers in their homes, use is largely confined to libraries and even that is still none too satisfactory. Easier loading projectors improve the desirability of films. Also, 8mm film cartridges have some advantage over conventional films, in that they provide easy access to a small subject without the viewer having to endure a long reel in order to reach a specific point of interest. Forsdale says that the 8mm is to the 16mm as the freely circulated book is to the manuscript that was chained to the monastery table.[16]

Cost Factors

On the basis of financial considerations one may judge that a book or two on a subject represents a better buy than a filmstrip, since the book can be used longer and more conveniently. However, the filmstrip may present matter not found in any book or may offer it in a more effective fashion thus justifying its purchase. After the three or four leading books on a subject have been obtained, the law of diminishing returns (owing to repetition of matter from title to title) may indicate that a filmstrip is the next wise purchase. Obviously, also, there are stimuli which a printed item simply cannot convey.

The task is complicated by the fact that seldom is there a simple question of book or periodical versus film or recording for a given topic. Masses of material overlap one another rendering it difficult, if not impossible, to make exactly the right selection in each case. One should recognize that mistakes will be made, and that even if correct choices were wisely made each time, others might not recognize and appreciate the fact. Nonetheless, the librarian would like to make intelligent choices for the maximum benefit of the library program.

Building a Collection

Once a collection is established, the process of further building is often one of considering each item available and making one of three decisions about it: (1) to select and acquire it at once, (2) to reject it, or (3) to reserve judgment and file notes for later consideration. Each decision should be based on factors such as those previously discussed, and on such questions as:
(1) Is the content of the item useful, important? Are extraneous or distracting elements filtered out?
(2) Does the item present the facts? Is it accurate and up-to-date? Is it truthful? These are not easy questions to answer for an informational item, in printed or nonprint format. Even if the librarian is expert, there will always be some doubt. The most reasonable course is to obtain a consensus of competent opinion, and to act on that. Some items thought to be untrue may be obtained anyway, for historical use or as examples of unusual points of view.
(3) Is the item's arrangement satisfactory? At higher levels of study a logical order may be best; but for some purposes a progression from known to unknown, or from simple to difficult, may be preferable. If there is a summary or review, is it handled well?
(4) Is the subject one which is well presented by the particular medium used? Does the specific format teach this subject better than is possible with other media? If the purpose is to preserve or store information (rather than to teach), is the medium selected for this purpose the most effective and practical?
(5) Is an item appropriate for college level? This criterion is particularly difficult to apply. The claim made for some films is that they may be used in kindergarten through college. This may

be but it is rather uncommon. However, a slide of a tarantula may be fascinating to a small child and educationally valuable to a graduate student. Even a reproduction of "Whistler's Mother" may be appropriate for young and old. Pictures without accompanying words can appeal to a wide range of levels, as can phonorecords, especially those containing certain kinds of music. It is the use of words which usually limits an item to specific age levels. Even here, there are exceptions such as Walt Disney films, which appeal to children as well as their grandparents. Moreover, a children's book on a technical subject may be read with profit by an adult. As a general rule, though, printed materials are likely to have a smaller range of use level than visual items. Sound films and tapes of personal interviews tend to be restrictive, while purely pictorial or other nonverbal materials have an advantage in this regard.

(6) Regarding films, is commercialism held to an acceptable level, not distracting from the central theme and informational content?

(7) Finally, is the technical quality acceptable? Is it artistic? Are physical size, format, and color satisfactory? Is the workmanship of high quality? Are background music, narration, and other presentation devices of particular items handled well?

References

1. David O. Lane. "The Selection of Academic Library Materials: A Literature Survey," College and Research Libraries 29: 364-72 (Sept. 1968).
2. Felix Reichmann. "Purchase of Out-of-Print Material in American University Libraries," Library Trends 18:332 (Jan. 1970).
3. Eugene A. Pringle. "Audiovisual Materials and College Objectives," Choice 3:1108 (Feb. 1967).
4. For suggestions on filing, see John K. Bertrand, "Media Reference Service: Neglected Step-Child of the New Era," Audiovisual Instruction 12:16-22 (Jan. 1967).
5. C. K. Ogden and I. A. Richards. The Meaning of Meaning, 10th ed. (New York: Harcourt, 1952), p. 50.
6. For some suggestions, see Guidelines for Audio-Visual Services in Academic Libraries, Audio Visual Committee (Chicago: Assn. of College and Research Libraries, 1968), p. 14-15.
7. C. Robert Haywood. "Old, Bold Librarians," The Library-College Journal 1:11-14 (Summer 1968).
8. Loran C. Twyford. "Educational Communications Media," Encyclopedia of Educational Research, 4th ed. (New York: Macmillan, 1969), p. 367.
9. Thomas Risner. "NICEM, Mediated Media Index," Educational Screen and Audiovisual Guide 49:15-17 (Jan. 1970).
10. C. J. Duncan. "A Survey of Audio-Visual Equipment and Methods," in Media and Methods: Instructional Technology in Higher Education, edited by Derick Unwin (London: McGraw-Hill, 1969), p. 14-15.
11. William H. Allen. "Media Stimulus and Types of Learning," Audiovisual Instruction 12:28 (Jan. 1967).

12. Frank Johnson. "Audio-Visual Aids, " in University Teaching in Transition, edited by David Layton (Edinburgh: Oliver and Boyd, 1968), p. 126.
13. See Review of Educational Research 38:111-96 (Apr. 1968). This number is devoted to a review of the literature on "Instructional Materials: Educational Media and Technology" for the six-year period since 1962.
14. See AV Communication Review 16:333 (Fall 1968).
15. Charles F. Hoban. "Communication in Education in a Revolutionary Age, " AV Communication Review 18:375 (Winter 1970).
16. Louis Forsdale. "8mm Film-in Education: Status and Prospects--1968, " in To Improve Learning: An Evaluation of Instructional Technology, vol. 1, edited by Sidney G. Tickton (New York and London: Bowker, 1970), p. 231-32.

INSTRUCTIONAL MATERIAL ASSESSMENT TOOL

By Namu Olaolorum Orderinde

A growing concern of school administrators, teachers, and media specialists is how to properly select appropriate learning materials that relate to the objectives of the school and the needs of the learners. The awesome task of selecting materials from the vast array of commercially prepared print and nonprint items points to the need for a systematic guide for materials assessment.

With increasing demands upon the school's learning resources center, the media specialist is expected to manage, coordinate, design, develop, implement, and evaluate educational media. Subsequently, media specialists need reliable tools and techniques to reduce the hazards on selecting learning materials: materials which could lack relevancy and purposefulness.

In a recent survey of literature, we found considerable information on concepts and techniques for media selection. In many cases, these were descriptive statements relating to factors which should be considered when reviewing materials. As an example, Quisenberry (1973) developed a set of criteria for the selection of learning materials by focusing upon how content and design variables relate to the developmental aspects of the learner: aesthetic value, concept development, personal relationships, language development, and so on. Other sources have developed extensive standards for analyzing and evaluating specific materials (Erickson, 1970; Brown, 1965; Rufsvold, 1967).

Many school media centers have developed standardized feedback forms that are used by local educators to assess a school's audiovisual services operation and the suitability of specific learning materials. This type of monitoring is generally directed toward improving the services operation and determining how singular materials relate to a specific instructional sequence. Although this assessment is important and essential, it seems that an orchestrated effort is needed to bring together a list of items that would meaningfully and efficiently evaluate the diverse quantities of learning materials available.

It is important that those educators who are to be involved in the selection of learning materials be provided with sets of evaluative criteria that will assist them in assessing materials. The evaluators should address themselves to the presentational variables of the ma-

Reprinted from Audiovisual Instruction, vol. 19, no. 4, April 1974, pp. 22-24, by permission of the publisher.

terial. Design, purpose, objectivity, validation, and learner interests and ability levels must be considered in addition to the personal assessment of the evaluator.

The faculty of the School of Library Media at Alabama A & M recently completed a survey that focused upon the factors to which professional educators address themselves when examining the design qualities and informational properties of learning materials. University professors, school administrators, librarians, media supervisors, library media specialists, and teachers were surveyed. Opinionaires were mailed to 180 professionals in the southeastern United States, and 97 satisfactorily completed forms were returned. The Opinionaire Survey Form listed 15 brief statements which required a yes/no response or a short statement. The survey had essentially three focal points:

1. Major considerations when reviewing learning materials.
2. Supplemental information that is helpful in assessing validity.
3. Elements that are most often scrutinized when reviewing learning materials.

After analyzing the input from the 97 responses, it appears that learning materials might be assessed under eight points:

I. Goal and Objective Oriented. The content of the presentation related to the explicity of implicitly stated goals and/or objectives.

The goals and objectives are defined and are evidenced in the content of the material.

The material seemed to achieve its stated goals or objectives.

The content of the material is free from implied messages which contradict the stated goal(s) or objective(s).

The goals, objectives, and general content of the material are most adequately conveyed through this particular medium.

The content of the material adequately represents the subject(s) concept(s) for which it was developed.

II. Objectivity. The content presents information in a fair and impartial way. It does not favor one aspect, event, issue, or group over another.

Positive and negative aspects are presented in an objective manner.

The material presents a study of real people, real issues, and/or real things.

The material is free from promoting or propagandizing special interests.

The material's content presents controversial points of view but all positions are presented in a fair and impartial way.

The material is free of portraying one group, place, thing, issue, or event over another.

The presentation excludes the use of harmful generalizations and stereotypes.

III. Promotes Understanding. Content presents other people, places, and things without negative undertones.

The presentation is free of loaded words, i. e., "backward", "primitive", "dirty", "savage", "uncivilized".

The presentation is free of making value judgments toward ethnocentrisms ("mine is better than yours").

The material presents instances of nonsegregated social relationships and human groupings.

The material portrays racial, religious, and ethnic groups in such a way as to build mutual understanding, appreciation, and acceptance.

The material should help the learner appreciate the many important contributions to our civilization made by members of the various human groups.

IV. Level of Sophistication. The material seems suitable for the entry level and competencies of those learners for whom the presentation is directed.

The material (content) reflects an experiential commonality ... a sameness of experiences which can be shared by the learners for which it was designed.

The students for which the materials are designed should be able to interpret signs (pictures and visuals) and symbols (words and other abstractions).

The content of the material will be challenging to the students for whom it is directed, yet not too difficult and thereby frustrating.

The material has applicability to similar concepts or issues which might confront those users for whom the material was developed.

V. <u>Validation</u>. A listing of other sources and agencies that assessed the material, and with what results.

I personally know someone who used these materials and found them to be instructionally satisfactory.

The information accompanying the materials showed the material to be meaningful and effective in other places with similar learners.

There is a description of field tests which states who conducted the testing (individual, organization, or agency), when and where the testing was conducted, with what subjects, and with what results.

The informational content of the material adequately presents the knowledge and/or understanding of the particular area of concern.

The agency which produced the material has a good reputation for having developed and designed other meaningful educational materials.

The material meets the standards established by this school system.

VI. <u>Design Variables</u>. The methods by which the content was organized and developed, in terms of the use of language and visual elements, technical clarity, production techniques, etc.

The length of the material is just about right for those students for whom it was designed.

The illustrations and/or descriptive content (audio-to-visual, word-to-picture) are compatible and reinforcing.

The audio and/or visual elements of the material are clear and understandable.

The material is not too large or bulky and can be presented with little physical effort.

The concepts introduced in the content are well developed and sequentially presented.

The material has a feedback mechanism for assessing the student's attainment of the objective(s).

The material clearly identifies major points of understanding.

The material's content has an immediacy ... an up-to-date focus on events, issues, people, things.

The designer(s) of the material provided for student and/or teacher interaction before, during, and/or following the presentation.

The material uses prompts and cues (pointers, arrows, underlines, etc.) to assist the learner in attending to the important aspects.

The material is free of confusing and/or conflicting concepts.

The content is reasonably free of any designer/producer subjective distortions.

VII. Personal Assessment. The personal and professional judgments of that particular evaluator.

The content of the material would not be offensive to any of my learners.

The content of the material should stimulate and challenge the learners.

The information presented through this material is as good as or better than any known alternate method.

The price listed for the material seems reasonable.

The material would make a meaningful addition to our media center.

I would gladly write the publisher and tell him these materials are well designed and appropriate for those learners for whom they are intended.

I would recommend the purchase of this material.

Our school maintains suitable facilities and/or equipment for the proper presentation of the material.

VIII. Other. Basically directed at material developed on technical, vocational, professional, and special interest areas.

The content of the material supports and documents all conclusions reached.

The information is presented in suitable bits for understanding.

The presentation of the information is within the grasp of the intended learners.

There is an accompanying guide or manual to assist the instructional leader in utilizing proper approaches, procedures, and evaluative techniques.

The material suggests and prescribes other learning activities which the learners might explore.

The issues and terms are well defined within the context of the material.

The concepts presented in the material relate throughout the presentation.

This school or system provides suitable facilities and/or equipment for the proper utilization of the materials.

This material assessment device has proven a viable tool for providing educators--especially media specialists and their materials selection committees--with more effective and systematic means for selecting appropriate learning materials.

I feel Edgar Dale best summarizes this article when he candidly reminds us, "some educators discuss instructional technology as though there were a real choice as to whether we should introduce it in schools and colleges. There is no such choice. It is already there in greater or lesser degree. Our only choice is whether we use educational technology wisely and purposefully."

References

Dale, Edgar. Audiovisual Methods in Teaching, third edition. New York: Holt, Rinehart and Winston, 1969, p. 612.

Erickson, C. W. H. Administering Instructional Media Programs, fourth edition. New York: Macmillan, 1970.

Quisenberry, Nancy L., et al. "Criteria for the Selection of Records, Filmstrips and Films for Young Children," Audiovisual Instruction, April 1973, pp. 36-39.

Rufsvold, Margaret I. "Guidelines to Selection and Evaluation of Newer Educational Media," Audiovisual Instruction, January 1967, pp. 10-15.

CRITERIA, CHOICES, AND OTHER CONCERNS ABOUT FILMSTRIPS

By Diana L. Spirt

In the beginning there was the image, albeit internalized. On the universal time clock oral and written language arrived later. It is commonly believed that man has always expressed his thoughts in ideograms. Witness the cave drawings of early man. The multiple mechanical developments that clustered around the written word after the Renaissance, however, have tended to obscure the primacy of the pictorial element as a basis for man's communication. Scribes, printer's devils, and others associated with written language flourished. The development of an enlarged elite was assured. Since the late 1800s, however, librarians and others "in the trade" have become part of an undercurrent to re-establish the balance between verbal and visual symbols.

The reappearance of the image reproduced through a lens has slowly reminded us of the importance of visually thinking about things. Today we are the possessors of traditional audio-visual media which recapitulate what man has designed to extend his senses from fresco pictures to various sizes of film and tape to sound in any of its manifestations. We have representations of reality in one to three dimensions (holography), where cave men with a local artist in residence had only one. Although book illustration has developed as an art form, many books still depend solely upon words. In this era of the parallel book and film forms, however, some books do become transmuted into feature films.

The breakthroughs for the past 20 years have been in sound. Early in the 20th Century, when slides and still pictures were increasingly a vogue, if sound was deemed necessary, the lecturer's voice served as accompaniment. When the silent films developed around the same time, the rickey-tickey piano of the local clubhouse or movie theatre was the only added sound. Some middle-aged citizens (those who were fortunate enough to have seen excerpts of Flaherty's documentary film, Nanook of the North, in their elementary classrooms during the '30s) do not necessarily remember that originally there was no narration. The final stages in this redress of balance between verbal and visual images seem to revolve around the disbursement into the educational system of these "toys and entertainments" of an earlier period. History suggests that a wide distribution of ideas is a hinge on which the gate of social change swings. Elitism is presumably to be leavened further. As selectors of materials for our marketplace of ideas, this puts librarians in a difficult position. Unless we understand the historical process, we could find ourselves in a role similar to the priest-caste in Egypt during its decline.

We adjust by setting up rigidly specified criteria by which we evaluate and choose. Either that or we use none. Criteria, however, are only as sound as the judgments of the people who use them. There are really only two main and one sub-criteria for selection of media (I am purposefully ignoring the controversial question of guidelines for materials for young people). The criteria are as follows: (1) What is the idea, intellectual content, etc. in the material and how is it presented?; (2) Is the medium that is used to present the idea the most suitable one for its treatment? Each medium does vary in what it can do well in relation to the idea expressed. The sub-criteria is perhaps the most important consideration. The individual is unique, bringing knowledge and experience (or lack of it) to bear on the viewing and listening. In a pluralistic, non-melting pot society this condition is equivalent to our social idea of "good." Your uniqueness and reaction to the material will finally insure sufficient flexibility to give our educational system as broad a base range as possible. Rigidity of selection is anathema and self-defeating. Consequently, criteria must be studied, learned and applied, and finally cast aside when the occasion dictates.

Some choices that depend largely on the second criteria will illustrate. The picture book Rosie's Walk by Pat Hutchins (Macmillan) is a colorful and lively example of a book for the young. The motion of the animals, the chicken's confident strut, and the fox's doomed stealth are visible to the individual viewer or small group. Even the youngest children for whom the book is intended can understand the representation of good and evil in the animals portrayed, as well as the subliminal moral with its double message, "For safety, stay in your own back yard." An extra bonus is the 95¢ price of the paperback (Crowell-Collier).

At this point it should be said that a natural inclination for the imaginative--making a sound slide or filmstrip story from the book is undoubtedly a fine idea, even though an illegal one. It is perhaps too sweeping to say that librarians who are quite ethical in all other things tend to think of this type of infringement of the copyright law as permissible. It is not. The picture book can be extended by using the book in an opaque projector or by cutting it up and using the pages to make transparencies. The word "using" is vital because the author, as well as others, ourselves included, makes a livelihood from this product.

In trying to reach a larger group, much of the inherent motion is lost in displaying one book. So a problem remains for the librarian who is dealing with groups, as well as individuals. The film and filmstrip versions of Rosie's Walk (both Weston Woods) are alternatives to the problem of group use. Both use the catchy tune, "Turkey in the Straw." It is appropriate to the farmyard scene while the tempo provides great pacing, thereby increasing the illusion of motion. However, the resemblance ends with the sound.

The 16mm film has the fluidity of movement that many well made films possess, enhanced in this case by excellent animation. The 35mm strip does not have this added dimension of motion. This is strange because the same sound track would normally give it some illusion of motion. However, the horizontal half frame shots (except for the title and last two frames) diminish, if not negate, any effectiveness the strip might have. By using the second criteria alone, the choice of the 16mm film for group use or, as an alternate, paperbacks in quantities for individual use are better choices.

Robert McCloskey's story, Time of Wonder (Viking), demonstrates a different selection problem. The book is a good example of what is generally called a "mood" book. It is a lovely-to-look-at, but static children's book. In 16mm film (Weston Woods) it becomes a visual tone poem about a family on an island off the coast of Maine. The camera pans and uses iconographic techniques well suited to the visual quietude of the story; the colors and narration correspond. What motion is needed is there.

The filmstrip (Weston Woods) has almost the same forcefulness, if the image is projected to maximum capacity. The story doesn't seem to need motion. The choice here seems to be reversed: the filmstrip or, once again, paperbacks in quantity.

A basic misunderstanding about film in whatever width film stock can be seen in the 8mm film rendition of Wanda Gag's folktale, Millions of Cats (Coward-McCann). The black and white woodcuts are splendid on the white pages of the book, stylized and properly solid looking, giving the work a timeless quality. But, in either the 8mm or 16mm film (Weston Woods), the projected static sense becomes extremely impersonal, thereby dissipating much of the quaintness and truth of the tale.

The two main criteria are often interdependent. Several filmstrips demonstrate this condition. Geoffrey Chaucer, Poet and Pilgrim (Guidance Associates) is a first-rate package with a Teacher's Guide that alone is worth the price. Yet, the treatment of Chaucer in a filmstrip--even in this artful package--seems both alien to the medium and unfaithful to the idea of the earthy Chaucer, here abstracted and fossilized.

Living Poetry: Poetry and Pictures (AIDS) unsuccessfully attempts to merge the poesy metaphors of such artists as William Blake and Langston Hughes with beautiful photographs. Poetry is sound and is heard in the mind rather than seen. Consequently, it belongs in emphasis to a sound medium. It takes an exceptionally inspired and artistic treatment to wed it to images.

An illustration of a good merger of medium and idea exists in a new set, America! The Poetry of a Nation (Guidance Associates). It accomplishes the feat of tying poetry to pictures and, in the process, provides a rich storehouse for the student and teacher. Another type of package with filmstrips, records, and photographs from which the frames were made is Scholastic's Images of Man. It is a noble effort conceived in the "Concerned Photographers" group. The idea of formulating a non-hackneyed presentation of the fundamental dignity and beauty of the human condition through the photographs and narration of four well known camera men is fully realized in this filmstrip set. The addition of the photographs on card stock gives the package tremendous potential. When both criteria are fulfilled and the evaluator's visceral reaction says, "Yes, Indeed, " the work at hand is going to affect others.

Just how we will respond to the current trend toward the cartoon format will be revealing. (Remember the Walt Disney cartoon factory controversy among children's librarians?) A renaissance in the cartoon format is here and growing. We're bound to see more of it in 35mm--with a slight difference. It is coming back as Head Comix in the same way that these strips exist in the world of magazine comics. This trend toward Head Comix which began in magazine format already extends to the general public. It has been a part of the history of public movie entertainment since the Beatles' movie, The Yellow Submarine; television's "Sesame Street" and lately Ken Berry's "Wow" show. It can currently be recognized in the feature film, Fritz the Cat.

A raunchy but interesting satire, Fritz is in some ways the quintessence of the celluloid cartoon. Aside from its intellectual content--and it does have it--it is arresting in its animation, color, sound, use of nostalgia, etc. It is a far cry from a 1967 cartoon filmstrip, John Henry, A Legend (Guidance Associates), but still of the same genre. It is not so far removed from a newer cartoon filmstrip from the same producer, What Do You Do About Rules?, which follows closely in the fashion of the comics of the '50s. (Many of the young people who worked on it grew up with its television progenitors.) The comic art form in ... Rules? is compelling. It delivers and powerfully, moved along by the upbeat accompaniment. The message it relates, however, may be open to question. At least the producer hopes so because it is a discussion strip in an elementary series devoted to values.

This current trend may provide more controversy in the selection of media than we have had recently. However, it may also show some persons that the influence of our selection policies upon the dissemination and democratization of ideas can have but a momentary negative or beneficial impact on the grand scale of time. Meanwhile, our choices will be important to the individuals for whom we select for the here and now. As many thoughtful people have written, all the more reason to try to surmount the barriers of self.

HINTS FOR FILM EVALUATION

By James L. Limbacher

Content Values

1. Does the film have unity?

2. Is the film or its contents dated or obsolete? Will it soon become so?

3. Is it free from stereotypes?

4. How does the film give examples or comparisons? Does it make use of emphasis?

5. Are these effectively presented?

6. Is it useful for the audience intended by the producer?

7. Is the film of any permanent value?

8. Does it have general appeal?

9. Are there any obvious factual errors?

10. Were all the possibilities of the subject matter fully realized?

11. Should the film have been longer? Shorter? Does it try to cover too much?

12. Were you glad the film was made?

13. Does the film consider the point of view of its audience?

14. Is it really a film or could it be presented just as well as a set of slides, a tape, a record or a filmstrip?

Psychological Values

1. Does the film stimulate interest?

2. Is the main objective clearly and concisely presented?

Reprinted by permission of author from mimeographed copy dated January, 1977.

3. Does the viewer identify himself immediately with the film?

4. Does the film provide motivation for further discussion and participation after the showing?

5. Are there too many ideas in the film?

6. Does it have a unity of purpose? Does it achieve or over-achieve this purpose?

7. Does it fill a definite need?

8. Is it similar to a dozen other films on the same subject or does it take off on a new facet of the subject?

9. Is it adequately developed and brought to a logical climax?

10. Does the viewer feel "cheated" or "irritated" at the end of the film in any way? If so, is this necessarily bad?

Artistic and Technical Values

1. Is the direction characterized by a "wholeness" of units?

2. Is the film visually pleasing? Are the shots well composed?

3. Is the film in good taste? If not, is there a reason for its bad taste?

4. Is the photography clear enough to enable the viewer to see all objects without straining? If not, is there a reason for it?

5. Is the film equipped with an adequate beginning to orient the viewer?

6. Do the actors or narrators have good voice quality, diction and timing?

7. If narrated, does it match the visuals on the screen? Is the narrator condescending in mannerisms and style? Is the narration "age-levelish"?

8. Do the settings and clothing contribute to the mood of the film?

9. Do scenes move forward in a logical progression? If not, is there a reason why they don't?

10. Can the sound be heard? Is it well modulated and recorded?

11. Is the musical score unobtrusive yet effective in underscoring the film?

12. Does the film have good rhythm and pacing? Is the editing smooth and devoid of static qualities and poor matching?

13. Are closeups used effectively and whenever possible to pinpoint and clarify the ideas?

14. Are animation, flash-backs and process photography, when used, effective?

Social and Ethical Values

1. If controversial, does the film give both sides of the story?

2. If not, is this fact so stated in the titles or by the narrator?

3. Is the film constructive? Does it encourage a feeling of responsibility toward humanity and the world?

4. Does it stimulate general good will? Is any race, religion or profession held up to ridicule? If so, is there a reason for doing so?

5. Is the film truthful without distorting facts?

6. Does the film influence behavior toward a positive goal?

7. Could any misunderstandings arise from the film?

8. Are unusual examples presented as typical?

9. If sponsored, does it spend too much time in advertising?

10. Does the film allow for discussion or social action at the end?

Entertainment Values

1. Is the film entertaining?

2. Is the story well told or the information well presented?

3. Are the players and/or the narrator well cast?

4. Does a feeling of reality pervade the film?

5. Is it produced with imagination, style, originality and humor?

6. Is the medium of the motion picture used effectively and artistically?

7. Is the resultant film a work of art?

Audience Reactions

1. Does the viewer react favorably on seeing the film? Is this important?

2. Does the film hold the attention?

3. Could any parts of the film be misunderstood by the viewer?

4. Does the audience have to view it twice to completely understand the content?

5. Does the film take on new aspects under subsequent viewings? Does it hold up on a second viewing?

CRITERIA FOR SELECTING REALIA

By Jean Rustici

The establishment of specific criteria for the selection of realia is best accomplished by a group at the local level who are familiar with the specific needs and interests of the children for whom they are providing the realia collection. The group process should reflect the opinions of adults, who interact with children in a variety of settings: home, school, church, recreational areas, libraries, stores, hospitals, etc., and should be based on actual observations of children's interests as they are free to pursue them. Testing tentative selections with actual groups of children is a necessary part of this process.

In establishing standards upon which a judgment or decision for selection might be based, what are the primary considerations which lead us to the primary objectives of the realia experience for the child?

We know, for instance, that concepts grow through experience. Is our primary objective then, just to provide different objects to extend the child's experience beyond his present experience? This would suggest that we provide more things in greater variety, perhaps several sets of each thing, and this could limit the possibilities for children.

It would be misleading to set up criteria about such things as design, durability, etc., without acknowledging the fact that experience is not simply contact with an object, but reflection and thought about it, particularly thought which relates it to personal goals. The more varied the child's experiences, the more opportunities for the development of self concepts of adequacy and security, the basis for all future learning.

Therefore, criteria for the selection of realia should be based on the needs of the target group, but in addition, inherent in the selection process should be a specific consideration of the child's freedom to select and use materials in his own experiential context, and this is equally important as the suitability of the objects being provided.

All of this is by way of saying that it is more detrimental

than useful to subject each piece of realia to a "standards" or age
level test, but perfectly possible to apply such criteria to the suitability of a total collection.

The following questions are intended as guidelines for the establishment of criteria for the selection of realia:

1. **Is a Child Able to Select Materials in the Library...**

Which cover a wide range of difficulty reflecting the fact that he develops at uneven rates, not according to rigid chronological patterns?

Which are procured by children and adults from their surroundings
as well as those from manufactured sources?

Which fit into his own grand design as well as those which provide
him with a connection to the adult world?

Which allow for his own deep involvement as well as those which
provide a contact between him and his parents?

Which release feelings as well as those which challenge his problem
solving ability?

Which give him the opportunity to develop his own values as well
as those which reflect the values of our larger society?

Which give him the opportunity to touch objects of different textures
and weights?

Which give him the opportunity to listen to a variety of sounds?

Which give him the opportunity to watch and to create a variety of
movements?

Which give him the opportunity to return to an object many times to
explore various play possibilities with it at several different levels
of development?

2. **Questions Relating to Considerations of Basic Materials**

Are a wide variety of raw materials, natural materials and man-
made materials represented, such as wood, water, sand, glass, metal, textiles, plastic, etc.?

Are materials particularly indigenous to the area being served represented?

3. **Quantity**

Are there many sets of the same thing or are sets of increasing complexity provided? Are there possibilities of having one complete set of realia for in-library use, so children and parents may be constantly aware of the variety that is available and also so a child may try out that which he may borrow at a later date?

4. Design

Is the shape of the toy related to its function?

Is color used as a tool, not as a useless decoration? That is, does it relate directly to the design and function of the toy?

Is the toy simple in design and are there multiple ways to use it?

If there is a mechanism involved, is it visible to the child and does it work properly to show a simple procedure?

Is the detail incomplete, not specific, in order to challenge the child's imagination as he uses it?

5. Durability

Is the toy well constructed of a solid material?

Is it structurally insulated against breakage?

Are replacement parts available for the toy?

Can it be useful without all of its parts?

6. Safety

Is the toy able to be washed and cleaned if necessary?

Is it non-flammable?

Has it been checked out with the Consumer Products Safety Commision banned toy list (available from State Department of Consumer Protection)? Toys cannot always be declared safe because of the problem of providing safe play environment which is ultimately the function of parents and other guardians.

Bibliography

International Journal of Early Childhood Education, Supplement, 1972, pp. 58.
Parent Cooperative Preschools International Journal, Volume IV, Number 1, fall 1973, pp. 14-15.
Toys All Over the World, OMEP, 1971. (OMEP is Organisation Mondiale pour L'Education pre scolaire.)

Epie Report No. 42, 1972. "How to Select and Evaluate Materials."
Ross, Donald. "How to Do a Toy Safety Survey", in A Public Citi-
    zen's Action Manual. Grossman, 1973.
Beck, Helen. Don't Push Me, I'm No Computer. McGraw, 1973.
Safe Toys for Your Child. Children's Bureau pub. no. 473-1971,
    Dept. of Health, Education, and Welfare.
Bits and Pieces, Imaginative Uses for Children's Learning. Asso-
    ciation for Childhood Education International, 1967. (pam)
More Recipes for Fun. Par Project, 1972.
Parent Guide I. How to Play Learning Games with a Preschool
    Child, by Far West Laboratory for Educational Research and
    Development. General Learning Corporation, 1971.

THE ACQUISITION OF MAPS FOR SCHOOL
(AND OTHER SMALL) LIBRARIES (Excerpts)

By Charles E. Current

The importance of maps in the school library has often been underestimated. Usage is not confined to geography or history courses in today's modern school curriculum.

Maps are usually regarded primarily as place media but their scope is not limited to showing geographic locations. By employing combinations of diverse symbols they also visualize many other important topics such as ethnic relationships, physical, social and economic conditions, and historical, artistic, and literary development.[1]

Almost all subject areas being taught today can utilize them in one way or another. "Unlike many other reference sources, the map is a form which crosses all disciplines, all subject areas. It is a highly specialized topic with its own variations in cataloging, acquisition, and maintenance."[2]

The proposed Standards for School Media Programs reflect educators' recognition that maps are one of the vital resources that should be included in the library. Recommended as a part of the basic collection for libraries which serve 250 students or over are:

One map for each region studied and special maps (economic, weather, political, historical, and others) for each area studied.

Duplicate maps available for each class section requiring maps at the same time, the number of duplicates to be determined by sections of students and the availability of maps on transparencies and filmstrips.

Wall maps for teaching stations.[3]

The acquisition of these important cartographic materials is often a major problem for the school librarian. Aside from the limitations of the amount of money available to spend on these materials there is always the question of what to purchase. It should be kept in mind that maps are of two basic classes. One is the general map which is either physical or political or a combination of the two; the other is the thematic map which serves some special purpose. The library should consider acquiring both types.

There are three main reasons libraries collect maps: 1) educational, e. g., collecting maps so as to learn the basic geographical, historical, geological, and/or other facts about the regions of the earth and its place in the larger celestial systems; 2) utilitarian, e. g., collecting maps so as to be able to compile new ones as old ones become obsolete; and 3) scholarly, e. g., collecting maps in order to understand better the many aspects of the disciplines of geography. [4]

Regardless of the purpose for acquiring maps, certain guidelines need to be established for evaluating them. Some might be relatively expensive purchases produced by commercial companies whose main purpose is to provide materials for a profit. Others are available quite inexpensively from organizations or companies which bear the major financial load by providing educational materials in order to promote good will for the organization. Then there are others which are products of government agencies, groups or perhaps an individual. Whichever is the case, there are factors which need to be taken into account before a decision is to be made as to acquiring them. Criteria for selection are:

1. Visibility: Maps, like charts, graphs, and diagrams summarize information, teach a process, and offer statistics pictorially. Thus good visibility is a must.

2. Size: The map usage is of primary importance. In some cases it will be designed to serve a group and at other times the individual. The important thing is to make sure the map to be purchased will be able to serve the patron who is going to be using it. In connection with this, the storage and display facilities in the school library often are factors in determining the size of maps to be purchased.

3. Amount of detail and suitability for grade level: Often maps are unsatisfactory because they contain too much or too little material. Thus the maps to be purchased should relate to the needs and abilities of those who will be using them.

4. Color: It is the use made of color and not just its presence or absence which indicates its value. Good use of color in maps not only makes these materials more attractive, but also shows relationships and emphasizes contrasts.

5. Durability: The main concern here is with potential rather than initial quality. The commercially prepared map may include a washable finish and a cloth backing which is desirable. However, library processing can often add similar features. The decision to purchase cloth-backed materials or to process them in the library will depend largely on the available equipment, the staff time available, and the size of the map. Generally speaking, it is a wise expenditure to buy the large wall maps in plasticized or cloth-backed paper.

6. Accuracy: Last, but not least, accuracy is a must for any map that is to be added to the collection. The authority of the geogra-

pher, the precision of scale, the projection, the clarity of symbols used and the date of publication are all factors to be considered whether the map be simplified, or highly detailed. [5]

In essence, in buying maps it is necessary only to follow a few simple rules which also pertain to the selection of books and other library material.

> A map is supposed to convey a picture. If it does this clearly, without confusing the reader, the chances are it is a good map. And if a map is drawn to scale, with clean lines carefully laid down, with parallels of latitude and meridians of longitude indicates, the chances are it will be a fairly accurate map, though not necessarily so. Whether we realize it or not, all of us are capable of editing a map or chart which is badly done. Good maps are almost never badly printed. [6]

The cost of purchasing and maintaining a map collection should not be the serious problem it is often made out to be. This often appears to be a protective device employed by some librarians when faced with unfamiliar material such as maps and charts which do not fit neatly into the library scheme of things. The truth is that the importance of administrative costs dwindles with the proper appreciation of the intrinsic and extrinsic value of the material under consideration. [7] Furthermore, many of the cartographic materials purchased are from government agencies from which the cost is a minimum rate.

The question of when to purchase maps and other geographic materials is another concern for the school librarian. The obvious consideration is that of budget allocations for such material.

References

1. Warren B. Hicks and Alma M. Tillin. Developing Multi-Media Libraries (New York: R. R. Bowker Company, 1970), p. 25.
2. William Katz. Introduction to Reference Work, Vol. I (New York: McGraw-Hill, 1969), p. 285.
3. Standards for School Media Programs (Chicago: American Library Association, 1969), p. 32.
4. Lynn S. Mullins. "The Rise of Map Libraries in America During the Nineteenth Century," SLA Geography and Map Division Bulletin, LX (March 1966), p. 2.
5. Della Thomas and Helen Lloyd. Practical Storage and Use of Maps and Posters (Stillwater, Oklahoma: Oklahoma State University, 1964), pp. 8-12.
6. Lloyd A. Brown. "The Problem of Maps," Library Trends, XIII (October 1964), p. 224.
7. Ibid., pp. 218-219.

MICROFORM PUBLICATIONS: HARDWARE
AND SUPPLIERS (Excerpts)

By Ralph J. Folcarelli and Ralph C. Ferragamo

In addition to criteria generally applied in the selection of
print materials, such as scope, authority, authenticity, and treatment, a set of special criteria for microforms should be considered.
Most of these criteria relate to the technical quality of the image reproduction itself in such areas as resolution, density and contrast.
We are generally dependent on the reputation of the micropublisher
for meeting these criteria.

When libraries have a choice of micropublishers publishing
identical titles (as is true of many government documents), various
criteria must be considered, including type and capabilities of existing reader/printer equipment, user needs and policies, film size
and image legibility, archival permanence, and even packaging. All
of these points and others, such as film stock and film coatings, are
also considered when libraries are themselves involved in reprogra-
phy (filming for preservation) or in choosing a commercial reprogra-
pher. Allen Veaner deals with these problems extensively in The
Evaluation of Micropublications.[1] His handbook would also prove useful in establishing an overall microform selection policy. In many
instances, however, a particular micropublisher may be the sole
source for a specific microform title or project. In this case, the
voices of librarians must be heeded to ensure consistently high quality and standards.

The points considered by reviewers of microforms, which may
be interpreted as additional criteria, also deserve attention. Microform Review, a leading reviewing source, includes the following criteria in their regular microform evaluations: microformat, film
type, reduction ratio, film polarity, external and internal finding
aids, sequence, hard copy availability, replacement policy and payment considerations.

Other than Microform Review, there is a virtual void of critical reviewing sources of current microform projects. However,
there are several other journals which either announce new microform projects or offer occasional critical reviews (and thus may be
considered as current selection aids): Advanced Technology Libraries, Journal of Documentation, Library Resources & Technical Services, Microdoc, Microfilm Newsletter, Microfilm Techniques, Mi-
croinfo, Micrographics Today (formerly Micro-News Bulletin), Publishers Weekly, and Special Libraries.

Reprinted from Library Trends, vol. 24, no. 4, April 1976, pp.
716-717, 725, by permission of the publisher and authors.

When choices are possible, the problem of choosing a format (microfilm, microfiche, or microprint), size of film, or negative or positive reproduction are all dependent on individual library policies and user needs. The advantages and disadvantages of each of three major formats are outlined in an account by Veaner,[2] and are discussed in greater detail by Bernhardt.[3] While no definite conclusions are reached, the many points considered will aid most librarians, particularly those whose libraries are just beginning to develop microform collections.

References

1. Veaner, Allen B. The Evaluation of Micropublications; A Handbook for Librarians. Chicago: ALA, 1971.
2. Ibid., p. 6.
3. Bernhardt, Homer I. "Formats," in Diaz, Albert J., ed., Microforms in Libraries. Weston, Conn.: Microform Review, 1975.

A SUPPLEMENTARY PAMPHLET FILE
IN AN ACADEMIC LIBRARY (Excerpts)

By Doris Snyder

Traditionally, the term "vertical file materials" refers to those items which are housed vertically in file cabinets or similar containers. The collection may contain any or all of the following: flat pictures, charts, maps, pamphlets, posters, newspaper and magazine clippings, sheet music and art prints. They are non-book materials and may be filed separately or interfiled with the books. We are concerned only with pamphlets.

For our purpose, and with our ultimate aim in mind, the descriptor "supplementary materials" rather than "vertical file materials" is more appropriate for this is, in essence, what our pamphlet file is to be--a supplement to other materials in the library.

What Is a Pamphlet?

Pamphlets are sometimes referred to as "ephemeral" and "fugitive" materials. These are misnomers. Pamphlets are difficult to arrange, to catalog and to file because of their varied format but instructional and reference pamphlets certainly are not "ephemeral" and well organized brochures not "fugitive."

Pamphlets are "different" from books but there is little agreement on where a pamphlet ends and a book begins. It is defined as "a thin limp book" (Cutter), a "single sheet, center-stapled or stitched non-serial" ... as long as it has a paper cover but then too, only up to a point. The American College Dictionary says "generally less than 80 pages." In current usage, however, a paperback of less than 80 pages is still not a pamphlet, and sometimes a paperbacked book of 160 pages is pamphlet handled.[1] Bloomberg defines a pamphlet as "an independent publication of 49 pages or less, bound in paper covers."[2] A definition in effect at Harvard is:

> ... a small piece of printed matter, ordinarily containing eight or more pages, not treated as part of serial publications and not originally intended to be separately bound. But for the purposes of the record ... a pamphlet which is treated like a volume--by being bound--is counted as a volume; and an unbound volume which is treated like a pamphlet--by being bound with others, tied up in a bundle

Reprinted from Oklahoma Librarian, vol. 24, no. 4, October 1974, pp. 8-17, 34-35, by permission of the editor.

with others or sent to the so-called 'pamphlet files'--is
treated as a pamphlet.³

UNESCO defines a pamphlet as "... a non-periodical printed publication of at least 5 but not more than 48 pages." Webster's Third
New International Dictionary carefully avoids the issue by the definition "an unbound publication other than a periodical having fewer
than a fixed number (as 50, 80, 100) of pages ..." and the ALA
Glossary agrees: "... in local library practice, there is a variation
in the maximum number of leaves or pages allowed under the term."

What then is a pamphlet? A pamphlet is "what we make it"
(Condit), and "treatment counts more than format" (Miller). Perhaps the definition of an advertising executive is the most realistic:

> 'Do you see this booklet?' he said, holding up a small, un-
> bound publication. 'In this office, if I call this a book, it's
> a book; and if I call it a pamphlet, it's a pamphlet.'⁴

The Value of a Pamphlet File

The value of pamphlets has been recognized since the Queen
Anne period. The efforts of Miles Davis were seconded by William
Oldys, who gave the following four reasons for their preservation:

1. The regard we owe to the preservation of good writings.
2. Pamphlets stand in greater need of attention than bound
volumes.
3. They are the liveliest pictures of their times.
4. They are the truest images of their authors.⁵

Though the worthiness of pamphlets has not been challenged
by librarians, the task of preserving them is an unwelcome responsibility. Because of their general characteristics, handling them
presents many problems.

> To condemn any pamphlet to innocuous desuetude ... mere-
> ly because it is innocent of a stiff cover, is to despoil
> the temple of learning and reject the good things of Provi-
> dence ... that it forms a rather troublesome asset in the
> wealth of a library cannot be doubted. Pamphlets taken
> singly will not stand upon the shelves; they will curl up,
> become dog-eared, accumulate dust, and get in the way of
> the books. If kept in piles, as is most frequent, it is
> very hard to get at any one that is wanted in the mass.
> Then it is objected to them, that the majority of them are
> worthless, that they cost too much money, and time, and
> pains, to catalogue them, and that they are useless if not
> catalogued; that if kept bound, they cost the library a sum
> out of all proportion to their value; that they accumulate
> so rapidly as to outrun the means at the disposal of any
> library to deal with them; in short, that they cost more

than they come to, if bound, and if unbound; they vex the
soul of the librarian day by day. [6]

What does the pamphlet collection offer in return for the effort, time and money in spite of their inherent problems? Some of
their unique contributions are listed as:

1. Currency. Despite many technological advances in publishing
there still is a time lapse in the production of books. Pamphlet
file publications can help to fill this gap. Because these materials
are quick and relatively inexpensive to produce, new ideas and the
latest statistics often appear in this form long before they laborious-
ly work their way into book format. They are also frequently revised.

A research library attains distinction not merely by acquiring traditional publications but by collecting the unusual
item that may shed great light on an issue. Such items
often constitute one of the most useful research elements ... their value is based on their treating a specific
problem which is timely and may at some later date be
treated in a chapter of a monograph. [7]

A dramatic demonstration of the up-to-the-minute quality
of vertical file materials occurred when the State of Michigan announced restriction on the sale of DDT. Extension service bulletins were quickly revised to substitute
alternate methods of control. Our book collection could
not duplicate this rapid and complete realignment. [8]

2. Uniqueness. Difficult subjects sometimes receive only sparse
treatment in a book. The file may help to fill the gap. Often the
answer to a trying question is found in a pamphlet.

... pamphlet collections help greatly to meet the varied
demands of libraries since they provide kinds of material
not always found in books. They permit selective coverage of some subjects which would have to be left out in a
book collection of a reasonable size.... Pamphlets can
be superb--and often the only--sources of data not published in book form. [9]

3. Multiplication of sources. Pamphlets offer a way to
bolster the book collection with a variety of supplementary offerings
on popular topics. Because they are free or relatively inexpensive
they can be added without serious budgetary implications.

4. Compactness and accessibility. When time is limited,
the pamphlet file becomes all the more important because of the
concise nature of the material it contains. It offers a quick approach
to the specific subjects.

5. Extension. The pamphlet file offers an opportunity to
provide information in areas of occasional or sporadic demand. Be-

cause of the low cost of the materials it is possible to be much more liberal in selection.

6. Authority. If chosen wisely, the materials in the file possess an authority which matches and even surpasses that of books. The reports of organizations, research reports, Health Information Series, etc., have long been accepted for their authoritative feature.

7. Reference. Many institutes and associations issue bibliographies relating to their areas of special interest. Government agencies are also active in compiling lists of informative sources. A growing number of libraries now offer their bibliographies for distribution on a national scale. The library may not own all the materials listed but they can often be obtained through interlibrary loan or photocopying services. This is one of the most neglected resources in most supplementary pamphlet files and one that would greatly extend and enhance the service function of a pamphlet collection.

References

1. Wyllie, John Cook. "Pamphlets, broadsides, clippings and posters," Library Trends, 4 (October 1955), p. 198.
2. Bloomberg, Marty. Introduction to Public Services for Library Technicians. Littleton, Colorado. Libraries Unlimited, 1972. p. 224.
3. Currier, Franklin T. "Harvard rules for counting volumes and pamphlets," Library Journal, 43 (1918), p. 241.
4. Condit, Lester. A Pamphlet about Pamphlets. Chicago: University of Chicago Press, 1939. p. 1.
5. Ibid., p. 21.
6. Ibid., p. 23.
7. Rogers, Rutherford D. & Weber, David C. University Library Administration, N.Y.: H. W. Wilson, 1971, p. 268.
8. Miller, Shirley. The Vertical File and Its Satellites. Littleton, Colo.: Libraries Unlimited, 1971. p. 3.
9. Gould, Geraldine N. & Wolfe, Ithmer C. How to Organize and Maintain the Picture/Pamphlet File. Dobbs Ferry, New York: Oceana Publications. 1968, p. 3.

Bibliography

American Library Association. Manual of Library Economy. Pamphlets and minor library material. Chicago: ALA Publishing Board, 1917. Chp. 25.

Ball, Miriam Ogden. Subject Headings for the Information File. 8th ed., New York: Wilson, 1956.

Bloomberg, Marty. Introduction to Public Services for Library Technicians. Littleton, Colorado: Libraries Unlimited, 1972.

Christine, Emma Ruth. "Revitalizing the vocational life," School Libraries, 17 (Winter 1968), 41-2.

Condit, Lester. A Pamphlet about Pamphlets. Univ. of Chicago Press, 1939.

Currier, Franklin T. "Harvard rules for counting volumes and pamphlets," Library Journal, 43 (1918), p. 241.

Fahringer, Peggy Louise. "A classification of knowledge for the arrangement of a library school pamphlet file with a manual of instruction." 1958. ERIC Microfiche ED 060 901.

Fairfax, Virginia. "Pamphlets and Clippings in a Business Library," Journal of Electricity and Western Industry, San Francisco, 1921.

Ford, Stephen. The Acquisition of Library Materials. Chicago: ALA, 1973.

Gauthier, R. "Pamphlet Service," UNESCO Bulletin for Libraries, 24 (May 1970), p. 172.

Goldsmith, Stephanie. "Pamphlet collections: the defense rests," in The School Media Center. Pearl L. Ward & Robert Beacon, comp. Metuchen: Scarecrow Press, 1973.

Gould, Geraldine N. & Wolfe, Ithmer C. How to Organize and Maintain the Library Picture/Pamphlet File. Dobbs Ferry, New York: Oceana Publishers. 1968.

Ireland, Norma O. The Pamphlet File in School, College, and Public Librarianship. Faxon, 1954.

Jones, Margaret. "Pamphlet classification," RQ, 8 (Spring 1968), 17-19.

Miller, Shirley. "From abacus to zoos. Or the care and feeding of the vertical file," Library Journal, 92, (Dec. 15, 1967), 4477-79.

_____. The Vertical File and Its Satellites. Littleton, Colorado: Libraries Unlimited. 1971.

Public Affairs Information Service Bulletin. N.Y.: Public Affairs Information Service.

Readings in Nonbook Librarianship. Jean Spealman Kujoth, ed. Metuchen: Scarecrow Press, 1968.

Rogers, Rutherford, & David C. Weber. University Library Administration. New York: H. W. Wilson, 1971.

Shaffer, Dale E. The Pamphlet Library. Use of the Sha-frame System. From the author, 437 Jennings, Salem, Ohio. 1972.

Sears List of Subject Headings. 9th ed., New York: H. W. Wilson, 1965.

Veitch, Natalie. "Free and Inexpensive," RQ, 12 (Fall 1972), 64-65.

Vertical File Index. New York: H. W. Wilson. Monthly.

Weber, Olga. "Trimming the clipping files by the 7 R's," Special Libraries, 60, (Fall, 1969), p. 82-6.

Weihs, Jean Riddle, Shirley Lewis & Janet Macdonald. Nonbook Materials-the Organization of Integrated Collections. 1st ed., Ottawa, Ontario: Canadian Library Association, 1973.

Wilson, Louis R. & Tauber, Maurice F. The University Library. New York: Columbia University Press, 1956.

Wyllie, John Cook. "Pamphlets, broadsides, clippings and posters," Library Trends, 4 (October 1955), 195-202.

POPULAR MUSIC COLLECTIONS AND PUBLIC LIBRARIES

By Frank Hoffman

The development of significant archival collections of popular music recordings has, to this time, been largely limited to a few university and special libraries. Creation of such holdings in public libraries, the appropriate collectors of this segment of Western culture, will be similarly limited in the future unless record librarians make a radical change in their collecting policies. Yet in an era characterized by the proliferation of nonbook materials on a widespread scale, few if any of the audio-visual media can match the spectacular strides which have been made by the popular music phonorecord. Given this fact, it would seem a foregone conclusion that increased openmindedness and foresight in the planning of phonorecord collections are necessary if public libraries wish to realize their fullest potential in the paramount functions of conscientiously chronicling contemporary events for future generations and of acting as agents in the dissemination of information.

A few years ago a highly respected music trade journal devoted the bulk of one of its issues to the "classical crisis" afflicting the otherwise healthy phonorecord industry. The introductory articles made the following observation: "Industry leaders point to the shrinking percentage of the 'total record market' accounted for by the classical 'product,' citing among other figures a decrease from eighty-five per cent for classical sales in 1910 to less than five per cent today. "[1]

Music librarians would do well to observe the practicalities embodied in the above statement as it relates to their profession-- that is, a large segment of public taste is being overlooked when libraries fail to give popular music (a term which can be used to loosely embrace such seemingly diverse styles as country-western, jazz, blues, folk and rock, the latter accounting for by far the largest percentage of commercial sales) fair representation in their record collections. If a certain book, possessing a modicum of "artistic merit" and without the likelihood of attracting the concerted wrath of censors, were outselling its nearest competitors by a ratio similar to that of moderately successful popular music recordings over the more lucrative classical ventures, could libraries conceive of not stocking it? Being service-oriented institutions, public libraries can't afford to remain ensconced in ivory towers with respect to the planning of phonorecord collections any more than they can in the building of book holdings. Yet the acquisition of popular music

Reprinted from Southeastern Librarian, vol. 23, no. 4, Winter 1974, pp. 26-31, by permission of the editor.

discs is rarely given more than secondary attention by public librarians.

A search of the library literature on the subject of sound recordings during the past five years provides ample evidence of the tendency of record librarians to treat popular music as ephemeral material. Joan Smith's "A Basic Stock List" typifies this way of thinking. [2] Of the 400 works she recommends for the "average record library," not one popular disc appears. "Popular" titles, according to Ms. Smith, are adequately represented in the works of composers such as Gilbert & Sullivan and Vaughn Williams. Marc Faw's somewhat more ambitious and diversified listing, which chronologically reaches back as far as the High Middle Ages and includes annotated commentaries evaluating the recorded interpretations of each work, also overlooks the inclusion of popular titles in a basic phonorecord collection. [3] Although these and other writers might very well be open to the acquisition of popular works, the implication of such listings appears to be that such material should only be considered when the foundation has been laid in the form of a well-balanced classical collection.

Aside from the ever-present deterrent represented by the lack of sufficient funds, there are two major roadblocks to the development of comprehensive popular music phonorecord collections in public libraries. First, record librarians must be made to see that the shifting of emphasis in collection development from classical to popular music should be viewed in the positive light of attracting a vast audience of non-users to library resources, rather than simply as a policy resulting in severe inroads on the services available to serious music enthusiasts. Second, it is necessary for record librarians, as professional public servants paid to provide for the interest of their respective clientele in the most efficient way possible, to separate personal preference from the objectivity which is to be desired in the building of a phonorecord collection. [4]

A regrettable corollary to the intellectual snobbism exhibited by many record librarians is the lack of foresight exercised in the acquisition of unfamiliar or comparatively new materials. As illustrated by Carlos Hagen, a librarian at the University of California at Los Angeles, in his article, "The Struggle of U.S. Sound Archives," this sad state of affairs can apply to sectors outside the record collection:

> In the 1960's librarians faced the explosion of the underground press. Granted, the materials produced by these presses are often controversial and even shocking to some people. However, anyone with some social and historical sensitivity should have seen that the underground papers were documenting a most important social change, not only in the U.S., but throughout much of the world. American librarianship has an admirable record of supporting freedom of expression and fighting censorship. Given these facts, one would have expected that librarians would have

recognized the importance of the new publications and avidly supported them. Unfortunately, nothing like this happened; on the contrary, practically every major academic and public library seemed to take the same attitude. 'This is junk, and as such has no place in any respectable library.' Now, only a few years later, one finds that first writings of some of the most influential poets, writers and thinkers of an immense social revolution were published by the underground press. Libraries are now spending thousands of dollars trying to acquire back runs of issues of underground papers and publications. Early issues of underground papers have become collectors' items. Publications that any enterprising librarian could have obtained for a few cents (or even free in some cases) are often selling for as much as $50 apiece or more. [5]

While representative serious music collection is vital to any public library, it is an unfortunate circumstance that many librarians tend to visualize the phonorecord collection as being divided into distinctly separate and antagonistic camps which are given terms such as "cultivated" vs. "unsophisticated" genres; "enlightened" as apposed to "unenlightened" styles. The comparatively recent development of rock music (as well as such closely related fields as country, blues and soul) into a mature art form, despite its admitted superabundance of mediocrity and ballyhoo, would seem to undermine the logic of such labels yet further. Apply any evaluative criterion and the finer creations of popular music need not blush when compared with the musical masterpieces of classical literature--whether it be structural complexity (witness the albums produced by the Beatles between 1967 and 1969), depth of expressive feeling (as is self-evident in the songs of soul queen Aretha Franklin), or technical prowess in execution. One must take into account that each musical style has its own house rules. For example, an operatic voice would hardly provide as convincing a setting as a harsh, gutsy vocal delivery in putting across a pulsating hard rock number.

Popular music--particularly rock music at this time--merits attention above and beyond the mere considerations of widespread demand and consumate artistry. On the strength of its sociological value alone, popular music deserves increased attention in the form of archival collections. Perhaps more than any other media of mass proportions, this music mirrors the thoughts and conditions of today. Following a tradition which has included among its proponents the dramatists of classical Greece, the orators of imperial Rome, the enlightenment philosophers of eighteenth century Europe and the reform-oriented journalists of late nineteenth and early twentieth America, popular musicians offer, to an extremely large audience which is gaining countless adherents daily, social commentaries and proposals acutely relevant to the present day. When a fourteen-year-old boy hears Bob Dylan sing that equality and religion are only concepts taught in schools, it is foolhardy not to believe that his future values and behavior will be affected by this message. [6]

The ideas embodied within the lyrics of popular songs are usually easy to understand in their uncompromising directness. The songs of the Rolling Stones represent an expansive catalog of the experiences and feelings of man searching for self realization and fulfillment within the strictures imposed by his environment--e.g. the social alienation of "Get Off of My Cloud," the experimentation with drugs found "In Another Land" and "Sing the Song Altogether," the mood of protest and revolution communicated in "Street Fighting Man," and love affairs ranging from the platonic relationship in "Lady Jane" to the raw sexual overtones of "Stray Cat Blues." The impact of these messages can be better appreciated when one realizes that many English groups have become household words in the United States even before they have stepped within the borders of our country. Conversely, American aggregates, including the Beach Boys and the Grateful Dead, perform to sellout audiences in Germany and are honored by having the lyrics to their songs sung by Japanese youth who can't even speak the English language. (It should be noted in passing that a great opportunity exists here for the enterprising translator who is willing to produce bilingual librettos of rock music texts.)

Although the popular music of the late 1950's lacked the self-conscious reformist spirit of the post-Dylan era, many of the songs from this period can now be seen to possess a special relevancy of their own. The compositions of Chuck Berry, the Coasters, and others have pictured this era for us in the most vivid of colors--the humdrum existence of high school, young love and objects permitting personal expression within their own social sphere such as clothes and cars. The blatant sexuality reflected in the then new primitive rhythms and exhibitionist theatrics of many of its performers at this date represent sufficient sustenance in themselves for researchers in the fields of sociology, psychology and musicology.

While most librarians might be aware of the potential for the healthy circulation statistics to be gained by allotting a greater portion of their phonorecord budget to popular music, many are discouraged by the fickleness of public tastes as reflected by the rapid turnover in hit tunes (a problem further aggravated by the time lag involved in the ordering and processing of phonorecords) in addition to the high costs incurred by the replacement of discs lost or misused.

Skeptics should note, however, that these problems aren't sufficient to justify their use as a means of rationalizing the neglect of the popular music sector of phonorecord collections. The rash of recent 1950's rock and roll revivals and compilation of scholarly jazz discographies are but two bits of evidence which would seem to indicate that longevity in appeal can be a characteristic of popular music as well as of the classics. Since the majority of stores handling phonorecords deplete their stock of the average long-playing popular album within six months and since many of these albums go out of print fairly rapidly, libraries can serve an important function in providing the opportunity for these albums to be heard at a later date.

The establishment of a non-circulating collection within the general phonorecord collection which could be listened to inside the library only, on library equipment, while handled only by trained library personnel, would be one way of cutting down on monetary costs resulting from theft and damage. Important factors to consider in applying the reference label to discs might include age, intrinsic artistry, musicological or sociological significance, and whether or not a disc is in print. Other approaches meriting consideration in providing for the safety of library phonorecords would be the institution of informal training sessions on the care of discs and the enforcement of stringent controls similar to those imposed on all film borrowers.

The production of additional copies of a disc by means of tape recording represents perhaps the most practical means of providing for both the archival and circulation functions of the phonorecord collection. It should also be pointed out that while librarians tend to be rather cautious about acknowledging the availability of library discs as an opportunity by which patrons can build their own personal tape collections, the benefits in terms of circulation this activity brings to libraries cannot be overlooked. As concerns the ethical and legal ramifications involved in passively condoning this practice, the following assertion by Abe Goldman is particularly worth noting:

> A library that lends phonorecords may know or have reason to believe that some borrowers will make duplicates of the sound recording for their own private collections. The library would not appear to incur any risk of liability on that account. The house committee also dealt with home recordings as follows: 'In approving the creation of a limited copyright in sound recordings it is the intention of the Committee that this limited copyright not grant any broader rights than are accorded to other copyright proprietors under the existing Title 17. Specifically, it is not the intent of the Committee to restrain the home recording, from broadcasts or from tapes or records, of recorded performances, where the home recording is for private use and with no purpose of reproducing or otherwise capitalizing commercially on it. This practice is common and unrestrained today, and the record producers and performers would be in no different position from that of the owners of copyright in recorded musical compositions over the past twenty years.'[7]

The archival function of a well-balanced popular music collection can be of as much practical value to a public library as high circulation figures. Some of the benefits which might ensue are: (1) the education of area patrons, (2) prestige sufficient to attract visitors and scholars from outside the local scene, (3) publicity which would stimulate community pride as well as serve the more practical function of acting as a catalyst in attracting increased local funds and gifts. Any project offering the wide spectrum of services possible with the existence of an archival collection of popular music possessed of a clearly defined purpose can hardly fail to stimulate public support.

Given the premise that the music department of a public library is receptive to the idea of placing primary emphasis upon the development of a popular phonorecord collection, the greatest problem becomes one of understanding this field in an authoritative manner. Relatively few librarians seem to possess a close acquaintance with the pop scene together with its constant fluctuations in taste. The decision as to which reviewing media to employ in the construction of acquisition lists is as baffling a proposition as the selection of the phonorecords themselves. Many periodicals which treat the rock scene in depth are erratic as regards to quality of content as well as the types of evaluative criteria employed. The cliche vocabulary of "hip" reviewers is often hard for those outside the mainstream of the youth subculture to appreciate, let alone understand. An objective and authoritative view can best be obtained by comparing the opinions of a commercial trade publication devoted to this field such as Billboard or Cash Box with a magazine emphasizing the aesthetic values of music (e. g. Stereo Review, High Fidelity, Creem, Rolling Stone) and with the various library journals which include reviews of popular recordings.

Additional measures should be employed to ensure the success of a popular music archive. Librarians should not be hesitant about actively seeking special discount rates with certain record companies. The vast number of promotional copies of albums mailed out to not always interested reviewers often would be of more use in spreading the word if displayed on a shelf in the local public library. Smaller labels are particularly receptive to such overtures. These companies usually operate on much tighter budgets than the larger ones, aiming at quality rather than quantity as the key to commercial success. These outfits also tend to specialize in a particular style of music, such as country and western or rhythm and blues--a philosophy ideally suited to the purposes of most special collections. Therefore, it might in many cases be highly feasible, both in terms of expenditure savings and the value of the collection to be had, if a library agreed to purchase the entire catalog of a specific company.

Sufficient advertising in order to acquaint the general public with the collection is also advisable. Pamphlets, circulars, newspaper features and instructional radio and television programs in which these holdings are utilized represent just a sampling of the public relations projects possible.

Perhaps the cardinal rule in building popular phonorecord collections should be that the public library take advantage of the local environment. This would seem a practical step in keeping with both the economics of collection building and the musical tastes of local patrons. For example, it would be hard to visualize the advantages to be derived from pouring a sizeable amount of money into

the development of a country music archives by the Boston Public
Library at the expense of other genres more highly favored in that
region.

A noticeable degree of uniqueness in relation to record collections of a comparable nature provides yet another excellent means
of publicity. Important variables to consider in this respect are:
(1) the location of recording studios nearby (cities like Muscle
Shoals, Alabama, and Nashville and Memphis, Tennessee are known
to many people only for the music produced there by world-famous
recording artists); (2) historical significance (e. g. the birthplace,
home or artistic starting point of a widely known musician); and
(3) opportunities of a less definite sort such as the precedent set by
the philanthropic activities of particular individuals or groups.

The need for public librarians possessing the willingness and
capability to exploit the possibilities of popular music archives cannot be overstressed. For many years the establishment of sound
collections of jazz phonorecords was hampered by intellectual snobbism. Another important factor in the neglect of these older recordings was the lack of acceptance of the 78 r. p. m. disc by librarians
as an information format worthy of a concerted effort at preservation.
By the time enough musicologists and archivists awoke to the significance of jazz as a vital and creative art form which should be documented in its historical development, much material had been irre-
trievably lost. Carlos Hagen appears to view the problem as reaching far deeper than the antipathy on the part of librarians toward any
particular art form or the formats utilized in presenting them.

> By ignoring the new media and the techniques necessary to
> handle them, librarians are, perhaps unconsciously, causing
> immense damage to our cultural heritage. Looking to the
> immediate past, there has not been much enthusiasm in li-
> brary circles for accepting the new and unfamiliar. [8]

The 45 r. p. m. record, which became the primary vehicle for
rock and roll during the decade beginning roughly with the mid-1950's
and continuing uneclipsed until the rise of the long playing album as
the preferred artistic medium by the mid-1960's, has suffered neglect on the part of librarians similar to that of the 78 r. p. m. disc.
With the exception of selected songs that various record companies
decide to include on album anthologies (e. g. Roulette's monumental
"Golden Goodies" series, Original Sound's "Oldies But Goodies"),
many important old singles dating back to the youthful period of rock
will never be heard by anyone besides a few knowledgeable private
collectors who can afford the time and money necessary to acquire
the hits of vintage rock and roll artists such as the Spaniels, the
Nutmegs, the Harptones and the Flamingoes. This deplorable situation is complicated by the possibility of suit being brought upon librarians by the record industry if the free exchange and taping of
recorded material among libraries throughout the nation becomes
commonplace. In his column contained within the Music Library Association's Notes, [9] David Hall cited a paper given by H. William

Krasilovsky at the 1969 meeting of the Association for Recorded
Sound Collections (ARSC). In this paper the author set forth the
proposition that

> phonorecord librarians as a group, whether through MLA,
> ARSC, or both, should engage in an organized and con-
> certed effort to help develop legislation and a proposed
> code of fair practices, which on the one hand would pro-
> tect the legitimately vested interests involved in the pro-
> duction of sound recordings, and yet allow the educational/
> library community and the bona fide scholar reasonably
> easy access to all sources of sound recording material
> coming within their sphere of interest.[10]

By means of their close ties with the general populace, public
libraries possess an inherently better vantage point than do university
or special libraries for the assimilation of the sometimes subtle
nuances of popular tastes. This superior degree of perspective together with the realization of prodigious quantities of music constantly being produced in this genre, renders it necessary that as many
public libraries as possible serve the important function of becoming
depositories dedicated to the preservation and documentation of popular phonorecords for future generations.

References

1. Freed, Richard. "Crisis in American Classical Music Recording," Stereo Review, 21:57, February, 1971.
2. Smith, Joan Pemberton. "A Basic Stock List," Phonograph
   Record Libraries: Their Organization and Practice, edited
   by Henry F. J. Currall. 2nd ed. Hamden, Connecticut,
   Archon Books (c1970) pp. 162-75.
3. Faw, Marc T. "A Basic Record Collection: an Annotated Dis-
   cography," Oklahoma Librarian, 22:15-17+, July, 1972.
4. Hagist, Barbara. "Resistance and Reluctance in Record Selection," Library Journal, 93:518-520, February 1, 1968. Ms.
   Hagist's article documents the glaring gulf existing between
   the listening tastes of users and non-users of the Tulsa Public Library record collection in a survey taken by the patrons
   of that library. Also included is a plea for objectivity in
   record selection policies on the part of music librarians.
5. Hagen, Carlos B. "The Struggle of U.S. Sound Archives," Library Trends, 22:49-50, July, 1972.
6. Dylan, Bob. "My Back Pages," available on his Greatest Hits
   album on the Columbia label. Another well known interpretation is the hit single version released by the Byrds in
   1967, which was also included on their Younger Than Yesterday album for Columbia.
7. Goldman, Abe A. "Copyright and Archival Collections of Sound
   Recordings," Library Trends, 22:153-54, July, 1972.
8. Hagen, Carlos B. "The Struggle of U.S. Sound Archives," Library Trends, 22:49, July, 1972.

9. Hall, David. "Record-Industry Notes," <u>Music Library Association Notes</u>, 26:726-30, June, 1970.

10. <u>Ibid</u>., p. 729.

RECOMMENDED READINGS

The topic of evaluation of materials is covered widely in the literature. Books dealing with administration of libraries, collection development, services to specific audiences as well as books on the use of media frequently include sections on the evaluation of materials. These standard works are frequently revised and the reader is advised to check for the latest edition of the works cited below, which are samples of the range of approaches used.

Two works dealing with collection development are: (1) Mary Duncan Carter, Wallace John Bonk, and Rose Mary Magrill, Building Library Collections, 4th ed., Metuchen, N.J.: Scarecrow Press, 1974 (5th edition, 1979); and (2) Robert Newton Broadus, Selecting Materials for Libraries, New York: H. W. Wilson, 1973. These general works discuss many aspects of collection development, as well as presenting criteria to be used in evaluating specific types of materials, such as works from a particular discipline.

General works on the characteristics of non-print materials discuss related technology and utilization, which are matters that must be considered in evaluating the potential value of such materials to a collection. Compatibility of materials to equipment owned by a library are also discussed. Examples of works that focus on non-print materials and have sections on evaluation of materials are: James Wilson Brown, Audio-Visual Instruction: Technology, Media & Methods, 5th ed., New York: McGraw-Hill, 1977; Walter A. Wittich and Charles F. Schuller, Instructional Technology: Its Nature and Use, 5th ed., New York: Harper & Row, 1973.

Frequently works that discuss a specific format include sections on selection. Two such examples are Andrew D. Osborn's Serial Publications: Their Place and Treatment in Libraries, 2nd ed., Chicago: American Library Association, 1973, and Bill Katz' Magazine Selection: How to Build a Community-Oriented Collection, New York: R. R. Bowker, 1971.

Another useful guide is Emily S. Jones' Manual on Film Evaluation, revised edition, New York: Educational Film Library Association, no date.

A number of journals which regularly feature articles on evaluation have published anthologies. For the reader who has missed the original articles these collections provide an overview of recent and sometimes conflicting views on the topic. Examples of such anthologies include: Issues in Children's Book Selection: A School Library Journal/Library Journal Anthology, New York: R. R. Bowker, 1973; Crosscurrents of Criticism: Horn Book Essays 1968-1977, edited by Paul Heins, Boston: Horn Book, 1977; and Selecting Media for Learning: Readings from Audiovisual Instruction, Washington, D. C.: Association for Educational Communications and Technology, 1974. The information provided may be organized by moving from the broad overview to specific criteria for unique formats, or to criteria for materials for certain audiences.

While the articles in this chapter and the recommended readings do not cover every conceivable form of material found in library collections, they do provide a beginning and basic look at the criteria librarians must consider. The appearance of new methods of presenting information creates a need for librarians to be ever alert to the developments. Reading current literature and attending exhibits at conferences provide two means by which librarians can add to the basic knowledge presented in this chapter.

CHAPTER 7

ROLE OF PUBLISHERS, PRODUCERS
AND DISTRIBUTORS

For librarians to be knowledgeable consumers, they must be cognizant of the factors influencing the provision of materials. Factors such as the operational aspects of publishing, distribution patterns, economics, and the diversity of sources for various formats of materials affect the availability of desirable and attainable materials for our collections.

Publishers work within certain strictures, such as the cost and availability of materials; access to printing press time; talent and work of authors, illustrators, translators and other individuals involved in the creation of materials; and warehousing. These strictures indirectly affect library selection, as does the changing structure of publishing houses, which limits our ability to "know our publisher." This ability formerly provided a point of reference as to the anticipated quality and type of works issued by a particular house. Editorial affiliations, as well as ownership and management patterns, are in such a state of flux that the librarian needs to read up-to-date news sources about the industry in order to have a sense of the possible future direction of publishing within a company.

Producers of audiovisual materials also face strictures including ones imposed by those involved in the creation of materials, or the need for various types of facilities to produce their materials, and changes brought about by technological advances. Unfortunately, there is a paucity of information in the literature about the operation of, and unique situations faced by, the audiovisual industry.

Publishers, like librarians, are concerned with the quality of books and their contribution to mankind. This idea is expressed by Herbert S. Bailey, Jr. in "Epilogue: On Quality" from his book on the management of publishing houses, entitled The Art and Science of Book Publishing. One way for librarians and publishers to share their concerns is for them to work together. Thomas M. Schmid, in "Libraries and Publishers: The Uneasy Partnership, " offers specific suggestions about this relationship as it applies to university presses. While acknowledging benefits to both publisher and librarian, Schmid sees this involvement as a means of providing librarians with an education into the realities of publishing. These realities are explored further when Harald Bohne addresses the frequently raised question: "Why Are Book Prices So High?" Using that question as the title for his article, Bohne writes from the perspective of the university press and provides insights applicable to other publishing organizations. The influence of economics and management of the publishing industry are examined from a different viewpoint by Crittenden, who comments on the phenomenon of "Merger Fever in Publishing" and its possible impact on the publishing of the more experimental, high-risk works. These writings provide an introductory glimpse into the world of publishing.

But these sources of materials (publishers/producers) do not always provide direct distribution to libraries. Our selection of materials calls for knowledge of the distribution patterns that exist. Certain materials are available only by direct approach to the publisher/producer, as is the case with government publications, some audio-visual materials, subscription publications, and ephemeral materials. Other materials are indirectly distributed by means of wholesalers/jobbers, periodical subscription agencies, or special dealers (rare or out-of-print books, audiovisual materials).

The roles and services of distributors are explored in several of the selected articles. Harold Roth delineates the operations of the book jobber in "The Book Wholesaler: His Forms and Services" and provides practical advice on the selection of the wholesaler. The paperback, now an important alternative to the hardcover format, is the focus of Marilyn Abel's "Paperback Practicalities." The increasing use of paperbacks, their distribution, jobbers and customer services are described as they relate to paperback in school and public libraries. The inclusion of audiovisual materials in libraries has been accompanied by the growth of companies that act as dealers and suppliers for these materials. Excerpts from Edward J. Hingers' article, "The Audiovisual Supplier: Dealing with Dealers and Distributors," point out the role of such companies. Other agencies serve as both producer and distributor. One example is the Government Printing Office. Wellington Lewis, in writing about "The U.S. Government Printing Office Today," details the functions of the Public Documents Department as a distributor.

These articles point out concerns about accessibility, availability, economics, and distribution which affect the ability of libraries to carry out selection and collection development in the patterns they might consider desirable. For the library, these concerns translate into problems with the quality and price of materials, speed of delivery, and non-availability of materials caused by the decreasing number of printings of a work, which leads to a shortened "in-print" status for that work. Furthermore, the cost of warehousing and materials is increasingly reducing the retention of titles on publishers' backlists.

These concerns are not those of just the publisher/producer or librarian; rather, they are mutual concerns and reflect the interrelatedness and interdependence of those providing materials and those purchasing them. This point is emphasized when one considers that for some types of materials, libraries constitute the principal market, e.g., children's literature and reprints.

EPILOGUE: ON QUALITY

By Herbert S. Bailey, Jr.

A publisher is known not by the skill with which he runs his business but by the books he publishes. The history of publishing is the history of great houses that published great books; it is also the history of literary taste, which itself is made in part by publishers. The purpose of the activity we have been analyzing is to produce and distribute books, and it is worthwhile only to the extent that the books are worthwhile--and only to the extent that they are read.

It has been said that printing, like architecture, is a servant art. Printing serves publishing, and publishing serves civilization. Books reach every aspect of our culture, interpreting the past and the present, anticipating the future, carrying necessary information, portraying life as it was and is and as it can be imagined. All kinds of books do this, and all kinds of publishers have opportunities to exercise judgment on quality--on the effects of what they publish, for books do have effects, both good and bad. If a publisher runs his business well, he has greater opportunities to favor quality, to distribute it widely, and thus to contribute something worthwhile to mankind.

LIBRARIES AND PUBLISHERS:
THE UNEASY PARTNERSHIP

By Thomas M. Schmid

Frank Wardlaw, when director of the University of Texas
Press, used to liken the editor-author relationship to a porcupine
that backed into a prickly pear and murmured, "Is that you, honey?"
I'd like to borrow that characterization and extend it to the uneasy
connection between publisher and librarian. As one who spent a
goodly number of years in publishing before becoming a librarian, I
am thoroughly persuaded that a strong symbiotic tie exists. It
seems equally evident, unhappily, that this tie is frequently strained
by both parties.

Libraries represent the overwhelming market for scholarly
books. I wonder how many university presses have a librarian from
their institution serving on the press committee or board of gover-
nors. It seems possible he/she could be of more than ornamental
value, if only to question occasionally that well-loved assessment of
a manuscript as one "which every library will have to buy." More
positively, the librarian could help in certain policy decisions faced
by most presses today. One of these involves the format in which
information is to be published. I get the distinct impression that
publishers decide on format--e.g., microfilm or microfiche, positive or negative, high or low reduction ratio, filmstrips or slides,
phonodisc or audiotape, A-V materials bound into the book or offered separately--without regard for the technological trends and
capabilities of libraries; without regard, in brief, for the preferences of the greatest single segment of their market. The presence
of a librarian, either formally on the press committee, or infor-
mally as a consultant, might prevent the scholarly publisher from
making some of the more egregiously wrong choices.

Another benefit resulting from such association would be the
education of the librarian to the harsh realities of publishing. In
such an event, his/her attitude toward publishers might change from
focused dislike to vague compassion. The basic aim should be to
establish communication at the level of workaday concerns, rather
than relying on high-level inter-professional committees such as
ALA and AAP, whose great goodwill has traditionally been exceeded
only by their ineffectiveness.

Cooperation between librarian and publisher is crucial, more-

Reprinted from Scholarly Publishing, vol. 6, no. 1, October 1974,
pp. 3-7, by permission of the University of Toronto Press; copyright © University of Toronto Press, 1974.

over, if we are ever to come to grips with a set of problems which
will yield only to a willingness on both sides to abandon dearly held
concepts in favor of real change.   I mean no less than a basic alteration in the economics underlying the publication of information,
the distribution of information, and the compensation of its authors.
This alteration was not planned, nor were plans made to cope with
it.   However, it is upon us and must be dealt with.

Traditionally, the economics of publishing has rested upon the
physical number of copies sold--of a book, of subscriptions to a
journal, of recordings, of microfiche sets, or whatever.   A well-
defined compensation scheme has been in force, involving purchase
price, royalties, extra rights.   This traditional scheme, which,
with variations, has worked quite well since the time of Gutenberg,
has now been badly upset by technological and societal changes.
Among these changes are: scarcity and consequent high prices of
paper, ink, and binding materials; cheap, convenient photocopying;
computer storage and manipulation of information; relatively cheap,
convenient electronic transmission of information; and increasing
eagerness of libraries to form consortia, networks, and other con-
structs to further the sharing of resources.

All these factors are interrelated; all tend to work against the
sale to libraries of large numbers of physical information packages
(all right, books).   As materials become scarcer and prices of
books go up, libraries avail themselves of technological and cooperative means to share them, which means the price per copy goes up
still further, and so on.   The spiral ends when the price of books
exceeds the willingness of taxpayers of trustees to carry the burden.
We have seen this point reached at more than one institution, which
has then had to make even greater use of photocopying, interlibrary
loans, etc.

Quite apart from considerations of economy, there is the
temptation, posed by the photocopying machines in libraries, to substitute wholesale copying for tedious notetaking.   In the process, the
copyright law takes a fearful beating.   Articles, diagrams, poems,
and even entire books are duplicated.   To be sure, such duplication
often violates copyright, but when the technology becomes irresis-
tible, can it be stopped?   An old legal tag applies here: A right
without a remedy is no right at all.

There are still some librarians around who are parochial
enough to think that this is mainly the publishers' problem.   In a
vague sort of way, they believe that the high calling of service to
research and scholarship carries with it a dispensation from certain
laws of the land, and they regard it as a "victory" for libraries
when a ruling goes against a publisher in favor of a library: "[The
Williams & Wilkins decision] is a victory for NLM and NIH and for
libraries generally. " (The quotation is from the ARL Newsletter of
10 January 1974.)   It does not require a great deal of reflection to
determine just how hollow such a victory is.   Given enough such
victories, in the courts or in the more relevant arena of day-to-day

practice, the sources of publication will surely wither. They won't disappear entirely, given people's apparently inherent drive to communicate, plus the Diktat to "publish or perish," but quantity and quality will inexorably tend to decrease.

This cannot be in the interests of libraries. We are the preservers and disseminators of information, not the originators. If our sources dry up, we will become museums, fascinating ones to be sure, but hardly places where the action is. Let me illustrate. A year or so ago, a respected reprint house announced a major project which would make widely available in microfiche an important research collection encompassing several thousands of volumes. The price was high but not exorbitant, reflecting, I assume, the publisher's break-even point if a reasonable number of research libraries were to buy the set.

What happened then? If one may extrapolate from the experience of a library at the foot of the Wasatch Mountains, my guess is that telephones were picked up all through the little universe of the Association of Research Libraries (the logical marketing target for the set), and groups of libraries--ad hoc congeries as well as established consortia--informally decided that perhaps a dozen institutions purchasing this set would be sufficient to serve the needs of their patrons. In the particular instance cited the copyright law does not even play a role, since the overwhelming bulk of the material is old enough for the copyright term to have expired. Since the format was to be microfiche, and since fiche can be reproduced at a cost of about four cents apiece, access to individual titles would be both cheap and fast for a library unwilling to incur the hefty purchase price for the whole set but prepared to go to the designated repository to fill its needs. Score one for libraries. But really? At this point, the publisher may well decide that there is no possibility for profit, and abandon the project. If that should be the case, everybody loses: the publisher, the library, and the researcher, who after all is what the whole thing is about.

So far, this discussion has been a bit hard on librarians. It is time to point out that publishers have done their ample share to contribute to the problem. What other industry would rely so trustingly on a law passed in 1909* to protect it from all the advances in technology since that date? This reliance creates a wonderland where what ought to be (according to law and statute, right and precedent) becomes what is flying in the face of experience and reason. It is perfectly possible to be comforted by counsel and upheld in every legal test, and yet be vanquished by what happens in real life. There are no winners in a struggle in which the protagonists try to ignore the twin powers of economics and technology.

After writing the previous paragraph, I was struck by the fact that I seem to have fallen into the prevailing rhetoric almost without

---

*This law has now been superseded--Ed.

being aware of it--using words like "struggle" and "protagonist" to describe what should essentially be a partnership between librarians and publishers. To restore that sense of partnership, I suspect that some traditional attitudes will have to be abandoned by publishers as well as librarians. I do not mean to suggest that we have already arrived at some sort of technological millennium. It was very much the fashion, ten or fifteen years ago, to predict that books and journals would soon be published in a single copy. That copy would, according to the futurists, be keypunched into a national computer, from which it could be called up on a cathode ray tube anywhere in the country (or indeed the world), and reproduced in hard copy or microform. There is no question that the technology to do this is present in full measure. The only reason that particular prophecy has not been fulfilled is that the cost would be prohibitive.

What we are dealing with, therefore, is a much more subtle problem, involving not a technological breakthrough, but a sort of technological creep-through. The book has surely not been replaced, but the number of physical copies sold is not keeping pace with the increase in costs. It thus seems inevitable that publishers must abandon "number of copies sold" as the index of profitability. This, however, requires also that libraries in their turn abandon the concept of unrestricted access--by circulation, copying, interlibrary loan, microfilming, computerization--to the published product.

At this point, my cloven hoof will have become apparent to any librarian who might be reading this paper. It's true: the logic of the situation as perceived from at least one university library seems to dictate some form of per-use fee, a prospect that has been singularly unpalatable to librarians ever since the idea of "free access to information" gained wide currency in the nineteenth century. What's worse, I believe that librarians themselves must volunteer to make this change, for publishers do not have the power to impose it, either politically through legislation or economically through sanctions. It seems passing strange for a librarian to regard the powerful publishing establishment as something of a helpless giant. But if libraries continue to lend to each other, and their patrons continue to copy, so that one book does the work formerly performed by many, what can the publisher ultimately do? He can win the quintessentially Pyrrhic victory of going out of business, and I don't think that's what anybody has in mind.

WHY ARE BOOK PRICES SO HIGH?

By Harald Bohne

The question I have been asked most frequently during some twenty years of bookselling and publishing has been: "Why are book prices so high?" For someone who loves and uses books every day it is difficult to understand why the question persists. Books are no more expensive than other commodities, but rather less so, once one moves from the bare necessities of life (food and shelter) to forms of recreation, entertainment, self-improvement, and professional activity. But the question is asked (and has been asked, it seems, in all times) by people from all walks of life: students, scholars, housewives, professional people, readers who buy books for entertainment and escape, readers who buy books to improve their minds--even authors who buy other authors' books. Why should this be so?

One answer may be that the pricing policies of publishers so mystify the reader that he suspects them. Why else would an otherwise well-informed public question the price of a book when, on the average, it is less than the cost of a normal meal in a medium-priced restaurant, or when a drink in a hotel bar now costs approximately as much as a 300-page mass-market paperback? Which involves the most labor--the meal, the drink, or the book?

Or why should the question be asked when the average retail price of university press books in North America in the last five years has gone up less than 30 per cent,[1] while the consumer price index has risen 34.4 per cent,[2] and academic salaries 31.9 per cent?[3]

It is true that some book prices are too high in relation to their content. This, however, is not generally because the publisher's pricing policy is outrageous, but because the book is not a good one, or has been presented by the publisher in a format which is too luxurious or inappropriate for the subject. Most scholarly publishers have at some time or other been guilty of overediting and re-writing manuscripts, of presenting a simple, straightforward monograph as if it were a trade book which might attract thousands instead of hundreds of readers.

But there are basic publishing functions which pertain to all books--the scholarly monograph, the popular novel or biography, the

Reprinted from Scholarly Publishing, vol. 7, no. 2, January 1976, pp. 135-143, by permission of the University of Toronto Press. Copyright © University of Toronto Press, 1976.

textbook, and the paperback. The pie is cut into pieces of different size, but there is also one pie: the list price. This article will attempt to explain why the pie has to be the size it is to feed all those who are involved in its making: author, editor, designer, production planner, printer, binder, salesman, invoice clerk, accountant, shipper, wholesaler, and bookseller.

Two pieces of the pie are easier to accept than the others. By coincidence they are parts over which the publisher has only indirect control: the discount to booksellers and wholesalers, and the cost of printing and binding.

Every reader knows and accepts the fact that the retailer from whom he buys a book must make a living, and that the bookseller relies on the publisher to allow him a discount off the retail price large enough to pay his staff, rent, and taxes, with a little left over for himself. Publishers can decide whether to allow an educational (or short) discount of 20% or a trade discount of 40%; but they must realize that the 20% discount practically excludes the book from being stocked regularly by all but a handful of college or specialist booksellers. Any book, then, for which the publisher expects to reach a market beyond libraries, institutions, and the limits of a scholarly sub-discipline must be priced to allow a booksellers' discount of 40% or more. Some may argue that this is an exorbitant margin, but that it is not may be seen in the economic plight of practically all independent booksellers who offer more than current bestsellers and publishers' remainders. Forty per cent margin is not a great deal in a business where every item sold is unique, where expertise and professional training are expected from the staff, where the distribution system is cumbersome and expensive, and where the customers complain constantly about the price of the product, the fact that the bookseller does not have a complete range of all the several hundred thousand books available in the English language, and that it takes too damn long for a book specially ordered to reach its anxious reader. On short-discount and special-order books the retailer in fact is apt to lose money.

The other area over which the publisher has only limited control is the cost of printing. He is, of course, in a position to shop for the best price for the quality desired. But he has little room to maneuver in the face of industry-wide increases in the cost of labor and of paper and other materials, and the uncertainties of whether paper and binding cloth will be available when typesetting is completed--both matters of great consequence to the cost of the book.

Yet these are, to repeat, the two areas the book buyer does understand best. Most people can relate easily to the expense of running a retail business. And the costs of paper and cloth, printing and binding, involve tangible products, things that can be held in one's hand, felt, measured, weighed, and judged by their appearance.

Somewhat more remote from public awareness is the compen-

sation due to the author--his royalty. Writers of books are among
the few professional groups in the world whose earnings are, in
most cases, completely unrelated to the amount of work they undertake, the time they spend in writing, and the contribution to knowledge and entertainment their writing makes. Often the publication of
a book heralds the author to his friends as a new member in the
ranks of the Arthur Haileys and Jacqueline Susanns, whose income is
legend in the press, when the truth is that the revenue from the average author's royalties would drive most of his readers to the picket
lines. It is true that authors of academic books draw other benefits
from their publications--prestige, promotion, tenure--but even so a
royalty of 10 per cent (whether of the list price or of the net proceeds received by the publisher after discounts) spread over a sale
of 1,000 to 3,000 copies during a period of five to ten years is very
small compensation indeed. And let us not forget another peculiarity
of royalties, that (except for advances, which are rare in scholarly
publishing) they are paid only after the publisher and bookseller have
managed to sell the book to the consumer. The author normally is
anxious to have his book distributed and read as widely as possible.
Yet not only his readership, but his earnings as well, meagre as
they may be, depend entirely on the publisher's ability to get his
book to the marketplace in a format that will attract the potential
purchaser.

And this is where we enter the grey area in the price of
books: publishers' overhead expenses. What does the publisher do--
after the bookseller and manufacturer and author have all had their
shares--with the rest of the pie? Depending on the discount the book
carries, and assuming that the manufacturing cost accounts for 20
per cent of the list price, the balance remaining may be anywhere
from one-third to one-half. This is what the publisher has available to assess manuscripts, prepare them for publication, promote,
stock, sell, and distribute the finished books, and provide a margin
of profit if any is expected--which is not usually the case with academic books.

Overhead expenses are really the cost of doing business. In
a publishing house, this means list-building and manuscript appraisal, substantive and technical editing, design and production planning,
estimating and scheduling, promoting and advertising, selling and
distributing, warehousing, invoicing and shipping, accounting and collecting, and holding all this together through an administrative unit.
The overhead expenses in a house which published primarily trade
books of interest to the general public, or textbooks used in schools
and universities, obviously vary from those of a small poetry house
or a university press concerned primarily with scholarly monographs.
The number of titles published by any one of these may be the same,
but the number of copies sold of any title will differ greatly. The
cost of promoting and selling twenty-five thousand copies of a popular
novel is not twenty-five times the cost of promoting and selling a
scholarly monograph published in an edition of one thousand copies.
The base against which the trade publisher can charge his overhead
expense is far greater than that available to the academic publisher.

Part of this larger base is, of course, absorbed by higher discounts to booksellers and higher royalty payments to authors. But because each title published is a unique product, it requires individual treatment in all areas of publishing, whether its publisher's list consists of popular books or specialized monographs. Obviously, the scholarly publisher, operating from a much smaller base, must retain a larger piece of pie to survive.

Publishers of academic works are, of course, assisted by their universities, by government-sponsored agencies, or by private foundations, and this keeps the pie from growing too large to be attractive to all but the largest libraries. But support from these bodies, which are experiencing their own financial difficulties, has not been able to keep pace with inflationary increases in all areas of book production and publishing, so that retail prices of books have had to increase even though, as we have seen, these increases run below those in comparable areas.

But back to the question of what happens with the part of the retail price retained by the publisher. What are the benefits the author and his readers derive from the publisher, and are they worth the money the publisher needs to pay for them? Let us examine the various stages through which each book must pass, considering what it gains in the process and at what expense. [4]

The first stage, the assessment of manuscripts, in scholarly publishing is a complex and often time-consuming process. In most cases, the senior editors of a university press make only a preliminary evaluation of a manuscript in general terms and rely on the opinions of the author's peers before deciding to propose it for publication. The in-house assessment, and equally the selection of appropriate readers, require knowledge and expertise which can be gained only by years of experience. At its best, this process provides many positive benefits. Even before transmitting a manuscript to an outside reader, the editor may make suggestions for revision and improvement which will give the manuscript a better chance of favorable assessment. The readers too will have suggestions. The author may not wish--or be able--to incorporate all such suggestions, but more often than not the result is a better book than would otherwise have been.

In-house appraisal costs editors' time, and outside assessment costs readers' fees (which are nevertheless little more than token payments) and postage (which can amount to a remarkable sum in a year). But only a fraction of the manuscripts submitted can be published, and many hours must be spent reading and judging works which in the end have to be rejected. This cost, too, must be met, and in the long run (unless this is covered by a university subsidy) the reader must pay not only for the books he reads but for the cost of screening those which do not merit publication. This last is no small service in a world of increasing verbal pollution.

A manuscript that is accepted for publication undergoes copy

editing--a highly skilled craft with benefits that are difficult to identify, for in the finished book successful copy editing is invisible.
The reader of a well-edited book is in direct communication with the
author, unaware of the word-by-word editorial scrutiny that has assisted the author's efforts to present his ideas clearly without ambi-
guities, obscurities, or repetitions, without the irritating distrac-
tions of faulty syntax or misspelled names, without inconsistent de-
viations from accepted usage in notes, bibliographies, charts, graphs,
and tables.   Readers of ill-edited books may be all too well aware
of the lack of editing by the presence of such "static" in the communication.

It is difficult, and of only limited usefulness, in any industry-
wide survey, to analyze the expenses of publishing in terms of individual titles.   Instead, in such surveys the operating costs are normally expressed as a percentage of total net sales.   University Press
Statistics for 1974, compiled by John P. Dessauer for the Association of American Publishers and American University Press Services,
shows that for the thirty-two presses participating in the survey, the
costs of editorial appraisal and copy editing absorbed 8% of the total
revenue from sales.   The economy of scale referred to earlier in
the comparison between scholarly publishers and trade houses applies
also among university presses: the average editorial expense decreased from 23.7% reported by presses with net sales under
$250,000 to 7% for presses with sales above $1 million.   It must be
remembered that this 8% also includes the very real cost of deciding
what not to publish.

The book designer's contribution, like the copy editor's, is
often not easily visible to the public.   His aim is to ease communication between author and reader.   This he does by manipulating
type and the space between type on a size of page and a stock of paper he has chosen with care, guided by budgetary as well as aesthetic considerations.   The complexity of much scholarly writing, involving tables and charts, foreign languages, extracts and notes,
mathematical or chemical formulae, poses special problems for the
designer.   His choice of typeface and format, except for budgetary
restraints, is large, with corresponding possibilities for error.   The
best design cannot turn a poor manuscript into a good book, but a
badly designed book can impede the communication which is the purpose of publishing.

To be effective, the designer obviously has to be fully familiar with methods of production; without that expertise, book design
would exist in a vacuum, either asking for the impossible or producing a book which might price itself out of the market.   Production planning and supervision are therefore equally important facets
of the publishing process.   This is a stage which, moreover, normally can lead to economies as well as costs.   Experience with the
problems most commonly found in scholarly manuscripts is leading
many presses to develop standard formats which can be used, with
only minor modifications, for a variety of books.   Production planning also involves the selection of typesetter and printer, and the

exploration of advances in printing technology. Careful and experienced shopping in this area, together with the establishment of streamlined procedures between a select number of printers and a publishing house, can save many dollars in the long run.

The cost of design services and production planning, in the 1974 university press statistics, averaged overall 2.9% of net sales. The figure varies from an average 9.7% of sales among the smaller presses to 2.4% among the larger ones. These statistics (as well as those given for editorial costs) include fees paid to freelance editors and designers in addition to the salaries paid to permanent staff. Some aspects of copy editing and design can be done more cheaply by employing freelance labor, if such help is available, because the latter does not normally have to carry all the overhead expenses incurred in a business office. But many of the functions described above require the kind of permanent expertise and dedication which cannot readily be acquired in the freelance market.

There is no point in writing or publishing a book if it is not read, and in the interests of the author each book should be brought to the attention of, and made available to, the widest possible readership. Because most scholarly books are addressed to very specialized audiences, their publishers cannot rely exclusively on the book trade's normal channel of distribution: the bookseller. A good deal of the academic publisher's promotion must be by direct mail. This may take the form of extensive mailings of circulars announcing individual titles, brochures promoting specific series, or catalogues covering the publisher's total output or his titles in given subject areas or publishing seasons. This form of promotion is expensive, relying as it does on the building or acquisition of appropriate mailing lists, the design and printing of attractive mailing pieces, and the vagaries and rates of the postal service. But no more effective means have been found to tell the potential reader about a new book in his field or in a field related to his interest which, because of its limited market, is unlikely to appear on bookstore racks, and might otherwise escape his notice. Reviews of scholarly books often do not appear until months after publication and in the interim--to speed cash flow and reduce interest charges--the publisher must find how to bring his titles to the attention of possible readers by whatever ways are available. Direct mail is one, display advertising another: both are expensive if related to the net result. The university press statistics for 1974 show the average cost of promotion to be 12.9% of sales. Only 2.5% of this cost related to salaries of the publisher's promotion staff; the balance included such items as space advertising (2.6%), catalogues and trade advertising (1.7%), direct mail promotion (3.1%), free copies (1.7%), and exhibit costs (0.7%).

The publisher's role in bringing the author's book to the attention of the public does not end with this, however. He must also employ a sales force to bring books to the attention of booksellers, college and university bookstores, and trade and library wholesalers. That expense accounts on the average for another 3.8% of sales, approximately half of it in salaries and commissions, the rest in travel expenses.

The mechanics of distribution require efficient systems of warehousing, stock control, order fulfilment, invoicing, credit control, and bookkeeping. Since university presses often deal with purchasers directly rather than through the limited number of wholesalers and booksellers that trade houses can use, virtually thousands of accounts have to be established and maintained. And although the market for scholarly books is the world, it is simply not large enough in number (as opposed to diffusion) of purchasers for university presses to sell foreign editions or rights as a matter of course; as a result they must maintain this extensive network of accounts on a world-wide basis, with all the attendant problems of shipping, documentation, and collection. The shipments they make to customers, both domestic and foreign, are generally small, averaging fewer than three books; this increases the cost of wrapping materials as well as handling. Moreover, scholarly books are held in stock for much longer periods than the average lifetime of a trade book, and this results in higher warehouse costs and higher costs of interest on the capital invested to produce them. Even so innocuous a factor as the titling of scholarly books can drive up costs. The complexity and similarity of many academic book titles, and the variations on them-- sometimes no more than approximations of the title--that appear in correspondence, require special care in order fulfilment and the preparation of invoices, if the expense to the publisher and the annoyance to the customer in receiving the wrong book is to be avoided. Order fulfilment cost on the average 5. 6% of net sales, according to the 1974 survey. Of that, 4% covered salaries. Warehousing and shipping costs weighed in at 6. 4% of sales, with 3. 1% going to salaries.

What is left in the list price pie has to cover the publisher's administrative expense of doing business. What does this include? Management, accounting, and general office salaries took 7. 3% of net sales, rent or occupancy charges 2. 6%, employee benefits 2. 4%, and all other administrative and general expenses (including telephone, office supplies, insurance, membership fees, depreciation of office equipment, copying costs, share of data processing costs, bad debt and collection expense) 6. 9%.

Let us translate these percentages of net sales into portions of list-price pie--for a scholarly monograph selling at $15. 00 (not an unusual price these days) with an appropriately short discount. (The average discount over all university press books is probably closer to 30% than 20%; but there seems to be a general trend towards more short-discount books, and such specialized works are the subject of this article. Moreover, the so-called trade books that have long discounts assist their short-discount brothers by generating, through larger orders, a contribution to overhead, without which prices might be even higher. Whatever figure is chosen will involve some distortion.)

Clearly the scholarly publisher is not usually left with any surplus after all expenses have been met. As noted, the cost of investment in inventory, for those presses which have to carry it,

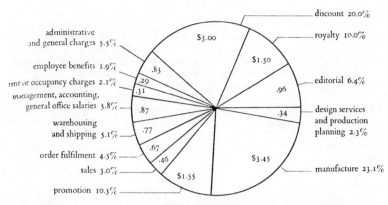

has been yet another major obstacle towards achieving anything approaching solvency. The need for subsidization of titles and/or operations has become greater than ever. The gap between cost and income is growing wider and wider. And retail prices, we are often told, are now as high as they can go.

References

1. AAP/AAUP statistics.
2. U.S. Bureau of Labor statistics.
3. American Association of University Professors.
4. For some of the descriptions of publishing procedures I am indebted to Values in Publishing, a booklet recently issued by the Association of Canadian Publishers/Association des Presses Universitaires Canadiennes.

MERGER FEVER IN PUBLISHING

By Ann Crittenden

The book publishing business is in the throes of a major shakeout. As a result, what was once a cottage industry is rapidly becoming part of one of the world's most-high powered industries-- the fast-growing "media" business.

Unlike an earlier wave of concentration in publishing, in the late 1960's, when textbook publishers eagerly eloped with computer companies, the present round of marriages is taking place within the media set. Hard- and soft-cover publishers are joining forces and publishers and bookclubs alike are being sought by giants of the television, newspaper, and magazine business.

Indeed, the urge to merge is such, according to J. Kendrick Noble, a publishing analyst for Mitchell, Hutchins & Company, that "almost every major company in the media field is looking for more media acquisitions. "

With an abundance of cash to invest but held back from expansion in their immediate areas by antitrust considerations, big firms are rapidly widening their scope. In recent months, for example:

Time Inc., a major conglomerate in magazines, book publishing, and cable and pay television, has proposed acquisition of the Book-of-the-Month Club, the nation's oldest and largest book club, and David Susskind's television producing company, Talent Associates.

CBS Inc. has acquired Fawcett Publications, a family-owned paperback and special-interest-magazine publisher, and Frederick Praeger, a hard-cover house--adding to a complex that already included a mass-market paperback publisher (Popular Library), a hard-cover publisher (Holt, Rinehart & Winston), a science-textbook house and some 25 magazines.

The Bertelsmann Publishing Group, West Germany's largest book and magazine publisher, purchased 51 per cent of Bantam Books, the largest and one of the most successful mass paperback publishers in the United States, from IFI International, which is affiliated with the Agnelli Group of Italy.

302 / Publishers, Producers, Distributors

A number of major film studios, including Columbia Pictures and 20th Century Fox, are exploring ways to enter book publishing. Conversely, Harcourt Brace Jovanovich, which publishes hard- and soft-cover books, operates radio stations and produces educational films, is moving into feature film production.

The latest consolidations follow more than 300 book-publishing mergers in the last 20 years, according to the Authors Guild. Data gathered by the professional authors' association indicate that the trend is changing the face of a once-fragmented industry.

Seven paperback publishers now control the bulk of the mass paperback industry, and all of them are part of larger corporations. Ten companies accounted for 89 per cent of all book-club sales in 1976. According to industry analysts, only 40 of the estimated 6,000 hard-cover trade houses in the country can successfully publish a book on a nationwide basis. Moreover, even these houses are rapidly being absorbed by larger conglomerates, such as Gulf and Western, or are themselves becoming the nucleus of a conglomerate. Doubleday, for example, now owns a paperback house and a book club.

"If this trend continues," Richard E. Snyder, president of Simon & Schuster, commented in a recent interview in Publishers Weekly (the book-industry publication whose parent, R. R. Bowker, was itself acquired by the Xerox Corporation a few years ago), "like the seven sisters of the oil business, we will have seven giant publishing companies of varying size, either as part of a conglomerate or we will become like Doubleday, which in itself is a bit of a conglomerate."

The phenomenon has aroused concern in the Authors Guild and among numerous writers and members of Congress that book publishing is losing its rich diversity, and that return on investment, rather than aesthetics or public responsibility, will come to dominate the print media. It has also pricked the interest of the Justice Department and the Federal Trade Commission, which are investigating the antitrust implications of the merger trend.

Even in purely economic terms, some in the book business wonder whether the emergence of the multimedia companies makes sense.

"You just can't make money in publishing," says Daniel Okrent, former editor-in-chief of Harcourt Brace. "In five or 10 years these guys will be saying, 'What is this business--I want out.'"

Book publishing is a notoriously low-profit business. Last year the industry showed a pretax earnings margin of only 7.2 per cent, primarily because hard-cover trade books, the weakest link in the industry, earned only 1.7 per cent in 1976, down from 4.4 per cent the year earlier.

Excluding subsidiary rights income from the sale of paperback and book club rights, the average hard-cover trade publisher
lost 16 per cent last year, according to the Association of American
Publishers.

Certain areas of book publishing, however--those that have
attracted the most investor interest--have done considerably better:
educational, professional and special interest books, for example,
and book clubs. Over the last five years industry sales have gone
from $2.9 billion in 1971 to $4.2 billion in 1976, an annual increase
of 7.8 per cent. Yet virtually all of these gains resulted from
higher prices--the number of books sold actually declined between
1972 and 1976. According to Book Industry Trends, 1977, published
by an industry study group, sales dropped from 1.373 billion copies
in 1972 to 1.360 billion last year, a fact attributed largely to the
inflation in book prices.

Clearly economic pressures account for part of the publishers' willingness to sell out to larger houses, particularly when the
capital required to compete in the business is escalating. Because
of the rise in bookstore chains, which are interested in buying fewer
titles and more best-sellers than the Mom-and-Pop stores they are
replacing, the demand for top authors is soaring, as are the prices
paid to them.

Small independent publishers often do not have the money to
meet the $1 million-plus demands made by today's best-selling
writers. To stay in the bidding, hard- and soft-cover houses are
merging or are looking for highly capitalized conglomerates to help
them raise the new ante.

As one example of the forces at work, Gail Sheehy, who received a $35,000 original advance for her best-selling book Pas-
sages negotiated an advance of more than $1.2 million for her next
book.

The demand for "big" books in the paperback market is particularly fierce, for only with a list headed by probable best-sellers
can a publisher gain all-important display space in retail outlets,
such as supermarkets and drugstores. Paperback rights to The
Thorn Birds, by a relatively unknown writer, Colleen McCullough,
sold for $1.9 million, and industry observers believe that record
will be broken by the end of the year.

There is another side to these windfalls: Books by unknown
authors are becoming harder to publish or to sell. According to
Bowker's Weekly Record, fewer new books were published in 1976
than in 1974. One reason, analysts say, is the publishers' response to the chains' hunger for fewer, bigger titles.

Moreover, advances paid to the majority of writers are now
less favorable than just two years ago, according to semi-annual
surveys conducted by the Authors Guild. In the latest survey more

than 60 per cent of the responding authors said they had received advances of less than $10,000.

Thus the trend toward concentration among publishers is in part a result of increasing concentration in book retailing as well as from economic concentration in related media industries.

The rate of return on equity in the highly concentrated radio and television industry, for example, was 23.3 per cent last year, far higher than the all-industry average of 14.1 per cent. Television companies--particularly CBS with a rate of return of 25.3 per cent and a 33 per cent earnings rise to a record $164 million last year--are cash-rich and looking for acquisitions. Time Inc., with record earnings and an internally generated cash flow from operations of $107 million last year, has also been compelled to find ways to spend the money.

In most cases these media companies have few avenues of expansion in their immediate fields, often for antitrust reasons. The networks cannot buy any more stations or expand into cable, and Time would have problems if it cast covetous eyes on any existing magazines. Moreover, unit-sales growth in many areas of the media, including newspapers, motion pictures and segments of the magazine business, has slowed significantly in recent years-- thus, the appeal of a new, but related field such as the book business.

Some conglomerate executives are describing their expansion into publishing in terms of what they used to call "synergy" in the go-go days of the 1960's, and which they now prefer to call "complementarity." Television and film companies in particular, with heavy appetities for production ideas, reason that by acquiring book publishers, they can obtain rights to such material at a lower cost than that for the same rights in the marketplace.

For their part, some big publishers are eager to contract for authors' film and television rights, traditionally reserved by the writer, in hopes of spinning them into profitable productions.

As Mr. Snyder of Simon & Schuster has put it, the book business is "the software of the television and movie media." Said Joseph L. Dionne, senior vice-president for corporate planning at McGraw-Hill: "It's like having your own raw material. It's like backward integration."

Mr. Dionne, and numerous publishers and editors, are skeptical about the actual degree of "complementarity" that results from multimedia matchings. They point out that the films produced by motion picture and television companies owned by media conglomerates are rarely based on books from affiliated publishers. And in spite of publishers' pressures or entreaties, sophisticated authors still refuse to relinquish their rights in other media.

More fundamentally, Mr. Dionne and other industry experts wonder whether the corporations now enthusiastically gobbling up book publishers can avoid the indigestion that followed the merger gluttony of the 1960's. Then, giant companies such as International Business Machines, Raytheon and Xerox busily absorbed textbook publishers, expecting to obtain material to program into their teaching machines. But the conversion of books into software was not at all simple, and a decline in the birthrate and a cutback in Federal education expenditures starved more than one ambitious project.

Some more recent mergers have been equally disappointing. Warner Communications has struggled for years, and at some cost, to succeed with Warner Books, a mass paperback house acquired in 1970. But by 1976 Warner's publishing group, including comic books and a distribution company, still had a lower pretax income than 1970.

Random House, the hard-cover house acquired by RCA in 1965, is still earning only a 4 per cent pretax profit, far less than RCA's other lines of business. Random House editors used to joke that RCA could have made more money simply by leasing out the publishing company's office space, a former employee recalled. RCA's management earlier this year, almost sold Random House to The Times Mirror Company, publisher of the Los Angeles Times. The deal was never consummated, partly because of Justice Department concern over possible antitrust aspects.

"The low rates of return of these publishers reflect the fact that these huge companies can't just wave a wand and bring earnings up," said T. H. Lipscomb, the president of Times Books, a subsidiary of The New York Times Company. Times Books, like Quadrangle Books, another subsidiary, went through years of losses and management changes before its reorganization this year.

Nevertheless, executives of the acquiring companies emphatically insist that they have not overestimated the earnings possibilities in bringing efficiencies to a business in which "99 per cent of the people don't know how to read a profit and loss statement," as Erwin A. Glikes, vice president of Harper & Row, put it recently.

Off the record, they rhapsodize about the savings that can result from applying modern management techniques and strict financial controls to family enterprises operated more like hobbies than businesses. In fact, figures published by the A.A.P. recently show a correlation last year between the size of publishers and their profit margins--the larger companies showed the highest rates of return.

There is some industry speculation that if current trends continue, with book publishing companies growing larger and increasingly profit-conscious, more and more experimental, high-risk works will be published by the small regional publishing houses that seem to be cropping up all over the country, particularly in the West. These publishers, which may produce as few as five books a year, may well become farm teams, in effect, developing new talent for the majors.

Similarly, as the larger publishers place increasing emphasis on the mass market, such works as poetry and translations of important foreign books will gravitate more and more to the university presses--much as cultural television programming has been relegated largely to public television.

In this process, the few remaining independent publishers are those most likely to be affected, according to John Dessauer, book-industry analyst. "They do seem to be in a squeeze, " he notes, "and most will probably sell out if they can. "

THE BOOK WHOLESALER:
HIS FORMS AND SERVICES

By Harold L. Roth

The book wholesaler, sometimes called a jobber, is probably
the oldest commercial library supplier in terms of continuous service. One such firm, which claims to be the "oldest and largest,"
notes a founding date of 1828.[1] For the purpose of this paper in a
library centennial issue, we will assume a continuous service to libraries of one hundred years and note that the major function of
wholesalers has not changed. The book wholesaler is a significant
part of the book distribution process; he buys and stocks quantities
of newly published books from publishers, and acts as a middleman
selling mainly to libraries and bookstores. The wholesaler's customers deal with that wholesaler as a means of consolidating shipments from as many as 3,000 publishers, reducing the cost of ordering individual titles, speeding up the ordering process, and obtaining a discount as large as possible on all purchased books.[2]
The wholesaler acts as a specialist in serving libraries, is usually
aware of the problems of the libraries with which he deals, and is
concerned with the needs of this specialty customer. The similarity
between wholesalers becomes a bit vague at this point.

Literary Market Place 1975-1976 lists seventy-two wholesalers
to schools and libraries. It also lists thirty-eight, not all different,
who claim specialist status for dealing in special subject areas.
There are also wholesalers who specialize in dealing with bookstores,
export and import, and remainders. Within each category there are
differences in size of stock, areas served, number of branches, number of publishers carried, and other services. Closer study shows
other differences. Some have large sales staffs, others have very
small staffs. Some firms limit the number of customers they will
handle, others handle all types of accounts except the smallest. A
library has difficulty in determining the wholesaler's capacity to
serve and is encouraged to visit its prospective wholesaler and his
competitors to determine the nature of the service to be expected and
to verify the statements of capacity which might originally have been
used to pique an acquisition librarian's interest in the wholesaler's
service.

The Way a Wholesaler Works

As in any business, the book wholesaler survives by his prof-

Reprinted from Library Trends, vol. 24, no. 4, April 1976, pp.
673-82; by permission of the publisher and author.

itmaking skill. He has chosen service to libraries because he feels that the business of selling books in quantity can be an efficient one which should deliver a solid bottom line at the end of the year. As part of the distribution process, the wholesaler is basically not concerned with any single title or with the titles of any one publisher. He does not sell titles nor a publisher's stock; he sells service based on long experience in dealing with libraries and satisfying their needs.

The wholesaler's key to service is his staff of book buyers. The buyer of new books is frequently a "book man" who deals with a publishing salesman--also a "book man"--and together they play the marketing game of determining the optimum number of copies to be stocked by the wholesaler in the initial order. The decision is based on a subjective evaluation to which is added some knowledge of previous sales records of similar types of books, a general knowledge of the success of the publisher's output with libraries, and a discussion of the type and extent of publicity and promotional money to be allocated to promoting individual titles. If the book receives the proper press and review coverage, the orders are bound to roll in from libraries. If the buyer guessed correctly, the wholesaler should be able to meet the initial requests and develop a base for reorder and regular stocking.

Books already stocked are reordered by other buyers. Reordering of backlist titles, sometimes standard ones, is done by many wholesalers on a basis of computer-scoring of the movement of materials by title over a given period of time. This is a fairly scientific method but is flawed in that it assumes that the publisher retains material in stock or reprints to the same rhythm that motivates the wholesaler's buyer to order. Stocking is a science that is not always scientific; it is subject to economic vagaries and affected by print orders, print schedules, paper prices, availability of printing time, inventory cycles, and the cash-flow situation, to name a few factors. It also assumes a knowledge of the marketable life of a book. In a tight cash market with high costs, the wholesaler who succeeds best with his customers is the one who guesses correctly most often and develops his buying and stocking cycles most effectively. In large corporate entities the freedom to make correct decisions on availability of materials is frequently affected negatively by suddenly increasing inventory without concurrent increases in the amount of business done.

After the books are ordered from the publisher, the process is relatively simple. The books are received, stocked on shelves after noting the receipt of the material, orders for titles in-house are matched immediately, the books are brought together with other books for the same customer, the material is checked, invoiced, boxed and shipped. The customer receives the material, reverses the process of checking against invoice, passes books to the next phase and the bill is passed for payment. Any problems not resolved by telephone or mail are referred to the saleman for the territory, who handles the complaint on a regular call. It is to the wholesaler's advantage to handle all orders with a minimum of personnel involvement to keep his costs down and the customer satisfied. The wholesaler also depends for his cash flexibility on regular payment of bills which can be held up by unnecessary errors.

It must be remembered that the wholesaler is in a business in which his profit comes from sharing the difference between the list price and his cost with the customer. Books range in cost to the wholesaler from net price to as much as 50 per cent. The economics of the business requires the wholesaler to save some profit for himself; therefore, he has different prices for books bought at different prices or requiring different ordering procedures. His prices vary with the quantities and also with the services the customer requests.

Each action taken adds a cost to the process; thus, the wholesaler often develops his operation in order to minimize his costs and increase his efficiency. Small wholesalers do this through personal service, cutting in-house personnel costs, and limiting their business to a select number of clients. Larger wholesalers achieve their efficiency by modernizing their activity, increasing the flow of business, providing additional services at a fee, concentrating more heavily on scientific marketing strategy, and/or dealing in more profitable aspects of the business.

What One Can Expect from a Book Wholesaler

A library doing business with a wholesaler has a right to expect his orders to be filled expeditiously, a major percentage of his requests to be filled on the first shipment, and the balance available within a 30- or 60-day period. Reports on the state of the order should be made at least once, and an agreement should be reached whereby at a set time it is possible to cancel and reorder, so that the order can remain current and the librarian and wholesaler can develop a better control on the outstanding state of the orders.

One should not expect 100 per cent fulfillment on all orders. The nature of the book trade makes that impossible. Even if the library anticipates its needs it is difficult to foretell when a book will be delayed in production, or when a publisher will decide not to publish, to reprint or to remainder the edition the library is seeking. [3]

The library may also expect other services since the wholesaler, in his attempt to provide a more complete service at a price that the library will pay, may make it possible for books to be provided in a shelf-ready state. Commercially produced cataloging kits, plastic jackets, completely cataloged collections sometimes known as "instant libraries," leased books, order by wire, order by magnetic tape, and on-line ordering using machine-readable language are all possible today. They are services worth considering when the problem of maintaining expensive technical services areas must be reconsidered.

With library personnel costs accounting for as much as 65-80 per cent of the overall library operating budget, a search for cost-effectiveness has found commercially provided services becoming more attractive. The use of machine-readable language, the development of standard coding systems such as ISBN, and the development of CIP and the entire concept of on-line interchange of information[4] has made it feasible to order on a more frequent basis, maintain a reasonable ordering cost, and to provide immediate access to uniform bibliographical information on a large scale. This latter development has also caused the demise of several of the most innovative and successful wholesalers in their prime, partly because of continually growing research and development costs and partly because of start-up before fully testing the new procedures. However, some wholesalers have benefitted and have added these additional services to their stock of traditional services.

Access to Wholesaler Services

The wholesaler has come a long way from its operation out of a warehouse lined with storage bins. Many wholesalers have modern plants to which they welcome visitors. They frequently employ professionals in all areas of operation so that the customer and the wholesaler can discuss problems on the same level. The modern wholesaler is willing to travel to investigate problems, to discuss the service on all levels, to handle a demonstration, and to act as a partner in dealing with administrations which must learn the needs rapidly and be approached on purely cost/benefit terms. The modern wholesaler is also ready to consider other solutions to library service problems on a profitability basis.

Many new libraries have been started on an "instant library" basis by some wholesalers who selected and stored material after processing to library specifications in anticipation of library construction completion. This service was solicited by the wholesalers aware of the need. Libraries had asked about the possibility and the dealer decided there was a way of handling the problem within the constraints of profitability.

Bid proposals have frequently been discussed in the literature with proponents and opponents being vociferous in their support and denial of value. In his landmark popular work on acquisitions, Melcher discusses the bid procedure and the problems, ranging from inability to fulfill to restrictions on service from the wholesaler by the resulting overall unprofitability of the contract.[5] Bids are frequently required by governments which are accustomed to buying in bulk. Books and other library materials have been considered bulk purchases and thus amenable to fixed-price bid purchase. The bid procedure is usually a restrictive measure and found too inflexible to purchase material of a dated nature. The purchasing agents are

strong for the procedure because it seems to effect control on expenditures.   The librarians are less sanguine; they know the problems of missing out on books and other materials which disappear
from the market or are not provided by the wholesaler because of
a later evaluation of the costliness of the process.

There are many governments which, under the blandishments
of librarians, have concluded that the purchase of the book is a
unique process and worthy of exemption under the bid resolutions.
Other governments find that the total figure for purchases requires
a bid contract.   Frequently, the bid contract is drawn with enough
exemptions to maintain flexibility for the library in its ordering
procedure.

The wholesaler likes contract work if it is profitable, and it
gives some guarantee of service to the library.   It is possible to
work with a dealer without a bid in a very profitable fashion.   If the
library is considering a contract, it is worthwhile to have some discussions beforehand with many wholesalers to see what the possibilities are before the contract is drawn.   Dealing with suppliers requires everything to be provided with a similar set of specifications
if competition is in the offing.   Some understanding of the effect of
restrictions should be discussed in economic terms.   Wholesalers
should be approached with the desire to solve a problem effectively
rather than to create one.   If a purchasing agent must be involved
he can be brought in on a pre-qualifying meeting so that he understands what is being discussed and can have input.   It is important
to remember that the wholesaler will cooperate because it is to his
advantage to have agreement on the terms of the bid throughout the
entire process.   The wholesaler frequently has an opportunity to
point out that bids are two-way streets and the effectiveness of the
contract is based on the willingness of both parties to abide by the
agreement.   In this case it usually means that the wholesaler can
take this opportunity to work out more simplified and assured payment procedures.   Libraries and purchasing departments should expect to find the wholesaler upset by billing practices which take additional discounts from bills which have been past due for as long
as six months or one year.   If the bid conference does nothing more
than set an effective payment agreement, the relationship between the
wholesaler and his customer has been advanced tremendously.

Approval Programs

One of the services that has had a recent history as a general
wholesale service is the approval plan.   The literature has many articles on the development of this means for libraries to receive on
approval (with permission to return) materials in subject areas in
which they collect broadly.   Originally started to meet the needs for
technical material not readily reviewed in the library literature, it
has grown to a more general service.   Many large wholesalers and
some small wholesalers have been involved in this type of business.
Refinements in the operation of this type of plan are still being made

and it is anticipated that it will continue to be a viable service, although the question of the size of library which can be served most effectively by this plan is still being discussed. [6]

Evaluation of Wholesalers

There are many checklists of steps to use in evaluating a wholesaler. They appear in a variety of acquisition texts but are not really current. It is possible to evaluate the wholesaler by asking him for a list of the publishers whose material he stocks and a list of those customers in the same area that are served by him, by sending through a variety of test orders compared with similar materials ordered at the same time from other suppliers, and finally by visiting his plant to see it in operation.

This writer, having been on both sides of the fence, can attest to the fact that no evaluation can assure service better than closely monitoring the receipt of materials and reporting back to the salesman, marketer or management type in the wholesaler's operation. This is a highly competitive business and each wholesaler tries to keep the customers that make his operation an effective one. Doing so means profitability and relates directly to the effectiveness of service and continuity of business over a long period of time. One does not establish himself with a wholesaler and move to another one immediately. The nature of the business is largely detail, which takes a long time to do correctly. It is based on agreement and interpretation of the meaning of that agreement. Change is costly, which is why it is essential to get everything correct as soon as possible. It is also the reason for trying to lock in the library with its supplier. Change is not impossible, and it is the library that must determine the need for such change. The wholesalers are aware of this, which is the reason for the addition of more professionally trained personnel to their staffs.

If one is looking for professional services beyong the service of materials, it is important to find the wholesaler with staff able to handle the requirements of the library in all its detail. The problem of communication and its resolution is so important that wholesalers are joining with librarians and publishers to make the business of distributing materials more effective. [7] To make the communications possible, marketing specialists from the library field are being brought in, conferences with specialists from the wholesaler's staff and the library staff are held by the wholesaler, presentation exhibits sponsored by the wholesaler are made available to bring new titles to the attention of librarians, and sales presentations involve specialists as well as the salesperson in the territory.

Evaluation of capacity to serve the library field today must be made as much from current input of the wholesaler as from the wholesaler's past history of service to the library. Library needs are different from those in the past, the types of services are expanded, and the basis for evaluation must be changed to consider the satisfaction of the new needs by the new services. Practical considerations of willingness to meet specification requirements and concern with the librarian's problem when presented help to guarantee a proper evaluation quotient of the wholesaler's services.

The Future of the Wholesaler

The future of the wholesaler is integrated with the future of the library. Management analyses are being made more frequently where personnel costs are overriding the capacity of the library to purchase new and replacement books and other library materials. Libraries are investigating the possibilities of buying many professional services as part of their book supply contract. The libraries are becoming more dependent on the wholesaler and the supplier who lists many services other than the traditional one of book supply.

The president of one large supplier of wholesale services to libraries credits the continuing growth of title output--and the increasing number of small publishers unable to support marketing organizations--with the development of the large single supplier. He sees the wholesaler becoming a service organization with two roles: (1) to gather, select and make available those books and materials which are in demand, and (2) to create and deliver services which librarians deem necessary. Libraries' needs should be met in the most efficient and economical way, using professional talent in specialty areas--bibliographic, selection, purchasing, sales, warehousing, manufacturing, fulfillment, and systems.[8]

There is a recognition of the need to overcome unnecessary redundancy. The growing support for the Ohio College Library Center (OCLC) as an intermediate step in the progressive battle to overcome redundant handling of the same information is significant for the wholesaler. This may well become the domain of a private agency, possibly the wholesale service agency, which has a vested interest in one-line access to the large-scale-ordering data base. The possibility of making a profit using this technique is a natural for the wholesaler, who can spread the costs of development and continuation over a broader service base than can OCLC.

There is a great need for technical services functions in libraries. There is a vision of the reduction of the number of processes which need to be performed in the library itself. Several wholesalers will be needed in order to perform this function competitively and at a reasonable price in the great general area of supply. A need for specialist wholesalers will persist because the nature of the library market is such that a general wholesaler cannot operate the specialty portion of the business in conjunction with his regular operation. There are variations in the handling of the requirements of the academic library, the public library, and the school library. Each function requires a different set of specialists in the plant and administration to meet those needs. Import requirements for foreign materials are going to be investigated further, with many domestic wholesalers attempting to bring this activity into the mainstream of their operation. The specialist in this area has the edge and, because of the loyalty of libraries to their efficient suppliers, it is believed that future change in this area will be slow and will be dependent again on the continued effective development of the on-line bibliographic data base from which to select.

Many wholesalers are trying to develop and handle proprietary products as part of their total regular services to libraries. This has not been very satisfactory because of the problems of monopolistic practice inherent in this procedure. The development of special products will continue but will probably operate more effectively under wholly owned subsidiaries rather than in the mainstream of wholesale practice.

More professionals will be employed by wholesalers to serve the library business. The wholesaler will continue to concentrate on the service aspect of the business and will develop effective ways of stocking to meet the library needs as they are expressed. The publications supported by wholesalers will attempt to anticipate the availability of materials, and concentrated efforts to develop approval-ordering plans that are efficient and geared to the availability of bibliographic information will continue and possibly tie in with library system development and group ordering.

The nature of library operations will continue to change and their relationship with the wholesaler will continue to develop. Materials which have not lent themselves to handling by wholesalers will be added to wholesale lines, probably starting in separate divisions and gradually phased into the entire ordering process. Films, microfilms, slides, other audiovisual material, periodicals, and serials will be reconsidered as part of the wholesaler's service practice.

The rationale is based on the fact that reduction of technical services and acquisition staff in favor of public service staff will require more efficient methods of ordering materials to extend the service coverage required by more public service requests. There will always be some people buying from individual publishers and some publishers may have large enough lines to continue to warrant individual sales and convention coverage. Special collections and rare book collections will require specialized bibliographic service not compatible with the large-scale service of the general wholesaler. Many sets of reference materials will also be sold on a direct basis.

In a market that presently includes at least 60,000 customers in the institutional area, investigation of the possibilities available for service sales shows that the wholesaler has a great potential ahead. With continuing education to be recognized once again as the province of libraries, the potential for continued library support and growth is assured. Now that the wholesaler has proven his willingness to listen to the librarian's needs, there will be more requests to investigate additional services to libraries.

References

1. Literary Market Place with Names & Numbers, 1975-1976. New
     York: R. R. Bowker, 1975, p. 368.
2. Ford, Stephen. The Acquisition of Library Materials. Chicago:
     ALA, 1973, pp. 58-60.
3. Melcher, Daniel, and Saul, Margaret. Melcher on Acquisitions.
     Chicago: ALA, 1971.
4. Baker, DeWitt C. Personal communication.
5. Melcher and Saul, op. cit., p. 63-69.
6. Spyers-Duran, Peter, and Gore, Daniel, eds. Economics of
     Approval Plans. Westport, Conn.: Greenwood Press, 1972.
7. Geiser, Elizabeth A., et al. "Book Marketing and Selection: A
     Publishing/Library Forum," Library Resources & Technical
     Services 20:65-69, Winter 1976.
8. Baker, op. cit., p. 2.

Additional References

Boyer, Calvin J. "State-wide Contracts for Library Materials: An
    Analysis of the Attendant Dysfunctional Consequences," Col-
    lege & Research Libraries 35:86-94, March 1974.
Fischer, Mary, comp. Los Angeles Public Library: Description of
    the Automated Library Technical Services (ALTS) Program.
    Los Angeles: Los Angeles Public Library, 1973.
Kim, Ung Chon. "Purchasing Books from Publishers and Whole-
    salers," Library Resources & Technical Services 19:133-47,
    Spring 1975.
McCullough, Kathleen. "Approval Plans; Vendor Responsibility and
    Library Research; A Literature Survey and Discussion," Col-
    lege & Research Libraries 33:368-81, Sept. 1972.
Richard Abel and Company, Inc. A proposal for the opening day
    collection of Nassau County Reference Library, Portland,
    Ore. April 5, 1974.

PAPERBACK PRACTICALITIES

By Marilyn Abel

This year marks the tenth anniversary of Daniel N. Fader's famous study, Hooked on Books (Berkley Books). It seems a good time to reflect on the importance to current educational and leisure reading of paperback books for young readers. In the past ten years, students and librarians, and teachers and publishers alike have come to recognize the vital role paperbacks play in the lives of young people. Confusion, however, still exists about paperbacks-- their publishing and distribution. There seem to be so many of them, coming from all directions and information is needed about how to find out about them, where to get them, why they seem different from regular books. Perhaps this article will answer many of the questions about paperbacks that I've heard during the years I've worked with paperbacks and young adult librarians.

The type of paperback which most frequently draws questions is the mass market paperback--the rack-sized (4 3/16"x7"), shiny covered book seen everywhere--in airports, drugstores, bookstores, and, in increasing numbers, in libraries, too. The history of this kind of paperback is interesting. Pocket Books was the first mass market publisher, followed in postwar years by Bantam. New American Library (NAL), Dell, and others. Mass market publishers are, by and large, reprint publishers. They buy the rights to reproduce a hardcover book in paperback form for a specific period of time. At the end of the term of the license, the rights are renegotiated or they revert to the original hardcover publisher. Today's mass market publishers also publish original books, sometimes placing the hardcover edition with a trade publisher before issuing their own paperbound edition.

Distribution

The secret, the very basis of success for Pocket Books and other mass market publishers was that, during World War II and in postwar America, they linked into magazine distribution. Thus paperback books, in those early days and even now, were published and distributed in much the same way as magazines. In fact, in my mind paperbacks still fall right between books and magazines. Instead of a seasonal publication schedule (as with hardcover juvenile trade publishers), mass market paperback houses publish a monthly

schedule of titles in specific subject categories. There will be a
book for the science fiction, romance, gothic, western, young adult,
self-help, reference categories--whatever. In addition, these schedules include fiction and nonfiction new releases--often called super
releases, blockbusters, or sub-leaders--each and every month.
Consider the monthly western paperback category to be rather like
a magazine's regular feature on western fiction and you will understand why mass market paperbacks fall somewhere between magazines
and regular books. "Leader titles" are generally those which will
receive the most advertising and promotion, perhaps even radio and
TV spots. They are often hardcover bestsellers or books for which
paperback houses have paid high advances expecting them to become
even bigger paperback sellers.

Mass market paperback publishing isn't called "mass market"
for nothing. The factors of high-speed presses, large print orders,
and shot-gun distribution have led to its success. There is high
turnover--last month's new releases must yield space to this month's
new releases. Returns must be cleared away--just as the dated issue of each magazine must yield to the next month's issue.

In mass market paperback publishing the cover of a book is
all-important. It becomes a mini-poster for the book and since paperback purchases are often impulse purchases, the poster-cover at-
tracts readers, ignites their interest, and asks them to read! The
psychology of paperback covers is one of the most fascinating aspects
of the business. Certain kinds of art instantly "categorize" the book
as one of a kind or type: a man's book, a woman's, a young adult's,
a gothic, a western. I think paperback cover art is so exciting and
attractive that libraries should display it and use it as much as bookstores do--to create excitement, color, and ultimately attract readers.

The magazine (and occasionally newspaper) distributors who
handle mass market paperback books are part of a nationwide network
of wholesalers usually servicing a specific geographic area. Called
independent distributors or "ID's," they are sometimes equipped to
service libraries with both new and backlist paperbacks. Where ID's
are seriously committed to the paperback business, they maintain
showrooms of children's and young adult titles and sufficient stock to
fill school and library orders as they come. They have staff to help
in purchasing, and, besides their own catalogs, a selection of publisher catalogs and promotion materials. They also provide quick
local service.

Jobbers

Historically, because ID's were not able to service the wide
ranging needs of schools and libraries in some areas, special paperback book jobbers developed. These firms are not involved in magazine distribution and concentrate solely on books. Sometimes they
specialize in book fairs, library business, in store rack service,

chain stores, bookstores, or in sales to the college market. Sometimes they choose to handle many facets of the business. They too
maintain showrooms, distribute publisher catalogs and catalogs of
their own inventory, and have knowledgeable staff to help the librarians through the thickets of the paperback ordering.

In addition to these channels of distribution, libraries may
purchase paperbacks directly from those publishers who are equipped
to handle their orders.

Customer Services

Whatever your source of supply for mass market paperbacks,
there are services you should expect and indeed demand. A personal contact with someone at a distributor or publisher is a must.
Just because their books are mass market paperbacks does not mean
that you cannot expect to get personal service. You need someone
you can call for special projects, sound information, new ideas, to
rush orders or make adjustments. If your distributor is nearby,
you should be a welcome visitor, allowed to roam through the stock-
room at will.

Since paperbacks are a trendy business and these books are
published so frequently, your distributor must keep you informed,
personally or by flyer notices. Working with your distributor, you
ought to be able to set up a monthly "prepack" of new children's and
young adult titles, school titles and leisure reading titles, so that
you can examine single copies of everything that is available and
pick and choose for your library's needs. Returns should be acceptable.

The educational staff of the distributor should alert you to
new books or ship them automatically--you should make the final
decision. If, after working with a distributor, you cannot reconcile
your needs for both information and books with the distributor's capabilities, by all means change your distributor. No matter where
your library is or how small the account, there are distributors who
can and will tailor their services to your specific needs.

Why Paperbacks?

The appeal and advantages of paperback books should be obvious. They are timely: in areas of current interest and news,
there will be a paperback book available long before a hardcover
title on the subject is published. Watergate books hit the stands a
mere ten days after the scandal broke. Avant-garde editorial staffs
in paperback houses and the high-speed presses permit nearly instant print response to a trend--a movie or television show, a national crisis or problem. Consider how the novel Jaws and several
other related paperbacks coincided last summer with the showing of
the movie itself--the talk of teenage and adult America!

To children and teenage readers, paperbacks are hip. They have a grown-up, pack-it-in-your-pocket, smart appeal which encourages reading and talking about books. Paperbacks are exciting-- even the traditional classics of literature are more interesting to young people when they are bound in sharp paperback covers.

The range of titles in print and available today is truly amazing. Paperbacks also come in boxed sets--mini-libraries of titles by a particular author or in a specific subject area. Check the latest edition of Paperback Books in Print (Bowker) to see just what treasures are available!

These books are a blessing to budget-weary librarians. Mercifully, paperback prices still represent the biggest bargain in books today. The bindings and glue are stronger than ever. Not infrequently, librarians report 15-25 readings per paperback. A low-price, high-circulation paperback book is a librarian's dream. For less money than you'd think, you can add depth and breadth, excitement and jazz and, above all, readers to your library.

Uses

Because of their flexibility, the wide range of titles, exciting covers and their high appeal, paperbacks offer possibilities for all kinds of creative uses. A school librarian can form sets of circulating classroom libraries, responding to a teacher's particular study unit or to students' general reading interests. The collection can circulate from classroom to classroom during the school year. Spinner racks, placed right at the library doors, can entice young readers to new and high interest paperbacks.

Public librarians can use paperbacks in connection with summer film screenings; in local day camps and child care centers--all to extend the role of the public library, as it should, into the lives of young adults.

Trends

Slowly but surely there are signs that mass paperbacks themselves are being assimilated totally into the traditional world of books. For those mass market publishers who traditionally did not conform to the International Standard Book Number (ISBN) numbering system, there are signs of change. Some mass market publishers now use ISBN codes; others are at least discussing it.

The New York Times Book Review and Publishers Weekly now feature a paperback bestseller list; both general magazines and Library Journal and School Library Journal now review more paperbacks than ever before. American Libraries notes in advance which publisher has purchased what bestseller hardcover rights and ALA's Booklist reviews paperback books now too. Several traditionally hardcover library jobbers are also carrying paperbacks now and plan to increase their services with these books.

You should know that mass market paperback publishers maintain education departments to serve the school and library market. You should know that many of the services of these departments are available to you, either via your distributor or from the paperback publisher itself. Graded and annotated elementary and high school catalogs are produced annually by most mass market paperback publishers. Many of these publishers produce teacher guides for specific titles or groups of titles which will be useful to the teachers in your school or to those who frequent your library.

Subject area brochures, dealing with the subjects of current educational interest, ads in library and educational media, and displays at state and local educational and library exhibits all serve to highlight important titles and new ways to introduce young readers to them. Sometimes posters and buttons are available and contests and author appearances can be arranged to add excitement to any library's program.

Most paperback publishers supply materials to their distributors, who in turn will gladly pass it on to interested customers. The educational managers of each publishing house are listed in the current edition of Literary Market Place (Bowker), and, in addition, a request for information on paperbacks for children and young adults, sent to the Educational Paperback Marketing Committee of the Association of American Publishers (AAP) 1 Park Ave., New York, N.Y. 10016, will be forwarded to the education department of member houses: Ace, Avon, Ballantine, Bantam, Berkley, Dell, Fawcett, New American Library, Penguin/Viking, Pocket Books, Popular Library, Pyramid, Scholastic, and Warner Paperback Library.

Rewards

As a publisher, it is rewarding and exciting to work with children's and young adult librarians who have themselves discovered the satisfying and fruitful use of mass market paperbacks in their libraries. Librarians and books go together like love and marriage, and the mass market paperback is a natural extension of this rapport. May all librarians who work daily in the rewarding effort of creating a new generation of informed citizens and of people who read for the love of it, find their pleasures enhanced by entering the wonderful world of paperbacks!

THE AUDIOVISUAL SUPPLIER:
Dealing with Dealers and Distributors (Excerpts)

By Edward J. Hingers

The audiovisual supplier--the dealer or distributor of audiovisual goods and services--comes in many shapes and sizes. Fortunately for us all, the majority of suppliers do not fall into the
"greedy dog" category. For the audiovisual librarian, faced with
new and ever-changing technologies and public demands, the establishment and maintenance of good relationships with suppliers is of
prime importance.

When a reliable dealer is found, he is to be cherished. His
role should continue before, during, and after the sale. Sound advice and guidance are needed before a transaction to help make a
wise choice which may not necessarily be the cheapest in the short
run. During the sale, especially if it is a large one requiring many
separate components (such as a video installation), the dealer may
suggest substitutes and other changes within the alloted budget. It
is after the sale, however, that may be the most critical time. Especially when dealing with expensive equipment (and to a lesser extent software items), the service follow-up is the most important
aspect of all.

Hardware Distributors

Any piece of mechanical/electronic hardware will need tender
loving care sooner or (preferably) later. This is one of the main
reasons for not automatically accepting the lowest bid. One reason
that a company may be able to offer the lowest price is precisely
because it has no intention or capability of offering vital services to
its customers after delivery.

After a few mistakes have been made and a certain period of
time has passed, anyone can separate the honest and reliable dealers
in his vicinity from the "greedy dogs." The first time around, however, is the most difficult. How does one find the reliable dealers?
Aside from the obvious method of looking in the local Yellow Pages,
one can talk to other audiovisual users in the community. This
might be another library, another school, or even an advanced hobby-
ist.

It is difficult, and frequently impossible, to obtain reliable,

Reprinted from Library Trends, vol. 24, no. 4, April 1976, pp.
737-743, 745, 748, by permission of the publisher and author.

objective reports about hardware items. Library Technology Report[1] can be of some help, but it does not cover every item. Although it does not evaluate equipment, an annual publication, The Audio-Visual Equipment Directory,[2] is a good place to start when looking for just about any item of hardware. This directory should be on every standing-order list. The sheer variety of items offered is bewildering and, unless one has special training and knowledge, the technical specifications can be virtually unintelligible. This is yet another situation where a knowledgeable dealer is an invaluable reference tool. He is usually prepared and eager to aid in the selection of equipment that is within the budget and will satisfy (and continue to satisfy) a library's needs.

Beyond the dealer who will actually sell to you is the manufacturer. Despite the wealth of information found in the Audio-Visual Equipment Directory and available from whatever dealer or dealers one has chosen, the manufacturer can often supply additional information to help make an intelligent choice.

For an expensive investment such as videotape equipment, the manufacturer or importer will frequently be willing to send a representative to discuss your needs and problems without obligation. This ploy, of course, would be most valuable after deciding upon a particular brand. The manufacturer will have advance knowledge of any imminent model changes, and can provide more detailed information about his product than any individual dealer is likely to have. While the manufacturer's representative will not really feel free to recommend a particular dealer, he will, if pressed, offer information about his largest clients. This information might be important if you are concerned with minimum delivery time.

The terms of a warranty or guarantee must be complied with in order to meet the manufacturer's conditions for keeping it in force. For example, if any modification of equipment is done, it may void the manufacturer's warranty. Both the manufacturer and the dealer can give advice about this.

Trade shows are regularly held in many major cities. The local Educational Communications Council or the equivalent (often associated with schools) may have exhibitions at these shows which are valuable to attend. On the national level, Business Screen is a good publication in which announcements will be listed; Variety and Billboard are other informative publications.[3] Once again, the dealer would be a likely source of information, even if he is not exhibiting. Surely, some of the manufacturers he represents will be there. Even if one has no immediate intention of buying it is good to know what is new. Such exhibitions are also a good opportunity to get on desired mailing lists.

An informed dealer can often steer his customers into new paths of thought. The most expensive solution to any given problem is not necessarily the best. If there is the possibility of acquiring videotape capability for a particular project, a good dealer might suggest the less expensive alternative: audiotape. If what is to be shown is truly visual (such as a dance demonstration), video-tape is a logical choice. If, however, material to be prepared for the archives is chiefly speech (perhaps a book-talk), audiotape would be the proper choice.

As examples of the types of questions to ask a dealer, con-sider the following:

1. When is audiotape better than videotape?
2. When is forward-projection of slides better than small-screen rear-projection?
3. When is open-reel format to be preferred to the audio-cas-sette?
4. Should one produce a filmstrip or a set of slides?

A good dealer should be able to outline the advantages and disadvantages of almost any situation based on his experience.

Concerning relative cost of equipment, there are two basic philosophies to consider. One philosophy opts for the most elabo-rate and expensive hardware it is possible to obtain with any given budget. The theory behind this is that good equipment will last much longer and is cheaper in the long run. The opposite philosophy con-tends that the cheapest equipment should be bought and disposed of or replaced whenever necessary.

Once again, the dealer's advice should be sought. Unless the model in question has recently come on the market, he will know, in general terms and for average use, how long it will pro-bably last. The dealer should play a role with respect to his clients that is more than that of an order-taker. Taking time to give the salesman a tour of the facilities and to explain in detail what is be-ing accomplished puts the dealer in a much better position to serve his customer. Conditions and needs can vary so widely that only a custom-tailored answer will do.

There is truly no "best" 16mm projector or other piece of equipment. The "best" is whatever is best for a unique set of cir-cumstances. What might be a perfectly suitable piece of equipment for permanent installation might not be at all suitable if it has to be transported to a variety of locations. When buying a piece of fairly delicate electronic equipment such as a television set, the dealer might not be able to make the best suggestion if he assumes that the set will be installed in a corner and never moved. If the customer does not explain that the television is to be moved around, the dealer will probably not suggest buying a sturdy, wheeled case lined with foam rubber to transport it. It should be remembered, however, that even the best dealer sometimes does not think to sug-gest an item he does not regularly stock.

Essentially, we have been talking about the wholesale rather than the retail dealer. In the context of audiovisual hardware, the wholesaler is one who is in business primarily to serve the industrial and educational markets. Most of his stock-in-trade will be illustrated in a catalog. Not every item will always be in stock and ready for immediate delivery. Usually the catalog will contain the list price as recommended by the manufacturer. The specifications and copy will probably come directly from the manufacturer and be printed up with no changes. (This accounts for the similarity of most company catalogs.) The market price is seldom the selling price, however. To begin negotiations, it is good to ask if there is a state contract price--if indeed the state in question negotiates such prices. Dealers will seldom volunteer this information, but invariably will answer directly if asked.

Some items, such as still cameras, lights, and turntables, might be purchased from a local retail dealer. Long before there is any need for such a person, it is wise to foster at least a nodding acquaintance with local retail dealers. If it is a camera shop, for example, requests for projector rental, etc., can be referred to him. If you publish a catalog of films available to the public, it might benefit circulation to leave a complimentary copy with the local retail dealer. When the time comes to buy smaller items, he will probably give you a substantial discount.

Software Distributors

Software comes in a variety of guises, each with its own merits and potential uses. The most familiar to librarians and teachers remains the 16mm film; other formats are rapidly gaining ground, however, particularly videotape in the one-half inch and three-quarter inch formats. An important trend just over the horizon is the videodisc. If, as reported, the discs will sell in the general price range of phonodiscs, the implications for libraries, schools and home users will be tremendous. Among the envisioned products is a player priced in the $400 range, in price competition with a moderately priced stereo system.

It should be noted in regard to 16mm film that, in addition to the usual pattern of outright purchase, the possibilities of leasing and short-term rental also exist as a growing trend. While a familiar favorite such as The Red Balloon is available by lease exclusively, the opportunity does exist to negotiate with distributors about many titles, particularly feature films. Films Inc. has long had a number of excellent titles for lease, including the classic film that belongs in every collection: Citizen Kane. Very recently, United Artists has also entered the leasing picture. Many other distributors have a list of titles available for leasing.

Because the situation is constantly changing, one could profit from asking about the availability of any film one might want. More companies are considering leasing films as time, the economy, and competition bring new pressures to the distribution business.

There are many times when commitment to a five-year or life-of-print lease is not desirable. The long-term leasing of features is most conveniently handled on a library-system level as a part of its regular service. However, an often-overlooked possibility is joining with several other local libraries or schools on a cost-sharing basis. The object is to bring an expensive feature film or series of films to a number of local institutions. Such cooperative effort can result in considerable dollar savings.

Most of the major distributors are willing to offer much help in planning a program. If, for example, a film normally rents for $100 per showing, many libraries would find it impossible to fit into their limited budget. However, if four libraries decide to band together and schedule the film during a two-week period, the distributor might offer the film for that period for $150. For $37.50, therefore, each library would be able to show the title that would normally cost it $100. This is the type of deal that can be worked out through individual negotiation. If a distributor's business relies on mail-order (and most frequently it does), a turn-around of two circulations a month is about average. Using the example given above, the distributor comes out ahead (he has received $150 instead of $100 for a film during a two-week period) and each of the renting institutions comes out ahead by $62.50.

While each case, each title, and each distributor will add a new factor to the equation, a rule of thumb based on several years' experimentation with precisely this type of program emerges. For any given film, double the lowest basic rental fee and multiply that figure by the number of months you intend to lease a title. The final sum should be a rough figure around which you can work with the distributor. If there is daily truck delivery, or if the libraries are willing to carry the print from library to library themselves, the number of libraries which can be served is much greater than the number of circulations the distributor can expect to handle with a mail-order business.

Once a rough figure has been determined and negotiations for the actual price have begun, the distributor may offer a much lower price than anticipated. This is particularly true with certain older films that may not have become major "cult" titles. Sometimes, however, a price larger than the estimate has to be paid for some of the great foreign classics or popular recent titles.

Sometimes the distributor will not be able to release a particular title for an extended period. He may have an insufficient number of prints to handle both special orders and his regular trade, or his distributor (the legal owner of the copyright) may not be willing to allow the sort of deal we are considering.

Occasionally, it will be necessary to negotiate on the basis of the number of showings rather than of the time period the film will be in your possession. In this case, the distributor might want the full regular fee for the first showing and a percentage of the full fee for each subsequent screening. In almost every case, however, the price turns out to be a bargain.

A word of advice: much time can be lost by indecisive planning. If, for example, five libraries decide to work out a shared-cost program of feature films, considerable discussion will inevitably arise about which titles are to be chosen. The distributors must then be contacted to check on prices and the shared-cost arithmetic done. If there are too many conferences, disagreements, disappointments, etc., the planning could drag out forever and cost more in staff time than the savings such cooperation could bring. What is needed is a group of program planners who have the authority to say "yes" or "no" immediately without needing to check back with a director about budgets, meeting room availability that week, and so forth.

Each person involved with the planning should be prepared to suggest titles, accept reasonable compromises based on availability from the distributor and the needs of his colleagues, judge when the programs can be realistically scheduled and make switches when the need arises, and commit money up to some previously set limit.

Once a good relationship has been established with a distributor, it is often possible to get quotes by telephone. Of course, the distributor might prefer to think about it for a longer time--if you have the time. However, as more and more library systems and individual libraries are making these arrangements, distributors are quickening the pace because they are getting accustomed to dealing with such needs. Especially in times of tight money, such deals are important both to the libraries and to the distributors.

On the subject of buying films outright, the story is a shorter one. Purchase is usually a matter of critical previewing and, if the decision is made to buy, of looking up the current price in the distributor's catalog. However, it does pay to reserve some funds for special sales or closeouts.

There are a few "rules" to consider and apply to the situation in question:

1. Be sure that you get on a lot of mailing lists and that your files are kept up to date.
2. Whenever a salesman calls (in person or on the telephone) ask for the latest catalog or list of his recent releases.
3. Since no one can possibly preview all the films released in any given year, ask the salesman which films have been good sellers to other libraries. This is a valuable checkpoint and not a substitute for regular previewing; the bandwagon approach is not always valid.

Occasionally, a used 16mm print can be picked up inexpensively. If the savings are considerable, the risk may be worthwhile, but it is better to determine beforehand whether there are return privileges.

Unfortunately, there is a negative side to film distributorship: the filmlegger. This is very dangerous territory, and it is best to avoid it totally. If someone can offer a brand-new print of a title at one-half price, he probably has some connection at a film lab. A legitimate distributor has sent in his negative to have some new prints made up, but a few extra were run off illegitimately. The temptation may be great, but such films are actually stolen goods.

The cost of films is constantly rising. Producers and distributors are faced with rising production costs and skyrocketing lab prices. For every print a filmlegger sells (and for every videotape illegally copied), the distributor is losing a sale. This, too, must be reflected in a general rise in price.

Fortunately, there is something buyers can do to help stop this trend. Distributors are usually willing to take legal action when they hear about violations from legitimate sources.

A major problem with distributors is the scheduling of prints for preview. Prints are increasingly expensive to have made up and to schedule. The ideal customer for the distributor is the one who schedules a preview date for a specific title and manages to return it on or before the due date. It is inexcusable for an organization to keep a print for any extended period, yet this practice is all too common. Indeed, why would anyone hold for six months a print he simply wanted to preview? The thoughtless handling of prints by the potential customer is yet another reason why the price of prints continues to go up.

One possible way of cutting costs, offered by an increasing number of distributors, is to bypass the preview print altogether. If you are dealing with an established classic, the distributor can afford to cut the price if preview is not requested. Sometimes it is also possible to request a new print which you can preview and then keep if you decide to purchase the title. In this case, too, the price can sometimes be discounted. While distributors do not always publicize these facts, it is a trend. Thus it is a good idea to ask when in doubt or when seeking a bargain, because both parties can benefit.

References

1. Library Technology Reports, offered on a yearly subscription basis from American Library Association, 50 E. Huron St., Chicago, Ill. 60611.
2. The Audio-Visual Equipment Directory, an annual publication of the National Audio-Visual Association, Inc., 3150 Spring St., Fairfax, Va. 22030.
3. Business Screen, published bimonthly by Harcourt Brace Jovanovich, 757 Third Ave., New York, N.Y. 10017; Variety, published weekly at 154 W. 46th St., New York, N.Y. 10036; and Billboard, published weekly by Billboard Publications, Inc., 9000 Sunset Blvd., Los Angeles, Calif. 90069.

THE U.S. GOVERNMENT PRINTING OFFICE TODAY
(Excerpts)

By Wellington H. Lewis

The U.S. Government Printing Office serves as the primary
producer and supplier of the vast array of documents which result
from the activities and research conducted by the Federal Government. Fulfillment of many of the printing and distribution requirements of the Executive departments and agencies is a principal task,
but service to the Congress has always been the GPO's foremost
responsibility. The GPO today faces many new challenges in view
of the increasing demand for information and the importance of
Government programs in our everyday lives.

Printing in the United States Government is a unique support
service--unique because the printing itself, and the equipment used,
are controlled by a special public law. Since 1777, when the Second
Continental Congress was evacuated from Philadelphia, there has
been the need for laws and regulations to bring order to the many
things printed by and for the Government. The GPO was established
in 1861. The Act of January 12, 1895 consolidated the laws relating
to public printing into Title 44, U.S. Code, "Public Printing and
Documents." Also, a permanent Congressional Joint Committee on
Printing (JCP) was established and the position of Public Printer of
the United States was created as head of the GPO.

The Joint Committee on Printing, in effect, is the Board of
Directors for the GPO. The Committee consists of the Chairman
and two members of the Committee on Rules and Administration of
the Senate and the Chairman and two members of the Committee on
House Administration of the House of Representatives. Under Title
44 of the U.S. Code, the Joint Committee on Printing may, "use any
measures it considers necessary to remedy neglect, delay, duplication, or waste in the public printing and binding and the distribution
of Government Publications." (44 U.S.C. 103)

Besides the actual printing responsibilities, in 1972, the Joint
Committee on Printing placed micropublishing activities within its
realm when it ruled that microforms are publications and, as such,
must be produced in accordance with Title 44.

To provide the services required of the GPO, an immense

This material was originally published in "The U.S. Government
Printing Office Today," by Wellington H. Lewis, in Drexel Library
Quarterly, vol. 10 (Nos. 1 & 2, January-April 1974), pp. 8-14,
16-19. Reprinted by permission.

physical plant, as well as a continuing program of technological advancement in the art and science of printing is necessary. Located four blocks from the Capitol, the GPO has four buildings ranging in age from 35 to 70 years. The three main buildings have eight floors.

Operating under frequently crushing Congressional schedules, hot metal type-setting techniques are still in use. Perhaps the basic reason for retaining hot metal in the GPO can be traced to the perpetuation of conventional copy-preparation methods in the Congress. But some cracks are appearing in the monolithic facade. Under the aegis of Congressman Wayne L. Hays and his Committee on House Administration, GPO is now setting House Committee business calendars from magnetic tape generated on the House computers. This material is being produced on two Linotron 1010's, which are among the most advanced high-speed photocomposers in the industry. The tapes are produced as byproducts of the Committee's information retrieval system. The hard core of Congressional copy generation, however, is still via stenotype, typewriter, and keyboard.

In addition to the many documents and publications issued by Government agencies, most of the necessary forms, manuals, and miscellaneous publications used by the Federal Government in the conduct of its business are also produced through the GPO.

Although the Central Office plant in Washington is one of the largest printing plants in the world, the GPO has very little specialty equipment which would put it in competition with private industry. There are no process color cameras or related types of equipment, and the Office has only five two-color offset presses. The GPO does not have the equipment to produce such specialty items as snapouts, tab paper, tab cards, decals, and other products requiring specialty equipment. The Office is basically a single-color book and job shop, geared for producing the printing requirements of Congress.

One of the most important tasks is the printing of the proceedings and debates of the U.S. Congress, better known as the Congressional Record. Fifty thousand copies of this publication are produced each day the Senate and the House of Representatives are in session. Its size can vary from 16 pages to over 300 pages. Its bulk depends, of course, on the amount of business conducted by our legislators on a particular day--and on how much material is inserted with their remarks. The average Record is about the size of a 38-page daily newspaper. Copy starts coming into the Office about 6:30 p.m. and the last copy arrives somewhere around midnight, despite a 9:00 p.m. deadline. Regardless of whether the Record is 16 or 300 pages, it must be set in type, printed and delivered to the Congressional Post Office at the Capitol before 6:30 a.m. the next morning.

The Public Printer is also charged with making Government publications available to the public. To accomplish both its printing

and distribution functions, the GPO has 8,500 employees. Most are
in the main GPO complex, but the Office also has field printing
plants, printing procurement offices, bookstores, and two document
distribution centers. In the main plant there are 141 presses and
379 typesetting machines spread over 32 acres of floor space.

Publishing and Printing Functions

The GPO does more than $300 million worth of printing
business each year. Approximately 60 per cent of this is procured
from commercial firms. Over 1,100 orders for printing are received per day, 22 carloads of paper are used each day, and well
over one million publications are printed a year.

As the Federal Government grew more complex, it reached
out to the states to serve the people better through field installations.
A 1967-68 study of Government printing, under the direction of the
JCP, indicated a need for decentralization of printing services, as
well as a need for more extensive use of the commercial printing
industry. Therefore, the JCP directed a new policy requiring printing to be done near the point of origin or where the product is to be
distributed, with stress being placed on procuring these requirements
from the commercial industry. Fourteen regional printing procurement offices are now operated by the GPO and the majority of agency
printing is procured from the private sector through these field offices and the Central Office. GPO procurement of almost every type
of printing imaginable is based on the competitive bid system, and
follows closely the Federal Procurement Regulations under which all
Government agencies operate.

The GPO has always supported and encouraged innovations in
the printing industry. Progress in printing production and computerized typesetting can do a great deal to improve the flow of Government information. There has been a trend over many years away
from the letterpress process of printing directly from type and plates
toward the lithographic process of printing from offset plates. Offset plate materials have vastly improved over the years with the capability of longer press runs which help reduce costs. Automatic
processing equipment has become available to process these plates
with reduced labor costs. Even in the letterpress field, new materials are being used to make plates today by the photographic process, which may help rejuvenate the letterpress process. There is
a tendency to convert more and more work from sheet-fed presses
to web-fed presses with automatic folders that run at more than five
times the speed of the sheet-fed presses. The bookbinding operations are improving with the availability of higher-speed equipment
and the concept of in-line production to decrease the amount of manual handling between various steps in production. Improved adhe-
sives have become available which have made possible the manufac-
ture of a serviceable bound book at lower cost.

Probably the most dramatic development in the printing industry is the use of computers and automated typesetting machines in the composing room. The fantastic growth in the number of computers in the Federal Government--from 531 in 1960 to more than 4,000 in 1970--has forced a change in the technology of reproducing printed copies of data generated and stored by computers. The GPO is a leader in this new technology of computerized composition.

In 1962, at the direction of the JCP, the GPO began a program to reduce the cost and improve the quality of printed material emanating from Government computers. A Federal Electronic Printing Committee, now significantly retitled the Federal Electronic Printing and Micropublishing Committee, was formed to provide technical guidance to the JCP on matters pertaining to electronic composition. A study undertaken by the GPO in 1962 proved the feasibility of using computers in typesetting to drive automated phototypesetting equipment, and culminated in the award of a contract to the Mergenthaler Linotype Company/CBS Laboratories, to develop and deliver the first high-speed cathode ray tube phototypesetting machines. The contract was signed in March 1964, and the first of two systems was placed in operation in October 1967, and has been in daily production since that time. A second system has been in operation since January 1969. These machines accept magnetic tapes from an agency computer and convert the data on the tape to images on a cathode ray television tube. A photosensitive film records the light images on the face of the tube, and the end product of the machine is a complete page, ready for offset platemaking.

At the present time, 100 different publications are produced on the Linotron 1010, as it is called, using more than 275 different typographic formats. The great majority of these publications were formerly produced by photographing a computer printer listing. The quality was poor and the number of pages needed to present the information was large. With the electronic composing system, the number of printed pages in the average publication has been reduced by approximately 40 per cent less than would have been needed for a computer listing. The reduction in the number of printed pages means fewer negatives, fewer plates, less presswork, less paper, and lower costs to print and distribute the publication. Last fiscal year, over 700,000 pages were composed on the two Linotron systems.

Public Documents Department

Printing operations are critical at the GPO. However, equally important are the sale and distribution of publications once produced. To accomplish these tasks, the Public Documents Department was established as an integral part of the GPO. The Department, however, receives its own regular appropriation, and also operated in part from the proceeds received from the sale of publications. When a Government agency prints a book through the GPO, the Documents Department places a rider on its requisition, ordering a specific number of sales copies. Printing costs for these sales copies are covered by a revolving fund, and sales revenue is returned to the fund. In this regard, it is the intent of Congress that the publications sales program be self-sustaining.

The Assistant Public Printer (Superintendent of Documents), heads the Public Documents Department and is responsible for four major programs: distribution of publications for Members of Congress and for agencies and departments of the Federal Government; the servicing of Federal depository libraries throughout the United States; issuance of catalogs and indexes; and the sale of Government publications.

Distribution and Sales

A major portion of the work force of the Public Documents Department is involved with the sale of Government publications. Sales activities include procurement of sales publications, marketing activities, inventory and warehousing, receipt of orders and remittances, and order-filling. Over 25,000 agency titles selected for their interest and educational value are available through the Documents Department.

In fiscal year 1973, 78 million copies were sold with a total sales value of $23 million. The workload seems to be an ever-increasing one; on an average day 19,000 orders plus some 2,000 phone inquiries are received. Besides a Central Office area for forward stock, three warehouses in the Washington, D.C. metropolitan area are used to store the inventory.

The Public Documents Department also operates a nationwide chain of GPO bookstores; six in the Washington D.C. area and 17 located in other cities. Two distribution centers, one operated entirely by Documents Department employees in Pueblo, Colorado, and another in Philadelphia, Pennsylvania, working in conjunction with the Naval Publications and Forms Center, have been established to process orders from the Department's announcement periodical, Selected U.S. Government Publications. Selected U.S. Government Publications is issued monthly and lists approximately 200 new and popular titles available for sale. It can be received free, upon request, and is currently mailed to 1.5 million addressees.

In terms of workload and number of employees, the distribution function is the Public Documents Department's second largest activity. Congress is the primary customer for the distribution of Government publications. In fiscal year 1973, over 95 million items were distributed for Members of Congress. The vast majority of this business is distributed through the U.S. Postal System and involves several large-scale operations, including the maintenance of mailing lists, storage of required stock, and the operation of inserting and mailing machines.

Problems in Improving Distribution and Service

Several major programs are presently being conducted by the Public Documents Department in an effort to improve service to customers and users of Government documents through refinements in sales and distribution operations. New warehouses have been established in recent years to help reduce storage problems. Modern technology is being employed wherever possible to speed up order processing, references, and mailing operations. A task force, comprised of GPO personnel and advisors from the National Archives and Records Service, is presently reviewing methods of operation to develop a plan for a totally automated receipt control and order processing system.

At this time, almost all Public Documents Department resources are being devoted to improving service and to operating the sales program in the most cost effective manner.

Historically, the publication sales program of the GPO has been self-sustaining. Title 44 states, "The price at which additional copies of Government publications are offered for sale to the public by the Superintendent of Documents shall be based on the cost as determined by the Public Printer plus 50 percent." (44 U.S.C. 1708) The cost of this program, including labor, materials, and overhead incurred in printing, warehousing, and distribution, is to be borne by the users of the publications rather than being subsidized by appropriations from the General Funds of the Treasury. A pricing formula was devised to take these factors into account in establishing the sales price of Government publications and, with rather modest and routine adjustments from time to time, worked well over the years in accomplishing Congressional objectives. Recent increases in labor and material costs, however, have upset this balance. The last routine adjustment in prices was made in 1968. Since that time, paper supplies have become much tighter and consequently more expensive. In recent years, GPO's paper costs have risen an astonishing 98 per cent. Add this to a postage increase of over 400 per cent (since the Postal Reorganization Act of 1971 when the Postal Service became a business and began charging all Federal agencies full postage) and a labor increase of 54 per cent, and the need for price increases is evident.

Based on recent policy guidelines, six major changes relating to the sale of government publications by the Superintendent of Documents may be seen:

1. Prices on individual books and pamphlets are going to increase, in most cases about 50 per cent.

2. Prices of dated periodicals and subscription services are going to rise even more dramatically than those of individual publications. Subscriptions will reflect the biggest price increases, because they are mailed to readers regularly and, are therefore most affected by postage rates.

3. Except for the "Table of Redemption Values," all subscriptions will be sold on a one-year basis only. This is because of the aforementioned price reviews.

4. No discount will be allowed when a mailing is to be to a third party except in the case of quantity orders. In this regard, purchasers of 100 copies or more of the same publication shipped to one point will receive a 25 per cent discount as in the past.

5. Back copies of a subscription will no longer be mailed as part of a customer's subscription order, just as with Time or Newsweek. The customer will receive the next issue. However, single copies of any issue will still be sold.

6. Prices printed in publications may differ from what you actually paid for them. That's because when a book is reprinted, the price usually changes, but since it is only a reprint and not a revision, copies with the old price line are distributed until they are exhausted, rather than destroy them or attempt to correct the prices manually.

The changes reflect an attempt by the GPO, after substantial losses for the past two years largely due to postage increases, to put the sales program back on a self-sustaining basis as is the intent of Congress.

Micropublishing

Another area of interest which primarily involves the Public Documents Department is that of GPO micropublishing. Broad guidelines for the program have been determined and, in perhaps the greatest step forward to date for the fledgling field of micropublishing, the GPO and five other prominent organizations in the field have settled on specific standards for the production of microfiche from source documents. In the near future, Federal depository libraries will be surveyed to determine if there is sufficient interest to warrant distribution of specific categories of publications in microform, rather than in printed copy. If sufficient interest/utility is indicated and with JCP approval, a small sample of publications will be produced in microform by commercial contract and distributed. After this pilot procedure, and if it proves satisfactory, the program could be expanded to include other categories of publications to depository libraries. Ultimately, this may mean that either microfiche or hard copy can be furnished for depository collections. However, only one format is supplied free; it would be necessary to purchase the other if wanted.

Meeting the continuing demand for Government publications and fulfilling the Federal printing requirements are not the only challenges facing the GPO.

The GPO, as well as the entire printing and publishing industry, is right now facing a very real paper shortage. Naturally, the
concern is rooted in the ability of this Office to meet its commitments in furtherance of national programs. Until several years ago,
the paper industry was systematically expanding. But today mills
are operating at near-maximum capacity. Experts have declared
that the demand for paper will outrun the supply for many months and
perhaps years. The GPO publication announcement periodical, Selected U.S. Government Publications, which is printed by a commercial
firm, has been delayed and has recently been printed on newsprint,
because 100-pound offset paper has not been available. It may soon
be printed on recycled paper. There is a growing list of documents
affected by the shortage.

From the Government's aspect, this shortage is a serious one,
because often the programs which documents are intended to activate
or maintain are slowed as well. Also, the documents are frequently
regulatory or informational in nature with impact on the public interests of every American.

Procurement standards for paper are becoming more flexible
and Federal departments and agencies are accepting wide departures
from long established formats because of the paper procurement
situation. Publications and periodicals are also being regularly reviewed for necessity.

In fiscal year 1973 the GPO bought from commercial printers
or itself produced over $300 million worth of printing. This figure
includes about 136 million pounds of paper used in its own plants.
In the past 15 months paper costs have risen on the order of 60 per
cent. The paper supply situation is being monitored carefully and
the Public Printer has appealed to the paper industry for assurances
that the Government's paper requirements will be met. In the past,
the industry has acted voluntarily and the Government's programs
have been carried forward. No public program has yet suffered ir-
reparably from the lack of paper for printing. However, paper
needs are pressing and no short-range solution appears in sight.

Overcoming the paper shortage, micropublishing, computerization in typesetting, and streamlined order processing systems are
major factors in the future of the GPO. The Office looks forward
to the continued cooperation of the library community and especially
to the assistance of the Advisory Council to the Public Printer for
Depository Libraries, in working together to serve the needs of the
American public for Government documents.

RECOMMENDED READINGS

While the preceding articles have discussed operational aspects of the publishing, production, and distribution, librarians frequently need current information on trends, statistics, and activities about publishing and production. Useful for obtaining such facts and figures are several publications from R. R. Bowker. The Bowker Annual of Library and Book Trade Information and Educational Media Yearbook pull together trends, expenditures, and other information on a regular basis. The reported facts and figures found in these annuals can be updated by consulting Publishers Weekly. The latter publication includes current information about the book trade and its products.

An account of the changes that occurred in the 1960s and 1970s which are influencing the publishing of books and journals is found in Michael H. Black's article, "National and International Publishing in Relation to the Dissemination of Information in All Disciplines," ASLIB Proceedings 26, no. 11 (November, 1974), pages 418-424. A similar approach to the topic, but limited to the United States, is presented by Dan Lacy in "An Overview of Publishing in the Seventies," Information--Part 2, 2, no. 5 (1973), pages 1-7. These two articles show the impact of population growth, library funding, educational trends, and technology upon the world of publishing. The possible impact of the "sales syndrome" on the world of publishing provides Robert Hector an opportunity to take the devil's advocate position in "Books as 'Product'" in Library Journal 101, no. 10 (May 15, 1976), pages 1180-1182. These selections illustrate the many factors which influence the availability of books.

For an overview of the publishing industry, two general works are John P. Dessauer's Book Publishing: What It Is, What It Does (R. R. Bowker, 1974) and Chandler B. Grannis' What Happens in Book Publishing, 2nd ed. (Columbia University Press, 1967). These works describe the many facets involved in the manufacturing and distributing of books.

"The Federal Government as Publisher" by Robert E. Kling, Jr. (Information--Part 2, 2, no. 5 (1973), pages 25-29) provides insight into the activities of this agency and complements the Lewis article found in the readings. This issue of Information--Part 2 is entitled "Publishing in the Seventies" and includes other informative papers presented at a Colloquium of the School of Library and Information Science, State University of New York at Albany (April 25-26, 1972).

An informative account of the creation of a book is presented by Howard Greenfield in Books from Writer to Reader (Crown, 1976). Enhanced by illustrations, the Greenfield work shows many pieces of equipment, as well as processes such as camera separation of color.

The world of audiovisual production has not received similar attention in the literature. However, an informative article by Angie Le Clerq entitled "The Filmstrip Industry--A Guide to the Production, Distribution, and Selection of Educational Filmstrips" is found in Library Technology Reports 12 (May, 1976), pages 257-269.

As was mentioned in the introduction to this chapter, librarians face special problems when they are trying to locate out-of-print books. Methods of obtaining materials as reprints, microtexts, and exchanges are extensively covered in Ernest R. Perez' "Acquisitions of Out-of-Print Materials," in Library Resources & Technical Services 17, no. 1 (Winter, 1973), pages 42-59. D. G. Parsonage describes the "Role of the Specialist Dealer" and explains the differences between library catalogs and auction catalogs in AB Bookman's Weekly 54, no. 21 (November 18, 1974), pages 2155-2156, 2158, 2160, 2162.

CHAPTER 8

RECENT DEVELOPMENTS CREATING CHANGE
IN COLLECTION DEVELOPMENT

In this final chapter, the editors have attempted to select articles dealing with issues already evident that could affect library
selection and collection development in the years immediately ahead.
These concerns have been the subject of much discussion in the
1970s, but the issues raised have not been resolved.

One of these issues has been the impact of technological developments, the "ogre" or "angel" that has occupied so much of librarians' thoughts and speculations in recent years. All around us
we see the evidence--new information services being created; existing ones being added to a library's resources; discussions of the
merits of competing cataloging systems; meetings at which vendors
and librarians debate who should access the services.

With regard to this technology, a key question for the future
of librarianship is whether librarians will have any part in the decision-making or will wait passively while economic and social forces
wrest out the decisions that will shape the library's future. Some
librarians may, of course, take an active role, eagerly "jumping on
the bandwagon, " but still without thought about what the ultimate effects may be.

Many of these developments, besides their impact on the
larger spectrum of librarianship, carry particular implications for
the areas of selection and collection development. The choice of the
material to be computerized has implications for intellectual freedom; the question of charges for information access also bears on
this; decisions on a choice of a computerized information service or
traditional print materials, forced by financial "facts of life, " can
greatly affect collection development.

Other current developments can also have far-reaching effects on libraries' collections. The 1976 copyright law revision has
several implications that may be realized in the years following
1978, when the law went into effect. Some questions that arise are:
Will libraries have to purchase more materials in order to have
them readily available, rather than depending on interlibrary copying? If a system of royalty payments becomes obligatory, how will
budgets for materials be affected? Other issues will become ap-

parent as the act is implemented and tested. Librarians should be aware that the legislation included a review date of 1982, so that records and information should be collected in order to provide data for that review.

Publishers, responding to inflationary pressures, may more generally adopt tactics which perhaps exist already and are viewed as irritating, but are not yet considered crucial. Differing means of publishing, e.g., the issuance of "papers" instead of full-fledged journals, may be adopted, with decided impact on libraries' collections.

Financial strictures, always present, are exacerbated by inflation and, increasingly, by opposing demands for more governmental services on the one hand, and for tax relief on the other. Libraries will very likely have to re-examine their conventional beliefs and practices in selection. There will be some hard decisions to make in choosing among the various alternatives. The challenge will be to select the most favorable options, in terms of good library service.

One of the alternatives being discussed is the concept of "no growth." Several writers are asking sharp questions about the use that is made of large portions of library collections. They suggest that more exact advance determination can be made of the usefulness of items being considered for purchase.

How can librarians best prepare to meet the challenges of these issues and to make effective, prudent decisions? In itself, this is a hard question, to which there are few indisputably good answers. One idea that few would question is the advice to be alert to the issues, to try to determine what is occurring and to think about the possible consequences and the alternative solutions.

The readings included in this chapter contain no definitive answers to all the questions at this time. They do serve as examples of articles that alert the librarian to the issues.

The first article, "Libraries in the Marketplace: Information Emporium or People's University?" by Fay Blake and Edith Perlmutter, deals with the issue of information services and library charges for their use. Quoting from many writers on this question, the authors present the arguments made for charges and for "entering the market place"; then proceed to analyze them, reducing their effectiveness by exposing what they consider anachronistic, retrogressive bases of thought.

In two selections, by Edward Holley and Richard De Gennaro, the current copyright law is examined and explained. In "A Librarian Looks at the New Copyright Law," Holley provides the historical background and lucidly explains several of the provisions significant for libraries, such as fair use, and copying for classroom purposes. De Gennaro, in "Copyright, Resource Sharing and Hard Times: A View from the Field," is more concerned with the possible effects of the law. His message is reassuring: he says that he foresees no real difficulty for librarians in complying with the provisions of the law. He thinks it will not significantly affect the way most libraries serve their readers, but he also urges a moderate, realistic reaction in which the librarian is not bluffed into paying for privileges unnecessarily. Furthermore, he believes librarians should exercise all the rights and privileges of the new law without fear or a misplaced sense of justice. His evaluation of the importance of resource-sharing aptly puts the whole issue into perspective.

Turning to another issue, that of the practices that publishers employ to make a sale or increase their profits, Daniel Melcher exposes and apologizes for unethical practices. His "Ethical Standards in Publishing" makes us aware of failings, but also points out the librarian's responsibility in curbing them. In the hard-pressed times ahead, librarians will need to be especially alert and assertive in their expectations of publishers' ethics.

Within the library walls, some reassessment of established attitudes will also be necessary. A traditional belief has been that a library, particularly an academic one, must continue to grow in order to be good. Now that belief is called into question by Daniel Gore in "Zero Growth for the College Library." He discusses various answers to the question, "How large should a library be?" and defines the bases underlying those answers. Different terms appear in his writings, "holding rate," "availability rate," and "cost effectiveness," causing old premises to be re-examined.

Another of our accepted premises, the right of the public to obtain information they need, is commented on in the editorial, "Medical Information Taboos." Here, John Berry supports that premise with his endorsement of the Community Health Information Network (CHIN) in Cambridge, Massachusetts. In doing so, he cheers the end of an old but still prevalent taboo, that medical or legal information for patrons should be handled with great caution.

LIBRARIES IN THE MARKETPLACE:
Information Emporium or People's University?

By Fay Blake and Edith Perlmutter

Several recent developments in the world of American libraries seem to foreshadow an ominous trend toward a new concept of library service. The concept is translated into a variety of proposals--the "information supermarket," "libraries for profit," "user fees," "user-based charges"--but what's really being proposed is an elimination of tax-supported library service.

Louis Vagianos in his article, "Libraries: Leviathanic Vagrants on a 'Titanic' Trip" (LJ, May 1, 1973, p. 1450), says libraries haven't increased their productivity in a century, so a "fair market price" or "real price" or user charge to the consumer of the information product is called for. "The information consumer," he says in attention-commanding italics, "has never really had to pay for his information and as a result has no conception of its cost, and therefore of its value to him as a product or service."[1]

Charles O'Halloran, Missouri state librarian, beats the same drum in a recent squib in Show-Me Libraries for September 1973. Libraries, he says, ought to take their chances in the "free market economy" just like franchise restaurants and Studebaker. Because of the "operation of the Law of the Marketplace which destroys the weak and the inept and the outmoded," he says, "some libraries would certainly die" but "some would flourish and prosper."

O'Halloran fails to specify how exactly libraries would operate in this "free marketplace" he airily wants to consign us to (yes, the man has heard about Lockheed--he says so), but presumably free means not free so libraries would charge users for their services just like all the other enterprises in the free economy we operate in.

From still another source, the Information Industry Association, comes a proposal to set up an "Information Supermarket," a proposal for the funding of at least some library services through user fees for personalized preprocessed information packages prepared by specialized entrepreneurial libraries run for profit in the free market. In April 1973 the HA Board Chairman, Eugene Garfield, testified before the National Commission on Libraries and Information Sciences that "user-based charges must inevitably prevail" and stressed that anything you get for nothing is worth nothing or, at any rate, valued at nothing.

At least one public library has already experimented with a user fee for some of its services. On April 1, 1970, the Minneapolis Public Library, in cooperation with the Greater Minneapolis Chamber of Commerce, inaugurated a special service to the business community of Minneapolis. For $18 per hour the library would provide abstracts, bibliographies, current awareness service, and searching within and outside of Minneapolis Public Library.

On the practical level, it is curious that, at this time when the "free market" is vanishing from what Galbraith calls the "new industrial state," suggestions for converting public agencies into for-profit businesses are increasing. Disenchantment with public sector performance has led to an irrational embrace of the market at a time when the market may itself be outmoded.

Now let's take a look at some of the rationale for this sudden flurry of proposals to turn economic history back to Adam Smith and to turn libraries loose in a "free market economy." Most of the reasoning seems to be based on muddy thinking and the uncritical swallowing of some undigested economic phrases. Vagianos, for example, says "The goal of society ... has been ... improvement in labor productivity ... and the concomitant ... [is] an improved standard of living for the individual...." Well, that sounds like an argument standing on its head. Even the greediest society would claim an improved standard of living as its goal and improvement of labor productivity as the concomitant, not the other way around. But be that as it may, Vagianos goes on to claim that the improvement of the library's labor productivity can be implemented through (1) the use of cost effectiveness to increase efficiency and, consequently, productivity, and (2) the use of a "fair market price" user charge.

O'Halloran says, "In a free market economy, popular choices and preferences, competition, skilled versus inept management, imagination and boldness, or fear and hesitation can bring prosperity or ruin and it's brutal and jungle-like." The citizenry, O'Halloran claims, ought to decide freely what their money should be spent on, and if it decides that a huge defense budget is what we all need rather than continued funding for libraries, then so be it. O'Halloran doesn't bother to mention that funds for libraries, even when chosen by the elected representatives of the citizenry, can be sidetracked by impoundment.

Zurkowski and Garfield both have personal association with the profit-making sectors of the information industry; they would naturally be expected to support more profit making. They don't confine themselves to such demands, however. Garfield says his association's existence in the free market will inevitably spur the development of new information technologies and an increased awareness of and expertise in the use of these new technologies.

Zurkowski on the other hand, speaks (<u>American Libraries,</u> May 1973, p. 258) of the HA user-charge suggestion "that in certain

specialized areas where the available information services are very
specialized and expensive, a for-profit library might well develop,
thereby relieving some competition for the ever-diminishing public
resources available for libraries. "

So, the arguments for libraries as profit-making or, at least,
fee-based information supermarkets are that they would: 1) increase
the productivity of libraries; 2) increase the economic efficiency of
libraries; 3) convince the user of the library's value; and 4) relieve
competition for public resources. We maintain that none of these
claims is true and that all these anachronistic proposals do the library user a serious disservice. We believe very strongly that today's library needs some drastic changes if it is to be an essential,
functional social institution, but the changes need to be in the direction of more public support, not less.

Vagianos, O'Halloran, et al. have placed themselves in the
position of the undergraduate who has taken the introductory course
in Principles of Economics and proceeds to instruct the World Monetary Bank (not that the Bank couldn't benefit from some wise instruction). These gentlemen have confused the market mechanism in a
private enterprise system with economic efficiency in public enterprise, in this case the provision of library services. Let us deal
first with increased productivity in libraries. Vagianos claims that
improved labor productivity has been an overwhelming success in the
private sector but has not improved in the library since the Industrial Revolution. How he arrives at this conclusion or even how he
defines productivity is left to the readers' imagination. We are defining increased productivity as either the increase of real output
with a given real input or the decrease of real input for a given
real output. The rate of growth of total productivity cannot be
measured without the measurement of the rate of growth of the real
product. How does Vagianos measure the rate of growth of real information product? The problems in measuring real input and real
product in the private sector are immense (see, for example, "The
Measurement of Productivity," Survey of Current Business, May,
1972). The problems of measuring productivity in service industries
in the private sector are even greater. The problems of measuring
real input and real product in a public service industry are still
more formidable. Vagianos' airy assertion about the libraries' stag-
nant productivity flies in the face of the economists' admitted inability to agree on how to measure the productivity of public service industries. Let us search for the best techniques to achieve efficiency
by all means, but productivity is only one aspect of efficiency.

Production is part of the question of supply in the economic
equation. The other side of the equation--the demand side--accord-
ing to Vagianos, O'Halloran, and Garfield, would be solved by
charging the consumer of the information product "real prices,"
"fair market prices," or "a user charge." These are not synonymous, although the proposers do not distinguish among them. Os-
tensibly, a fair market price is determined by Adam Smith's famous
"invisible hand" through the laws of supply and demand. Mr. Nix-

on's Phase 4 is ample evidence that the invisible hand is palsied. One would think that a fair market price for instance, could rather easily be determined, but somehow meat prices do not seem to be in equilibrium through the laws of supply and demand. What makes these pundits believe that such an elusive product price as the library's could possibly be so equilibrated?

Public goods are, by definition, goods that are not financed through the private exchange or market economy. We assume, therefore, that Vagianos and the others substitute a "user charge" for public goods since there can be no "fair market price" for them. We deny that a user charge for the information product would increase economic efficiency. The price of a product in a private transaction takes into account only the private costs and benefits of the product. The price of an automobile, for instance, is based on the internal cost of the manufacturer and the utility of the car to the buyer. When the production and consumption of the automobile results in pollution, however, society is affected. The price has not, thus far, reflected the social costs to third parties or society, costs which are called "externalities" or "spillovers." In a competitive market the pricing mechanism would generally reflect a more or less efficient allocation of resources, but when the social cost has not been included, the pricing mechanism has been skewed and resources have not been efficiently allocated. The "spillover" may be either a cost or, as in the distribution of the information product, a benefit to society or third parties. The whole point of a public service industry like libraries or education is precisely the benefit spillover to society as a whole. No user charge could take into account this nonquantitative "spillover" or "externality." Therefore, a user charge would inevitably fail the test of efficiency.

Maybe the proponents of a user charge consider it an efficient technique because it seems to rid us of the problem of "free riders." You want our service? Pay for it! Here, too, they're off the track. The socalled free rider may very well be benefiting all of society. The individual who makes use of the library's product is not engaged in a private transaction which benefits and concerns only himself. He may be using his information to build a bridge, to show others how to build a better bridge faster, to write an opera; to use the computer to compose music, to cure a disease, or to invent a new prosthetic device. In other words, he may be increasing society's total productivity in ways not immediately visible from his library transaction alone. The private sector's overwhelming increase in productivity, which has so impressed Vagianos, may very well be partly the result of the free rider's utilization of the library's product. Our carrying of the free rider is, in effect, our investment in human capital.

But it is not efficiency alone that must be considered in the concept of a user charge. Vagianos and Garfield and O'Halloran say the user has no conception of the cost or value of the library's product because he hasn't had to pay for it. Have they access to

some secret information which enables them to determine the value
of a service to a user and to equate that value with the price? If
two users each pay one dollar per unit of information service, one
with an income of less than $4000 a year, the other with an income
of more than $100,000 a year, do they assume that the value of the
information product is the same for both? Vagianos says: "... as
any economist knows, the best way of evaluating alternatives is by
comparing cost benefits"--or, given the alternatives, will you spend
your dollar on beans or books? But as any librarian knows, when
you're trying to live on welfare, you haven't got alternatives--beans
are more important than books. The library envisioned by these
writers reminds us of Thoreau's comments in Walden: "I respect
not his labors, his farm where everything has its price ... who
would carry his God to market, if he could get anything for him ...
on whose farm nothing grows free, whose fields bear no crops,
whose meadows no flowers, whose trees no fruits, but dollars; who
loves not the beauty of his fruits, whose fruits are not ripe for him
till they are turned to dollars. "

Even Adam Smith, the founder of laissez-faire economics,
concedes in his The Wealth of Nations that "... the duty of the sovereign or commonwealth is that of erecting and maintaining those
public institutions and those public works, which though they may be
in the highest degree advantageous to a great society, are, however,
of such a nature, that the profit could never repay the expense to
any individual or small number of individuals, and which it therefore
cannot be expected that any individual or small number of individuals
should erect or maintain.... After the public institutions and public
works necessary for the defense of the society, and for the administration of justice ... the other works and institutions of this kind
are chiefly those for facilitating the commerce of the society, and
those for promoting the instruction of the people.

That was in the 18th Century, yet in the last quarter of the
20th Century, our anachronistic library "economists" want to return
to a real jungle where public works will become nonexistent and
where the amenities public institutions have dispensed to all will become the possession of a tiny and moneyed minority.

The capstone argument for fee-based information supermarkets
is that competition for public resources would be relieved. What
makes these gentlemen think that removing an expenditure from a
public budget would automatically create an alternative public use
for the funds involved? The more likely outcome would be a decrease in taxes and the shift of resources to the private sector.
The income increase due to reduced taxes would be spent on private
goods, including information. And the resources formerly used to
service public libraries, would now be employed in private information industries.

Competition for public resources would not be relieved, but
on the contrary, increased by competition from the private sector
which plows profits into advertising its wares. In a competition for

the dollars of consumers and firms to buy private goods versus dollars for taxes which buy public goods for "others," the battle is rigged in favor of the private sector.

The thinkers who want to turn libraries into "efficient profit-makers" have succumbed uncritically to certain unwarranted assumptions. They have assumed without reason that the principles applicable to private enterprises can automatically be transferred to public enterprises. Beyond that, they have assumed that private enterprise in our society functions in a thoroughly free market, one that never existed fully free and is now an economist's chimera. The supermarket for information retrieval will resemble the telephone monopoly more than the competitive wheat market in economic textbooks or even the present-day grocery supermarkets. As in the telephone industry, duplications would be wasteful and technology would require large-scale operations for information retrieval. A third assumption is that private enterprise run with efficiency and a dash of imagination succeeds while "the weak go to the wall." A corollary of this assumption is, inevitably, that any private enterprise which survives must be efficiently run. We hate to be the ones to publicize the fact that some emperors are naked, but it is a fact.

There are private enterprises whose efficient management is not enough to overcome competitors with more sources of money, more political influence, more willingness or ability to cheat or connive or bribe.

The assumption that private enterprise produces what people need because of the exigencies of competition is also unwarranted. The supermarket which the library is to emulate is a prime example of the opposite. Milton Friedman, the eminent professor of economics at the University of Chicago and erstwhile advisor to President Nixon, supposes a fable in a recent New York Times article in which the retail provision of groceries has been organized like our elementary and secondary schools. "Would there be supermarkets and chain stores?" Friedman agonizes. "Would the shelves be loaded with new and improved convenience products? Would stores be using every device of human ingenuity to attract and retain customers?" Friedman fails to ask: Would stores be selling meats prepared with carcinogenic nitrites and nitrates? Would the shelves be stuffed with expensive and nutritionally useless foods? Would stores be adding to the cost of food a huge expenditure for vulgar, untruthful advertising? Would foods be offered in wasteful double or triple paper wrappings?

We already have an example of a few experiments in public services turned over to private enterprise. The U.S. Office of Economic opportunity contracted with private educational firms in 1970 to teach school children in several grades. Payment was to be made on the basis of performance by the educational firms, and comparisons were to be drawn with the performance of children in regular classes. The result of the experiment seems to be one big mess. OEO says the experiment was a failure. There is apparently no evidence that the private firms performed the teaching function any better than regular school teachers despite the performance payment incentive. Could it be even that the powerful profit incentive doesn't guarantee efficient and effective public service delivery?

As a matter of fact, where we really care about results nobody seems to suggest putting the project into private hands. When is the last time anyone proposed that the Army ought to be farmed out to private enterprise? We could argue that such a step would make it more efficient: why leave the organization of the Army to dunderheaded public servants when it could be done by captains of industry for a profit? We could make the Army more productive: pay private companies by body count? Or number and size of wars they could arrange? And we could institute a user fee: anyone who wants a sophisticated protection packet including the latest in nuclear weapons can damn well pay for it; otherwise, how's he going to know the value of what he gets--and that'll get all those peaceniks off our necks, too. If they don't like the armed forces, they have the freedom of any citizen to opt out. You can try the analogy out on police forces or space exploration. Why not sell all public parks off, too, while we're at it?

This is not to maintain that we regard libraries as they are now run as models of productivity or efficiency or just plain utility. This is not to say that libraries and the library's product should not be improved. On the contrary. Today's library needs drastic improvement, but not via the thoroughly anachronistic proposals for the pricing of a public service in a society which has been growing more and more affluent, in which leisure is becoming more and more widespread, and in which more and more public services have become necessities rather than the luxuries they used to be. The "rigorous procedural standards," "the new techniques," "the budgetary and cost controls" offered as panaceas are only useful if the library's real productivity is increased. That means expanding and improving the quantity and quality of its products without increasing input, and that means substituting new services to new populations which can and do find them outside the library. This is not the place for a full exposition of these new services, but a few examples to consider are massive programs to serve the ghetto populations with information on employment and training or with programs designed to develop a sense of community and increased opportunities; or programs designed to provide prison and jail populations with extensive legal, vocational, and general information. We could provide extensive new leisure services for our population--not merely the traditional recreational books. How about mediating between filmmakers and their huge potential audience? How about helping users learn how to become filmmakers themselves? We could be providing information on controversial community issues as well as the rostrum and meeting halls for the discussion of community issues. We could be serving very young children and their parents and teachers before they enter the public school system not only with books but with toys or games or pets or whatever we can think of that expands the world of the next century's adults.

What's the social benefit of all these nontraditional services? Why not serve those who've already made it, more or less, and forget about the losers? Well, some of the reasons we'll just have to take on faith--and the words of people who've told us what libraries did for them. When Malcolm X told us the prison library turned his head and his life around, we believe him. We think it's worth a lot to society in human terms--and even in just plain economic terms-- to turn someone away from a dead-end drug scene or a dead-end job or a dead-end holdup, and libraries can do something positive about this. Free and public libraries, that is, which accept their responsibility for serving everyone with the full range of information they need.

These services, especially those to populations the library has consistently failed to serve, will often have to be given instead of some of our extensive and expensive services to well-served populations, but the substitution could be economically efficient and could be increasing the library's real productivity. The library could become again the people's university we once were for the poor, the alien, the illiterate, and the disregarded as well as the source for information to a changing society.

A LIBRARIAN LOOKS AT
THE NEW COPYRIGHT LAW

By Edward G. Holley

Almost every journal we pick up these days features an article on the new copyright act or announces an institute or workshop
on the subject. Librarians are concerned about its effects on their
libraries as well as on their attempts to provide "user-oriented library and information service to all." Presumably, they hope that
the articles and institutes will provide quick and easy answers to the
problems they anticipate when the law becomes effective Jan. 1,
1978.

If so, they are doomed to disappointment. Certainly, the librarians are receiving much information and some guidance, but
there are no quick and easy answers, even from Register of Copyrights Barbara Ringer herself. An Act for the General Revision of
the Copyright Law, Title 17 of the United States Code,[1] otherwise
known as PL 94-553, is a complex piece of legislation with many
unresolved issues. Librarians will have to study the act carefully
and keep up with developments as they occur.

For my own money, the best current materials on the topic,
in addition to the law itself and the conference reports it emerged
from, are ALA's "Librarian's Guide to the New Copyright Law" and
two articles published by Professor John C. Stedman in the AAUP
Bulletin.[2] Both warn that the issues are complicated, the regulations and procedures as yet unwritten, and the developments of the
next few years likely to be as important as the law itself. Publishers also take this view, according to Publishers Weekly.[3]

What exactly does the new copyright act of 1976 attempt to
do, how does it differ from the 1909 law, and what new opportunities or constraints does it place upon libraries as they concern
themselves with library property entrusted to them?

Article 1, Section 8 of the United States Constitution is the
basis of all our copyright laws. It grants Congress the right "To
promote the progress of science and useful arts by securing for
limited times to authors and inventors the exclusive right to their
respective writings and discoveries."

The framers of the Constitution had a double purpose: 1) to

make it clear that copyright and other patents were designed to promote progress and creative effort, and 2) to limit the duration of the monopoly. The balancing of public right to utilize the knowledge of others against private right to benefit from one's creative efforts is at the heart of the matter. Depending on whether you are the user and consumer of a creative and scholarly work or its creator, you will doubtless come down harder on one side of the issue.

Over the years, copyright has undergone a variety of changes. Under the 1909 law, an author controlled a literary production for a total of 56 years: the first registration of 28 years coupled with a 28-year renewal. Unpublished manuscripts were covered only by common law, which gave author and heirs control forever.

The most vital change, and one destined to have a far-reaching effect on the ownership of literary property, is the new concept of copyright duration for both published and unpublished works. Following international practice, the new U.S. law provides that copyright extends from the act of creation to 50 years after the death of the creator. This extension of the time period disturbed a number of people, for, as the Senate Committee Report of 1975 noted, [4] about 85 per cent of the currently copyrighted works are not renewed. Thus the new provision of "life plus fifty years" will tie up substantial bodies of material which would have been freed for scholarship earlier under the old law.

Another important point to remember is that since a work now will enjoy copyright protection from the moment of its creation, the author, not the publisher, may sell, give, or distribute all or part of the rights to a publisher, a library, heirs, or anyone else. Clearly this is an advantage to an author; in this sense the revision can be called a "proprietor's bill."[5]

How will this provision affect librarians? Let me cite an example. If an author publishes a book in 1980 and dies in 1985, copyright protection will extend until 2035, when the work will go into the public domain. If the author left a manuscript in the custody of a library but did not also present the literary rights, the heirs can sell, publish, or otherwise dispose of these rights until the same date, 2035. Until that date, librarians and others who wish to use the work would need permission from the owners.

Most American Libraries readers won't be around when that work goes into the public domain, but they will have to deal with similar problems. If they want to publish a manuscript in their Friends of the Library magazine or bring out a small edition of a work, they must secure permission and pay whatever fee may be assessed. That was always the case, of course, but as David Martz has indicated in a recent issue of Manuscripts, [6] some curators have probably been violating the common law for quite some time. One suspects that much of the material librarians and dealers publish has no commercial value and the heirs may enjoy an ego boost from seeing grandfather's letter to General Robert E. Lee in print. Nonetheless, libraries with manuscript repositories should make sure that their procedures conform to the new law. And when they accept collections, they should compose letters of agreement that provide the flexibility they need to carry out their public duties.

For published works, the new law may also prove to be tricky. The requirement that the publisher include the copyright notice on the verso of the title page is retained, but if the notice is inadvertently omitted, the author may still be able to retrieve copyright. No one can be certain that a work is in the public domain unless a notice says explicitly that reproduction is permitted. [7] When in doubt, librarians will need to check with the Copyright Office.

Bibliographically, the copyright notice will continue to be important to librarians, but the major concern, with both published and unpublished works, is the date of the author's death, not the date of publication. The new law requires the Copyright Office to register the death of a creator. This will probably be done by computer, which should make it easy to retrieve.

Chasing down heirs can be a real problem for librarians. Anyone who has ever tried to put together an anthology either for classroom use or publication, can tell you how hard it is to find the owners. It's also difficult to determine whether or not a work was ever copyrighted. Authors who contribute to esoteric and scholarly journals are far more interested in sharing their ideas with their peers than in receiving compensation. [8]

Thus far, I have discussed only manuscripts and published writing. However, the new law also protects musical compositions, drama, pantomimes, choreography, pictures, graphics, sculpture, sound recordings, motion pictures, and other audiovisual creations (Section 102). Works produced by the United States government are still not copyrighted, although at the last minute the National Technical Information Service tried to add a five-year copyright clause to protect its publications. The Senate hadn't time to schedule hearings on the proposal, but NTIS will probably return to Congress with its request.

As Barbara Ringer pointed out at ALA's 1977 Midwinter meeting, the really radical copyright revision is in how the United States chooses to deal with creative and artistic people. Undeniably, the creator of a work of scholarship, literature, or art has greater rights under the new law. There are, however, certain restrictions on these rights, and it is these sections that receive the most attention from librarians. Since photocopying and reproduction are immediate problems for so many librarians, that concentration is understandable.

What are the restrictions on the author's rights and how can the librarian deal with them? The two sections of PL 94-553 which caused the greatest controversy were 107, Fair use, and 108, Reproduction by libraries and archives.

The doctrine of "fair use" developed in the 1930s to permit a scholar to make a single copy of a work for individual use without violating copyright. Through the years the courts have interpreted fair use, but now for the first time the concept is embodied in law.

Essentially, Section 107, "Limitations on exclusive rights: Fair use," states that one may reproduce a copyrighted work for criticism, comment, news reporting, teaching (including multiple copies for classroom use), scholarship, or research without infringing on copyright. That seems a very broad grant indeed but the determination of fair use involves these considerations: 1) purpose and character of use (is it commercial or nonprofit?), 2) nature of the work, 3) amount and substantiality of the portion used, and 4) effect upon potential market for the work.

The concern about photocopies for classroom teaching caused a coalition of educational associations (chiefly NEA) to confer with representatives of publisher and author groups on standards for copying from books and periodicals. The resulting guidelines (pp. 67-70 of HR Report 94-1476) state that multiple copies may not exceed one copy per student. These copies may be made for classroom use or discussion provided they meet certain tests for brevity (less than 250 words for a poem, less than 2,500 words for an article, story, essay), spontaneity (no time to ask permission), cumulative effect (not more than one copy per author and no more than nine instances during a term), and inclusion of a notice that the material is copyrighted.[9] Consumables, i.e. workbooks and standardized tests, are not to be copied. Guidelines for music were also developed and appear on pp. 70-72.[10]

The Association of American University Professors and the American Association of Law Schools disagreed with these guidelines; the AAUP dissent is published in the Congressional Record.[11] As Stedman has noted, voluntary agreements are binding only on those who agree to them.[12]

It seems entirely likely that classroom photocopying will be a trial-and-error process and that the various parties will be back at the conference table again. There was no agreement on audiovisual materials; the introduction of the videotape recorder Beta-Max was a real stumbling block here. The House Report urged the Register of Copyrights to keep the various parties talking to each other. I would advise the school/media center librarian to read the relevant sections of the House Report very carefully and proceed with caution in acting within these guidelines.

What is not so clear is fair use in photocopying for interlibrary loan purposes. Publishers are greatly concerned with this matter, especially after the Williams & Wilkins decision. Many journal publishers believe that libraries use their networks to avoid subscribing to journals and thus cut the publishers' income.

The new law permits libraries and archives to reproduce and

distribute materials for interlibrary loan provided 1) there is no substantial aggregate use by one or more individuals and 2) there is no "systematic distribution" of multiple copies. Thus libraries must not make interlibrary loan agreements that, in effect, substitute reproductions for subscriptions or purchases.

But how does one decide when the library is engaged in legitimate interlibrary loan activity and when it is avoiding subscriptions? Clearly a large library such as the British Lending Library or any other regional library reduces the subscriptions some libraries must carry. For such libraries, some kind of royalty agreement with the copyright owner would seem to be required.

What form royalty licensing will take, if it occurs at all, is uncertain, but such an approach does seem possible with the emerging state and national networks. Librarians will have a vital stake in such developments and should keep informed about hearings and other legislative activity relating to this problem.

The copyright act does provide for a 1982 review of library copying provisions and a report by the Register of Copyrights on how the balance between copyright owners and users has worked out after five years. Before that review, librarians will want to be sure that the user's access to information is not being curtailed, that record keeping does not require inordinate expenditures of the library budget, and that the user is able to take advantage of services aided by the new technology. On this point, CONTU should make valuable recommendations.

The aim is to have a bank of material on which all can draw. But what about the small college library requesting an occasional article from the Harvard Library Bulletin or the Journal of Library History? That would appear to be permissible as long as the request doesn't exceed five copies per year from either journal.[13] The burden also appears to be on the borrowing library, but the language of the guidelines is vague. I would advise both the borrowing and the lending libraries to keep careful records of every interlibrary loan transaction in the immediate future.

These particular guidelines on Section 108 (g) came as a result of the good offices of the National Commission on New Technological Uses of Copyrighted Works (CONTU), whose chief aim is to study the effect of computers and other new technology on copyright. CONTU asked librarians and publishers to develop fair and viable guidelines that could be incorporated into the House Report.[14] They can be found in the Conference Committee Report, HR Report 94-1733, pp. 72-73.

The guidelines on "Photocopying-Interlibrary Arrangements" state that violation would occur when any library or archives in one calendar year requests six or more copies of any article or articles in one given periodical published within the last five years of the request date. What the guidelines are saying is that if a library needs more than five copies of articles from a title less than five years old it ought to have that periodical in its collection. Similar guidelines apply to phonorecords and other copyrighted works. Musical works, pictorial, graphic, or sculptural works, motion pictures, and audiovisual materials not specifically news programs are excluded from this rule.

Libraries will need to keep very careful records of interlibrary loan transactions so that they will not exceed the five-copy limit for one title during one 12-month period.

I can predict with some confidence that the end of this affair is not in sight. During the next few years a number of studies will be made to determine how networks affect the sale and distribution of published works. Publishers would like networks to pay royalties on what they believe is large-scale copying.

The National Commission on Libraries and Information Science is funding a study to analyze library photocopying and to conduct a feasibility test of a royalty payment mechanism. The National Technical Information Service has already offered to set up a clearing-house.[15] And the Association of American Publishers recently announced it intends to set up a clearinghouse for royalty payments for photocopying.[16]

There are, of course, many other provisions that interest librarians. Vanderbilt University's success in preserving its Television News Archive is a plus for access to that medium.[17] The new act further provides for the establishment of an American Television and Radio Archives in the Library of Congress so that there will be a permanent record of this form of the American heritage.

The new act culminates two decades of hard work, but the work is not completed. What emerged from the various competing interests was a compromise, and compromises seldom satisfy anyone. Many of its provisions will have to be worked out over time.

Librarians must watch for additional regulations, administrative procedures, commission reports, and even modifications of the bill itself. In this dynamic situation, one must expect continuing change.

As I can vouch from personal experience, much of the literature and many of the meetings will be deadly dull, but no one should imagine that they are not vital. Librarians will need to become increasingly sophisticated on copyright law and how it affects library functions.

No one wants to deprive authors compensation for their works. But librarians are also committed to providing access to information for all--or, to use Melvil Dewey's message, "the best reading for the largest number at the least expense."

THE MOST CONTROVERSIAL SECTIONS OF THE NEW LAW

§ 107. Limitations on exclusive rights: Fair use

Notwithstanding the provisions of section 106, the fair use of a copyrighted work, including such use by reproduction in copies or phonorecords or by any other means specified by that section, for purposes such as criticism, comment, news reporting, teaching (including multiple copies for classroom use), scholarship, or research, is not an infringement of copyright. In determining whether the use made of a work in any particular case is a fair use the factors to be considered shall include--

(1) the purpose and character of the use, including whether such use is of a commercial nature or is for nonprofit educational purposes;
(2) the nature of the copyrighted work;
(3) the amount and substantiality of the portion used in relation to the copyrighted work as a whole; and
(4) the effect of the use upon the potential market for or value of the copyrighted work.

§ 108. Limitations on exclusive rights: Reproduction by libraries and archives

(a) Notwithstanding the provisions of section 106, it is not an infringement of copyright for a library or archives, or any of its employees acting within the scope of their employment, to reproduce no more than one copy or phonorecord of a work, or to distribute such copy or phonorecord, under the conditions specified by this section, if--

(1) the reproduction or distribution is made without any purpose of direct or indirect commercial advantage;
(2) the collections of the library or archives are (i) open to the public, or (ii) available not only to researchers affiliated with the library or archives or with the institution of which it is a part, but also to other persons doing research in a specialized field; and
(3) the reproduction or distribution of the work includes a notice of copyright.

(b) The rights of reproduction and distribution under this section apply to a copy or phonorecord of an unpublished work duplicated in facsimile form solely for purposes of preservation and security or for deposit for research use in another library or archives of the type described by clause (2) of subsection (a), if the copy or phonorecord reproduced is currently in the collections of the library or archives.

(c) The right of reproduction under this section applies to a copy or phonorecord of a published work duplicated in facsimile form solely for the purpose of replacement of a copy or a phonorecord that is damaged, deteriorating, lost, or stolen, if the library or archives has, after a reasonable effort, determined that an unused replacement cannot be obtained at a fair price.

(d) The rights of reproduction and distribution under this section apply to a copy, made from the collection of a library or archives where the user makes his or her request or from that·of another library or archives, of no more than one article or other contribution to a copyrighted collection or periodical issue, or to a copy or phonorecord of a small part of any other copyrighted work, if--

(1) the copy or phonorecord becomes the property of the user, and the library or archives has had no notice that the copy or phonorecord would be used for any purpose other than private study, scholarship, or research; and
(2) the library or archives displays prominently, at the place where orders are accepted, and includes on its order form, a warning of copyright in accordance with requirements that the Register of Copyrights shall prescribe by regulation.

(e) The rights of reproduction and distribution under this section apply to the entire work, or to a substantial part of it, made from the collection of a library or archives where the user makes his or her request or from that of another library or archives, if the library or archives has first determined, on the basis of a reasonable investigation, that a copy or phonorecord of the copyrighted work cannot be obtained at a fair price, if--

(1) the copy or phonorecord becomes the property of the user, and the library or archives has had no notice that the copy or phonorecord would be used for any purpose other than private study, scholarship, or research; and
(2) the library or archives displays prominently, at the place where orders are accepted, and includes on its order form, a warning of copyright in accordance with requirements that the Register of Copyrights shall prescribe by regulation.

(f) Nothing in this section--

(1) shall be construed to impose liability for copyright infringement upon a library or archives or its employees for the unsupervised use of reproducing equipment located on its premises: Provided, That such equipment displays a notice that the making of a copy may be subject to the copyright law;
(2) excuses a person who uses such reproducing equipment or who requests a copy or phonorecord under subsection (d) from liability for copyright infringement for any such act, or for any later use of such copy or phonorecord, if it exceeds fair use as provided by section 107;
(3) shall be construed to limit the reproduction and distribution by lending of a limited number of copies and excerpts by a li-

brary or archives of an audiovisual news program, subject to
clauses (1), (2), and (3) of subsection (a); or
(4) in any way affects the right of fair use as provided by section 107, or any contractual obligations assumed at any time by
the library or archives when it obtained a copy or phonorecord
of a work in its collections.

(g) The rights of reproduction and distribution under this section extend to the isolated and unrelated reproduction or distribution
of a single copy or phonorecord of the same material on separate occasions, but do not extend to cases where the library or archives,
or its employee--

(1) is aware or has substantial reason to believe that it is engaging in the related or concerted reproduction or distribution
of multiple copies or phonorecords of the same material, whether
made on one occasion or over a period of time, and whether intended for aggregate use by one or more individuals or for separate use by the individual members of a group; or
(2) engages in the systematic reproduction or distribution of
single or multiple copies or phonorecords of material described
in subsection (d): Provided, That nothing in this clause prevents
a library or archives from participating in interlibrary arrangements that do not have, as their purpose or effect, that the library or archives receiving such copies or phonorecords for distribution does so in such aggregate quantities as to substitute
for a subscription to or purchase of such work.

(h) The rights of reproduction and distribution under this section do not apply to a musical work, a pictorial, graphic or sculptural work, or a motion picture or other audiovisual work other than
an audiovisual work dealing with news, except that no such limitation shall apply with respect to rights granted by subsections (b) and
(c), or with respect to pictorial or graphic works published as illustrations, diagrams, or similar adjuncts to works of which copies are
reproduced or distributed in accordance with subsections (d) and (e).

(i) Five years from the effective date of this Act, and at five-
year intervals thereafter, the Register of Copyrights, after consulting
with representatives of authors, book and periodical publishers, and
other owners of copyrighted materials, and with representatives of library users and librarians, shall submit to the Congress a report
setting forth the extent to which this section has achieved the intended
statutory balancing of the rights of creators, and the needs of users.
The report should also describe any problems that may have arisen,
and present legislative or other recommendations, if warranted.

Notes

1. The Copyright Revision Act of 1976 (PL 94-553) can be requested from members of Congress and may also be found in
   U.S. House of Representatives Conference Report (H.R. 94-

1733, Sept. 29, 1976). Other material important for understanding the law includes the U.S. House of Representatives Judiciary Committee Report (H.R. 94-1476, Sept. 3, 1976 with corrections in the Congressional Record, Sept. 21, 1976, pp. H10727-28). A Senate report must also be studied for its discussion of sections 107 and 108: U.S. Senate. Committee on the Judiciary. Copyright Law Revision, S 94-473, Nov. 20, 1975.

2. For a single source, the ALA pamphlet "Librarian's Guide to the New Copyright Law" is unquestionably the best. I also highly recommend the two articles by John C. Stedman, "Copyright Developments in the United States," AAUP Bulletin, 62, pp. 308-19, October 1976, and "The New Copyright Law: Photocopying for Educational Use," AAUP Bulletin, 63, pp. 5-16, February 1977.

3. Three articles by Susan Wagner, "S. 22: Copyrighted 1976, Congress Approves 'Monumental' Bill," Publishers Weekly, 210, pp. 22-24, Oct. 11, 1976; "Copying and the Copyright Bill, Where the New Revision Stands on 'Fair Use'," Publishers Weekly, 210, pp. 28-30, Oct. 18, 1976; "Lawyers Warn Publishers: Copyright Countdown Has Begun," Publishers Weekly, 211, pp. 56-58, March 7, 1977; and Barbara Ringer, "Finding Your Way Around in the New Copyright Law," Publishers Weekly, 210, pp. 38-41, Dec. 13, 1976.

4. U.S. Senate. Committee on the Judiciary. Report on Copyright Law Revision, S 94-473, Nov. 20, 1975, p. 119.

5. The fact that the Congress had to reiterate its belief in balancing the rights of users and the rights of authors has a strange ring of protesting too much. See "Copyright Law Revision," Congressional Record, 122, pp. H10872-H10911, Sept. 22, 1976. For the author's view of this, see "A Look at Copyright: The Past and Likely Future," Journal of Library and Information Science, II, pp. 1-15, April 1976. Some members of Congress admitted to their constituents that it was a "proprietor's bill" but promised to try to see that libraries did not get hurt in the process.

6. David J. Martz, Jr., "Manuscripts as Literary Property: Everybody's Problem," Manuscripts, 29, pp. 23-27, Winter 1977.

7. For example, American Libraries and College and Research Libraries have for some time copyrighted the articles published therein but include with their copyright notice the following statement: "All material in this journal subject to copyright by the American Library Association may be photocopied for the noncommercial purpose of scientific or educational advancement." Other scholarly journals might consider a similar statement.

8. As Stedman says in his article on "The New Copyright Law," op. cit., "While authors of many works of educational value write with the expectation that they will be compensated if their work is copied, other authors are interested primarily in the maximum dissemination of their ideas, not in remuneration. Typically, the latter receive no compensation from

the publisher ... and indeed, often must pay for the privilege of having their pieces published. In such circumstances, who possesses the right to permit, or prohibit, copying?", p. 7.

9. U.S. House of Representatives, Committee on the Judiciary. Report on Copyright Law Revision, H.R. 94-1476, Sept. 3, 1976, pp. 67-70.

10. Ibid., pp. 70-72.

11. Congressional Record, 122, p. H10881, Sept. 22, 1976. The entire letter is reprinted in Stedman, "New Copyright Law," p. 7.

12. Stedman, "New Copyright Law," p. 12.

13. House of Representatives. Conference Report on General Revision of the Copyright Law, 94-1733, Sept. 29, 1976, pp. 72-74. Also in ALA's "Librarian's Guide."

14. Ibid., p. 71.

15. Reported by Barbara Ringer at the 1977 ALA Midwinter. Ms. Ringer noted that the publishers seemed opposed to this.

16. A recent issue of BP Report published by Knowledge Industry Publications indicated that the Association of American Publishers had chosen Ben Weil, Exxon Research and Engineering, to develop a nonprofit copyright clearinghouse that would channel payments from libraries to publishers.

17. This is an example where one individual citizen, Paul Simpson of Nashville, Tenn., almost single-handedly preserved the right to tape national TV news broadcasts for scholarly study and research. See S. Report 94-473, p. 69; H. Conference Report 94-1733, p. 73. See also the remarks of Senator Baker "Copyright Law Revision--Conference Report," Congressional Record, 122, p. S17251, Sept. 30, 1976.

COPYRIGHT, RESOURCE SHARING, AND HARD TIMES

By Richard De Gennaro

Remember the bumper stickers from the Vietnam peace movement that read: SUPPOSE THEY GAVE A WAR AND NOBODY
CAME? We could use a slogan like that to help end the long and
tedious war of words between publishers and librarians over the fair
use and photocopying provisions of the new copyright act scheduled
to take effect Jan. 1, 1978. Our line might read: SUPPOSE THEY
GAVE A NEW COPYRIGHT ACT AND NOBODY CARED?

That is what may happen once the unfounded fears of publishers and librarians are allayed, after they live with the new law for
a time and discover that it changes virtually nothing for the vast majority of them. But right now, many librarians are worried sick
about complying with the new act. It is complex and unfamiliar and
they are afraid of the adverse effects that its provisions, particularly
sections 107 and 108(g), may have on their capacity to continue to
serve their users in the usual ways. These fears stem in part from
the publicity given to early proposed versions of these sections which
threatened to seriously limit or even put an end to "fair use" and
photocopying in interlibrary loan operations.

But that is behind us now. I believe the final versions of
Sections 107 and 108 and the CONTU (National Commission on New
Technological Uses of Copyrighted Works) guidelines are fair to
authors, publishers, and librarians. I can foresee no real difficulties in complying with them, and I do not believe they will significantly affect the way most libraries serve their readers. Most librarians in public and academic libraries need not try to master the
legal intricacies of the new law or make elaborate preparations to
implement it. The leaders of library associations and their legal
counsel should and will continue to monitor and influence the implementation and administration of the new law; the rest of us should
set the copyright issue aside and turn our attention and energies to
other more critical matters.

The continued preoccupation of the entire profession with the
copyright issue will keep us from coming to grips with such pressing
problems as escalating book and journal prices, mounting losses
from theft and mutilation, rising personnel costs, and steadily declining budgetary support. In comparison to these and other problems

facing us, the impact of the new copyright law on libraries will be relatively slight.

This article has three aims. One is to put the matter of copyright and its possible effects on libraries and publishers into better perspective by offering some data and insights based on practical experience. Another is to urge librarians to exercise freely all the considerable rights the new law grants them. They should not permit themselves to be bullied or bluffed by hard-sell publishers into buying copyright privileges they have always had and which the new law reinforces.

The third is to dispel some of the exaggerated fears and hopes that many publishers and librarians have about the harmful or beneficial effects that increasingly effective interlibrary loan, networking, and other resource sharing mechanisms will have on their finances and operations. Some publishers fear that library resource sharing will seriously diminish their sales, and some librarians hope it will save them from the crunch that is coming. Both views are quite unrealistic.

A special issue of the ALA Washington Newsletter on the new copyright law is a readily available and indispensable guide through the complexities of the law.[1] It contains brief highlights of the new law, a librarian's guide to it, recommended preparations for compliance, and excerpts from the law and the Congressional Reports, including the CONTU guidelines. (Also of interest is the May 1977 issue of American Libraries, which has two excellent articles--one by librarian Edward G. Holley and the other by attorney Lewis I. Flacks).

Our interest here is not the entire copyright law but the Fair Use provisions and CONTU guidelines.

In Section 107 of the new law, the Fair Use doctrine is given statutory recognition for the first time. Section 108 defines the conditions and limitations under which libraries can make copies for their internal use and for interlibrary loan. Nothing in Section 108 limits a library's right to fair use of copyrighted works; the new law reconfirms most of the rights librarians had before and even extends some. It prohibits "systematic copying," but this is no problem since few academic or public libraries engage in systematic copying as defined in Section 108(g) (2) and the CONTU guidelines. Librarians are not liable for the unsupervised use of photocopying machines by the public provided certain conditions are observed. This is no change from the existing situation.

The most serious limitation appears not in the law itself but in the CONTU guidelines. They recommend that libraries refrain from copying for interlibrary loan purposes more than five articles a year from the last five years of a periodical title. They also stipulate that libraries must maintain records to document this use, placing responsibility for monitoring it on the requesting library.

What do these limitations really mean in practical terms?

If the University of Pennsylvania Library's experience is in any way typical, then the five-copy limitation will not seriously interfere with present interlibrary loan operations and services to users. Why not? Because interlibrary loan photocopying constitutes a relatively insignificant portion of our total library use to begin with. Once we exclude from our total interlibrary loan photocopying requests those that are from monographs, from journals more than five years old, and from journals to which we subscribe, those that are left will be a fraction of the total--probably on the order of 20 per cent. As much as 90-95 per cent of this remaining 20 per cent will be requests for less than six articles from the same title in a year. Of the 5-10 per cent that may exceed the guideline limitation, some will be for articles from journals whose authors and publishers have no interest in collecting royalties and from foreign journals which may not be part of the copy payment system. In the end, a library could simply decline to request more than five copies from any journal which required the payment of royalties.

The record keeping required by the guidelines is a trivial matter and involves only maintaining and analyzing a file of the third copy of a new three-part interlibrary loan form being developed. It could produce some interesting and unexpected consequences by reminding librarians that their subscription decisions should be based more heavily on actual rather than potential use. Librarians may identify some journals whose use will justify a subscription and a great many others whose lack of use will invite cancellation. [2]

These conclusions are based on statistics gathered at the University of Pennsylvania and on a report of a sampling of photocopy statistics from Cornell.

Applying the CONTU guidelines (no more than five copies in a year from the last five years of any title), the Penn Interlibrary Loan Office (excluding law and medicine) reported the following experience during the year from July 1976 through June 1977.

Articles were requested from 247 different journal titles. Of these, 173, or 70 per cent, of the journals had requests for only one article. Five had five requests, two had six requests, and one had seven requests. [3]

In every case where five or more articles were requested from a single journal, all were requested by one person working on a specific project or an annual review article. A total of four scholars were responsible for all these requests; two of them were working on annual review articles. The authors and publishers of the papers requested for mention in annual review articles should be grateful to have their works cited and not ask for royalties. Indeed, there were only two commercial journals listed which might qualify for royalty payments. The rest were nonprofit, scholarly journals. In any event, this type of occasional use hardly justifies a library subscription.

Last year Penn circulated nearly a half million volumes from its libraries, not including periodical volumes, which do not circulate. The total of home loans and in-building use is estimated at well over 2 million. During that year, we borrowed 2,941 volumes and received 3,726 photocopies from other libraries for a total of 6,667 items (less than one half of one percent of our total use). We lent 7,748 volumes to other libraries and filled 7,682 photocopy requests--a total of 15,430 items. The sum of all such extramural transactions--borrowing as well as loans--was 22,000, or about one per cent of our intramural use.

Penn is not unusual in this regard. The median for all university members of the Association of Research Libraries in 1975-76 was 11,053 loans and 4,505 borrowings for a total of 15,558 transactions. All these libraries together borrowed a half million originals and photocopies in 1975-76 and lent about two million. [4] Even if this traffic doubled or tripled in the next few years, it would still be relatively insignificant.

What can we conclude from these gross statistics? Simply that the total amount of interlibrary loan and photocopying in lieu of interlibrary loan is and will always remain a relatively small fraction of total library use. The point is not to denigrate the value of interlibrary loan or resource sharing but to emphasize the overriding importance of the local use of local collections. Publishers, librarians, and particularly network planners should keep this basic truth in mind.

Last year Penn spent $1.3 million on books and journals, and we would spend considerably more if we had it. We saved virtually nothing by using interlibrary loan and photocopying; in fact, we incurred substantial additional costs using interlibrary loan channels to obtain some important little used materials for a small number of users who might otherwise have done without.

The Cornell experience with the five-copy limit is similar to Penn's. Madeline Cohen Oakley, Cornell interlibrary loan librarian, reports it as follows:

> The new restrictions on photocopying pose a number of questions of policy and procedure for Cornell interlibrary loan operations. Although the five article per journal photocopy limit may seem low, our experience in interlibrary borrowing (the term covers both requests for loans and for photocopy) at Olin Library has not, for the most, borne this out. We consider a journal for which we have four or more photocopy requests to be frequently ordered, and all such journals are considered for purchase. To give an example, in the 1975-76 fiscal year, out of a total of 188 different journal titles represented in one group of requests, only 15 involved multiple copies of four or more from one journal. (Of those 15, nine were for more than five articles.) [5]

She remarks that the five-copy limit is likely to be a problem when a single individual or research project requires a number of articles from one journal. This is Penn's view as well. In such cases some restrictions will have to be worked out, and our users will have to be more selective in what they request. In those few cases for which we need to exceed the five-copy limit, we can presumably choose to pay a reasonable royalty to a payments center or do without. The mechanism for paying such fees may be in place by next year.

Ben H. Weil of Exxon has been appointed to serve as program director of the Association of American Publishers/Technical-Scientific-Medical Copy Payments Center Task Force, which is expected to design and implement a payments system by Jan. 1, 1978. The center would periodically invoice the users and allocate the payment, less a processing charge, to the appropriate publisher. I wish the center luck, but my guess is that the processing charges will far exceed the royalty payments, making it a financially precarious service.

It is important that librarians exercise all the rights and privileges the new law gives them, uninhibited by the fear of lawsuits or by an exaggerated or misplaced sense of fair play and justice. Section 504(c) 2 relieves employees of nonprofit libraries from personal liability in case of infringement if they had reasonable grounds for believing their use of the work was a fair use under section 107. Librarians must comply with the law as best they understand it, but they are not obliged to do more. Even the Internal Revenue Service encourages taxpayers to take all the deductions to which they are legally entitled and to pay no more taxes than the law requires.

Some librarians are already going to great lengths to establish elaborate and far more restrictive procedures than the law or the guidelines require in order to demonstrate their intent to comply with the spirit as well as the letter of the law and to show their good faith. By so doing, they appear defensive and guilty and run the risk of losing the rights they are too cautious to exercise. It is a time for boldness and courage.

Based on past performance, we can be sure that the publishers will not be cautious or diffident about exercising all the rights the law allows them--and even a bit more on occasion. Last fall, for example, one publisher misrepresented the provisions of the new law in a letter to his library customers offering to sell copying privileges that the law already gives them as a right.

Libraries that buy subscriptions with strings attached may forfeit their rights under the law. "Section 108(f) (4) states that the rights of reproduction granted libraries by Section 108 do not override any contractual obligations assumed by the library at the time it obtained a work for its collections. In view of this provision, libraries must be especially sensitive to the conditions under which they purchase materials, and before executing an agreement which would limit their rights under the copyright law, should consult with their legal counsel" (ALA Washington Newsletter, Nov. 15, 1976, p. 5).

Actually, urging librarians to consult legal counsel in copyright matters may not be very helpful advice. Because of its vagueness and complexity, the new copyright law is already being called the "full employment act" of the legal profession. The typical general counsel that the typical librarian can turn to will know little about copyright law and will, as lawyers customarily do when asked for advice by cautious clients on unfamiliar matters, give the most conservative opinion possible in order to be on the safe side. Librarians might be better advised in general to study the appropriate sections of the law and have the courage to make their own interpretations and decisions.

The vast majority of academic and public librarians have nothing to fear from the new copyright law. The amount and kind of copying that is done in their libraries will not require the payment of any significant amount of royalties, and the dollar amounts involved will be trivial to publishers and library users alike. I think that time and experience will show that the whole publisher-librarian controversy over copyright, interlibrary loan, and photocopying was the result of fear and misunderstanding--largely on the part of the publishers.

Resource sharing and networking give publishers nightmares and librarians hope, but both groups are seriously overestimating the impact these developments will have on their financial status and operations. Inflationary trends and market forces at work will soon change much of our current thinking about these matters.

Libraries are cutting their expenditures for books and journals because they do not have the acquisition funds, not because they are able to get them on interlibrary loan or from the Center for Research Libraries or the British Library Lending Division. Publishers still have the idea that if they can discourage interlibrary loan and photocopying, libraries will be forced to spend more money to buy books and journals. This is bunk. Libraries can't spend money they don't have. The fact is that with or without effective sharing mechanisms, with rising prices and declining support, libraries simply do not have the funds to maintain their previous acquisitions levels. If we cannot afford to buy the materials our users need, and if the law prohibits us from borrowing or photocopying what we do not own, our users will simply have to do without. Moreover, there is an increasing recognition that librarians and faculty members alike have developed highly exaggerated notions of the size, range, and depth of the library collections that are actually needed by most library users.

Studies have repeatedly shown that in general roughly 80 per cent of the demands on a library can be satisfied by 20 per cent of the collection. Journal use is a Bradford type distribution where a small number of journal titles account for a large percentage of the use. Eugene Garfield's numerous studies using citation analysis and the Institute for Scientific Information's Journal Citation Reports also corroborate it. A recent University of Pittsburgh Library School study showed that 44 per cent of the books acquired by one major research library in 1969 were never used in the succeeding five-year period. [6] A recent study at Penn produced a comparable finding. Earlier studies on library use by Fussler, [7] Trueswell, [8] and Buckland[9] showed similar use patterns.

Large collections confer status and prestige on librarians and faculty members alike, but when the budget crunch comes to a library, many of these status purchases will be foregone or dropped and the essentials will be maintained. Although we will rely on interlibrary loan or a National Lending Library to obtain these missing items when needed, they will rarely be called for, for they are rarely, if ever, used. [10] Libraries will continue to buy and stock as many of the high use books and journals as they can possibly afford.

It is also worth noting here that the word "research" is much overused to describe what professors do and what libraries support. This is another legacy of the affluent 1960s when there was seemingly no end to the increase in the numbers of Ph.D. candidates and professors in our universities and the wide variety of their research needs and interests. The economic decline in the 1970s is changing this attitude. Apart from those located at the major research-oriented universities, the primary mission of most academic libraries is or should be to support the instructional needs of their students and faculty. This function can be documented by a quote from the 1975 Ladd-Lipset survey of U.S. faculty members reported by the authors in an article entitled "How Professors Spend Their Time," which appeared in the Chronicle of Higher Education (Oct. 14, 1975, p. 2).

> The popular assumption has been that American academics are a body of scholars who do their research and then report their findings to the intellectual or scientific communities. Many faculty members behave in this fashion, but that overall description of the profession is seriously flawed.
> Most academics think of themselves as 'teachers' and 'intellectuals'--and they perform accordingly.
> Although data on the number of scholarly articles and academic books published each year testify that faculty members are producing a prodigious volume of printed words, this torrent is gushing forth from relatively few pens:
> --Over half of all full-time faculty members have never written or edited any sort of book alone or in collaboration with others.
> --More than one third have never published an article.
> --Half of the professoriate have not published anything, or had anything accepted for publication in the last two years.

--More than one quarter of all full-time academics
have never published a scholarly word.

They summarize as follows:

American academics constitute a teaching profession,
not a scholarly one. There is a small scholarly subgroup
located disproportionately at a small number of research-
oriented universities.

These conclusions about how faculty members spend their time
correlate well with what library statistics show about faculty use of
libraries--namely, that it is on the order of ten per cent of the total
and that much of it is for instructional purposes rather than research.

As for the publishers, they may make themselves feel better
by blaming journal cancellations and shrinking book orders on increasingly effective library resource sharing via systematic photocopying and interlibrary loan rather than on inflation and declining
library budgets, but they will be deceiving themselves.

Resource sharing will not seriously erode publishers' profits,
nor will it help libraries as much as they think. Interlibrary loan
will increase, but it will still continue to be a very small percentage
of total library use. The high cost of interlibrary loan and the needs
and demands of library users will not permit it to grow into something major. Its importance will always be as much in the capability for delivery as in the actual use of that capability. Like the Center for Research Libraries, it serves as an insurance policy. We
do not justify our annual membership fee in the center by the number
of items we borrow every year but by the fact that our membership
gives us access--if and when we need it--to several million research
items which might otherwise not be available to us.

In the long run, librarians cannot count on interlibrary loan
or their regional consortia or networks for the major economies they
will need to make to weather the hard times that are ahead. This
is as true for the many small college library consortia as it is for
the prestigious Research Libraries Group and the now defunct Five
Associated University Libraries cooperative. All too frequently, cooperation is merely a pooling of poverty. Many consortia members
are vulnerable because the magnitude of the cuts they will have to
make to counter inflation and declining support will far outweigh the
relatively minor savings regional cooperation will yield in the end.
In fact, like many automation projects, regional consortia may actually be costing their members far more than the benefits they derive if one includes the very substantial cost of staff time needed to
make them work. This cost will become more apparent when the
grant money that supports many consortia runs out.

Why can't consortia and resource sharing fulfill their promise?
Because they focus almost exclusively on reducing expenditures for
books and journals and only incidentally on reducing expenditures for

personnel. But in the end, any significant savings in library expenditures must come from eliminating positions, because that is where the money goes.

A typical large academic or public library spends 70-75 per cent of its budget for personnel and benefits, 20-25 per cent for books and journals, and only 5 per cent for other purposes. Thus, the amount of cost savings that can be made through resource sharing in any one year is necessarily only a small percentage of the book and journal budget. With these costs rising at the rate of 15 per cent a year, the savings will be largely absorbed by inflation.

The unpleasant fact is that we must eliminate positions if we are to make significant cost reductions to cope with inflation and no-growth budgets. To reduce staff will require a drastic curtailment of the intake of materials, reduced services, and increased productivity. There is no other way. Resource sharing is essential but it is not a panacea.

The cheap and easy victories come early in library cooperation, but what do we do that is cost effective after we have agreed to reciprocal borrowing privileges with our neighbors and saved a few positions by joining OCLC? What do we do for an encore after we have reduced our staff, journal subscriptions, and book acquisitions by five or ten per cent through cooperation, resource sharing, automation, and improved management? In the year 1975-76 inflation and declining support caused a 10 per cent decrease in the median number of volumes added to ARL libraries and a 5 per cent decrease in the number of staff employed.

Academic libraries are sharing the financial troubles of their parent institutions, and public libraries those of the local governments that support them. These troubles come from long-term economic, social, and demographic trends; they will probably get worse in the decade ahead. The troubles that publishers have are caused by rising costs and changing market conditions and not by library photocopying or deficiencies in the copyright law. These troubles will not be resolved by the collection of royalties on a few journal articles or the sale of a few more library subscriptions.

The library market is shrinking and hardening, and publishers--both commercial and scholarly--will have to accept that fact and make adjustments. Librarians will have to accept that the savings they make through networking, cooperation, and resource sharing in the next several years will be quickly absorbed by the continuing inflation in book and journal prices and rising personnel costs. Moreover, library budgetary support will continue to decline and the pressures to reduce expenditures will increase.

The fact is, libraries can no longer afford to maintain the collections, staffs, and service levels that librarians and users have come to expect in the last two decades. Libraries are experiencing a substantial loss in their standard of living as a result of inflation, increasing energy costs, and changing priorities in our society. We can rail against it and search for scapegoats, but it would be better if we came to terms with this painful reality and began to reduce our excessive commitments and expectations to match our declining resources.

The importance of resource sharing mechanisms, and particularly the most cost-effective ones--the centralized libraries' libraries, such as the Center for Research Libraries and the British Library Lending Division--is not so much that they will save us funds we can reallocate to other purposes, but that they will permit us to continue to have access to a large universe of materials we can no longer afford, spending our diminishing funds on the materials we need and use most. In sum, effective resource sharing will help ease the pain that will accompany the scaling-down of commitments and expectations we face in the years ahead.

Notes

1. Special Issue, ALA Washington Newsletter on the New Copyright Law, Nov. 15, 1976. (Reprinted and available from ALA Order Dept. for $2.)
2. For more on the need for a new attitude toward journals in libraries see: Richard De Gennaro, "Escalating Journal Prices: Time to Fight Back," American Libraries, February 1977, p. 68-74.
3. The eight titles which had five or more requests are American Orchid Society Bulletin, Harvard University, Botanical Museum, Cambridge; Fizika, Yugoslavia; Journal of Electroanalytical Chemistry, Elsevier Sequoia, Lausanne; Nukleonika, Polska Akad. Nauk, Ars Polona Ruch, Warsaw; Pramana, Indian Academy of Science, Bangalore; Revue Roumaine de Physique, Bucharest; Synthesis, George Thiene Verlag & Academic Press; and Worldview, Council on Religion and International Affairs, New York.
4. ARL Statistics, 1975-76. Washington, D.C.: Association of Research Libraries, 1976, p. 14.
5. Madeline Cohen Oakley. "The New Copyright Law: Implications for Libraries," Cornell University Libraries Bulletin, No. 202, October-December 1976, p. 5.
6. Stephen Bulick, and others. "Use of Library Materials in Terms of Age," Journal of the American Society for Information Science, May-June 1976, pp. 175-8.
7. Herman H. Fussler. Patterns in the Use of Books in Large Research Libraries. Chicago: Univ. of Chicago Press, 1969.
8. Richard W. Trueswell. "User Circulation Satisfaction vs. Size of Holdings at Three Academic Libraries," College & Research Libraries, May 1969, pp. 204-13.
9. Michael H. Buckland. Book Availability and the Library User. New York: Pergamon Press, 1975.
10. For a more extended discussion of these points see: Richard De Gennaro, "Austerity, Technology, and Resource Sharing: Research Libraries Face the Future," Library Journal, May 15, 1975, pp. 917-23.

ETHICAL STANDARDS IN PUBLISHING

By Daniel Melcher

One man's "ethic" may, of course, be another man's exploitation. I have heard many a bookseller decry "price-cutting" as unethical, but have never found anything against it in Consumer Reports. The college professor does not quite see why he should not Xerox sections of a copyrighted book without payment to the author--until he becomes an author. The Canadian distributor can give a hundred reasons why it is often necessary to put an $8 Canadian price on a book that sells in England for under $5, but many a prospect within "his" market area still feels fully justified in "buying around" when he can do so to advantage.

Now that the USA has become the world's most important source of translation rights and other kinds of literary property, we believe all countries should observe international copyright. However, we did not think so during the 19th century when we were happily helping ourselves to the works of British authors without payment.

Actually I think ethical standards in publishing will bear comparison with any other industry. Whether our ethics are higher, or perhaps our temptations lower, I am not altogether sure. Book publishers can concentrate on pleasing the reader, free of the need to also please advertisers. The publishing profession lacks the power over its members that is exercised by lawyers and doctors--but it also lacks the temptations that go with such power. Publishing is not yet bureaucratized as under civil service. The technology is still fairly simple: You can successfully go into publishing on a much smaller scale than into, say, television. Monopolies of the means of production and distribution have been weak and have not occurred naturally.

I suppose if I were out to do a muckraking report on the book industry, I could get a lot of mileage out of the recent Justice Department consent decrees under which a number of publishers agreed never to conspire to fix prices on school library books (without admitting they ever had); and out of the FTC files about various alleged abuses in the areas of encyclopedia selling, mail-order advertising, etc. But I think the responsible people in either the Justice Department or the FTC would be quick to say that the book publishing industry is pretty clean.

Reprinted with permission from Law Library Journal vol. 63, no. 1 (February 1970), pp. 123-128. Copyright © 1970 by the American Association of Law Libraries.

I am, of course, prejudiced. At least Marvin Scilken of the Orange Public Library thinks so. He thinks some publishers often times put "excessive" prices on their books. I agree. He favors regulation to limit this. I do not.

No doubt about it, this is an interesting area. Under present and contemplated copyright law, authors are given a legal monopoly on their writing for the express purpose of encouraging them to write. They are given, you might say, a legal license to price their literary property at whatever level they feel will bring them the maximum return. They are under no obligation to price their work for the widest possible distribution; they may, in fact, price it for an extremely limited sale. Is this just? When a public utility is granted a local monopoly, it expects some public surveillance of its rates. Should authors and publishers, operating as they do under publicly-granted monopoly rights in their literary property, come under similar surveillance as regards the "reasonableness" of their rates or service?

I believe I am stating fairly the point Scilken raises. And I may say that my conditioned reflexes, after a lifetime in book publishing, tell me that he just has not thought it through; he does not realize the extent to which even copyright books are vulnerable to competition, or how overpricing may reduce rather than increase net gains. I react to his point as I suspect many a lawyer reacts to "How to Avoid Probate." I say, "But this is the way things are; these are the ground rules under which we work."

All right. Let us suppose that typically an author and publisher intelligently follow the line of their own best self-interest and plan their pricing for maximum distribution--which also, happily, tends to be the best route to maximum gain. They bring out low-priced editions just as soon as the bloom is off the hardbound sales, they license translations into French, German, etc., etc. When, however, a publisher in India applies for the Punjabi language rights and offers a flat fee of $100 (less $50 in taxes, deducted at the source by the government of India), they turn him down. Question: Have they the right to turn him down?

Traditionally they do have that right, under either the Bern Convention or the Universal Copyright Convention, to which India is a party. As a matter of practical international relations, they probably do not have that right, because India, in advancing the so-called Stockholm Protocol, has made it clear that, if the "have" countries insist on asking what India regards as excessive payments for translation and other licenses, she may just authorize her nationals to take the property anyway, perhaps at a statutory fee. So Scilken is not alone; the government of India is also wondering whether the granting of copyright protection should not be contingent on a "reasonable" pricing policy.

In another small infringement of traditional rights, West Germany is experimenting with a legal requirement that a copyright owner <u>must</u> <u>answer</u> <u>his</u> <u>mail</u> or risk unauthorized (but legal) use of his literary property under statutory fees. The inquirer who seeks permission, but can not get a response, is given a remedy.

Are these problems of ethics?

They can be treated as if they were mere matters of commerce, but we would surely have been on stronger ground, both morally and commercially, if we had taken an earlier initiative in helping the Punjabi publisher rather than forcing him to get his government to move us through threat of withdrawal from full participation in international copyright.

The idea that the owner of a piece of literary property is under any <u>obligation</u> to correspond with would-be licensees or to quote them "reasonable" rates may seem strange by any analogy with other kinds of property, but then literary property <u>is</u> a strange kind of property.

One day I ran into Ronald Mansbridge, head of the New York office of the Cambridge University Press, who was troubled that some of the Cambridge titles were being picked up by American reprint publishers without authorization. He proposed that <u>Publishers Weekly</u> editorialize against it.

I was sympathetic. U.S. publishers have generally agreed with their British colleagues that the U.S. copyright law was unfair in its refusal of U.S. copyright protection to an English-language book not manufactured here. Other countries treated us better than we treated them. U.S. publishers have generally respected the British rights, even in books technically unprotected here. But I was also surprised. Because, whenever you find fairly wide observance of an "ethical standard," you usually find some more tangible support for it other than just good will. And there has always been basic <u>economic</u> reasons for observing that particular ethical standard--notably if you hoped to do business with the British publishers in other areas.

I said: "But, Ron, surely your edition is priced under the unauthorized one, so how could any reprinter sell any of his? After all <u>you</u> can sell both here and abroad and he can sell only here, so you can presumably make larger printings than his, and thus undersell him even after paying a royalty. Hasn't it always been that way?"

He said: "Well, our edition is out of print."

Well, well, and well! Must several hundred U.S. university libraries wait an unpredictable period for a possible Cambridge reprint, when there is a U.S. reprinter prepared to supply it now? And does it make any difference whether the original edition was unprotected in the U.S. on a technicality, or perhaps is even still in copyright? Does a copyright confer both the exclusive right to publish and also the right not to publish? And, if the latter, for how long?

Once a work has been "published" (i.e., made public, and, in a sense, dedicated to the public), does the public have any rights? Can it insist on the right to read? on the right to buy or make a reading copy? Can the author or publisher deny it this right? And to the extent to which these questions are answered in law or interpretation, are they answers that we want?

To a significant extent, the publishing ethic does say that there is some kind of obligation to keep a work in print. University presses sometimes reprint completely uneconomic quantities just to be able to keep a work available. In many author/publisher contracts, there is provision for the author to demand that the book be kept in print--or he may recapture the publishing rights. To an extent unparalleled in other industries, a publisher will generally accept and fill an order for a single copy of a single book (imagine a shirt manufacturer doing that!). It is perhaps a tribute to the special status we give to books, as extensions of the human mind, that we feel that an author's message, once made public, must remain accessible to the public. It was not always technically or economically possible to keep a book in print--but it is now possible to make reprints, even in quantities of one, and it will perhaps become a fairly universal practice (or ethic?) to make such arrangements, so that, in effect, no book will ever again go "out of print" in the sense of becoming unobtainable.

A practice that warrants clarification is that of deliberately reporting books "out of stock" when, in fact, they are really "out of print" in the sense that the publisher has no present intention or expectation of reprinting them. This clogs library ordering records by making it impossible to be sure whether a wanted work is temporarily or permanently unobtainable.

The problem is that, while any stock clerk can pronounce a title "out of stock," the decision to reprint or not to reprint has to be made higher up; and a decision not to reprint can be reversed at any time. In fact, with the recent rapid increase in the number of research collections anxious to round out their holdings of older books, it would be a bold publisher who felt able to say "This will not be reprinted, ever." Reporting a book as O.S. instead of O.P. is, therefore, both the easiest initial decision and the one that leaves the publisher with all his options.

A library's best strategy is probably to recognize that any book a publisher seriously intends to keep in print will (or at least should) be reported not just as "O.S." but as "O.S.--expected on such-and-such a date." A report of "O.S.--no date" inevitably implies either inefficiency (failure to exercise the foresight that would have anticipated the problem and enabled the stock clerk to make a more precise report) or indecision, i.e., doubt about the feasibility of reprinting.

The library that wants and needs a book that has been reported as "O.S.--no date" has a problem. It would be a great step
forward if publishers would, as a matter of course, indicate in their
trade order lists an authorized source for a Xeroxed facsimile of
both "O.P." and "O.S.--no date" books. It is sometimes argued
that the making of Xeroxed facsimiles will undercut the sales potential of any ultimate regular reprint; but, on the other hand, it can
also provide a mailing list of prospects who might like to replace
their Xeroxed facsimile with the real thing when it again becomes
available.

The question of "ethics" in publishing probably comes up
most often in:

The "hard sell" by encyclopedia salesmen;
An alleged trend toward emphasizing "profit" at the expense of
"quality";
Lack of candor on title and copyright pages;
Pre-censorship by overly timid publishers;
Questionable pricing and discounting practices.

It would be a great thing for society and for the more ethical
members of the industry if "hard sell" practices could be done away
with. Unfortunately, the "hard sell" will probably always be with us
as long as it pays. Without in any way intending to justify some of
the more dubious "hard sell" practices, as a practical matter, it is
the victims who must act if they are really to be curbed.

At the heart of the "sale" of an encyclopedia is (a) the need
to get into the home to make the sales presentation; and (b) the need
to get the prospect to sign on the dotted line, now, tonight. The old
reliable way to get into the home is to make the prospect believe
that he is going to get the encyclopedia free. Of course, there is
always a gimmick, such as showing "good faith" by signing up for
10 years' of updating material on which the price just happens to be
enough to cover the cost of the encyclopedia as well. The usual way
of keeping the prospect from saying that he will "think about it" is to
tell him that the terms--or certain extras--hold good only if he signs
now; later will be too late to get this once-in-a-lifetime bargain.

All this is clearly unethical--not only the usual double-talk
about "something for nothing," when clearly the amounts to be paid
must and do cover every item in the "package," but also the pretense
that the price quoted is "special," when in fact it is the standard one.

On the other hand, it is not necessarily a favor to a household,
or to the children in it, to urge them to take the same money to their
local bookstore, because, in point of hard fact, not one pater familias
in a hundred is going to do this. The practical choice in most house-
holds is probably between some books in the house and no books in
the house. If the money does not go into the encyclopedia (and the
dictionary, and the atlas, and the annuals), it very well may go into
whitewalls, tail fins, and completely superfluous extra horsepower in
the next family car (where the "hard sell" is equally rampant).

Librarians themselves are not necessarily immune to the blandishment of hard selling (albeit sweet-talking) salesmen. It pays to remember that the salesman's primary job is to increase his employer's share of your book money. He costs his employer from 12 to 20 per cent of what you pay. This cost may be recovered out of lowered printing and binding costs if the effect of his sales calls is to increase his employer's sales and thus permit larger printings to be made. However, if you buy more from him and, consequently, less from a publisher without a sales force, the ultimate effect of his activity will be to reduce the sales and increase the costs of the other publisher, which, in turn, could lead to an increase in the price of the other publisher's books or a reduction in the number of books he could accept for publication.

If one larger publisher gains an advantage through having his own direct-selling salesmen calling on libraries, then other large publishers must set up direct-selling library sales forces in self-defense, and other small publishers must perhaps share "commission men." And, in the end, a new balance will presumably be achieved with a new ingredient in the prices, namely, what the salesmen receive.

In defense of salesmen, it is often argued that they "create" new business--and "plus" business is highly profitable. But in the matter of book sales to libraries, do they really create new business or just fight over the division of the existing business? Is the sales interview a good method of book selection? In fact, what about the "ethics" of book selection by sales interview? Salesmen will be sent if librarians will see and buy from them. How many do librarians want to see? How many different sources do they want to buy from?

The ethics of library-wholesaler relations may also warrant some examination. Suppose a library has been giving all its business to wholesaler X and getting a basic discount of 36 per cent. Salesmen from publishers D, M, and R arrive soliciting direct orders and offering a bit more than 36 per cent.

Clearly if wholesaler X has quoted 36 per cent in the expectation of receiving all of a library's business, it is not quite cricket to place part of the library's business elsewhere. A bid that averaged together both the "creamy" business (e.g., books on which the number of copies per title is higher than average) and the skim-milk singles cannot be expected to hold if the "cream" goes elsewhere.

A good ethical standard for buyer/seller relationships is for the buyer to treat the seller with no less consideration than if the relationship were one of employer/employee. It goes without saying that the buyer/seller relation must be "arm's length," but this must not require "dumping" a supplier who has been giving satisfaction, in favor of any new source offering an extra percentage of discount.

In my opinion, a good way to protect all parties--the library,

the old supplier, and the would-be new supplier--would be a policy
of never giving a new and untried supplier more than a portion of
the library's business in any one contract period. The portion might
be one-third the first year, another third the second year. This
would help eliminate "feast or famine" problems for both bidders; it
would make possible a fair comparison of both discount and service;
it would protect the new man from the possibility of underestimating
his costs and losing his shirt; and, of course, the transition period
might enable the old supplier to rethink his discounts or service.
Firms too small to bid on all the library's business might, nevertheless, be able to bid on some of it.

Unethical practices sometimes surface in the form of offers
of unusually high discounts. Inasmuch as even the biggest wholesalers seldom buy better than at $5.40 for a book they will sell at
$6.40 (leaving a one-dollar spread, out of which to cover transpor-
tation, warehousing, picking and packing, billing, interest on money
tied up, and profit), it goes without saying that there has to be a
catch to any offer of discounts in the neighborhood of 50-off or more.
The books may be remainders; they may be special reprints or perhaps book club editions. They may even be worth what is asked.
But it can be considered certain that any supplier offering 50-off or
better is simply not offering the same "mix" as the supplier offering 30-37 per cent. It cannot be done.

One unethical practice is that of the low-bidder who then does
not deliver. Perhaps his competitor was prepared to take the sweet
with the sour and give the same basic discount whether he himself
got 43-off or 47-off. This fellow, however, instructs his buyers not
to touch anything not available at 46-off or better. He is simply always "out of stock" of anything on which he cannot get the kind of
discount he likes on the quantities in which he buys. I heard of a
case where a wholesaler always billed University Press books at 10
per cent off list (when he himself was getting full trade discounts),
for no better reason than that he found he could get away with it.
Any customer who complained was told that this wholesaler's definition of a "trade" book was one he stocked!

Monitoring a supplier's performance is not easy, but nothing
less is fair, either to the library or to the supplier's more conscientious competitors. One way to do it is to make a practice of
checking on the "unavailability" of any title by placing an order direct with the publisher. In some cases this will produce the book
through no fault of the wholesaler: he may have made an honest error; he may have been the victim of an honest error made by the
publisher; his stock order for 25 copies may have been refused because the publisher had only 7 copies; the publisher may actually
have been out of copies when the wholesaler ordered, but have received a reprint since; the publisher may even have reported the book
unavailable and then had some returns from a bookseller.

Anything can happen--but it should not happen too often!
Otherwise the supplier must be suspected of--well, inefficiency, at
least.

What can librarians do to throw their weight on the side of higher ethical standards in publishing? I think the first thing to note is that their views and their buying power do carry weight. They spend close to $500 million a year on books. They are almost the only market for some books and some publishers.

Two of the most potent weapons against overpricing are: (a) refusal to buy and (b) buying around.

I have a feeling that the "refusal to buy" could be invoked more often than it is. Somehow there ought to be some better response to a book that is overpriced, badly printed, and on inferior paper, than to say resignedly, "Well, we would be open to criticism if we did not have it. "

If you have been victimized by publishers who solicit your order, encumber your funds, and then don't publish when they promised, berate them if you like, but a far more effective defense is a rethinking of your internal encumbering procedures. Lots of libraries have worked out devices to avoid the paperwork, annoyance, and loss of funds from this source.

One reason some publishers "announce" a book even before they have really made the decision to publish it is to feel out the demand. They have learned that a probe in the form of "Would you buy this if we did publish it?" just does not produce many responses, apparently due to a belief on the part of many librarians that they cannot legally make a response that could be taken as "committing" funds as yet unappropriated. What is probably needed here is an "approved" wording understood by all parties to be uncommitting-- but still indicative. The result could be noticeably lower prices. I once took a gamble that a lower price on the latest 5-year cumulation of New Serial Titles ($37. 50, as I recall, vs. the customary $65. 00) would double the sale. It worked.

With just a little more arm-twisting, it should be possible to get enough publishers to specify acid-free book paper to ensure that all the book paper mills would change to the alkaline side. Happily, paper made with a neutral pH can apparently be made without cost penalties.

It is often asked whether the conglomerates that have been buying into publishing will not put an end to quality publishing by a hard-nosed insistence of "profit first. "

I can only say that I cannot get worried about it. Books just do not divide into the good ones on the one hand and the profitable ones on the other. If the big companies do not publish the "good" books, someone else will. Fortunately, good books do sell, unless you equate "good" with obscure or precious.

I will confess to a bit of apprehension over the possibility that the good books of the future may have progressively less chance of making the bestseller lists unless issued by one of the publishers with a big sales force, but even then a good book may get a second chance through paperback channels. Any company that tried to publish only conservative or noncontroversial books would, in my opinion, simply lose out in the marketplace. The "market" for such reading does not read.

The concept of copyright, seemingly simple, is actually an extraordinarily complex and fast-changing thing, seen vastly differently depending on whether you sit in Washington, Moscow, Formosa, or New Delhi; whether you are an author, publisher, educator, student, broadcaster, juke-box operator, or printer; and whether your concepts about copyrights were formed in the letterpress era, the offset era, or the Xerox era.

Many people still act as if the protection of rights of copyright owners lay in the copyright laws. It may be as valid to argue that past protection depended less on the law than on the difficulties of successful evasion. Where once it was a practical impossibility to make a single unauthorized copy of a book, it is now easy. Where once an infringer could expect prosecution, because if he was making any unauthorized copies he was making a thousand, now he can make so few it would hardly pay to try and call him to account.

Right now there are machines that can copy at costs as low as a cent a page. With such radically changed rules, there is bound to be a radically new ball game in which the defense of the copyright holder lies in making unauthorized copying unnecessary and unattractive rather than just illegal.

For example, a U.S. publisher cannot with impunity import an edition of a British book selling at 25 shillings ($3) over there and offer it at $10 here. His more knowledgeable prospects, who might not have baulked at a $5 U.S. price (which, less U.S. discount, might not be too far from the cost of buying in England), will, quite without compunction, buy around him rather than accept the $10 list price. In similar fashion, it can probably be expected that books priced in excess of 4 cents a page will be more freely "copied around" than books priced lower.

I do think a fair "ethical standard" involves respect for rights lost only through a technicality. In writing the so-called manufacturing clause into the U.S. copyright law, the Congress may have intended to help U.S. printers, but presumably did not intend to hurt foreign authors. In the same way, it seems only fair not to take advantage of an accidental failure to act in the 28th year of U.S. copyright to renew it for another 28 years. That renewal provision was . put in to help authors, not to hurt them.

On the other hand, it is surely going too far to suggest that royalty payments should be continued past the 56-year term of a U.S. copyright. If the Congress had intended to give authors longer protection than that, it would have done so. (The Mark Twain estate tried to claim royalties past the 56-year period on the ground that the pseudonym "Mark Twain" had been registered as a trademark. Ingenious, but in my opinion unethical.)

If these few probes into the ethics of publishing were being made under conditions where the floor could be thrown open to discussion, I should be tempted to conclude with just a few questions, such as the following:

What about the wholesaler who says, in effect, to a publisher: "Here is a library that has authorized me to send $1000 worth of books drawn from a list of $1500 worth. I plan to exclude yours unless you give me some extra discount."

When a publisher finds himself with 1,500 copies of a book selling 100 a year, should he (a) sell them all to a remainder house and declare it out of print; or (b) keep the book in print by keeping a five years' supply, despite the fact that for a time the book will be selling at two prices, the list price and the remainder merchant's price?

What of the publisher who just happens to omit the publication dates of his older books from his catalog? who presents a new printing as a new edition, even though the revisions are inconsequential? who presents a portion of an earlier work without sufficient identification of its source to enable a library to determine whether it already owns the material?

Is it ethical for a subsidized book to appear without clear warning to the reader as to the source of the subsidy?

To what extent is it a proper function of a tax-supported public library to satisfy all demands upon it for novels like The Love Machine? Has our society outgrown the need to assume that anyone cannot afford to read Jacqueline Susann without public subsidy? Could we perhaps better think of the library's function as that of making available what is not in every bookstall?

Does an ethical publisher produce a biology text that skirts the subject of evolution? or offer a "consulting fee" to a school superintendent for his advice on how to make a basic reading textbook more acceptable to his school system?

ZERO GROWTH FOR THE COLLEGE LIBRARY

By Daniel Gore

> All the rivers run into the sea; yet the sea is not full.
> --Ecclesiastes 1:7

When Abraham Lincoln was asked how long a man's legs should be, he replied, "Long enough to reach the ground."

One feels comfortable with such an answer: it makes sense, it conforms to reality, it offers no strain on the imagination.

When one asks a librarian how large a library should be, the invariable answer is, "Larger. And with provision for further expansion 15 years hence."

One used to feel comfortable with that answer too, because it made sense of a sort (at least to academicians, who intuitively know there is no such thing as enough books), and it certainly conformed to the only reality we have known since the foundation of the Alexandrian Library 2,300 years ago. Libraries have always grown until fire, flood or fighting put an end to them.

But lately the answer has begun to weigh upon the imagination, at least of those who pause to reflect upon the consequences of the observed geometric growth rate in academic libraries in the 20th century.

For several decades now academic library collections have been doubling every 15 years or so. University libraries that held several hundred thousand volumes in the 1930's hold several million today, and at that rate many of them would become, in just 50 more years, about the size of the Library of Congress today--a library of such gargantuan dimensions it calls upon the resources of a whole nation to sustain it.

The budgets of some present-day university libraries exceed the total institutional budgets of some small colleges. Yet some of those colleges have libraries whose growth rates will, if maintained over the next 50 years, bring them up to multimillion volume levels of the great university libraries.

Is anyone prepared to believe that the nation will ever sup-

Reprinted from the August/September 1974 issue of College Management Magazine, by permission of the publisher. Copyright © 1974 by Macmillan Professional Magazines, Inc. All rights reserved.

port a hundred university libraries the size of today's Library of Congress, whose annual budget is approaching $100 million?

Or that colleges 50 years hence will be able to devote to their libraries the constant-dollar equivalent of their current total institutional budget?

The imagination collapses under so ponderous a prospect, and one turns away from this problem, as from so many others, with the soothing conviction that the next generation will surely solve it-- especially since they will have the benefit of four times as many books as we have today to guide them in their thinking.

A dilemma arises here, for the library buildings we have today just will not hold four times their present content, and the money will not be available to expand them. During the last decade more than $1 billion worth of new academic library buildings were constructed in the U.S., and paid for mainly with federal money. But in a few years most of those buildings will be filled to capacity, as will their associated storage facilities, and relatively little federal or other funding is in sight to provide the usual remedy of more space. So the problem of coping with the geometric growth of academic libraries just will not wait for the next generation to solve it. We will have to solve it for them.

One solution that has been tried, and proved a failure, is miniaturization, through microfilming or computer storage, or any other technique. While certain results are achieved by those measures--for example vast and probably useless expansion of total resources, and reduction of data-retrieval times--they contribute nothing to the solution of the physical growth problem. The highest growth rates in the history of academic libraries have occurred precisely during the 30-year period when microtechnology was on the ascendant. That microtechnology has had no effect on the space problem is partially accounted for by the fact that librarians typically acquire publications in microformat only when, for whatever reason, they cannot or will not acquire them on paper. Microform collections have thus generally developed not as substitutes for something bulkier, but as collections that simply would not have existed in any form had they not been available in microform.

Determining Ideal Size

The solution to the growth problem will be found, I believe, not in the development of new technology to shore up the cracking foundations of the ever-climbing Tower of Babel, but in thinking about that most perplexing question, "How large should a library be?"

Such answers as have been given fall into three categories. First there is the heroic-impulsive, or Alexandrian answer, so called because it arose with the formation of the Alexandrian Library in 300 B.C., almost coincidentally with the origin of the peculiarly Western attitude that bigger means better, and that limits are inherently bad. The Alexandrian answer is simply that the library should acquire everything and keep it forever, lest something of inestimable value perish from the earth through negligence or misvaluation. The Alexandrian librarians are said to have collected hundreds of thousands of scrolls while that library existed. But despite their heroic efforts, and those of all succeeding generations of librarians, only 500 titles from classical antiquity have survived.

More recently there is the philosophical answer, which stipulates that an academic library should be large enough to hold whatever books are needed to support the curriculum, to support research where graduate programs are conducted, and to permit some "recreational reading." The philosophical answer has the merit of plausibility, but gives no clue as to the actual size of the library beyond the relative indication that a larger library will be required to support a "larger" curriculum. The philosophical answer avoids any forthright mention of what will happen to the collection if, say, a segment of the curriculum is simply dropped, or course content is updated in such a way that much of the existing collection proves to be either irrelevant or erroneous. By default, it amounts to agreeing that an academic library shall always be larger.

Finally there is the scientific answer, which has the virtue of providing exact numbers of volumes required, by means of a formula based on such variables as enrollment, size of faculty, number of graduate fields, etc. The principal value of the scientific answer is that it may favorably impress a fiscal officer who is not disposed to pry too deeply into your bedrock scientific formula, and discover that the whole thing miraculously floats upon a bottomless swamp of pure impressionism. It should be noted that the scientific answer applies only to questions of "How small may a library properly be?" It is calculated to frighten administrators into believing their library is too small, and is thus couched exclusively in terms of minimums. It resolutely ignores the question "How large should a library be?" as its proponents assume that anyone in his right mind knows a library should be just as big as it possibly can be, and always growing bigger.

The Alexandrian, the philosophical, and the scientific approach to libraries all require that they always grow larger, world without end. So potent and pervasive is this trinity, one would not dare speak out against it unless its ultimate outcome was manifestly absurd. Now that race car drivers are publicly declaring that speed limits are needed on the Indy 500, it may be permissible for a librarian to propose that size limits are needed for libraries.

What Is a Library for?

If we put aside our Alexandrian prejudices for a moment, and ask what is the main function of an academic library, rather than how large it should be, I think we will get general agreement that its primary function is to provide books for readers who want to read them now. (No suggestion is intended that academic libraries have no proper archival, or preservational role. Undoubtedly they do, but the proportion of their holdings devoted to that function is insignificant in relation to the space problem.) Though we may fret ourselves in a high-minded way about the imagined needs of our patrons in the 21st century, the needs we must actually fill are those of the student standing on the other side of the circulation desk.

When we suspend the perplexing question of collection size and ask instead questions about performance rates in relation to necessary functions, some unexpected results ensue, one of them being that by making your collection smaller you can actually provide more and better service.

Let us first ask what is an acceptable performance rate with regard to recorded holdings. To an Alexandrian the required rate is 100%--that is, the library should own, and the catalog record, every book that every patron, present or future, may ever ask for. To achieve that ideal rate you will have to own some 50,000,000 books, and add about 400,000 new ones every year, plus 300,000 new serial volumes.

If you will agree to a rate less than 100%, some surprising things happen. Several years ago the Yale Library discovered it owned about 90% of the books its patrons wanted to see, yet it owned only 2,500,000 titles, or 5% of the total that might be asked for. By falling off the Alexandrian ideal by a mere 10%, the Yale Library could forego the purchase of 47,500,000 books--and the construction of a building twice the size of the Empire State to hold them.

Consider now another measure of library performance: the availability rate, by which I mean the rate of success in finding on the shelves a book you want that the catalog says the library owns. Recent inquiries into this phenomenon indicate that an availability rate around 50% may be the norm. Assume now that you can find entries in the catalog for 90% of the books you want to see, and that you will find 50% of those actually on the shelves. The new result is a performance rate of 45%, which is dismal, but not because the library is too small. The cause lies elsewhere, and the remedy is not to add more titles.

Supply and Demand

During the 1960's R. W. Trueswell, now Chairman of the Industrial Engineering Department at the University of Massachusetts, published a series of statistical studies of library inventory phenomena, showing that a very small proportion of an academic library's collection accounts for nearly all the use. He makes the intriguing suggestion that 40% of a collection may account for 99% of the recorded use; and, if that be so, then at least half the collection may be removed without perceptibly affecting the availability of books that people will actually read. Trueswell's predictions so offend the Alexandrian temperament, they have met with the most devastating possible response from the library profession: they have been ignored.

Corollary to the proposition that most books in a large library are rarely or never used is the proposition that a small percentage of books are always in very heavy demand, and thus frequently unavailable when you want to borrow them. Hence in most libraries you are likely to fail nearly half the time to find the book you want, though the library owns it. The demand is too heavy for the supply, and libraries usually give no systematic attention to the problem. One library that did--the University of Lancaster's--discovered that when measures were taken to improve the availability rate from 60% to 86%, by shortening the loan period of high-demand books, the per capita use rate more than doubled. Had they instead doubled the number of titles in the collection, the availability rate would have been imperceptibly affected.

At the moment one can find very little data to answer these three essential questions regarding an academic library's performance:

What percentage of books wanted by patrons are recorded in the catalog? (The Holdings Rate)
What pecentage of wanted books recorded in the catalog are available on the shelves? (The Availability Rate)
What percentage of all books a patron wants are available to him on the shelves? (The Performance Rate: Holdings Rate times Availability Rate)

From the patron's standpoint the third question is the one that really matters, and the librarian's problem is to decide what combination of Holdings Rate and Availability Rate will yield the best results with the available resources.

Though scant, data now available on these matters are sufficient to make it worthwhile for any library to begin testing certain hypotheses aimed at improving Performance Rates while reducing collection size. I will present an illustration here to show what is realistically possible, using estimates which, though they certainly will not apply exactly to any one library's situation, should prove close enough to suggest a suitable point of departure.

Assume a university library with the following characteristics:

Collection size	1,000,000 vols.
Current additions	50,000 vols/yr.
Enrollment	20,000 students
Holdings Rate	90%
Availability Rate	50%
Performance Rate	45%

The Performance Rate in this library is quite poor, but probably typical of such libraries. A decision is made to improve it, by going the traditional route of adding to the holdings. Consider now the result that will be obtained by the most extreme imaginable application of the Alexandrian ideal: by some miracle you create a library holding every book under the sun, and add to it everything that is published everywhere, as it comes off the press. Your library now holds 50 million volumes, and each year you add 700,000 new ones. Your Holdings Rate climbs to 100%, but your Availability Rate remains 50%, for you have done nothing to affect it. The Performance Rate (the product of Holdings Rate and Availability Rate) thus moves up from 45% to 50%. Though you have spent two billion dollars on the project, your patrons perceive things to be far worse than they were before--because they now have to walk ten times as far in order to suffer about the same number of disappointments as before.

The tenure of university librarians over the last 15 years parallels in brevity that of university presidents, because they sought to improve Performances Rates by zealously attending to Holdings Rates, while ignoring the availability problem. Nothing really happened, except that their libraries got bigger, and they got another job.

Fewer Books Better Used

Keeping in mind the Trueswell predictions regarding collection size and performance rates, and the University of Lancaster's experience with availability rates, let us now consider how we may radically improve performance rates by cutting collection size.

Using Trueswell's simple statistical criterion for predicting which books in the collection will receive little or no use in the future, we remove 500,000 of them at one fell swoop. The Holdings Rate now drops from 90% to 85%. Why so little? Because the Holdings Rate applies to books that people will want to read, and you have statistically contrived to leave practically all of those books in the library.

At the same time, by statistical methods we identify those books whose predictable demand is so great that one or more added copies will be needed to achieve a certain predictable Availability Rate. By computer simulation we determine that 100,000 added copies will bring the Availability Rate to 95%, which is the best we can afford.

We have now a collection of 600,000 volumes, a Holdings Rate of 85%, and an Availability Rate of 95%. Although the collection has been reduced by 40%, the Performance Rate has climbed from a dismal 45% to a sterling 81%. Though the library has shrunk in size, everyone miraculously perceives that it has grown enormously--because suddenly, for the first time, patrons find books when they want them. Per capita use rates will probably double, while collection maintenance costs plummet.

And the new building that was going to be needed five years hence will never be needed, because the number of volumes required to maintain any specified Performance Rate will remain constant (assuming enrollment does) as the years go by. While the titles held by the library will change from year to year, as patron demand shifts from one book to another, the total number of volumes remains constant. The intake rate of new volumes may be any figure you like (or can afford), because the outflow rate will exactly equal it, if you are firm in your resolve not to attempt minor improvements in your Holdings Rate by vastly expanding the number of different books in your collection.

The Alexandrians will be tragically depressed by all this, and curse you both loud and deep for your rampant philistinism. But even they will make the astounding discovery that the books they actually want to read are, as if by magic, suddenly available when they wish to read them. As the opportunities multiply for them actually to read the books they have always wanted to, but never could because the library was so big, their lifelong frustrations with the library will diminish, and eventually they may forget what a wicked trick you played on them.

Cost Effectiveness

Collection maintenance costs do not usually show up in an academic library's budget, but they are there all the same. They consist of such things as lighting, heating, cooling, janitorial service, and the capital and depreciation costs of real estate. Assuming standard stack capacity of 15 volumes per square foot, average annual maintenance costs are about 20¢ per volume. Total maintenance costs, of course, grow exponentially as long as the collection does. A million-volume library today has annual collection maintenance costs of $200,000. If the collection doubles every 15 years, those costs will climb, in 45 years, to $1,600,000 per year.

With what you save in maintenance costs by creating a no-growth collection, you can easily afford a full-scale, rapid-delivery interloan service, to keep your effective Holdings Rate even higher than it was with an exponentially growing collection. You can even buy a Gutenberg Bible every year with a portion of the savings left over, or a Shakespeare First Folio if there are no sellers of the Bible that year. That should convince the Alexandrians that you are not a Philistine after all, but a person of discriminating judgment who prefers to spend his money on things of permanent value--things you just cannot get from anybody on interloan.

What to do with the half million volumes you discarded and the 50,000 per year you will discard hereafter? Regional and national storage centers are the obvious answer, since they can, by eliminating multiple copies of discards that will flow in from many libraries, cut aggregate storage space requirements by 90% or more.

All multiples of more than two or three (or whatever figure turns out to be operationally prudent) will be pulped, so new books can be made without laying forests waste.

"Unto the place from whence the rivers come, thither they return again." That is why, according to Ecclesiastes, the sea is never full. And that is why, once your library has reached a certain size, it need never be full again. How large should that library be? Large enough to satisfy a Performance Rate that is substantially better than what you now have, but always less than 100%, which nobody can afford.

When that size is reached, based on your own judgment of what is a satisfactory Performance Rate, you have a no-growth collection, and the means for keeping it. Your head and your bookstacks are out of the clouds, and your feet have reached the ground.

MEDICAL INFORMATION TABOOS

By John Berry

The taboos connected with the provision of legal and medical information to the general public have been around librarianship for a long time. Many of the basic reference courses in our library schools still teach that fields like law and medicine are super-sensitive, and that any public information service in these fields ought to be handled with extreme caution. Most public libraries, as well as most special libraries in hospitals, courts, law firms, or professional schools in these fields, have decided, as a matter of policy, that information service to the general public ought to be severely restrained, if it is provided at all.

At a recent meeting of the New York Regional Group of the Medical Library Association, we advocated abandoning these traditional taboos that restrain information service in medicine. While we were impressed with the large number of medical librarians who were reaching out to nearby public libraries with information service, we were also assaulted by some of those present who were afraid of the risks they would take if they provided such services. Many claimed that giving medical information to a general public would place them in legal jeopardy. Some librarians said they would be subject to criminal penalties for such crimes as "practicing without a license" or "malpractice." More important, a great many of these librarians felt that most citizens were insufficiently educated or knowledgeable to properly handle full disclosure of information about their illnesses, or the potential emotional strain caused by it. There was agreement that most librarians were incompetent to provide the kinds of medical and legal information most often requested.

While there are some good reasons for restraint, since it is not the role of librarians to second-guess lawyers or doctors, it is important to avoid over-reaction. We must be sure that in our fear, we don't over-proscribe or censor such information from our collections or our publics. Although the line between information provision and "practicing without a license" may be ill-defined, we have tended, traditionally, to be so cautious that the average citizen is rarely able to get any useful legal or medical information from us.

Those taboos still exist, but there are heartening signs of change. For the past several years we've heard an increasing number of reports of cooperative arrangements among specialized libra-

Reprinted from Library Journal January 1, 1978. Published by R. R. Bowker Company, a Xerox company. Copyright © 1978 by Xerox Corporation.

ries in law and medicine and nearby public libraries. Many public libraries have acquired and are providing pre-packaged legal and medical services, usually such things as taped messages by telephone, that provide certain highly proscribed information. There are even stronger programs in medical information now.

One of the more interesting experiments at medical-public library cooperation is the Community Health Information Network (CHIN) which links the Health Sciences Library at Mount Auburn Hospital in Cambridge, Massachusetts with the public libraries of nearby Arlington, Belmont, Cambridge, Lexington, Somerville, and Watertown (see LJ, December 15, 1977, p. 2464). A three-year, $150,000 grant from the National Library of Medicine plus a $19,312 LSCA Title III grant awarded to CHIN by the Massachusetts Bureau of Library Extension will be used to finance access to CHIN by community-based health professionals and "increase the availability of health information resources for consumers. "

CHIN's first priority will be to strengthen and simplify interlibrary lending among the libraries. Collection development is underway, and each public library in the network will build a basic collection in medicine and health, including some of the basic indexing tools in the field. The project also includes inservice training for reference librarians from the libraries. Questions from the public are already being answered.

We asked Ellen Gartenfeld, the enthusiastic Health Services Librarian who serves as CHIN coordinator about the taboos: "As long as librarians don't pretend to be doctors, there's really no problem for them ... I don't apply any other cautions... " she said, and continued, "You know, we're not providing 'do-it-yourself' medicine; we're supporting people in their interaction with their health professionals. " We asked her about librarian competence and she replied: "The time has come for librarians to develop these skills and provide this service. If we don't someone else will, and we'll have allowed another of our responsibilities to go to some other kind of new 'information professional. '"

Ellen Gartenfeld is right! We hope CHIN will be highly successful. It, and projects like it, are major steps forward in an information service area where taboos have reigned for much too long.

RECOMMENDED READINGS

From an extensive literature, the following have been selected to provide further reading on the issues highlighted by the articles selected for this chapter.

Concerned with the impact of new technology is the article, "Today Is Tomorrow: A Look at the Future Information Area, " by Louis Vagianos in Library Journal, 101, no. 1 (January 1, 1976), pages 147-156. He examines the whole range of possibilities and problems posed by computers, long distance telecommunication, cable television, etc., and ends with a discussion of information management and its implications for library service.

The discussion of payment for library information services by Fay Blake and Edith Perlmutter in this collection generated responses in the "Letters" section of Library Journal, 99, no. 5 (March 1, 1974), pages 593-594. Assessing the probable effects of user charges on library service, as they see them, and considering the possible alternatives, Blake and Perlmutter make an additional contribution to the discussion in "The Rush to User Fees: Alternative Proposals, " Library Journal, 102, no. 17 (October 1, 1977), pages 2005-2008. In response, in the "Letters" section of Library Journal, 103, no. 2 (January 15, 1978), page 114, a writer contests their arguments and accuses them of simplistic solutions.

The objectives of the National Commission on Libraries and Information Science (NCLIS) in regard to a national plan for the provision of library and information services are outlined by Alphonse F. Trezza in "The NCLIS View--A Full-Service Network, " Journal of Library Automation, 10, no. 2 (June, 1977), pages 170-176. The concept of a network capable of providing all kinds of information, transmitted in a variety of ways, to different types of patrons, among all types of libraries, is described and envisioned by the author.

Related to the idea of interlibrary cooperation is a study made by Ellen Altman and reported in the article, "Implications of Title Diversity and Collection Overlap for Interlibrary Loan Among Secondary Schools, " The Library Quarterly, 42, no. 2 (April, 1972), pages 177-194. The feasibility of establishing interlibrary loan systems among secondary schools was explored, with results that indicated potential large benefits in expanding the resources of the individual school.

For a thorough and balanced explanation of the copyright system, "Copyright Developments in the United States" by John C. Stedman is recommended. Appearing in the AAUP Bulletin, v. 62, no. 3 (Autumn, 1976), pages 308-319, this article includes underlying premises of copyright, a history of the copyright revision bill, a consideration of the controversial issues, and discussion of some of the specific provisions. An examination of the copyright revision bill from the publisher's point of view is provided by Sanford G. Thatcher in "Publisher's Guide to the New U.S. Copyright Law," Scholarly Publishing, 8 (July, 1977), pages 315-333.

In his article, "The Free Mind: Intellectual Freedom's Perils and Prospects," Library Journal, 101, no. 1 (Jan., 1976), pages 237-242, Eli Oboler considers the threat to intellectual freedom represented by the information industry and the control of intellectual property in the copyright legislation.

The question of the amount of use made of a library collection was the subject of research conducted at the University of Pittsburgh. Thomas J. Galvin and Allen Kent reported on the study in "Use of a University Library Collection: A Progress Report on a Pittsburgh Study," in Library Journal, v. 102, no. 20 (November 15, 1977), pages 2317-2320. They project plans for developing a tool to assess possible use of selected items.

"Limiting College Library Growth: Bane or Boon?" by Evan Ira Farber, Journal of Academic Librarianship, v. 1, no. 5 (Nov., 1975), pages 12-15, explores several alternatives for coping with space problems, more limited budgets, and continuing pressures for acquisitions. The differences in purpose between a university and a college library are pointed out, with the conclusion made that limiting the size of the college library collection could permit the librarians to devote resources and energies to developing a library program especially tailored to their constituency.

BIOGRAPHICAL SKETCHES OF CONTRIBUTORS

MARILYN ABEL is marketing director for Penguin Books. She has previously been affiliated with the American Booksellers Association, Wayne State University Press and the New American Library.

LESTER ASHEIM holds the position of William Rand Kenan, Jr. Professor of Library Science at the University of North Carolina-Chapel Hill. He has held numerous library positions, been active in professional associations and written extensively in the field of library science.

HERBERT S. BAILEY, JR. is director of the Princeton University Press, a position he has held since 1954. An active member of the Association of American University Presses and the American Book Publishers Council, he has been an officer of both professional groups.

JOHN BERRY III has been editor-in-chief of Library Journal since 1969. Earlier in his career he was an academic librarian, served as managing editor of the New Books Project at R. R. Bowker, and handled other editorial responsibilities with Library Journal.

FAY BLAKE is a lecturer at the School of Library and Information Studies, University of California at Berkeley. She has had academic library experience and has worked with the New York State Education Department as an associate in academic and research libraries.

HARALD BOHNE was associate director of the University of Toronto Press at the time he wrote the included article.

CALVIN J. BOYER is currently director of the University of Mississippi Libraries in University, Mississippi. Previously he held academic library positions in acquisitions and administration.

ROBERT N. BROADUS is a professor at the University of North Carolina-Chapel Hill School of Library Science. Formerly with the library science faculty at Northern Illinois University, DeKalb, Illinois, he has held several academic library positions.

JANE CAMERON was a trustee of the Birmingham, Michigan Public Library from 1965 to 1977. Appointed to the Michigan State Board for Libraries in 1974, she is chairman of that board.

ANN CRITTENDEN in 1977 won the Newspaper Guild's Page 1 Award.

CHARLES E. CURRENT is department chairman for Learning Resources Center, Indian Hills Community College, Ottumwa, Iowa. Previously, he had been a college librarian/teacher and a library science/media instructor. Active in AECT, he has also been president of the Nebraska Educational Media Association.

FRANCES C. DEAN is director of the Division of Instructional Materials, Montgomery County (Maryland) Public Schools. She served as president of the American Association of School Librarians in 1977-78, is a member of the Board of Trustees of the Freedom to Read Foundation, and is chairperson of the A. L. A. Intellectual Freedom Committee.

RICHARD DE GENNARO is director of the University of Pennsylvania Libraries. He is on A. L. A. 's White House Conference Planning Committee and has held numerous academic library positions and offices in professional associations.

MARGARET DOBBYN was a social science librarian at Kansas State University Library, Manhattan, Kansas, when she wrote the included article.

ROBERT B. DOWNS is Dean Emeritus of Library Administration at the University of Illinois. During his career he held numerous positions in public, college, and university libraries, was an advisor to universities and governments of several foreign countries, and was president of A. L. A. during 1952-53.

LOLLY EGGERS has been director of the Iowa City Public Library since 1975. She previously held other positions with that library.

ELAINE FAIN is an assistant professor at the University of Wisconsin at Milwaukee School of Library Science. She has worked in various special and academic libraries.

RALPH FERRAGAMO held the position of National Accounts and Training Manager with Xerox University Microfilms at the time he was joint author of the included article.

CAROLYN W. FIELD is coordinator, Work with Children of the Free Library of Philadelphia, a position she has held since 1953. Active in professional associations, Mrs. Field served as president of the Children's Services Division of A. L. A. in 1959-60.

LEO N. FLANAGAN is currently a freelance writer pursuing doctoral studies. He has had experience in the public library area.

RALPH J. FOLCARELLI is a professor of Library Science at Palmer Graduate Library School, Long Island University. Prior to faculty service, he held school and academic library positions.

RICHARD K. GARDNER is a professor at the Graduate School of Library and Information Science, University of California at Los Angeles. A former editor of Choice, he has held academic library positions in the U.S. and abroad, and has served as an advisor on library service to foreign governments.

MARY VIRGINIA GAVER, the original editor of this work, is Professor Emeritus of the Graduate School of Library Service, Rutgers University. She held various library positions and offices in professional associations, including the presidency of A.L.A. in 1966-67. She is a consultant for the Bro-Dart Foundation.

LILLIAN N. GERHARDT is editor-in-chief of School Library Journal. She served as president of the Association of Library Service to Children, A.L.A., in 1978-79. She has held editorial positions with Kirkus Services and School Library Journal. She has been a reference librarian and a children's library consultant.

BARBARA GOLDEN was with the Gene Eppley Library, University of Nebraska at Omaha at the time she wrote the included article.

DANIEL GORE is library director of Macalester College, St. Paul, Minnesota. He has been an academic librarian and cataloger, coordinated public services in various institutions, and is a frequent contributor to the library science literature.

RUTH GREGORY was head librarian at the Waukegan, Illinois Public Library when she wrote the included article. She has held various public library positions and elective and editorial offices with A.L.A. and other associations. She served as president of the Illinois Library Association in 1947-48.

EDWARD J. HINGERS is audiovisual consultant for the Nassau Library System, Garden City, New York.

FRANK HOFFMAN was on the staff of the Area Resource Center, Memphis Public Library and Information Center, Tennessee when he wrote the included article.

EDWARD G. HOLLEY is dean of the School of Library Science at the University of North Carolina-Chapel Hill. Prior to his service in library education, he held various academic library positions. He served as president of A.L.A. in 1974-75. As chairperson of A.L.A.'s Legislative Committee, he helped uphold library interests in the 1976 copyright act.

GEORGE M. JENKS is university librarian at Bucknell University, Lewisburg, Pennsylvania. He previously held various public and academic library positions.

MARY FRANCES K. JOHNSON is a professor at the School of Library Science at the University of North Carolina-Greensboro. She held various school library positions, and prior to entering library educa-

tion was director of the School Library Development Project of
A.L.A. in 1961-62.

EMILY JONES has been involved in the film world as a producer,
consultant, and lecturer since the early 1940's. She served as the
administrative director of Educational Film Library Association and
as editor of Sightlines.

JUDITH KRUG is director of the A.L.A. Office for Intellectual Freedom and executive director of the Freedom to Read Foundation.
Mrs. Krug has also worked as a reference librarian, cataloger, and
research analyst. In the summer of 1978 she received the Robert
B. Downs Intellectual Freedom Award (University of Illinois) in recognition of her contributions to intellectual freedom and the cause of
individual rights.

PHYLLIS LEVY (now Mandell) has been editor of Previews since
1972. Her career has been primarily in publishing. She has also
been a freelance editor and researcher.

WELLINGTON H. LEWIS is the assistant public printer (planning)
for the Superintendent of Documents. He joined the Government
Printing Office in 1970 and held various positions before assuming
his present one in 1975.

JAMES L. LIMBACHER is audio-visual librarian at the Henry Ford
Centenniel Library, Dearborn, Michigan. He has been active in
film library associations, was president of the American Federation
of Film Societies and of the Educational Film Library Association.
He has written extensively in this field.

LINDA MAHAN was a graduate research assistant at the University
of Illinois when she co-authored the included article.

PHYLLIS MANDELL see PHYLLIS LEVY

ALLIE BETH MARTIN was active in public library service for many
years, serving in a variety of positions, including that of director
of the Tulsa, Oklahoma City-County Library. She was active in library associations at both state and national levels, and served as
president of A.L.A. in 1975-76.

DANIEL MELCHER held various positions in the publishing world
since 1934, including several years with R. R. Bowker as general
manager, vice-president, and president. He wrote and lectured extensively, and was active in A.L.A.

LEROY CHARLES MERRITT was dean of the School of Librarianship
at the University of Oregon. Prior to that he held various library
positions and served on the faculty of the School of Librarianship at
the University of California-Berkeley. He was president of the
American Association of Library Schools in 1966 and editor of the
A.L.A. Newsletter on Intellectual Freedom from 1962-1970. His

concern for intellectual freedom was recognized by the establishment of the A. L. A. sponsored Leroy C. Merritt Humanitarian Fund.

KATHLEEN MOLZ is a professor at the Columbia University School of Library Service. From 1969 to 1974 she was chief of planning in the Bureau of Libraries and Educational Technology, U. S. Office of Education. Previously she held public library positions and edited Wilson Library Bulletin. She served as the 1978-79 president of the Freedom to Read Foundation's Board of Trustees.

TINA NOVASEDA was assistant editor of Previews at the time she wrote the included editorial. Currently she is a producer of audio-visual materials.

NAMU OLAOLORUM ORDERINDE (pseudonym for HOWARD G. BALL) is a professor and dean of the School of Library Media at Alabama A & M University. Previously he was a classroom teacher, public school administrator, consultant for the Ohio Department of Education, and held teaching and administrative positions in higher education.

EDITH PERLMUTTER is a faculty member at the Department of Economics, Loyola Marymount University, Los Angeles, California.

ELEANOR PHINNEY was a research specialist at Rutgers University and at A. L. A. She held executive secretary positions with A. L. A.'s Adult Services Division and the Association of Hospital and Institution Libraries.

HAROLD ROTH is director of the Nassau County Research Library in Garden City, New York. He has had a varied career with service in public libraries, as an education editor with the New York Times, and with the Baker and Taylor Company.

JEAN RUSTICI is an early childhood consultant with the Connecticut State Department of Education.

THOMAS M. SCHMID is acquisitions librarian for Marriott Library, University of Utah.

RITA JAMES SIMON is head of the Department of Sociology and a professor in the University of Illinois' Institute of Communications Research. Her career has been devoted to research and teaching in sociology.

DORIS SNYDER (now STEPHENSON) was a student at the University of Oklahoma's School of Library Science at the time she wrote the included article. She has worked in public and seminary libraries.

DIANA L. SPIRT is a contributing editor to Previews and is a professor at Palmer Graduate Library School, Long Island University. She has worked in public school libraries and has written extensively in the field of library science.

DORIS STEPHENSON see DORIS SNYDER

LESTER STOFFEL is director of the Suburban Library System, Burr Ridge, Illinois. Previously he held various public library positions and served as president of the Pennsylvania and Illinois Library Associations.

ZENA BAILEY SUTHERLAND is editor of the Bulletin of the Center for Children's Books and lecturer at the Graduate Library School of the University of Chicago. This article was taken from her keynote speech for Book Discussion Day sponsored by the Velma Varner Memorial Fund at Columbia University's School of Library Services on December 14, 1974.

LINDA WARD was collections librarian for music at the University of Western Ontario when she wrote the included article. More recently she has held positions with the Catham, Ontario Public Library.

INDEX

399

Manchester, William 57
Mandrell, Phyllis see Levy,
  Phyllis
Mansbridge, Ronald 372
Manual on Film Evaluation
  (Jones) 284
Manuscripts
  copyright provisions 350-
  351
Maps
  acquisition 265-266
  criteria 230, 266-267
"Marketing, Selection, and
  Acquisition of Materials
  for School Media Programs,
  Part I" (Theme issue of
  School Media Quarterly)
  163
Martin, Allie Beth 110, 122,
  173, 396
Martin, Lowell 57, 133
Martin, Sandra 61
Martz, David 350
Maryland. Department of
  Education. Division of Li-
  brary Development and
  Services 166
Mason, Ellsworth 194
Mass media 13, 14-15, 52-
  54
Materials Selection for Hospi-
  tal and Institution Libra-
  ries 150, 151-155
Maugham, Somerset 93
Mayo Clinic Library. Selec-
  tion policy 149
The Measurement and Evalua-
  tion of Library Services
  (Lancaster) 164
Media--selection 166
Media Programs: District
  and School 164, 170, 171
"Media Selection: Six Con-
  cerns" (Johnson) 166
Medical and legal information,
  access to 340, 388-389
"Medical Information Taboos"
  (Berry) 340
Medical libraries 148, 388
Melcher, Daniel 340, 396
Melcher on Acquisitions (Mel-
  cher) 156
Men at War (Hemingway) 32

"Merger Fever in Publishing"
  (Crittenden) 287
Mergers in publishing 301-306
Merritt, LeRoy C. 7, 63, 107,
  396-397
"A Method for Quantitatively
  Evaluating a University Li-
  brary Collection" (Golden)
  110
Metropolitan Public Library
  Users (Bundy) 173
Michigan Association for Media
  in Education. Intellectual
  Freedom Committee 107
Michigan Department of Educa-
  tion. Library Services Di-
  vision 164
"Microform Publications: Hard-
  ware and Supplies" (Folcarel-
  li and Ferragamo) 230
Microform Review 268
Microforms 120-121, 243, 381
  criteria 230, 268-269
Micropublishing 328, 334
Midwest Consortium for Politi-
  tical Science Research 124
The Mighty Soo: Five Hundred
  Years at Sault Ste. Marie
  (Judson) 233
Mill, John Stuart 7, 30, 39-41,
  43
Miller, Henry 233
Miller, Robert 117
Millions of Cats (Gag) 255
Minimum Standards for Public
  Library Systems 1966 165
Minneapolis (Greater) Chamber
  of Commerce 342
Minneapolis Public Library 342
Molz, Kathleen 8, 397
Montgomery County (Maryland)
  Public Schools 158-161
"More Effective Management of
  the Public Library's Book
  Collection" (Eggers) 110
Morgan, Robin 32
Multi-media see Nonprint mate-
  rials, Print materials
"Multimedia and the Information
  Requirements of Researchers"
  (Holley) 110
Music library 64, 95-106
Musical recordings (popular)
  230, 275-283